BETWEEN SHADOWS
MODERN IRISH WRITING AND CULTURE

BY THE SAME AUTHOR

Literature and Culture

Forces and Themes in Ulster Fiction (1974)
Fictions of the Irish Literary Revival: A Changeling Art (1987)
Colonial Consequences: Essays in Irish Literature and Culture (1991)
The Poet's Place: Essays in Ulster Literature and Society (co-ed. Gerald Dawe, 1991)
The Achievement of Seamus Heaney (1995)
The Nabob: A Tale of Ninety-Eight by Andrew James (ed. 2006)
The Cambridge Companion to the Irish Novel (ed. 2006)
Irish Novels 1890–1940: New Bearings in Culture and Fiction (2008)

Politics and Culture

The Idea of the Union: Statements and Critiques (ed. 1995)

Science and Natural History

Nature in Ireland: A Scientific and Cultural History (co-ed. H.C.G. Chesney, 1997)
Recoveries: Neglected Episodes in Irish Cultural History 1860–1912 (2002)

Titanic Studies

The Titanic Complex: A Cultural Manifest (1997)
Titanic (ed. 1999)
The Age of Titanic: Cross-Currents in Anglo-American Culture (2002)

BETWEEN SHADOWS
Modern Irish Writing and Culture

John Wilson Foster

Foreword by
Edna Longley

IRISH ACADEMIC PRESS
DUBLIN • PORTLAND, OR

First published in 2009 by Irish Academic Press

2 Brookside
Dundrum Road
Dublin 14, Ireland

920 NE 58th Avenue, Suite 300
Portland, Oregon,
97213-3786, USA

www.iap.ie

British Library Cataloguing-in-Publication Data
An entry can be found on request

978 0 7165 3005 3 (cloth)
978 0 7165 3006 0 (paper)

Library of Congress Cataloging-in-Publication Data
An entry can be found on request

Printed in Great Britain by the MPG Books Group, Bodmin and King's Lynn

CONTENTS

For Liam Kennedy
Historian and campaigner – distinguished among the less deceived

PREFACE

Between Shadows: Modern Irish Writing and Culture was written over the past fifteen years and is meant now to form a sequel of sorts to *Colonial Consequences: Essays in Irish Literature and Culture* (1991). Much has happened in Ireland since the early 1990s. The Celtic Tiger arrived, roared for a decade or so, and just yesterday fell silent. With its departure, Ireland threatens to become once again an emigrant society, after some years of unprecedented inward investment and of immigration, both from the Diaspora (what was starting to be called 'Greater Ireland') and from fellow nations in the European Union. What I say about Irish affluence in my essay on Conor McPherson's *The Weir*, for example, has become historical virtually overnight. It remains to be seen whether what one might have said about the welcome extended to foreigners and the emerging multiculture, or about the endangered status of the Christian churches in Ireland, has also become outdated. In any case, one cannot continuously bring criticism up to date in order not to be historically wrong-footed, so I have contented myself with some necessary dating and updating in endnotes.

The state of affairs in Northern Ireland has been even more fluid, with ceasefires, pacts and agreements, violations or rejections of those pacts and agreements and then, for the past decade, a semblance of peace, security, stability and growth. The years in which much of the book was written were those in which the 'peace process' was suffering birth pangs, which explains some of the cultural anxiety and partisanship expressed in this book, particularly in 'Getting the North: Yeats and Northern Nationalism' and 'Guests of the Nation', written during the bicentenary of the 1798 rebellion. They may now seem old-hat, if not foolish and over-reactive, but they too are captions to the Irish *Zeitgeist*. Besides, if Irish political history teaches us anything, it teaches us the folly of unbridled optimism. The so-called 'End-of-History' claim proved false beyond Irish shores, which makes it doubly unlikely to prove valid for Ireland.

Particularities in standards of living aside, the broadening of cultural outlook in Ireland, with increasing European contacts and perspectives, reductions in social and political tensions between

Ireland and Great Britain, and the assimilation of western worldwide youth culture (now increasingly indistinguishable from adult culture) have gone on apace and are probably irreversible. All this must surely be connected to what I detect in the study of Irish literature and culture today: more elbow-room than before, a broadening of the syllabus, as it were, with welcome enlargements to the body of discussible work and cultural productions and healthy transgressions of the bad old binary mindset. There have been welcome, if hesitant, rehabilitations, not only of neglected Irish women writers and gay writers, of Irish scientists and fieldworkers, but also of those Irishmen who fought in the Great War (hitherto a tense or sidestepped subject) and those who served in the Royal Irish Constabulary and Dublin Metropolitan Police, all of whom are increasingly seen as tragic human beings rather than simply deluded lackeys. Recently for me, the Great War and Yeats (who at some level denied it) are indeed the stones in the midst of all.

In my own case, the dubious stimulation of the political turbulence after 1985 (the year of the Anglo-Irish Agreement) that I noted in *Colonial Consequences* lost pressure a decade later, soon after I edited an intervention in cultural politics (1995), during which I had debated Gerry Adams in Vancouver in a forum organized by the Vancouver Board of Trade in 1994 when Adams's visit to Canada was newly approved. (A local Celtic magazine likened me unfavourably to a pit bull, which astonished my mild-mannered self.) But perhaps in the detours from the Troubles I was taking in my work, was betrayed the weariness of taking sides: the partisanship in 'Guests of the Nation' is balanced by the wish in that essay (once expressed by the Ulster-Canadian Brian Moore) for a pox on both their houses. Of course, under pressure of events there are bound to be reversions and returnings to base. To that extent, criticism in Ireland can exhibit journalism's shortfall in objectivity as well as its strengths of engagement and immediacy. Were my sorties outside literary criticism more than simply evidence of diverse interests, perhaps traceable back to the fact that I had taken a general degree – in zoology, history, social anthropology, philosophy, English – rather than an Honours degree in English that I somehow failed to enroll in?

In any case, I was drawn to the *Titanic*, both the tragedy and the ship, and the applied science culture of Ulster that produced them. This culture was one I grew up with on my father's side. I was also drawn to natural history and its history, and the culture they too emerged from, though I had no family link to it (beyond my father's enthusiasm for animals) and was surprised in my teens by the joy of birds, which has remained as strong as ever. These attractions issued in books, most of which could indeed be titled *Rehabilitations*, but sprang from deeper and perhaps less cultural origins. But later? A friend once said to me, probably in the late 1990s: you've interested yourself in the *Titanic*, the British connection and (which was true) the American passenger pigeon, the last specimen of which died in 1914. Do you see any connection? he asked. I didn't answer, but I think he was suggesting some kind of quixotic rearguard action on my part.

JWF
Vancouver, B.C., 1993 – Portaferry, Co. Down, 2009

NOTE ON THE TEXT

In earlier versions, portions of this book have appeared in the pages of *The Canadian Journal of Irish Studies*, *The Irish Review*, *The Irish University Review*, *Yeats Annual* and *The Yellow Nib*.

'Emblems of Diversity' is a revised version of a plenary lecture to the Yeats Summer School, Sligo, August 2007.

'The Islandman' began as a talk to the inaugural Ceiliuradh Blaithin/Robin Flower Celebration, Great Blasket Cultural Centre, Dunquin, March 1996.

'Stretching the Imagination' is a revised version of a lecture to the 'William Trevor at 80' symposium, Trinity College Dublin, April 2008.

'All the Long Traditions' appeared in *Out of History: Critical Essays on the Writings of Sebastian Barry*, ed. Christina Mahony (Dublin: Carysfort Press, 2006). It began life as a Leverhulme Visiting Professor to the United Kingdom public lecture, Ulster Museum, Belfast, November 2004.

'Guests of the Nation' began as a plenary talk to the International Association for the Study of Irish Literatures, University of Limerick, July 1998.

FOREWORD

If Irish literary and cultural criticism has taken off since the 1970s – and it has – John Wilson Foster is one of the main reasons. He has widened its conceptual horizon, provoked new debates, redefined old debates, and helped to make other critics as historically conscious as he is himself. The writings collected in *Between Shadows* develop Foster's earlier work on the Irish Revival; on Irish literary genres, especially fiction; on the culture of science and natural history; on cultural politics. A powerful link between all these interests is the autobiographical element that grounds all his criticism, as when he says: 'I am interested in the prevalence of proverbial thought in [Tomás] O Crohan's reminiscences, for I grew up with the vestiges of it in post-war Belfast'. Foster's formative immersion in Belfast idiom also underlies his sensitivity to the hybrid dramatic speech of Conor McPherson and Martin McDonagh. And we might read autobiography into the closing sentences of a rich essay on Strangford Lough: 'The gannets ...penetrate the Lough in ones and twos and seem to bring messages from the open sea beyond ... The traffic of Strangford is ceaseless and sometimes unexpected'. That vista could symbolise Foster's intellectual journeys, his 'messages from the open sea', his unexpectedness. He does not interpret Ireland as an 'exile', a term he rightly suspects in its Irish uses, but as a migrant whose different compass-points inform one another.

In his Preface, Foster wonders about the 'cultural anxiety and partisanship' which, he feels, inflect his concern with Northern Ireland. That is, he sometimes writes deliberately (and deliberatively) as an 'Ulster Protestant': now assimilating the Orange protest at Drumcree; now 'wrestling Wolfe Tone'; now mapping cultural zones excluded by cultural nationalism, by the Revival, by Irish academic orthodoxy. He attends to the problematic issues of W.B. Yeats, the Great War, and both together. In fact, the 'peace process' (which requires eternal vigilance) has outdated none of this. At the same time, attitudes have changed on several questions that Foster was first to raise. He should take due credit for what he calls 'more elbow-room' in Irish studies and elsewhere, rather than revert to his pessimistic sense, in 'Guests of the Nation', that 'Protestant Ulsterness' is 'a necessary but insufficient and comfortless affiliation'. Foster also wonders whether he has been engaged in 'some quixotic rearguard action'. Yet perhaps that defines all critical thought as it swims against the tide of received opinion. The recuperations in these essays – Oscar Wilde's scientific bearings, forgotten war-fiction, Thomas Kettle, Robert Lynd, William Trevor's Anglo-Irish 'loneliness', Belfast literati before the 1960s – are essential to Ireland, if not the 'nation'.

'Guests of the Nation' begins with a reflection on 'categories' as 'an engine of the Irish problem'. Foster deconstructs ethno-religious categories by facing into them, as well as subverting them; and he does the same with a different (if related) 'two cultures' split: that between arts and science. Nobody, for instance, could be better equipped to situate the blackbird in Irish natural and literary history. A key category that Foster opens up, not always overtly, is 'northernness'. If 'Guests of the Nation' is his most politically driven essay, 'Criticism and Benedict Kiely' carries the greatest emotional charge. Here one recuperator recuperates another. And Foster, whose wit, style and quirky enthusiasms take him beyond academic discourse, clearly identifies with Kiely's inclination to 'see Ireland as an immense hedge-school, a vast roofless academy and field-laboratory as busy as Joyce's streets'. Further, when noting Kiely's own identification with William Carleton, his perspective as 'a Catholic Ulsterman' in Dublin, or his 'patriotism that is not nationalism but local pride (and affection)', Foster seems to demarcate northern common ground that is more pre-Partition than anti-Partitionist: hospitable ground, where he ceases to be a 'guest'. Like Kiely, he writes Irish literary and cultural history from a neglected northern angle. This angle, which colours even Foster's view of O Crohan and the Blaskets, is crucial not only to any northern future but also to how the whole island continues to reconfigure itself.

Edna Longley
August 2009

I
WRITERS

1

EMBLEMS OF DIVERSITY: YEATS AND THE GREAT WAR

EAGLE INTO PLANE

Lady Gregory informed Yeats by letter on 4 February 1918 that her son Robert had been killed in Italy. In a postscript she invited the poet to commemorate her son in writing.[1] A week or so later, she suggested to Yeats themes he might consider.[2] Yeats published a short appreciative article on Robert Gregory in the *Observer* of 17 February but Lady Gregory clearly wanted a poem and supplied Yeats with further ideas, and later in the month he began the pastoral elegy, eventually entitled 'Shepherd and Goatherd', which he finished on 19 March (Foster, *A-P*, p.119). In mid-June he finished a second poem on Gregory, 'In Memory of Major Robert Gregory', and sometime later in 1918 he wrote 'An Irish Airman Foresees his Death'.[3] A fourth poem, 'Reprisals', was written in 1921 which, instead of commemorating Gregory, alleged that current events in Ireland rendered his death futile, thereby understandably upsetting the dead pilot's mother.[4]

Yeats was particularly pleased with 'An Irish Airman' and later read it, broadcast it and anthologized it in his *Oxford Book of Modern Verse* (1936).[5] It entered the anthologies of English poetry and has stayed there. I remember being puzzled by this poem when I read it as a grammar school boy in Northern Ireland in the late 1950s. My father used to recount the exploits of Paddy Finucane, DFC, DSO, who was born in Dublin and lived in England. He was the youngest ever wing commander and an air ace who downed thirty-two German planes before his Spitfire was disabled by ground fire in 1942 whereupon Finucane calmly flew out to sea, communicating with his fellow pilots until his engine was empty and he ditched his plane, which sank below the waves with him still at the controls. He was a 22-year-old Second World War version of Robert Gregory, who always, one online biography states, dreamed of flying through the heavens. But I knew that Finucane was a member of the Royal Air Force, and was therefore more properly a *British* airman so that '*Irish* airman' in Yeats's poem struck a peculiar chord with me since I had never heard of the Irish Air Force. But then, the entire poem puzzled me, since it bore no relation to my expectations of a wartime pilot's thoughts and feelings. Since Lady Gregory liked the way Yeats's article in the

Observer underplayed her son's military exploits (Foster, *A-P*, p.117), perhaps in the poem her friend was honouring what he might have interpreted as his commemorative brief. Yet I will suggest later that he was actually doing very much his own thing. We are told that Lady Gregory's reaction to the poem is unknown (Hill, *Lady Gregory*, p.302).

What struck me about the poem is the absence in the speaker of the expected motives for flying and fighting. I don't know if then I connected this oddity with the poem's silent shift in scene. The airman's thoughts begin on the ground, as he looks up at the clouds, as though he were a pilot before he undertakes a mission, and they end *among* the clouds and are, moreover, posthumous (his future 'seemed' a waste of breath: past tense). The clouds 'above', in which he foresees his airy fate, give way at the end of the poem to '*this* tumult in the clouds ... *this* life, *this* death' – my italics. His thoughts include the assertion that neither law (for example, conscription – there was to be Irish resistance to the idea of conscription), nor duty (for example, patriotic duty), nor hatred of the enemy (the Germans), nor love (presumably of the English he was protecting, though he was guarding the Welsh, Scots, Irish and European allies as well), nor political propaganda, nor desire for fame – none of these have played a part in his being at the joystick of his warplane. Since the poem does not attribute its sentiments to a named individual, to the historical Major Robert Gregory, Military Cross, Legion of Honour, it is, strictly speaking, incontrovertible. But if the poem is read as one in memory of Major Robert Gregory (and the references to Kiltartan make this essential, surely), then there is a disconnect between those sentiments and the known facts of Gregory's life.

As far as I can tell, Gregory was pretty much the kind of chap who joined the armed services to fight the Bosch in the Great War. Following Gregory family tradition and at the insistence of his mother, he attended Harrow, the famous English public school, where he expressed imperialist sympathies and conservative and unionist views, in part because the Conservative party supported strengthening of the Royal Navy, then considered to be dangerously weak in the face of a possible German threat. Lady Gregory thought a career in politics might suit him, starting with a clerkship in the (British) House of Commons, but instead he went up to Oxford. (As the career of Erskine Childers demonstrates, of course, a clerkship in the Commons would not have guaranteed sound British patriotism: Childers was an English patriot and soldier who turned Irish republican but enlisted for duty in the British armed services during the Great War *after* running guns for the Volunteers.)

Gregory became legal owner of Coole and although he took some interest in the Irish Revival, decided on a career in art, and made sketches for an Abbey Theatre production of Yeats's *The Hour Glass*, he nonetheless comported (and disported) himself as a country gentleman and Irish landlord. When war broke out he sought a commission in the army, soon securing one in the Connaught Rangers, later transferring to the Royal Flying Corps in which he had a distinguished war career before being shot down.[6] For her part, Lady Gregory favoured Irish participation in the war effort after the Home Rule for Ireland bill passed, and wanted to kill Germans after the torpedoing of the *Lusitania* with her nephew Hugh Lane on board, though Robert was less bloodthirsty (Hill, *Lady Gregory*, pp.290, 276, 283). In Anglo-Irish tradition (one should simply say *Irish* tradition), whole families were involved in the War; eleven of Lady Gregory's nephews fought in the War, some dying in Ypres, Gallipoli and other battlefields (Coote, *W.B. Yeats*, p.276). Judith Hill remarks that Lady Gregory was a nationalist at the Abbey and at Coole a unionist. She did have second thoughts about the War and Irish participation, like many Irish, especially after the executions of the Easter Rising leaders, and Yeats's own ambivalence about the War must surely have fed into 'An Irish Airman', draining it of all partisanship. But Robert seems himself not to have become anti-war (Foster, *A-P*, p.118), unlike, say, Siegfried Sassoon, so I think we can say that whoever is talking in Yeats's poem, it is not the historical Robert Gregory. In a letter to Yeats in 1915, Maud Gonne expressed sadness that Gregory had enlisted, believing enlistment was 'so outside his life and duty' (Coote, *W.B. Yeats*, p.359), but his biography surely suggests otherwise.

Indeed, before this poem, Yeats had been intent on creatively misreading Gregory and turning him into a figure in a purely Yeatsian landscape (or cloudscape). In 'Shepherd and Goatherd', Gregory is depicted as someone who (reading between the pastoral lines) did not take a great interest in Coole, declining to improve it (in real life this was understandable since Lady Gregory remained effective mistress of the house) – a restless and unsettled man. In fact, the cuckoo that announces the opening of the elegy ('That cry's from the first cuckoo of the year./I wished before it ceased') later becomes Gregory himself, a cuckoo in the Coole nest. This stanza may have released some of Yeats's resentment at being ousted himself as chief nestling when Gregory and his wife came to live at Coole, where Yeats had spent unrivalled summers pampered by Lady Gregory. The cuckoo analogy is succeeded by the recognition that not much is left to testify to the achievement of the unnamed dead subject: 'but half a score/Of sorrowful, austere, sweet, lofty pipe tunes'. And though it has been said that Lady Gregory herself was aware of her son's failure to fulfil his promise (Hill, *Lady Gregory*, p. 299) – though surely his war record alone puts him beyond the commonality of men – it is a back-handed compliment the shepherd pays the premature deceased. What then to *do* in 'An Irish Airman' but situate Gregory in cloud cuckoo-land?

The unsettled cuckoo is perhaps harder to identify with Yeats's rooted man about to fly, whose 'country is Kiltartan Cross', and 'countrymen Kiltartan's poor'. However, he cannot be the caring landlord at one with the people, his tenants, because he speaks in the tones previously used by the speaker of 'Upon a House shaken by the Land Agitation' (1909), the tones of a semi-detached, rather indignant Yeats standing on the touchline. The sentiment of

> Although
> Mean roof-trees were the sturdier for its fall,
> How should their luck run high enough to reach
> The gifts that govern men ...?

is echoed in the airman's belief that 'No likely end [of the war] could bring them [i.e. Kiltartan's poor] loss/Or leave them happier than before'.[7] What's it all to them? In 1918 it was, of course, natural to imagine that the outcome of the War would hardly affect the lives of Irish peasants and farm workers in the west of Ireland, far removed from the Front and from diplomatic writ. Still, the poor are not just *far away from* but *far below* Yeats's pilot, who entertains the 'sweet laughing eagle thoughts' of the Big House denizens alluded to in 'Upon a House', and does so on wings that have become the wings of an aeroplane in 'An Irish Airman Foresees his Death'.

APPALLED NEUTRALITY

Clearly the War and Major Robert Gregory MC are themselves far away from 'An Irish Airman Foresees his Death', and even 'this tumult in the clouds' is probably not in Yeats's intended meaning aerial combat but rather high emotional ferment, the 'ecstasy' Yeats excitedly referred to when tutoring an actor in 1927 to read the poem for a radio broadcast (Hone, *W.B. Yeats*, p.457). Yeats himself was far away from the War in most senses, though he did experience first hand a Zeppelin raid in London in October of 1915 (Coote, *W.B. Yeats*, p.359). True, he claimed in a letter of November 1914 that he wished a German defeat but chiefly, it seems, because that is what those friends engaged in the War as soldiers and nurses desired.[8] This sentiment was balanced by his peculiar confession to Lady Gregory early in the War: 'I feel, strangely enough, most for the young Germans who are being killed. The spectacled, dreamy faces, or so I pictured them, remind me more of men I have known than the strong-bodied young English foot-ballers' (Coote, *W.B. Yeats*, p.352), as though armed hostilities had broken out between the Cheshire Cheese Rhymers and the Philistines. Even in London in 1915, Yeats reported that he gave the War little thought, on one occasion reading Keats's *Lamia* in preference to the War news (Foster, *A-P*, p.5). John Quinn, the Irish-American patron of Irish art and literature, was hostile to Yeats's stance, as Roy Foster tells us, and thought that Yeats's verse declaration of neutrality, 'On being asked for a War Poem', unworthy of the poet (*A-P*, pp.5–6). 'I think it better that in times like these/A poet keep his mouth shut', Yeats wrote, surely disingenuously: Yeats rarely held his tongue when he wished to set public figures right. Coote calls Yeats's attitude 'appalled neutrality' (p.352), implying simultaneous engagement and disengagement, whereas Richard Ellmann remarks that Yeats had little to say (and thus presumably think and feel) about the War because its issues were too abstract and international.[9]

Ellmann's is certainly one interpretation of what Terence Brown calls a 'deliberately detached Yeats' that he detects in Yeats's 'remote response to the general crisis' by which Brown describes Yeats's five-line poem, 'A Meditation in Time of War' (Brown, *Life of WB Yeats*, pp.221, 219). There are other possible interpretations. One is that Yeats, like many Irish, saw the War as largely an English and imperial affair and none of his business. Coote believes Yeats was generally slow to hold a political opinion unless it concerned Ireland (Coote, *W.B. Yeats*, p.567). In any case, the hesitation and ambivalence of many Irish towards any war involving the British later became the official neutrality of the Irish Free State.

Another, related interpretation is that Yeats wanted to ground opposition to any involvement in the War in a sense of locality and local obligation set over against an awareness of the far-flung regions already being entangled in Continental turmoil and the obscure obligations thus created. The poet is explicit in identifying the airman's allegiances as local, though I have implied that the notion of the airman chivalrously fighting to guard his tenants and neighbours is rather at odds with the implied haughty loneliness and *causelessness* of the airman, threatening to make the chivalry notion an insincere rhetorical flourish which at the same time results in the airman's singing what is really descant with himself. Furthermore, this opposition of allegiances can be reversed. Without calling into question their patriotism, many soldiers must have thought they were defending not just small nations but their own neighbourhoods: the 36th Ulster Division seemed to think it was defending Ulster, even Belfast, indeed the Protestant working-class enclaves of the Shankill Road and Sandy Row. When he was asked why he wanted to enlist, the English poet Edward Thomas (who, like Gregory, was in his 30s when war broke out), is reported to have lifted up a handful of soil and replied, 'literally this'.[10] Was it *local* soil or *English* soil? And are they distinguishable?

For Yeats, both locality and nationality could be proof against the mass culture he detested. He considered the more Irish western vicinities to be innocent of mass culture and popular print culture (by contrast, he celebrated popular or traditional *oral* culture) whilst his Irish literary and cultural Revival was meant among other things to rescue Ireland from the mass culture that beset England. The War in its potential vastness of scale threatened to be an offensive outbreak of warped democracy and popular madness, and if England began badly with incompetent officers, as Yeats claimed in a letter to his father, that was because England 'is paying the price for despising intellect'.[11] A threatening world war later, in 1938, Yeats was sure that an Irish army led by properly schooled officers from select military families could repel 'the disciplined uneducated masses of the commercial nations' (Coote, *W.B. Yeats*, p.570). In 1914, if everyone was thinking and talking about this mass affair, the War, Yeats would not.[12]

Another, and also related, interpretation is that the ongoing simultaneous Irish problems (with their constant threat or actuality of violence) occluded the Great War. It was perhaps not just a case of limited emotional resources to be expended in political crises, but also a case of political priorities: it was priorities that separated Padraic Pearse and other republicans, and even Yeats, who shared an anti-conscription platform with Pearse, from Tom Kettle and other Home Rule nationalists. Pearse thought that Great War participation and Irish nationalism were incompatible. Kettle thought the great, European issues of the War required the Irish Question to be shelved until Armistice; the choice is simple, he maintained: it is between barbarism and civilization.[13] Kiltartan in Yeats's poem is, by implication, not just a local barony but an *Irish* barony that can stand for Ireland herself: the airman is neither a *Galway* airman nor a *British* airman but an *Irish* airman. If Gregory fought for the Allies (and Yeats must have thought him misguided in enlisting), then at least he must have been fighting for Ireland in a roundabout way. But ironically, this is precisely what Kettle and John Redmond thought:

Irish soldiers in British khaki were fighting *for the first time as Irishmen*, helping to safeguard small nations from German designs, perhaps reform the British Empire and of course copper-fastening Home Rule by earning the gratitude of Britain.

And we can say more. Kiltartan was not any old barony, but the place where Gregory's mother had collected folklore, fashioned a literary dialect and furthered the aims of the Irish Revival. Locality, especially in the Gaelic-speaking west of Ireland, was one of the strongest planks in the Revival platform. By a kind of densely coded shorthand, 'Kiltartan' in 'An Irish Airman' establishes Irish Revival, with all that that entailed, as the cause for which Gregory was fighting, having launched himself into the air from the peasant and tenanted soil of Coole estate. As though to confirm this idea, Lady Gregory in the journal that she began as soon as the War ended, devoted a chapter to 'The Folk-Lore of the War', appropriating the War for Revival purposes as Yeats, we could argue, had already done in a more oblique way in 'An Irish Airman'.[14]

Kiltartan meant also the visions and beliefs Lady Gregory had been collecting there, and at the time of the Great War Yeats himself was busy with his spiritualism. So seriously did Yeats take spiritualism that it was capable of causing him to rearrange values and priorities in a way that would surprise and puzzle disbelievers in the spirit world. It may be that he could not bring himself to admit that even a world war could affect and change affairs instead of being, in the occult perspective, a necessary and unavoidable episode in some even larger supra historical plan, one that Yeats in 1917 was formulating and that would eventually become *A Vision*. It is as though Yeats had bigger fish to fry than even a war that threatened to engulf Europe and murder millions of people. Even a world war had to know its cosmic place.

Aversion was perhaps one way of handling a public crisis too big for Yeats to influence and shape. His limitation (and capacity) in this regard were to be revealed at Easter 1916 when he fretted that he had not been made privy to the plans for insurrection and had been caught off guard, visiting in England when the republic was proclaimed from the General Post Office. This is a familiar story and we know that 'Easter 1916', while it may not have satisfied Maud Gonne's republican outrage, was nonetheless a highly successful late insertion of Yeats into the Rising and its aftermath. As it turned out, he wrote a poem that will live in the memory as long as the rebellion itself and thereby forever associate the poet's name with an event which occurred in his absence. Perhaps he knew no such intervention was possible with the Great War and I wonder would we be churlish to detect a certain rhyming sulk in his six-line reply to the request for a war poem (February 1915), quoted above, in which with unusual modesty he rejects war poetry as unhelpful 'meddling' with statesmanship, something he surely can't have really believed.

Yeats's engagement or disengagement with the War is fascinatingly complex. After the Great War, during the Troubles or Anglo-Irish war, Yeats in his 1921 poem, 'Reprisals', could *now* situate Major Robert Gregory and his military achievement in its real context and drop all allegory or pastoral.

> Some nineteen German planes, they say,
> You had brought down before you died.
> We called it a good death.

This new ingenuousness now suits Yeats, for we realize immediately that 'we' were wrong in thinking it a good death. In the light of the atrocities being perpetrated in the name of England by the Black and Tans and other Crown forces, Gregory's death can now be seen as futile, his cause retroactively discredited, his status now one of 'the cheated dead'. Yeats tells the dead Gregory to stop his ears with the dust of his own grave to prevent him from hearing the cries of the murdered and wounded. Yeats had had occasion to use this form of closure before when he told Parnell in 'To a Shade' to return to the tomb to escape the disgrace of the Sir Hugh Lane affair. Whatever its merits and effectiveness, I can't help but see Yeats exploiting, or at least appropriating, rather than celebrating Gregory in these poems. I understand why 'Reprisals' upset Lady Gregory (he was dragging her son from his grave to make an insincere poem, she objected). If Yeats, as he told John Quinn, was moved by Gregory's death more for her sake than for her son's,[15] then it is likely that he wrote his two early poems equally for the sake of his evolving poetic and philosophy, thereby revealing the predatory imagination of the major poet.

In any event, Yeats's slownesses and silences on the Great War still, I believe, spoke autobiographical and cultural volumes and so did the few poems he did write on the subject (including two on Robert Gregory, two on the War itself). The hesitations and ambivalences were not all uniquely his, but were shared in the Irish intellectual circles he moved in. Douglas Goldring, the English novelist, playwright and conscientious objector, moved to Ireland in 1916, and later recalled:

> On the subject of the war, the neutrality and detachment of the Dublin 'intellectuals' was astonishing ... They were not pro-German nor did they wish the Allies to be defeated. Their

> attitude was that of compassionate spectators of a world-tragedy, in which they were scarcely more involved than any other small, neutral country. Their freedom of thought and comment, combined with tolerance of opinion different from their own, produced the kind of intellectual clarity which was to become the ideal of Henri Barbusse and his friends.[16]

As a letter to Lady Gregory on 30 August 1914 reveals, Yeats was surprised by the preoccupation with the War in London in contrast to the remoteness of the War in the Stephen's Green Club.[17] Ignoring the War and being ambivalent about it are two different things, of course.

Certainly there is ample evidence that the imminence and outbreak of the War were occasions for vigorous debate and opinion in Dublin and Ireland, most of it for a year or two highly favourable to the Allies.[18] Irishmen meanwhile enlisted in the tens of thousands, in response to encouragement less from unionists than from Home Rule nationalists, but chiefly, I suspect, carried by the historical momentum of service in the British Army that was traditional and centuries' old. Then came the Rising in Dublin. For many, those who fought and died in the Rising exhibited a heroism that far outshone the heroism of Irish soldiers at the Front, just as the rebellion itself eclipsed the Great War because it was seen as a purely Irish crux and closer to home. This planetary event in the Irish firmament was caused in part by Irish reaction to the Rising executions and disillusionment with, by contrast, the protracted and unheroically lethal World War; in her novel *The Golden Rose* (1924), Katharine Tynan recreated this eclipse with some regret, she having given two sons to the war effort.

After the War, the negative feelings and opinions set fast and became a popular and winning orthodoxy that consigned Irish support for, and participation in, the War to a kind of heterodoxy, even an undeclared treason.[19] Evolving constitutional politics, of course, played a part and the Somme as unionist apotheosis was matched by the Rising as nationalist apotheosis: Ulster as it were got the Great War, the Free State (and later the Republic) got the Easter rebellion.

The semi-official and awkward silence maintained in the Irish Free State and later Republic about the Great War and the impressive Irish participation in it derived in part, one could argue, from the Yeatsian strain of the Irish Revival, for whom the Easter Rising became of iconic importance to Ireland. In a rather longer term, the literary orthodoxy that came to hold sway required such Irish writers as Patrick MacGill, St John Ervine, Lord Dunsany, George Birmingham and Alexander

Irvine, and of course Thomas Kettle, to be neglected *when they wrote about the war*. (Five of these writers had been soldiers.) Even those writers who depicted the 'sharp, bitter cleavage', as Tynan in 1922 called it, between allegiance to the War effort and allegiance to Irish rebellion[20] came to be ignored – I am thinking of Mrs Victor (Jessie) Rickard and Douglas Goldring as well as Ervine, Tynan and, again, Kettle.[21]

A KIND OF ARSON

Surely there is a link of sorts between Yeats's discountenancing of the War and what happened after in Irish literary history and historical writing, given Yeats's vast influence. For Yeats was not done with the War after its cessation. Two episodes in his biography that demonstrate his hostility to the Great War as a literary theme and an Irish theme are well known.

One is his dismissal of the English Trench poets from candidacy when he compiled his *Oxford Book of Modern Verse* in 1936, in the Introduction to which he announced famously that 'passive suffering is not a theme for poetry'. Wilfred Owen, Isaac Rosenberg and the others had failed to express tragic joy and so were inadmissible. His rationale is majestically Yeatsian: 'When man has withdrawn into the quicksilver at the back of the mirror no great event becomes luminous in his mind.'[22] But behind it lay a less elevated judgement which he expressed in a letter to Dorothy Wellesley: Owen was 'all blood, dirt and sucked sugar-stick'; he didn't know, he told her sarcastically, that in rejecting Owen he was excluding 'a revered sandwich-man of the revolution'.[23] The last comment hints that he might have found the younger poets something of a threat or at least an obstruction in his path. He might have entertained deep and genuine literary reservations, but surely Owen's candidacy could not have been strengthened by Yeats's opposition to the War as a literary preoccupation.

Especially an *Irish* literary preoccupation, as the second episode, Yeats's heavy-handed rejection for the Abbey Theatre of O'Casey's play, *The Silver Tassie*, in 1928, shows. We know that before Yeats wrote his notorious letter to O'Casey that the Abbey directors were already irked by O'Casey and that Lennox Robinson had already entered serious reservations about one act of O'Casey's Great War play. But Roy Foster remarks that, in addition, the late 1920s Irish Free State was not an officially congenial place for feelings of sympathy for, or even interest in, the Great War and Irish involvement in it (Foster, *A-P*, pp.366–7). But Yeats's hostile reaction to *The Silver Tassie* went beyond these. The subject was wrong, certainly for O'Casey, perhaps for any Irish writer: 'you have no subject ... you are not interested in the great war, you never stood on its battlefields or walked its hospitals and so write out of your opinions' (Foster, *A-P*, p.367). Beyond military involvement, O'Casey's experience of the War was entirely lacking in what Yeats dubiously attributed to Major Gregory: a sense of locality, of immediacy or even nearness. I seem to remember that O'Casey tartly reminded Yeats that as far he knew Shakespeare had never been to Agincourt. Certainly Yeats's objection was strange coming from a writer whose imagination has been described as essentially dramatic.

If the English war poets had *too much* direct experience which overwhelmed their verse, then O'Casey had *no* direct experience, which 'underwhelmed' his drama, as it were, and gave his play no centre or passion. If the former expressed formless passionate intensity, O'Casey lacked all conviction and masked it by theatrical contrivance. Yeats continued:

> The mere greatness of the world war has thwarted you, it has refused to become mere background and obtrudes itself upon the stage as so much dead wood that will not burn with the dramatic fire. Dramatic action is the fire that must burn up everything but itself ... Among the things that dramatic action must burn up are the author's opinions.

Perhaps this graphic imagery of fire and combustion was close to the surface of Yeats's mind, since in October of the previous year (six months before the letter) Yeats had composed 'In Memory of Eva Gore-Booth and Con Markievicz' which ends dramatically with a summons to some kind of arson, intellectual, imaginative, historical, temporal:

> Arise and bid me strike a match
> And strike another till time catch;
> Should the conflagration climb,
> Run till all the sages know ...
> Bid me strike a match and blow

Perhaps he thought O'Casey in *The Silver Tassie*, like Constance Markievicz, had lost some central passion in favour of withered opinion; in 'Men Improve with the Years' (composed in July 1916), Yeats belies the title with regret for his 'burning youth'. A little later, in the eleventh stanza of 'In Memory of Major Robert Gregory' (finished in June 1918), Yeats returned to the imagery of fire:

> Some burn damp faggots, others may consume
> The entire combustible world in one small room
> As though dried straw, and if we turn about
> The bare chimney is gone black out
> Because the work had finished in that flare.

Here was the implied explanation for Gregory's versatility and lack of central accomplishment: the consuming passion that necessitated early death *was itself* the work and the accomplishment.

A letter George Bernard Shaw wrote to Lady Gregory after Gregory's death gives some biographical support to this picture of the airman. 'When I met Robert at the flying station on the west front, in abominably cold weather, with a frostbite on his face hardly healed, he told me that the six months he had been there had been the happiest of his life ... war must have intensified his life as nothing else could; he got a grip of it that he could not through art or love'.[24] Lady Gregory in her reply said something that illuminates 'An Irish Airman': 'I am glad to know the last thing he looked at was the Italian sky and not bursting shells or the faces of enemies' (Laurence and Grene, *Shaw, Lady Gregory and the Abbey*, p.138). Yeats's father wrote from New York, with a comparable image of Robert Gregory: 'His happiness (for he says he was happy) [lay] in his forgetting of self. Pleasure lies in remembering yourself, happiness in forgetting it – & we can only forget ourselves by attaining to the maximum of strenuousness – he lived at the highest pitch of exertion ... Sometimes people live to be old because they have never lived' (Foster, *A-P*, p.118).

If John B. Yeats's letter must have fed into 'An Irish Airman', surely too must Yeats's letter of 1910 to Robert Gregory, quoted at length by Richard Ellmann in *Yeats: The Man and the Masks*. Lady Gregory had received an insulting letter from Edmund Gosse. Lady Gregory and her son expected Yeats to take up the cudgels on their behalf and were disappointed by Yeats's reaction. The poet wrote to Gregory to exonerate himself by explaining the personality that lay behind his failure to take Gosse firmly to task. It was not that he feared a quarrel with the important and highly placed Gosse. No: the cause was a failure of *instinct* (a word mentioned three times in the letter), a resort to *analysis* (four times), especially analysis of *emotion* (twice), and dependence on *reason* (four times). Above all, *impulse* was too often murdered in him, and *impulse* or *impulses* was mentioned six times in this extraordinary and strained letter. One sentence reads: 'As I look back I see occasion after occasion on which I have been prevented from doing what was a natural & sometimes the right thing, either because analysis of the emotion or action of another or self distrustful analysis of my own emotion destroyed impulse.'[25] One feels that either Yeats is protesting too much, or in the course of the letter he forgets his correspondent and engages in a kind of soliloquy. Later, in January 1915, this self-description found its way into his poem, 'The People', in which his implied opposite is not Robert Gregory but Maud Gonne, his 'phoenix'. He confesses that unlike she, who lives in deed, not thought, he,

> whose virtues are the definitions
> Of the analytic mind, can neither close
> The eye of the mind nor keep my tongue from speech.

Either way, is it not tempting to read 'An Irish Airman Foresees his Death' as a kind of posthumous redress, as a way of commemorating Gregory by awarding him the virtues Yeats thought he himself lacked, at least during that episode with Gosse and the insult and Yeats's passive response and failure to champion Kiltartan's most important citizens? Ellmann (*Yeats: The Man and the Masks*, p.179) tells us that a few days after writing his letter to Gregory, Yeats wrote the poem called 'The Mask', a dialogue poem in which the last speaker asks: 'What matter, so there is but fire/In you, in me?' Was Robert Gregory in 'An Irish Airman' his mask, his anti-self, his preferable and desirable self? In the poem the airman lives the apotheosis of direct experience: '*this* life, *this* death', in comparison to which even 'The years to come seemed waste of breath', a life achieving 'A lonely *impulse* of delight'. In 'A Prayer for My Daughter' (1919), Yeats was to extol the capacity of 'self-delighting' in which the soul finds its 'radical innocence'.

So far is the Great War from 'An Irish Airman' that the poem can be read as disguised wish-fulfilling autobiography, and as part of Yeats's entire mythography. Even while we might deplore Yeats's aversion to the War as a theme for poetry, seeing behind that aversion a broader Irish recoil from reality and obligation, we can't but admire once again the poet's capacity for absorbing events into his own vision and version of the world, one of extraordinary density and virtuality.

NOTES

1. According to Stephen Coote, she sent her note to Yeats on 2 February: *W.B. Yeats: A Life* (London: Hodder and Stoughton, 1997), p.408. According to Roy Foster he received it on 4 February: *W.B. Yeats: A Life: The Arch-Poet* [hereafter referred to in the text as *A-P*] (Oxford: Oxford University Press, 2003), p.117.
2. Judith Hill, *Lady Gregory: An Irish Life* (Stroud, UK: Sutton, 2005), p.300.

3. Neither Foster nor Jeffares in *A Commentary on the Collected Poems of W.B. Yeats* (1968) dates 'Airman' more accurately than 1918.
4. Coote, *W.B. Yeats*, p.447; Foster, *Arch-Poet*, pp.183–4; Hill, *Lady Gregory*, p.318.
5. Foster, *Arch-Poet, passim*; Joseph Hone, *W.B. Yeats, 1865–1939* (New York: St Martin's Press, 1962), p.457.
6. Hill, *Lady Gregory*, pp.102–27, 135–6, 165, 173, 238, 275.
7. Cf. Yeats's poem, 'Parnell': 'Parnell came down the road, he said to a cheering man:/ "Ireland shall get her freedom and you still break stone"'.
8. Terence Brown, *The Life of WB Yeats: A Critical Biography* (Oxford: Blackwell, 1999), p.218.
9. Richard Ellmann, *Yeats: The Man and the Masks* (1948; New York: Norton, 1978), p.236. Foster believes that Yeats's ignoring of the War was an 'Irish propensity to therapeutic forgetting' that the poet shared. Yeats's 'deliberate amnesia about the 1914–18 war' occurred despite the fact that the War 'had done so much to create the conditions for the Irish revolution': 'Yeats and War: Poetic Strategies and Political Reconstruction from the Easter Rising to the Free State', *Transactions of the Royal Historical Society*, 6th series, vol.11 (2001), p.144.
10. Eleanor Farjeon, *Edward Thomas: The Last Four Years* (Stroud: Sutton Publishing, 1997 [1958]), p.154.
11. Allan Wade, *Letters of W.B. Yeats* (London: Rupert Hart-Davis, 1954), p.588.
12. Any more than he had talked or written about the sinking of the *Titanic*, which international disaster and hugely popular reaction to it seem to have escaped his attention.
13. Professor T.M. Kettle, 'Under the Heel of the Hun', in *The Ways of War* (London: Constable, 1917), p.106. This volume is a collection of Kettle's war journalism, compiled by his widow Mary Sheehy Kettle.
14. Lady Gregory, *Seventy Years: Being the Autobiography of Lady Gregory*, ed. Colin Smythe (Gerrards Cross: Colin Smythe, 1974), pp.509–31.
15. Wade, *Letters of W.B. Yeats*, p.645, Hill, *Lady Gregory*, p.301. When he wrote to Iseult Gonne, Yeats did not quite make this comparative claim: 'I have been deeply moved by the loss for his mother's sake & for his own': Foster, *Arch-Poet*, p.119.
16. Douglas Goldring, *Odd Man Out: The Autobiography of a 'Propaganda Novelist'* (London: Chapman and Hall, 1935), p.175.
17. Lady Gregory, *Seventy Years*, p.513; R.F. Foster, *W.B. Yeats: A Life: The Apprentice Mage* [hereafter *AM*] (Oxford: Oxford University Press, 1997), p.523.
18. The diversity of opinion in Dublin at the time is wittily and satirically represented in Gerald Griffin, *The Dead March Past: A Semi-Autobiographical Saga* (1937).
19. The notion of an early Irish national amnesia about the Great War was until recently an orthodoxy. Keith Jeffery, however, has questioned this received notion and claims that although the Irish were indeed wilfully forgetful of the War from the 1940s until the late 1980s, there was some measure of commemoration from the early 1920s until the late 1930s. See '"Writing out of Opinions": Irish Experience and the Theatre of the Great War', manuscript of talk to the Canadian Association for Irish Studies annual conference, University of Toronto, May 2008, pp.8–9.
20. Katharine Tynan, *The Years of the Shadow* (London: Constable, 1919), p.205.
21. I discuss Irish novelists who fictionalized the dilemma of loyalty posed by the Great War and the Easter rebellion in *Irish Novels 1890–1940* (Oxford: Oxford University Press, 2008), pp.409–48.
22. W.B. Yeats, Introduction to *The Oxford Book of Modern Verse* (Oxford: Clarendon Press, 1936), p.xxxiv.
23. W.B. Yeats, *Letters on Poetry from W.B. Yeats to Dorothy Wellesley* (London: Oxford University Press, 1940), p.124.
24. Dan H. Laurence and Nicholas Grene (eds), *Shaw, Lady Gregory and the Abbey: A Correspondence and a Record* (Gerrards Cross: Colin Smythe, 1993), pp.137–8.
25. Ellmann, *Yeats: The Man and the Masks*, p.178.

2

THE ISLANDMAN: THE TELLER AND THE TALE

ONE

I opened the pages of Tomás O Crohan's *The Islandman* (1934) in 1975, a year after I had said my 'farewell to Ireland' (to borrow a phrase from the book), and I fell upon it with relief in the smother of Romanticism, mysticism and nationalism that was the Irish Literary Revival I was then investigating. The book was itself, in truth, a kind of island on which 'the everydays of nature' were set down without claptrap – to borrow Patrick Kavanagh, a poet whose work was also in healthy contrast to the despotic mastery of the previous generation of Irish writers. And Kavanagh, too, could have been charged, like the author of *The Islandman*, with 'pleading the poor mouth' (a routine phrase in my east Belfast home, incidentally), save that like Tomás O Crohan he fought resentment to an eloquent standstill and gave us a view of human life that does not impoverish but dignifies it.

But long before the western outposts of the Revival swam into my ken, my attention was fastened on islands as a young bird-watcher, for whom they were thrilling observatories where birds of passage rested or perished, having arrived there on moonlit or starry nights. I had been to the Copeland Islands off County Down, Rathlin Island off County Antrim and Bardsey Island off Wales before I had yet heard of the Blaskets. The ornithological seventh heavens of Heligoland and Fair Isle were to bird-watchers what the Aran Islands and the Blasket Islands were to Irish Romantics, antiquarians, language students and cultural nationalists.

It was on Lighthouse Island, in the Copeland group, that one night I listened to an unearthly song that froze me before I tumbled to it, when I recovered my wits, as a seal's song, and so when I later came upon Tomás O Crohan's recollection of his first experience of this song ('My heart leapt in me, and I felt very odd', he writes), I knew the truth of it.[1]

The 'people of the sea' (the seals who in Irish folklore take human form, for example in 'The Tale of Moore's Castle' that Peig Sayers told Robin Flower)[2] are reduced to absurdity in Myles na gCopaleen's creatures that sleep at night in Dublin bus depots (just as Myles tried in *The Poor Mouth* to reduce to absurdity *The Islandman* and other such works),[3] but the seals escape the satirist by their versatility of significance, their serious otherworldliness and their sheer weighty factuality. Seals are hunted in perilous caves and 'The Day of the Seal Hunt', a chapter in *The Islandman*, is recounted with a brisk adventurism: experience remembered at its source.

But setting out for the neighbouring island of Inishvickillaun, the boat of the hunting party from Great Blasket reminds O Crohan of the boats of the Fenians of old. Diversions in O Crohan's memory propel the story of his life; serendipities of the life and of the narrative are one and the same; even unexpected setbacks in the life are narrative salvage amidst a general shipwreck. (This duality his story shares with Defoe's *Robinson Crusoe.*) In an early chapter he is diverted from usable seaweed by a killable seal, though to do the job he must become a miniature version himself of a Fenian of old.[4] Seals are in any case candidates for humanity. The Copeland seal sounded human and stood the hair upright on my neck, but O Crohan heard *his* seals singing 'Eamonn Magaine' and when O Crohan's fellow-boatman started up with his own song the animals were singing in the west and the lobsterman in the east, in the symmetry of folklore. And in *The Western Island* (pp.125–9), Flower reproduces O Crohan's story of 'Poor Donnchadh' who, for his unfeeling insult to his sister's memory, dies while seal-hunting, the people of the sea being the agents of retribution. Here is experience formalized into the tradition of the folk-tale. *The Islandman* is the hybrid progeny of the authority of tradition and the authority of experience.

There is for the bird-watcher a disappointing scarcity of birds in O Crohan's book – there are a few more birds in O Crohan's *Island Cross Talk* (1986; a translation of *Allagar na hInise*, 1928) – and it would be good to have the list of Blasket birds Carl Marstrander asked O Crohan to send him, according to Muiris MacConghail.[5] In *The Islandman* there are only pet gulls and the gannets on Little Skellig which the poet Dunlevy tells of because once the islanders took the young for food only to be confronted by a guard-boat and a fatal engagement ensued. Gannets were no longer eaten by O Crohan's day. Around the same time the islanders (who 'held that there was no property in the birds of the air', Flower tells us) ran afoul of another absentee owner when they took young puffins from the Tiaracht, but we have to read of this in *The Western Island* (p.96). O Crohan makes no mention of that unearthly bird, the Manx shearwater, which had its biggest Irish breeding colonies in the late nineteenth century on the Skelligs and were said to breed on the Blaskets.[6] The truth, I suppose, is that what was not readily at hand and usable or edible was hardly noticed at all.

Indeed, there is in *The Islandman* an almost phagic relation to life:

O Crohan's register of food intake seems in excess of his wish to tell us how hard life was, how islanders had to hoard or search for food. The book opens with the infant O Crohan at the breast and being there until he was four years old. By the third paragraph he is tucking as a child into hens' eggs, lumps of butter, bits of fish, limpets and winkles. Food very nearly dominates the narrative. The food of that time required memorable teeth, it seems, and O Crohan is proud to remember how early he had all his teeth, 'good grinders', with which to despatch anything. His hymns to teeth are hymns to the old days before tea and white bread, when the coarse meal required a mill in your mouth to deal with it. Since in *The Western Island* Flower records Sean Eoghain (one of the Dunlevys) as of the same opinion ('there wasn't man on the island that didn't carry a whole set of teeth to the grave', p.61), there must have been something to the champion dentation of old. It was as if the islanders once 'ate' life, whereas their descendants, a frailer crew, merely pecked at it. O Crohan's pride in his teeth is his pride at being a survivor of a more rugged epoch in island history; these are the teeth of a fierce tradition.

In such wise is the quotidian in O Crohan's story epochal. The fiction writer John McGahern (who incidentally believes Flower's to be an impressive translation) draws our attention to a recurring phrase in *An t-Oileanach*, translated by Flower as 'a day of our lives'.[7] The basic unit of time throughout the book is the day, McGahern observes, and I can't help but think of Philip Larkin's

> What are days for?
> Days are where we live.
> They come, they wake us
> Time and time over.
> They are to be happy in:
>
> Where can we live but days?

Days for O Crohan are the habitations of experience, but also turning-points in life; the formula 'One day' often means 'On a day that changed everything' or, at the very least, 'On a day worthy of being recalled'. A day offers the unexpected – an accident, a lucky discovery, a death, a windfall, a sea-gift, a departure or arrival. A day might yield the salvageable or require to be salvaged itself, usually through song and drink at day's end. But together, the days compose the discernible pattern of life, a measurable tide: another phrase, remarks McGahern, is that rendered by Flower as 'in the running of my days'. They are little different from the running of the days of his fellow islanders.

Animals and fish, if not birds, parade plentifully through *The Islandman*, domestic and wild alike; the fauna of O Crohan's island life was surprisingly rich: hens, donkeys, cats, dogs, cows, sheep, goats, ferrets; and in the wild: porpoises, congers, gulls, fish of many kinds, sharks, lobster and crab, rabbits and seals. They were to be eaten or used, of course, but could be eaten or used in another fashion, too. Animals provide O Crohan with a rich stock of metaphors by which he can depict and assess his fellows; mostly these are original or familiar, but occasionally they go beyond his experience. After the Congested Districts Board introduced fencing around consolidated private holdings, the gardens were shipshape, writes O Crohan, 'so that neither deer nor eagle could go into them' (p.235). This confused me (might there have been deer on Great Blasket? Might O Crohan have seen a white-tailed sea-eagle?) until I realized it was probably a traditional saying, which Flower in *The Western Island* records O Crohan as employing to describe a snug cave 'that neither deer nor eagle come could at' (p.86), possibly some bardic formula.

TWO

In *The Irish Tradition*, Flower recalls listening spellbound to an old man (a Blasketman, I infer) reciting a long tale. 'I have kept you from your dinner with my tales of the *fiana*', the teller apologizes. 'You have done well', Flower replies, 'for a tale is better than food'.[8] In *The Islandman*, the two are curiously connected and co-dominant. Food is the very stuff of life – what is gathered, hunted, grown, and so too is the tale, be it anecdote (experience barely processed), the local legend (midway between the memory of an historical occurrence, and its complete processing into the tradition of a Finn tale or international folk-tale), or the folk-tale proper.

So authoritative is tradition that for the renowned tale-teller, to stumble is to receive a sign that death is imminent. Peig Sayers recalled for Flower her father Tomás beginning a long tale, 'The Red Ox', only to stumble during its telling; she reminded him that death must be on his way; her father replied: 'Death hasn't left Cork on his way to meet me yet', but he sickened that night and died two days later (*The Western Island*, p.54). In this episode of a fatal telling, Tradition seems even more despotic than the Irish Revival was to be.

I have to confess to a certain boredom with folk-tales and I am more enamoured of the pithy dicta, saws and aphorisms that enliven O Crohan's written reminiscence. (Just as I prefer improvised one-liners to more elaborate, memorized jokes with punch-lines.) In his

Foreword to *The Islandman*, Flower attests to O Crohan's natural stream of proverbs as well as tales and poems. In *The Western Island*, Flower recalls one of his reunions with a group of islanders and their each producing proverbs on the inevitability of death and the consolation of religious faith. One asks, 'Where is the snow that was so bright last year?' Flower leaps up in excitement and cries 'Ou sont les neiges d'antan?' When he identifies the author as François Villon, the island 'King' inquires: 'Was he a Connaughtman?' When Flower enlightens him, O Crohan interjects: 'Well. You can't better the proverb. I've always heard that the French are a clever people, and I wouldn't put it past them to have said that before we did' (p.vi).

O Crohan's proverbs in *The Islandman* are natural and unforced – 'the tide doesn't stay for high noon'; 'it's a rare thing to see a cat with a saddle on him'; 'Try the river before you venture into the current'; 'the lazy lounger doesn't catch fish'; 'God's help is nearer than the door', and so on. Flower records one of O Crohan's in *The Western Island*: 'When the Lord God made heaven and earth at the first, He kept the better of the two for himself'. And others: 'talking never brought the turf home yet'; '"More water, More water" cries the drowning Protestant' (p.73) – this last an obscure one which doesn't sound flattering to the 'Sasanach', translated by Flower as 'Protestant'. Arguing over the nature of the people who might have lived on the island a thousand years before, the King defends Flower's assessment of the stone ruins as prehistoric, despite the evidence of their excellent masonry, by pronouncing sagely: 'all things in the world are growing better but only poetry and the craft of stoneworking'. Flower adds: 'This settled the matter, for a proverb is a final argument not to be controverted' (pp.25–6).

I do not know whether these are always literal translations from the Irish or whether on occasion Robin Flower supplied English proverbial equivalents; it is the case that Flower's mastery of English idiom (he is a very fine prose stylist in his own right, as *The Western Island* and *The Irish Tradition* demonstrate) sometimes gives me pause.

In any event, I am interested in the prevalence of proverbial thought in O Crohan's reminiscences, for I grew up with the vestiges of it in post-war Belfast. Proverbs and sayings are not merely nuggets panned from a discursive gravel, nor are they merely decorative remarks, conversational embroidery or hemmings. They are at once the evidence and the produce of a way of thinking about and perceiving the world. They are common, indeed essential, in largely oral cultures. After all, how is thought preserved in such cultures? – by thinking memorable thoughts, as Walter Ong remarks.[9]

Proverbs by being formulaic are their own mnemonic aids; but the forms of the proverbs are the substance of thought itself. As Ong observes: 'In an oral culture, experience is intellectualized mnemonically' (*Orality and Literacy*, p.36). So to identify aggregation, say, as an oral formula (soldiers are brave, princesses are beautiful, etc.), one that helps the memory, is also to identify a way of interpreting human beings and the world. I myself grew up with a ready ability to classify people (and usually to their detriment), and this was due not just to the vestigial puritanism (by which we were quick to disapprove and spot backsliding) but also to the strength of orality in that community. Ong refers justly to the 'psychodynamics of orality', and in an essay entitled 'A Runagate Tongue', I had already tried to identify the communal frame of mind that lay behind the hundreds of sayings and epithets I recall from childhood and that are absent from the dictionaries and phrase books.[10] We could essay the same for the community that produced *The Islandman*. In *The Irish Tradition*, Flower writes:

> There is one characteristic of Celtic speech ... which gets little notice in modern criticism, although it was the first thing to strike the Romans when they came in contact with the Celts. The elder Cato tells us that the Celts were distinguished for their aptitude for fighting and for subtle speech. The Irish have maintained these two characters. Indeed, I think if one asked what characteristic was to be found everywhere in Irish literature from the first records down to the tales and popular sayings current among the peasantry to-day, the answer must necessarily be: a sharp and homely brevity of epigrammatic speech eminently calculated for the rapid thrust and return of contentious talk. (p.110)

The islanders in O Crohan's account combat the elements, the creatures of the sea, each other (bloodily at times), and even fate and fortune themselves. There are casually dismissive remarks by husbands about their wives – but in their wives' absence, and these might have been oral formulas, expected expressions of male independence. Everyone seems quick to take offence: speech is often pre-emptive or conclusive: the first or last word memorably and unanswerably expressed. The picture of life seems Darwinian, but if so, it is usually contained by a cultural and oral Darwinism that ensures that competition is less lethal, more virtual. Ong describes oral culture as 'agonistically toned' (*Orality and Literacy*, p.43), which is part of its traditional force and does not subvert the conservatism of oral culture. Oral culture does not lack originality, but originality and individuality, the experiences that overspill their formulaic comprehension, express themselves in the management of social interaction: the right proverb for the appropriate occasion, for example: Hamlet's 'the readiness is all', might be the catch-cry of the oral culture.

Experience, claims Chaucer's Wife of Bath, is sufficient authority for her to speak of the woe that is in marriage; but the text qualifies her claim. Experience might be sufficient authority for O Crohan to speak of the woe that is in life (he speaks of his marriage as cursorily as Crusoe of his), but his thought runs as naturally to oral structure. Like the good Wife, O Crohan lives dynamically between the authority of experience and the authority of tradition. It has been said that one of the crucial problems of the Middle Ages was the relation of orality to a world making ever-increasing use of texts.[11] Tomás O Crohan and the culture of late nineteenth-century Great Blasket re-enact this problem, because of the broken continuity of the Irish tradition, because of the remoteness of this relic area (to adapt the linguists), and because of the impingement on the island of scholars of Irish and scholars of English.

O Crohan's sense of the world is not, on the evidence of *The Islandman*, primarily theocentric or Christian, but rather anthropocentric in the manner, say, of the traditional ballad. The written version of his worldview shares with the ballad that primal sense of humanity's mysterious relation to fate; it shares that quality Padraic Colum identified in folk-tales as 'reverie', a state of mind midway between dream and reality: life distilled, purged of irrelevance and circumstance.[12] In so purging it, O Crohan casts a cold eye on life, on death. I find this as impressive as Yeats's cold eye and purged images, at once ennobling and dismaying. How he came to be so I do not know, but O Crohan is to me one of the old masters, and about suffering they are never wrong, aware of its leisurely occurrence, its casual inevitability. Tradition and the individual talent, convention and unique experience: this is part of the picture but not the whole of it.

On the strength of *The Islandman*, I believe it was on the older consolation of philosophy rather than on nineteenth-century Christianity that O Crohan drew. *The Consolation of Philosophy* was, of course, the title of the sixth-century work by the Christian Roman writer Boethius and a most valued book for the Middle Ages, and for Geoffrey Chaucer. What is chiefly remembered from the book is Boethius' notion of the vicissitudes of temporal existence as a Wheel of Fortune. The consolation is that God is above the Wheel, directing it, that the Wheel is not the final geometry of human fate. Recalling how around 1888 the islanders lost their boats to confiscation (resorting to canoes thereafter) but fought free of exorbitant and arbitrary rent demands,

O Crohan remarks: 'People say that the wheel is always turning, and that's a true saying, for in the part of the world that I have known it has turned many times; and if the world improved a bit round the Blaskets at that time, and God gave us much good fortune, I fancy we didn't take the care we should have done of it, for "easy come, easy go" is always the way' (p.167).

There are troubles galore in O Crohan's life after that, but still, 'God's help is nearer than the door'; and 'He who puts us on short commons at one time gives plenty at another time'; and 'the thing a man likes least in the world may be, for all he knows, the very heart of his fortune'; and 'However hard our masters may be after us sometimes, the Great Master of all often sends them to the rightabout'. The Wheel turns, and his acknowledgement of it salvages O Crohan's account from an exclusive pleading of the poor mouth. *The Islandman* is as much an inventory of the bountiful as of woes – ninety-six rabbits in one foray on Inis na Bro; a trove of brass bolts from a ship sold for 16 pounds to a passing vessel; seventy-two lobsters in one night's work, sold for three gold sovereigns to an anchored ship; 8,000 spring mackerel in a day's fishing, salted down in the absence of a market for fresh fish.

The Wheel turns and there are turning-points more significant than others. The most celebrated for readers is the day the poet Dunlevy commandeered O Crohan's attention and took him from the task of turf-cutting. It is not clear to me why O Crohan thought an ill wind blew against him ever since the day the poet and his songs kept him from the turf (though I will come back to this). It is clearer why the romp with the frisky girls did so, for it seems to have belatedly stung him with the pricks of sexual desire: in the horseplay, he *realized* women, as it were. In any case, such turning-points initiate him into the *directions* of life, some good, some ill, the influences on one's life seen as winds, some favourable, some adverse. Another turning-point is the exhausting struggle with the sea beast (basking shark or whale) when the author was 55, prematurely reminiscent of Hemingway's old man and the sea. Flower records a comparable turning-point for Peig Sayers in *The Western Island* – her marriage at 17, after which by her own account she never knew an entirely happy day, yet refusing to complain since it is God's will (p.59).

THREE

The Wheel of Fortune is one way of imagining how unique experience, the individual life, is inseparable from the impersonal pattern of human existence commemorated in tradition. Occasionally the wheel-turn of a man's life coincides with the wheel-turn of a community. So it was with Tomás O Crohan, whose life encompassed the beginning of the end for the culture of the Great Blasket. The record of that life is not merely happenstance: the crisis of the island culture and the record of it are one and the same: politics, demography and serious literacy impacted on the island and induced it to tell its story as the life of a condemned man might flash before his eyes on the eve of his execution. It is a curious conjunction and is epitomized for me in the case of Eileen Nicholls.

Most of O Crohan's children died prematurely; the fourth child, Donal, drowned when as a boy he tried unsuccessfully to save Miss Nicholls, who had got into difficulties while teaching a daughter of O Crohan's to swim; the girl was saved. O Crohan is as usual laconic and stoical in the recollection, recalling that he was anxious lest the Nicholls family thought him angry that a boy of his died while saving their daughter. Their own anxiety was unnecessary: 'If it was for her he died', he writes, 'it could not be helped. It was God's will' (p.198).

By chance, the antiquarian Thomas Mason was staying near Dunquin and was told of the calamity (without knowing anything of Tomás O Crohan). What O Crohan observed as the biggest funeral Dunquin had ever known was painted by Mason, in *The Islands of Ireland* (1936), on to a broader canvas. 'The funeral procession of currachs across the Sound', he writes, 'reminded me of a funeral that I saw in Venice where black gondolas take the place of the mourning coaches'.[13] He remembers being told that a phantom ship had appeared before the tragedy, a 'sure forerunner of misfortune', but O Crohan – who is recorded by Flower in *The Western Island* as believing in fairies (or believing in them sufficiently to tell the tale of a stolen woman) – fails to mention this in *The Islandman*, in which the spirit world is scanted in favour of a daylight realism; it is possible, of course, that the spectral sighting was kept from him.[14]

By a more significant coincidence, the Ulster playwright and theosophist James Cousins, and his wife Gretta, were staying in Ventry in the August of that year (dated variously as 1908 and 1909 by Cousins – it was in fact 1909). Cousins was later edged out of the Irish Dramatic Revival by Yeats and he and his wife emigrated in 1915 to India where they stayed until their deaths. In 1950 they published in Madras a joint autobiography of alternating chapters, *We Two Together*, which includes a chapter by Cousins that recalls in detail the drowning of Eileen Nicholls.

Miss Nicholls was staying in the same lodgings as Cousins, who had known of her as a considerable figure in the Gaelic League. She had headed to the Blaskets, like Synge before her, to get as far away as possible from English civilization and the English tongue. Synge was the last visitor to occupy the bed above Thady Kevane's shop in Ventry that Cousins now occupied, waiting for his wife to arrive. Miss Nicholls then left for Great Blasket, shouting *Beannact libh* [*leat* in Cousins's account] to the Cousinses. This is the farewell that Miss Ivors shouts to the gathering in James Joyce's story 'The Dead' and in Cousins's telling, Miss Nicholls resembles Miss Ivors (Joyce's rendering of one of the Sheehy sisters). Gretta Cousins from Roscommon – whose Christian name Joyce probably borrowed for his character Gretta Conroy in 'The Dead' – had arrived and improvised a suffragette meeting outside the church where Miss Nicholls had that day attended mass as a 'pious Catholic' (Cousins's phrase) but had nevertheless scandalized the local mass-goers by seating herself on the men's side of the church.

The next day the tragedy occurs as the Cousinses are being rowed to the island to visit Miss Nicholls by arrangement. Cousins recalls: 'With one of those conspiracies of fate that are called coincidences, a neighbouring priest had come on a casual visit to the island, and had given great service to the locating of the body of Miss Nicolls [*sic*] and performing such rites of the Church as were possible under the circumstances.'[15] There is a wake for Miss Nicholls in the home of the King. The priest leaves with wires for the press from Cousins. A wake for the boy is held in the O Crohan home, but Tomás O Crohan is unidentified by Cousins and clearly unknown to him.

Cousins – who must have relished them as an occultist – records signs and portents: the phantom ship of yesteryear's design sailing out from Dunquin a few days before; a ghost-cat in the Kevane home that went upstairs and disappeared in the room where Miss Nicholls stayed; a girl-friend of Miss Nicholls remembering that in a game in which each in a group was asked how she would wish to die, Miss Nicholls had replied 'to be drowned saving another' (according to Cousins, Eileen Nicholls had gone to the aid of the girl before she herself got into difficulties). The mysticism of the Literary Revival, the suffragette movement, the folk belief in the spirit world, patriotic Irish Catholicism, the Gaelic League and cultural nationalism: all converge in one day's event on Great Blasket and Tomás O Crohan might appear to us as its silent president. This is not to speak of the symbolism of a fruitless attempt by a cultural nationalist to save an islander, and an islander to save a cultural nationalist, and the loss of both.[16]

FOUR

The coincidences of events and conjunctions of cultural meanings are hardly separable from the convergence of orality and literacy that made possible *The Islandman*. My attraction to the worldview of the book bears little resemblance to that of cultural nationalists. I am attracted to O Crohan's rugged individualism, and to his sense of individuality that extends even to his understanding of traditional wisdom: 'even the proverbs', he remarks, 'had their beginning; some man said every proverb out of his own mind at the first'.[17] I like, too, his assured sense of island identity by which the rest of Ireland is 'the land' and to which you bid your farewell when you embark for the islands. Here is Irishness before ideology, before politics, before a problematic self-consciousness; hardly practicable, I suppose, but somehow reassuring for me to contemplate. Tellingly, the last chapters, with the author engaged in cultural work, are less interesting to me than their predecessors; I sense the familiar looming and my heart sinks a little, Pearse and 1916 troubling the living stream of island existence.

It is not O Crohan's patronizable 'peasant' humility that appeals to me; rather is it his maverick independence that speaks to an inheritor of religious Dissent like me. To the extent that this is shared among the islanders, it is an aspect of the oral worldview; to the extent that it was O Crohan's to an unusually high degree, it is an aspect of his genius. McGahern identifies a Homeric boasting running through *The Islandman*, much of it toned down or edited out, according to McGahern.[18] He quotes a deleted sentiment from the close of the book: 'there's not a country or neighbourhood or nation in which one person doesn't triumph above all others ... Now from the first time the fire was lit on this island no one has written about its life or its people. That leaves the *craobh* or the branch of victory with the person who did it' (p.15).

This qualifies through the rivalry of authorship, of pioneer annalism, O Crohan's celebrated and soulful remark: 'I have done my best to set down the character of the people about me so that some record of us might live after us, for the like of us will never be again' (*The Islandman*, p.244). Otherwise the remark might remind us of something Finnian, the Abbot of Moville, said in 'The Story of Tuan mac Cairill', James Stephens' adaptation of a tale in the *Book of the Dun Cow*. Tuan tells Finnian the story of Ireland's invasions, thereby transferring custody of Ireland's pagan lore to the Abbot (Patrick to Tuan's Ossian) who felt that 'it would be a pity if the people who came after us should be ignorant of what happened long ago, and of the deeds of their fathers'.[19] But why shouldn't the scribe salvage fame from his efforts into the bargain, one imagines O Crohan saying, with a proverb at the ready to clinch the matter.

Competitiveness was strenuous in the lives of the Blasket islanders, if O Crohan's book is to be credited. Literacy permitted O Crohan to indulge for a wider audience what Flower in his Foreword to *The Islandman* calls O Crohan's 'natural critical faculty'. This can be turned even on poetry itself when it is to the detriment of work. Flower records a tale of O Crohan's in *The Western Island* (pp.17–19), in which an official Gaelic League-type Board of Poetry encourages song and poem making until the people of a town in Kerry near Killarney neglect their land and it runs to waste, idle creativity distracting them (as thought distracts Swift's Laputans who sail over a neglected landscape that some critics say is contemporary Ireland). Flower seems discomfited by the tale and counterbalances it with one borrowed from Laurence Sterne about a town not ruined but regenerated by poetry. But O Crohan's tale accords with the incident of the poet Dunlevy and the turf-cutting. In O Crohan I sense some of the philistinism and realism that abides with the critical faculty; his book seems the more authentic to me for being somehow wrested from a practical spirit that suspects its own attempts at flight; in this he, again, reminds me of Patrick Kavanagh; in each case art seems achieved against the grain and is a truer poetry over the head of it.

The House of Fame, whose door O Crohan knocks at the end of *The Islandman* (in McGahern's version at least) is where Poetry traditionally wishes to dwell, but it has been suggested that Chaucer – that practical and worldly man – undermines the notion by subversively describing the House with threadbare and hand-me-down sayings and formulas. If, as it has also been suggested, this is literacy's disguised reservations about the authority of orality,[20] O Crohan might have come to share those reservations though, by doing so, paradoxically enriching his own writing by nourishing it on the rich oral culture whose laureate and elegist he is.

NOTES

1. Tomás O Crohan, *The Islandman*, trans. Robin Flower (Oxford: Clarendon, 1951), p.180. All quotations are from this edition.
2. Robin Flower, *The Western Island or The Great Blasket* (Oxford: Clarendon Press, 1945), pp.103–6.
3. Flann O'Brien, *The Poor Mouth* (London: Hart-Davis, MacGibbon, 1973); first published in 1941 as *An Beal Bocht* by Myles na gCopaleen. By 1941, *An t-Oileanach* (1929) by Tomás O Criomhthain had been translated by Flower as *The Islandman* (1934) and *Fiche Blian ag Fas* (1933) by Muiris O Suilleabhain had been translated by Thomson and Moya Llewelyn Davies as *Twenty Years A-Growing* (1933); it was of course the Irish originals of these 'peasant autobiographies' that captured O'Brien's dark imagination.

4. I discuss this episode in the chapter on *The Islandman* in my critical survey, *Fictions of the Irish Literary Revival* (Syracuse, NY: Syracuse University Press, 1987), pp.323–40.
5. Muiris MacConghail, 'The Blasket Islands: An Island Literature and Oral Culture', manuscript of a paper delivered to the Tenth International Congress of Celtic Studies, Edinburgh University, 28 July 1995.
6. Richard J. Ussher and Robert Warren, *Birds of Ireland* (London: Gurney and Jackson, 1900), p.392.
7. John McGahern, '*An tOileanach/The Islandman*', *The Canadian Journal of Irish Studies*, 13, 4 (1987), pp.7–15.
8. Robin Flower, *The Irish Tradition* (Oxford: Clarendon Press, 1947), p.106.
9. Walter J. Ong, *Orality and Literacy: The Technologizing of the Word* (London: Methuen, 1982), p.34.
10. 'A Runagate Tongue, or, English as We Speak It in Ulster', *The Irish Literary Supplement*, 12, 3 (1993), pp.24–7. Reprinted in *Causeway: Cultural Traditions Journal*, 1, 2 (1994), pp.19–26; 1, 3 (1994), pp.35–8.
11. Brian Stock, *The Implications of Literacy: Written Language and Models of Interpretation in the Eleventh and Twelfth Centuries* (1983), quoted by Leslie K. Arnovick, *Written Reliquaries* (Amsterdam: John Benjamins, 2006), p.177.
12. Padraic Colum, *Story Telling New & Old* (New York: Macmillan, 1968), pp.14–15.
13. Thomas H. Mason, *The Islands of Ireland: Their Scenery, People, Life and Antiquities* (London: Batsford, 1936), p.100.
14. The spectral ship, though Mason does not say so, is presumably the ghost of *Our Lady of the Rosary*, a Spanish galleon of the Armada which was wrecked off the Blaskets with great loss of life: see Flower, *The Western Island*, pp.78–83.
15. James H. and Margaret E. Cousins, *We Two Together* (Madras: Ganesh, 1950), p.151.
16. At the Robin Flower Commemoration (Great Blasket Cultural Centre, 29–31 March 1996), I had expressed during my talk a desire to know more about Eileen Nicholls. By one of those coincidences that help to justify such gatherings, there was an Irish-speaking teacher in the audience who had written an entire book on her: *Oigbhean Uasal o Phriomhchathair Eireann* (Dublin: Conradh na Gaeilge, 1992). In Micheal O Dubhshlaine's bi-lingual book, Miss Nicholls's role in the Gaelic movement is deepened by her friendship with Padraic Pearse (who had preceded her to Great Blasket in 1898), a friendship O Dubhshlaine believes was romantic love on Pearse's part, a claim earlier rejected by the historian Ruth Dudley Edwards in her biography of Pearse, *Patrick Pearse: The Triumph of Failure* (New York: Taplinger, 1978), p.126. It is clear, though, from O Dubhshlaine's book, that Eileen Nicholls was a highly articulate cultural nationalist of great intellectual promise. The two papers of hers he reproduces, 'Some Thoughts about the Future of Irish Literature' and 'Nationality in Irish Education', are brief but maturely eloquent manifestoes on the connections between nationality, education and language, claims of the kind I regard as largely foreign to Tomás O Crohan, whose island culture she clearly wished to bring under the authority of the Dublin-based Gaelic Revival. (She is referred to as Eveleen Nicolls in O Dubhshlaine's *A Dark Day on the Blaskets: The Drowning of Domhnall O Criomhthain and Eibhlín Nic Niocaill on the Blasket Islands* [2003].)
17. Quoted in Flower, *The Western Island*, p.94.
18. McGahern, *An tOileanach / The Islandman*, p.14.
19. James Stephens, *Irish Fairy Tales* (New York: Macmillan, 1920), p.259.
20. Both suggestions come from Arnovick, *Written Reliquaries*.

3

AGAINST NATURE? SCIENCE AND OSCAR WILDE

YEATS, WILDE AND SCIENCE

Late and soon, W.B. Yeats identified science as a culprit standing in dangerous opposition to art and imagination. In 1897, in 'The Celtic Element in Literature', he welcomed a widespread reaction 'against the rationalism of the eighteenth century' which was mingling 'with a reaction against the materialism of the nineteenth century', a reaction he identified in literature as 'the symbolical movement'.[1] In 1900, he told Shaw in debate that Shaw belonged 'to a bygone generation – to the scientific epoch – and was now "reactionary"'.[2] Shaw was not amused. In 1921, the poet recalled his detestation of T.H. Huxley and the famous (Irish-born) physicist John Tyndall who had deprived him of 'the simple-minded religion' of his childhood.[3] His 1934 essay, 'Louis Lambert', put the nineteenth century's most famous scientist in the dock for 'what our instinct repudiates, Darwin's exaltation of accidental variations'.[4] Given such sentiments, one detects approval in Yeats's 1936 remembrance of Lionel Johnson as a Rhymers' Club-man who asserted that 'science must be confined to the kitchen or the workshop, that it could discover nothing of importance'.[5]

It was in Ireland, Yeats believed, that could be found the most fertile and hospitable ground available for the counter-Renaissance and counter-Enlightenment. Science was particularly uncongenial as a way of engaging with Irish nature (landscape and its creatures) that is, by turns, magical, dreamlike, mysterious, spiritual and symbolic, something inspiring local and national patriotism, subjective yet ancestral, most suitably expressed in poetry and art. Long after the Celtic Twilight (which promoted such an idea of Irish nature), Yeats's hostile attitude to science remained influential in Ireland. Of course, the exclusion of science from received 'native' Irish culture antedates Yeats, but the poet and his literary movement copper-fastened it.[6]

Yeats's dislike of science, if it owed something to Matthew Arnold's notion of Celticism (which helped to sponsor the Twilight), also flourished in the midst of the aesthetic movement of the close of the century. We might, then, expect it to have owed a debt to his fellow Irishman, Oscar Wilde, whom Yeats first met at the house of the poet W.E. Henley in 1888. We can find in Richard Ellmann's

Eminent Domain (1967) some of Yeats's other intellectual and artistic debts to Wilde eloquently tallied as borrowed ideas: the superiority of the imagination (and 'lying') over reason and observation (and 'truth'); the inferiority of life beside art and the latter's capability of imposing its images upon the former, and life's imitation of art; the crucial significance for western civilization of Hellenism, of 'the spirit that is Greek', as Basil Hallward terms it in *The Picture of Dorian Gray* (1890); the rejection of art as mere self-expression or mere fidelity to externalities.[7]

Although we might wish to ascertain the precise extent of Yeats's reading of Wilde and keep in mind how easy it is to confuse influence with affinity (many late Victorian British writers, after all, fell under the sway of French Symbolism), we could, unsupervised, lengthen Ellmann's tally. For example, Yeats was to explore in his verse dialogues, and systematize in his prose, Wilde's distinction in *The Critic as Artist* between the contemplative man and the man of action.[8] Secondly, Wilde's elaboration of the pose became Yeats's theories of the mask and the anti-self. Thirdly, if Wilde and Yeats shared the influence of Arnold, Wilde's acquaintance with the English poet's criticism predated Yeats's. It is true, of course, that by the time Wilde was endorsing Arnold's identification of the Celtic spirit in art Yeats was already steeping himself in Celticism.[9] We cannot, then, claim Wilde's interest in Celticism as a fourth anticipation of Yeats – unless, that is, we broaden Celticism to include those attributes we would now regard as amounting to a damaging stereotype of the Celt as lazy, imaginative and unrealistic (and most certainly unscientific), a stereotype that Wilde toyed with and that flourished before Yeats undermined it in his own peculiar way: i.e., by retaining it whilst dignifying it and draining it of condescension.[10] Wilde proudly regarded himself as a Celt (in England at any rate), and thought, not wholly seriously perhaps, that he and Shaw spearheaded 'the great Celtic school'. Ironically, Wilde and Shaw are the two major writers who are normally excluded, for nationalist reasons, from the canon of the Irish Literary Revival.[11]

Fifthly, Yeats's 'artifice of eternity' is Wilde's early ideal of beauty writ (and thought) large. Nature – that is, the natural condition of things – is in human beings impossible: 'Being natural is simply a pose, and the most irritating pose I know', cries Lord Henry Wotton in *The Picture of Dorian Gray*. 'To be natural is to be obvious', says Gilbert in *The Critic as Artist*, 'and to be obvious is to be inartistic'. In another sense, nature is the *substance* of things, and decorative art is for Gilbert the highest art because it deliberately rejects nature as a model in favour of that sense of *form* in which life is deficient and 'which is the basis of creative no less than of critical achievement'. *The Decay of Lying* (1889) begins: 'the more we study Art, the less we care for Nature. What Art really reveals to us is Nature's lack of design, her curious crudities, her extraordinary monotony, her absolutely unfinished condition.'[12] Aestheticism, Camille Paglia remarks, 'is predicated on a swerve from nature', and by nature we might mean variously human nature, the subject of the natural sciences, and the nature of things.[13]

None of this surprises, though I will return to it in an attempt to do just that. Nor does it surprise that Wilde praised Poe's 'Sonnet – to Science', in which science is humanized as a prying daughter of old Time (whose peering – in an interesting anticipation of Heisenberg – alters what it peers at), a failed muse; it is also animalized as a vulture feeding upon the poet's heart (like Prometheus' liver); in either guise it steals from the poet 'The summer dream beneath the tamarind tree'.[14]

Perhaps, if we wished a case-study of Wilde's attitude to nature and to science, of which the study of nature is a branch, we might choose the role of flowers in Wilde's life and work. The conventional imagery and symbolism of flowers in poetry assume a certain hothouse and florist's association in Wilde's writing, and indeed in his life, in which what Ellmann calls 'Pre-Raphaelite' and 'talismanic' lilies were frequent, not just as items of personal affectation (like the green carnations), not even just as emblems of beauty (and therefore uselessness), but also (and ranking in this regard with sunflowers) as 'perfect models of design, the most naturally adapted for decorative art'.[15] It was design more than appropriate symbolism that Wilde was thinking of when he wrote to the Rev. J. Page Hopps in 1885, expressing both his regret at not being well enough to attend a meeting of the Funeral and Mourning Reform group and his agreement (couched in a solemnity that skirts humour) with the group's aims: 'The habit of bringing flowers to the grave is now almost universal, and is a custom beautiful in its symbolism; but I cannot help thinking that the elaborate and expensive designs made by the florist are often far less lovely than a few flowers held loose in the hand.'[16] Tongue more obviously in cheek (or pistil in corolla), Wilde responded, in a letter that appeared in the *Pall Mall Gazette*, to a poet's botanically based correction of Wilde's pronunciation of the word 'tuberose':

> Sir, I am deeply distressed to hear that tuberose is so called from its being a 'lumpy flower'. It is not at all lumpy and, even if it were, no poet should be heartless enough to say so. Henceforth

> there really must be two derivations for every word, one for the poet and one for the scientist. And in the present case the poet will dwell on the tiny trumpets of ivory into which the white flower breaks, and leave to the man of science horrid allusions to its supposed lumpiness and indiscreet revelations of its private life below ground. On the roots of verbs Philology may be allowed to speak, but on the roots of flowers she must keep silence. We cannot allow her to dig up Parnassus.[17]

Like Miss Prism, Wilde spoke horticulturally, his metaphors drawn from fruits and flowers, and nowhere more so than in *Dorian Gray*, whose eponymous hero has a 'rose-white boyhood' and a 'rose-red youth', who eats the moon-chilled cherries that life (no, artifice) offers him and for which he lives (no, dies) to pay the penalty. The novel opens with the rich odours of roses mingling with the odours of lilac and thorn: nature's flourishes and fertilities are created to sustain a dangerous aesthesis – dangerous because it proves a moral anaesthesia – but that in turn is signified by nature's deficient form and threatening riot ('the sullen murmur of the bees shouldering their way through the long unmown grass') that is best turned from (it seems) in favour of human art and artifice. Almost immediately after this remarkable opening, nature is tamed into symbol and design before the reader eventually senses that the 'swerve from nature' – though granted not the nature of Basil Hallward's studio garden – is fatal.

SCIENTIFIC WILDE

We would expect such hostility to science from the man who, in Paglia's words, 'projected himself internationally as the ultimate aesthete'.[18] But on reflection the expectation seems shallow. To begin with, Wilde first knew that the 'marvels of design' achievable by decorative art were often absent from nature, not through studying Art (as he declares in *The Decay of Lying*), but through reading students of nature.[19] He wrote in his Commonplace Book while a student at Oxford: 'We have outgrown the theory of design and talk easily of the "silly maladaptations of organic nature" (Clifford).'[20] The editors of the Commonplace Book do not offer a precise William Kingdon Clifford source of Wilde's entry, and nor can I, but Clifford in his lecture 'On the Aims and Instruments of Scientific Thought' (reprinted in an 1879 volume of Clifford's essays and lectures that Wilde read studiously), does discuss purposeless or defective adaptations in organic nature.[21] 'Design' was a word shared by decorative artists and pre-Darwinian espousers of natural theology, but among naturalists in Wilde's time it was being superseded by the word 'purpose' so as to uncouple natural processes from an intelligent Creator, and pull back on teleological explanations of the organic world.[22]

But Clifford was only one of the major scientific thinkers Wilde read assiduously while a student at Oxford; others included Huxley, Tyndall and Herbert Spencer. His career at Oxford was timely in this regard: he matriculated two months after Tyndall's challenging, pro-evolutionist 'Belfast Address' to the British Association in August 1874, which provoked a controversy more important than the earlier Huxley–Wilberforce clash, in the assessment of one historian.[23] The thinkers young Wilde paraphrased and annotated in his Oxford Commonplace Book and College Notebook were grappling with the vexing issues of the day (often posed as disturbing oppositions), made more vexatious by the recent intervention of the evolutionists: mind v. matter, idealism v. realism, imagination v. reason, individuality v. race, experience v. heredity, consciousness v. external reality, freedom v. necessity.

We discover in Wilde's Oxford notebooks a surprising pleasure in science: witness his delight in Shelley's 'passionate enthusiasm for science' (*pace* Yeats) and in the claim that Goethe, 'a devoted pupil of science', was the first Darwinian.[24] Ignorance of Darwin was enough to condemn a putative thinker in Wilde's eyes as late as 1889, in which year he wrote to W.L. Courtney backhandedly thanking him for a copy of his *Life of John Stuart Mill*: 'As for Mill as a thinker – a man who knew nothing of Plato or Darwin gives me very little. His reputation is curious to me ... But Darwinism has of course shattered many reputations besides his.'[25] 'Unscientific' remained for the mature Wilde an indictment, 'scientific' a term of praise.[26] He had correspondents with scientific interests (for example, Grant Allen and Edward Heron-Allen), and of course his father was a practising scientist through whom Wilde would have absorbed to some degree the scientific element of Anglo-Irish culture and an implicit respect for it.[27]

Yet the early reading, the pondering of the weighty questions of the day, and the respect for science were all inferable from the epigrammatic shorthand of the imaginative works. I say 'were', for I had so inferred before coming gratefully upon *Oscar Wilde's Oxford Notebooks* (1989), edited by Philip E. Smith and Michael S. Helfand, which is the product of strenuous legwork and describes the bio-bibliographical base of that pyramid whose apex is the brilliant aphorisms. The text of the notebooks, the provision of sources, and the exhaustive and illuminating editorial commentary establish this book as the most important contribution to Wilde studies since the Hart-Davis edition of the letters in 1962. It is no longer possible to view Wilde as a supreme exponent of one, and only one, of what were once called the Two Cultures, as an artist blithely contemptuous of the other 'culture', or as a figurative inhabitant of Art, as Des Esseintes was a literal inhabitant of the sequestered artifice of his house at Fontenay-aux-Roses.

But even *A Rebours* (1884), translated by Robert Baldick under the title *Against Nature*, can give us pause in this regard, should we take our cue from Wilde. To the hero of the book that poisons Dorian Gray, nature has had her day: 'artifice was considered by Des Esseintes to be the distinctive mark of genius'.[28] But if Des Esseintes rebuffs nature in this peremptory way (and how far is he the object of Huysmans' irony?), he does not so rebuff the modern sciences by which nature has been studied. The narrator of *Dorian Gray* tells us that Des Esseintes was one 'in whom the romantic and the scientific temperaments were so strangely blended': that is, both unexpectedly and bizarrely blended, as they were more familiarly blended in, say, Goethe or (as we now know) the student Wilde. Wilde's novel, like Huysmans', is among other things a natural history of sensations, and includes (following Huysmans to the verge of plagiarism) a description and taxonomy of the hero's cabinets of collected exotica (strange perfumes, musical instruments, jewels) all reminiscent of both the Victorian collections of exotic natural specimens and the Victorian mania for cataloguing and classification. Dorian Gray also collects for a time stories about jewels, whereas Lord Henry Wotton collects epigrams; if Dorian's collection is secret, like Des Esseintes', Lord Henry's is for select public display; moreover, the epigrams are Lord Henry's own: he collects, as it were, himself. And the aphorisms and epigrams themselves, Lord Henry's and the others', we might even see as Wilde's social version of scientific axioms and theorems, summations of long observation and experience analogous to physical laws.[29]

Dorian Gray's passing addiction to collection and classification is an aspect of the connoisseurship practised by Lord Henry: both the artistic connoisseur and the scientific collector meet in taxonomy and nomenclature. When writing *Dorian Gray*, Wilde remembered his 1885 letter to the *Pall Mall Gazette*, for he has Lord Henry complain that scientific names for flowers do not emulate the beauty of the plants: he entertains the idea of renaming the organic world on aesthetic principles. Again, scientific method (that of nomenclature) is borrowed and adapted, not dismissed. As a dramatist and novelist, Wilde paid close attention to his characters' names, and in his most famous play founded a plot upon a pun and the nominal betrayal of the nature of the (mis)named.

As well as collector, Lord Henry is an experimenter who 'had been always enthralled by the methods of natural science, but the ordinary subject matter of that science had seemed to him trivial and of no import. And so he had begun by vivisecting himself, as he had ended by vivisecting others.' He jettisons the subject matter and retains the method: 'It was clear to him that the experimental method was the only method by which one could arrive at any scientific analysis of the passions; and certainly Dorian Gray was a subject made to his hand, and seemed to promise rich and fruitful results.'[30] 'He would be a wonderful study', Lord Henry tells Basil Hallward, choosing a word that suggests both pictorial composition and scientific inquiry (the case-study).

Like his literary forebears, Victor Frankenstein and Dr Jekyll (doubtful heroes in novels that, like *Dorian Gray*, exploit the *Doppelganger* theme), Lord Henry acknowledges that the price of substituting human life for the physical world is a hazardous participation:

> It was true that as one watched life in its curious crucible of pain and pleasure, one could not wear over one's face a mask of glass, nor keep the sulphurous fumes from troubling the brain and making the imagination turbid with monstrous fancies and misshapen dreams. There were poisons so subtle that to know their properties one had to sicken of them. There were maladies so strange that one had to pass through them if one sought to understand their nature. And, yet, what a great reward one received! How wonderful the whole world became to one! To note the curious hard logic of passion, and the emotional coloured life of the intellect – to observe where they met, and where they separated, at what point they were in unison, and at what point they were at discord – there was a delight in that! What matter what the cost was? One could never pay too high a price for any sensation.

'It often happened', he reflects, 'that when we thought we were experimenting on others we were really experimenting on ourselves'.[31] Shelley's Frankenstein, Stoker's Van Helsing and Wells's Time Traveller all learn this (while Jekyll learns its inverse), which might indicate a widespread cultural anxiety during the last century about science, not merely about the threatening illusion of its objectivity, but also about its generative capability that rivalled and therefore offended that capability exercised by God and nature.[32] 'To a large extent', Lord Henry concludes, 'the lad was his [i.e., Lord Henry's] own creation'.[33]

EVOLUTION AND THE INDIVIDUAL

Neither the suggestion of mock-science in *Dorian Gray*, nor the novel's moralistic, almost Christian conclusion (itself subverted beforehand by the celebrated Preface), nor the Faustian underpinning, nullifies in my opinion the importance of science to the book's conception or to Wilde's worldview and artistic vision. Nor do any of these nullify the novel's 'Hellenic ideal', its 'new Hedonism' that Wilde pits against what he calls, in *The Critic as Artist*, the 'new Puritanism' abroad in England. It is fascinating to discover that in his Oxford notebooks Wilde, drawing on Arnold, J.A. Symonds and others, thought it worth recording that 'the Greek attitude can only be gained by a recognition of the scientific basis of Life', that 'in early civilizations science is found intimately blended with poetry', that 'in modern science, the fourth dimension of space, infinity, eternity, &c are poetical conceptions', and that 'the early Greeks had mystic anticipations of nearly all great modern scientific truths'.[34]

Through Hellenism, Wilde associated science not with pessimism or glum materialism but with optimism and progress. Goethe, he wrote in his Commonplace Book, 'owed his sublime cheerfulness to his scientific training and this was the heritage of his Hellenism'.[35] But this did not entail emotionalism or sentimentalism. Lord Henry's belief that science is untouched by the emotions and therefore could enable us to solve social problems exacerbated by the nineteenth-century's 'over-expenditure of sympathy' is repeated by Gilbert, Wilde's spokesman in *The Critic as Artist*: 'That Humanitarian sympathy wars against Nature, by securing the survival of the failure, may make the men of science loathe its facile virtues.'[36] Wilde's systemic antipathy to philanthropy stands opposed to Dickens and may help explain Wilde's dislike of that novelist. Yeats shared the antipathy but not its Darwinian rationale.

The *a*morality of science, as Gilbert and Lord Henry (and Wilde) see it, is what some regard as its *im*morality, but Lord Henry interprets immorality as itself the occasion for individuality. Between morality and individualism 'the latter has really the higher aim. Modern morality consists in accepting the standard of one's age. I consider that for any man of culture to accept the standard of his age is a form of the grossest immorality.' Later in the novel, Dorian sits in front of his portrait, filled at times 'with that pride of individualism that is half the fascination of sin'.[37] Again, the moral penalty Dorian pays for that pride does not nullify individualism, which is a perennial virtue in Wilde's writings, from *The Critic as Artist* (1890) to *De Profundis*

(1897), maintained as it was by his concept of the Greek attitude. 'The longer one studies life and literature', Gilbert claims, 'the more strongly one feels that behind everything that is wonderful stands the individual, and that it is not the moment that makes the man, but the man who creates the age'.[38] If he jested that 'the whole of Japan is a pure invention. There is no such country, there are no such people',[39] Wilde seems quite serious in having Gilbert claim that Wilde's own century had been made by two men: 'The nineteenth century is a turning point in history simply on account of the work of two men, Darwin and Renan, the one the critic of the Book of Nature, the other the critic of the books of God.'[40] 'Progress in thought', Wilde wrote in his Commonplace Book, drawing on Clifford, 'is the assertion of individualism against authority'.[41]

At times Wilde called individuality 'self-preservation', a term that Darwinism would have suggested. He wrote in his Commonplace Book: 'The instinct of self-preservation in humanity, the desire to affirm one's own essence': these are the engines of progress, whereas puritanism, philistinism, sensualism and fanaticism are forces that seek to inhibit 'higher freedom'.[42] 'Essence' I understand as 'being', or more precisely the potential or blueprint for a possible fulfilment in the absence of repression, deflection or blockade; it is in one sense an Aristotelian, teleological idea, in another sense a Darwinian, hereditarian idea. In a Wildean paradox, Lord Henry – practitioner of influence for whom the natural is the greatest pose of all – is a disbeliever in nurture and a believer in nature; he practises fervently, that is to say, what he does not believe in. (The Christian martyr, Wilde was fond of saying, died for what he did not believe in.) 'The aim of life is self-development. To realize one's nature perfectly – that is what each of us is here for.' When Dorian Gray at the end of the novel accuses Lord Henry of having poisoned him with a book (*Against Nature*), Lord Henry replies: 'You and I are what we are, and will be what we will be.'[43]

There is, then, the obligation to one's own nature, and Wilde never abandoned as a virtue what he called 'self-realisation'. This unwittingly aligned him in an Irish context with George Moore and (in the future) with James Joyce, both of whom championed self-realization against the counter-individualist claims of the Irish Catholic church and the Irish nationalist revival.[44] In *De Profundis*, Wilde returns again and again to the desirability of self-realization. 'The supreme vice is shallowness', he tells Lord Alfred Douglas. 'Whatever is realised is right.'[45] 'I am far more of an Individualist than I ever was', he writes. 'Nothing seems to me of the smallest value except what one gets out of oneself. My nature is seeking a fresh mode of self-realisation.'[46] If in his moving letter he courts hubris in his self-identification with Christ ('Christ was not merely the supreme Individualist, but he was the first in History'), he at least rescues it from its shallower guise as mere eccentricity, flamboyant self-exhibition, perverse uniqueness: 'People used to say of me that I was too individualistic. I must be far more of an individualist than I ever was.'[47]

It was by his Oxford reading that Wilde discovered the evolutionary foundation of his belief in individuality, thereafter lifelong. Having defined progress in thought in his Commonplace Book, he then defined progress in matter, using Clifford's analogy between organic evolution and cognitive evolution: 'progress in matter is the differentiation and specialization of function: those organisms which are entirely subject to external influences do not progress any more than a mind entirely subject to authority'.[48] He derived this analogy from Clifford's 1868 lecture, 'On Some of the Conditions of Mental Development', in which the scientist defines individuality as differentiation from other organisms, and individuality in thought as differentiation from surrounding minds.[49] Clifford goes on to identify sharp mental differentiation as one of the characteristics of genius, which must have impressed the young Wilde. The evolutionary process of developmental differentiation ('the parts of the organism get more different'; 'the organism gets more different from the environment'; 'the organism gets more different from other individuals'), the evolutionary mechanism of natural selection, and the evolutionary concept of hierarchy in the organic kingdoms (arrangement in terms of organizational complexity) – all by analogy became Wilde's notion of cultivation, and gave a biological foundation to his aestheticism. Although in his Commonplace Book he joked that 'Nature kills off all those who do not believe in the Uniformity of Nature and the Law of Causation',[50] Wilde (like Lord Henry) practised artificial selection on himself: there is a suggestive analogy between Wilde's over-cultivation as an aesthete (a too great differentiation from his moral environment and other, hypocritically moral individuals) and the fate that natural selection visits upon those organisms that exhibit its counterpart in nature (unadaptable and self-damaging over-specialization); the analogy is both suggested by, and rendered ironic as a result of, Wilde's own readings in evolution and its exploitation in his works. It is tempting to see Lord Henry as another specimen of over-cultivation but Dorian Gray as one of devolution; that is, of the descent, rather than ascent, of man, a socio-biological reversion such as Spencer might have explained.[51]

THE POWER OF HEREDITY

Certainly Dorian is a specimen of flawed heredity as well as of malign nurture. He is a 'son of love and death': 'A beautiful woman risking everything for a mad passion. A few wild weeks of happiness cut short by a hideous, treacherous crime. Months of voiceless agony, and then a child born in pain. The mother snatched away by death, the boy left to solitude and the tyranny of an old and loveless man.' Dorian Gray's parentage (the quarrelsome, mean grandfather, the beautiful, romantic mother, the socially insignificant father) is for Lord Henry a fascinating tragic background for the decorative portrait of the boy he intends to 'paint': all pattern and 'symbolical value' after 'the new manner in art'. But it is also an influence, even a determinism, beyond Lord Henry's evil tutelage. What befalls Dorian Gray befell his mother, and what Lord Henry wishes to happen does, not just for reasons of sinister supervision (a self-fulfilling prophecy), but also for reasons of heredity: 'I hope that Dorian Gray will make this girl [Sybil Vane] his wife, passionately adore her for six months, and then suddenly become fascinated by some one else.' Along the way there is a mad passion, a hideous, treacherous crime, and voiceless agony. 'The men were a poor lot', says Lord Fermor of Dorian's family, 'but, egad! the women were wonderful'.[52] Dorian has inherited only his mother's wonderful beauty: otherwise he has inherited the character poverty of his male forebears.

But at least he did not succeed to what the narrator calls 'the inherited stupidity of the race'; that is, of the English, which Lord Fermor himself has come into. It was that stupidity that according to Wilde produced the philistinism, common sense and puritanism of the English to which aesthetes and the Irish were congenitally opposed (and the French, originators of aestheticism; Dorian's mother bears the surname Devereux).[53] Instead, Dorian has inherited tendencies from decadents and tyrants, exponents of a magnificent indifference portrayed in dramatic procession in the pages of Huysmans – Tiberius, Caligula, Domitian, Elagabalus – as well as tendencies from writers, including Petronius and Gautier. We are told, in a sentiment of which Borges would later have been proud: 'Yet one had ancestors in literature, as well as in one's own race, nearer perhaps in type and temperament, many of them, and certainly with an influence of which one was more absolutely conscious.'[54] And, of course, there is the inheritance of the human race itself, for Dorian Gray re-enacts the fate of Eve and the fall of man into sin and pain. It is as if through his mother's beauty he is female: or perhaps transvestite like Huysmans' Elagabalus, whom he imitates by attending a costume ball as Anne de Joyeuse, in a bejewelled dress. Like Des Esseintes, Dorian suffers from an inherited sickness, and both Wilde's novel and Huysmans' are studies in pathology, indeed of that pathological condition we call monstrosity and that so fascinated the Victorians in that age of moral and medical obsession.[55]

But the record of Wilde's reading at Oxford (1874–79) proves that his interest in heredity and pathology predated the publication of *A Rebours* in 1884. In one entry that might be a digest of Clifford, Wilde wrote: 'neither in the world of thought or in that of matter is the past ever annihilated'; and in another: 'the past is the key of the future'. From the pages of H.T. Buckle, Wilde thought it important to enter the names of William Cullen (1710–90) and William Hunter (1718–83), 'the earliest pathologists: their object was to show that there is a science of the abnormal'. And such a science is possible because 'even animal monstrosities', he writes down from Buckle, 'are now known not to be capricious but essentially natural; a new science is thus produced, that of Teratology'.[56] (Surveying his collection of fantastic musical instruments, Dorian Gray is delighted 'that art, like nature, has her monsters'.) If 'everything must come to one out of one's own nature', as Wilde wrote in *De Profundis*, 'there is no use in telling a person a thing that they don't feel and can't understand'. A refrain in *De Profundis* is the flawed heredity of the Douglases; he tells Lord Alfred: '[Your mother] saw, of course, that heredity had burdened you with a terrible legacy, and frankly admitted it, admitted it with terror: he is "the one of my children who has inherited the fatal Douglas temperament", she wrote of you'; 'Through your father you come of a race, marriage with whom is horrible, friendship fatal, and that lays violent hands either on its own life or on the lives of others'; 'the fact that the man you hated was your own father, and that the feeling was thoroughly reciprocated, did not make your Hate noble or fine in any way. If it showed anything it was simply that it was a hereditary disease.'[57]

Behind the allegation that Douglas betrayed a vicious mole of nature lay a contemporary idea, deriving from the theories of the Italian psychiatrist Cesare Lombroso, author of *Delinquent Man* (1875): that of degeneration.[58] Certain ironies attach to Wilde's belief in the power of heredity. If the biological concept of inheritance helped to sponsor the fashionable late Victorian notion of degeneration, the notion was for many people exemplified in literary and cultural decadence, of which Wilde was regarded as a vivid, even lurid embodiment. Also, seven months before he began *De Profundis*, Wilde petitioned the Home

Secretary for release from Reading Gaol, on the grounds that his misdeeds were due rather to a curable sexual pathology than to criminality, citing in evidence Max Nordau, author of *Degeneration* (1892, trans. 1895), a work which discussed Wilde as an example of 'a pathological aberration of a racial instinct ... a malevolent mania for contradiction ... the ego-mania of degeneration'.[59] *Degeneration* was dedicated to Lombroso, who wrote *Genius and Insanity* (1861), and in his petition Wilde professed his fear of losing his mind were he to remain in gaol (a rather *too* sharp mental differentiation, he might have added, remembering Clifford). Self-realization in the sense of fulfilment of the individual's heredity could, then, be a vice, as it was in Douglas's case and – as Wilde was ironically and implicitly claiming by petition – in his own. Yet beyond his petition, and Douglas's behaviour, he preferred to consider it as a virtue.

In Wilde is argued out the comparative forces of nature (or heredity) and nurture (including self-nurture, or self-cultivation) that so preoccupied his contemporaries at that junction of culture and biology that was called sociology. Self-realization could be the product of either, and nurture was not necessarily superior in this regard. Whereas for many of those contemporaries the weight of the past known as inheritance was a bleak proposition, for Wilde it was, on the whole, just the opposite (perhaps in part because he was immensely fortunate in, and immensely proud of, his own parentage and lineage). 'By revealing to us the absolute mechanism of all action', Gilbert says (as though fresh from Wilde's own scientific reading), 'and so freeing us from the self-imposed and trammelling burden of moral responsibility, the scientific principle of Heredity has become, as it were, the warrant for the contemplative life. It has shown us that we are never less free than when we try to act.' In compensation for our imprisonment in 'practical and external life' (though in *Dorian Gray* and *De Profundis* Wilde reinstated moral responsibility without endangering the imagination or minimizing heredity), we are at liberty 'to realize the experiences of those who are greater than we are': Leopardi, Theocritus, Pierre Vidal, Lancelot, Abelard, Villon, Shelley, Atys, Hamlet. As in *Dorian Gray*, literary-historical characters are – sociologically in Spencer's term, sociobiologically in contemporary terminology – in a very real sense our forebears. They constitute in *The Critic as Artist*, as in the novel, a 'terrible shadow, with many gifts in its hands', yet seem less oppressive, more liberating in the dialogue than in the novel. They are, in the former, at least in part the creatures of our own imagination; we are ordinarily more active in their summoning than was

Dorian, who seems merely to act out the consequences of Lord Henry's misguidance and (like Lord Alfred Douglas, as Wilde saw him) his own genotype. If the fate of Dorian Gray qualifies Gilbert's optimism, it still leaves his observation a considerable force: 'the imagination is the result of heredity. It is simply concentrated race-experience'.[60] For Wilde, Darwinism did not undermine the uniqueness of humanity or the freedom of the individual: rather it sponsored both by explaining the origin and direction of art (the product of imagination or recessive contemplation) and thereby vindicated art and the aesthetic life against the deluded claims of practicality and progressivism. Wilde was the aesthete who, in one of the larger paradoxes of his career, gave aestheticism a scientific foundation.[61] Life, he thought, imitates previous life as surely as it imitates art.

The concept of hereditary descent could also have sponsored, had Yeats but allowed it, the race-membership and race-consciousness upon which Yeats's Celtic Revival ultimately rested. Indeed, the invisible life Yeats championed was surely reconcilable with the ancestral life that Spencer championed and that was inexplicable in the exclusive terms of an individual's own experience. Clifford was persuaded by Spencer, and Wilde by Clifford, that all human knowledge derives from experience but not solely *individual* experience.[62] Such a view enabled a resolution of the dilemma posed by the exclusive empiricism of Locke and Hume on one side, and the transcendentalism of Kant (with his theory of universal truths, innately known) on the other.[63] Wilde absorbed the view into his work dramatically as well as polemically: for example, Gwendolyn's ideal Ernest (she seeks to marry the embodiment of Ernestness) is realized by the hitherto hidden heredity of Jack's ancestral Ernestness. Such a view also balanced the role of accidental variation (of pure, contingent individuality) to which Wilde, no less than Yeats, objected.

But an interest in science, including evolutionary theory, an admiration for Darwin, a respect for the nature of things, and the honouring of self-realization (even if he reconciled it with self-transcending imagination) – all distinguish Wilde from Yeats, who emulated him in so much else. It is possible to revise our perception of Wilde by demoting the Victorian aesthete in him and promoting the anti-English, wittily subversive feminist and anti-colonialist in him. This has recently been done for reasons of Irish cultural nationalism.[64] The revision is fine (if not dandy), but it threatens to backfire, since the case pursued reveals Wilde as a lifelong champion of that individualism that rejects the primacy of causes such as nationalism, Irish or otherwise. He is also revealed as an Anglo-Irishman who inherited the intellectual interests

– scientific as well as artistic – of his tradition. And its outdoor pursuits as well; those included fishing and shooting – encounters with nature in the flesh, so to speak. It is amusing to read the early and unexpectedly knowledgeable and enthusiastic letters about the action from the Wilde lodge at Lough Fee, County Mayo.

> The fishing has not been so good as usual. I only got one salmon, about 7 1/2 lbs. The sea-trout however are very plentiful; we get a steady average of over four a day and lots of brown trout, so it is not difficult to amuse oneself and as no fish are going in any of the neighbouring lakes I am fairly pleased. One week more of this delightful, heathery, mountainous, lake-filled region! Teeming with hares and trout! Then to Longford for the partridge, then home.[65]

Of course, Wilde soon after underwent a serious conversion to aestheticism, but nature and its scientific understandings stayed with him, translated rather than dispatched. No attempt at a recuperation and rehabilitation of natural history and nature writing in Irish culture, nor in late Victorian literary history, for that matter, need shrink from enlisting at some juncture the works and philosophies of this still surprising genius of Irish literature.

NOTES

1. W.B. Yeats, *Essays and Introductions* (London: Macmillan, 1961), p.187.
2. *The Letters of W.B. Yeats*, ed. Allan Wade (London: Rupert Hart-Davis, 1954), p.335.
3. 'Four Years: 1887–1891', in A. Norman Jeffares (ed.), *W.B. Yeats: Selected Prose* (London: Pan, 1976), p.50.
4. Yeats, *Essays and Introductions*, p.444.
5. Yeats, 'Modern Poetry: A Broadcast', in *Essays and Introductions*, p.491.
6. See my articles, 'Natural History, Science and Irish Culture', *The Irish Review*, 9 (1990), pp.61–9, and 'Natural Science and Irish Culture', *Eire-Ireland*, 26, 2 (1991), pp.92–103.
7. Richard Ellmann, *Eminent Domain: Yeats Among Wilde, Joyce, Pound, Eliot and Auden* (London: Oxford University Press, 1967), pp.9–27. I am using the edition of *The Picture of Dorian Gray* to be found in Isobel Murray (ed.), *The Writings of Oscar Wilde* (Oxford: Oxford University Press, 1989), pp.47–214. Basil Hallward's phrase is really Arnold's phrase, 'the Greek spirit' from the latter's essay, 'Hebraism and Hellenism', in *Culture and Anarchy* (1869). Wilde's interest in Greek culture derived as much from his Trinity College Dublin tutor, the celebrated Irish wit and Hellenist, John Pentland Mahaffy, as from the writings of Arnold: see W.B. Stanford, *Ireland and the Classical Tradition* (Dublin: Allen Figgis, 1976), pp.235–43.
8. See, for example, Wilde, *The Critic as Artist*, in Murray (ed.), *The Writings of Oscar Wilde*, pp.256–7, 274–5. Future references to *The Critic as Artist* will be to this edition. The distinction between the contemplative man and the man of action is implicit in Yeats's 'Easter 1916'. In 'Yeats and the Easter Rising', reprinted in John Wilson Foster, *Colonial Consequences: Essays in Irish Literature and Culture* (Dublin: Lilliput Press, 1991), I offered several sources of Yeats's famous phrase 'terrible beauty' without remembering Wilde's use of it in Chapter 8 of *Dorian Gray*.
9. Wilde wrote to Grant Allen in early 1891 praising his essay in the *Fortnightly Review* for its 'scientific demonstration' of the Celtic spirit of Art that Arnold had merely 'divined'. See

Rupert Hart-Davis (ed.), *The Letters of Oscar Wilde* (New York: Harcourt, Brace, 1962), pp.286–7. (Allen wrote several books on evolution.)
10. Laziness, imaginativeness and an attraction to the unrealistic are attributes of Wilde's Celt: see Hart-Davis (ed.), *Letters*, pp.429, 666, 751.
11. For the reference to 'the great Celtic school', see Hart-Davis (ed.), *Letters*, p.339. Although not an Irish nationalist, I have myself colluded in the exclusion of Shaw and Wilde, choosing in John Wilson Foster, *Fictions of the Irish Literary Revival* (1987), like most Irish critics, to see the Irish Literary Revival starting in Dublin with Standish James O'Grady, Yeats and Douglas Hyde.
12. I am quoting from the edition of *The Decay of Lying* in Murray (ed.), *The Writings of Oscar Wilde*, p.215.
13. Camille Paglia, *Sexual Personae: Art and Decadence from Nefertiti to Emily Dickinson* (New York: Vintage Books, 1991), p.523.
14. Without explanation, Hart-Davis believes Wilde may have been urging upon William Sharp (who was assembling an anthology of sonnets) the merits of Poe's sonnet 'Silence', even though the letter quite clearly says 'Edgar Allan Poe's sonnet to Science'; Hart-Davis (ed.), *Letters*, p.182.
15. Richard Ellmann, *Oscar Wilde* (Harmondsworth: Penguin Books, 1988), pp.43, 84, 158. The white carnation was dyed green, according to Ellmann, in homage to Huysmans' Des Esseintes, who preferred natural flowers that resembled artificial flowers to artificial flowers that resembled natural ones: Ellmann, 'The Uses of Decadence', *a long the riverrun: Selected Essays* (New York: Knopf, 1989), pp.3–4.
16. Hart-Davis (ed.), *Letters*, p.168. According to Hart-Davis, Hopps read this amusing letter aloud to the FMR meeting in Wilde's absence.
17. Hart-Davis (ed.), *Letters*, pp.172–3.
18. Paglia, *Sexual Personae*, p.512.
19. 'the art that is frankly decorative is the art to live with ... The marvels of design stir the imagination'. *The Critic as Artist*, in Murray (ed.), *The Writings of Oscar Wilde*, pp.288–9.
20. Philip E. Smith II and Michael S. Helfand (eds), *Oscar Wilde's Oxford Notebooks: A Portrait of Mind in the Making* (Oxford and New York: Oxford University Press, 1989), p.144.
21. William Kingdon Clifford, *Lectures and Essays*, ed. Leslie Stephen and Sir Frederick Pollock (London: Macmillan, 1901), Vol.I, pp.162–6.
22. Clifford, 'On the Scientific Basis of Morals', in *Lectures and Essays*, Vol.II, pp.88–9. 'The word "design"', writes Clifford, 'might then be kept for the special case of adaptation by an intelligence'.
23. Tess Cosslett (ed.), *Science and Religion in the Nineteenth Century* (Cambridge: Cambridge University Press, 1984), p.173.
24. The young Wilde was reading J.A. Symond's *Shelley* (1878) at this time, and possibly John Tyndall's 'Belfast Address', which discusses Goethe in such terms: see Smith and Helfand (eds), *Oscar Wilde's Oxford Notebooks*, p.206.
25. Hart-Davis (ed.), *Letters*, pp.236–7.
26. See, for example, ibid., pp.287, 489.
27. We can quickly gauge the importance of the scientific element of Anglo-Irish culture (which since the Irish Literary Revival has been consigned to the status of a 'hidden Ireland') from Gordon L. Herries Davies's essay, 'Irish Thought in Science', in Richard Kearney (ed.), *The Irish Mind* (Dublin: Wolfhound Press, 1985). More pertinently focused is T.G. Wilson's *Victorian Doctor; Being the Life of Sir William Wilde* (New York: L.B. Fischer, 1946), which recreates not only the varied pursuits of its subject (opthalmologist, archaeologist, ethnologist, statistician and naturalist) but also the commendable standard of Irish science during the Victorian period; see especially chapters 2, 8 and 14.
28. J.-K. Huysmans, *Against Nature*, trans. Robert Baldick (London: Penguin Books, 1959), p.36. Christopher Lloyd has suggested that *Against Nature* might better be titled *Against Culture*, on the grounds that it is not Nature itself that is rejected but a certain *conception* of Nature: 'facile notions of the picturesque', *J.-K. Huysmans and the Fin de Siecle Novel* (Edinburgh: Edinburgh University Press, 1990), p.95.
29. Clifford defines science as 'the getting of knowledge from experience on the assumption of the uniformity of nature, and the use of such knowledge to guide the actions of men': 'On the Scientific Basis of Morals' in *Lectures and Essays*, Vol.II, p.78. Much earlier, Bacon wrote

that a correct scientific method 'leads with constant path through the woodlands of experience to the open country of Axioms': *The Novum Organon* (Oxford: Oxford University Press, 1855), p.60. The cynicism of a Wilde character such as Lord Henry derives from his assumption of the uniformity (and therefore predictability and typicality) of human nature: the piquant humour is, of course, original.

30. Murray (ed.), *The Writings of Oscar Wilde*, pp.90, 92.
31. Ibid.
32. And, we might add, its destructive capability. Alan Campbell is the literal experimental scientist in *Dorian Gray*, blackmailed into getting rid of Basil Hallward's body through 'a certain scientific experiment' (ibid., p.173). (According to Ellmann, 'a friendly surgeon informed [Wilde] how this could be done by chemical means', *Oscar Wilde*, p.296.) But Campbell had already courted notoriety 'in connection with certain curious experiments' (p.171) and is unhealthily absorbed in biological research; it is implied he traffics like Frankenstein in the secrets of the charnel-house and frequents the world of Burke and Hare. (Science and crime conspired to initiate *Dorian Gray*, for it was at a dinner party in the presence of Arthur Conan Doyle that Wilde offered to write a novel in the spirit of friendly rivalry to Doyle's Sherlock Holmes mystery, *The Sign of Four*: Ellmann, *Oscar Wilde*, p.296.) In his secretiveness, Campbell recalls Des Esseintes the experimenter; in the amorality of his experimentation, he recalls Lord Henry Wotton.
33. Murray (ed.), *The Writings of Oscar Wilde*, p.91. For all the more important differences, it is diverting to compare Wilde's Lord Henry Wotton with history's Sir Henry Wotton (1568–1639). Sir Henry, like Wilde, was an Oxford man; he was interested in science (like Wilde's father, he studied the human eye) as well as literature, and, like his much greater friend John Donne, lived before that dissociation of sensibility we call the Two Cultures. He sent Bacon an account of experiments he witnessed at Kepler's house in Linz, and he procured foreign plants while he was James I's ambassador in Venice. He was an epigrammatist of note, and one of his paradoxes was to the effect that a diplomat should always speak the truth, for he shall never be believed. Another aphorism landed him in hot water with King James: 'an ambassador is an honest man, sent to lie abroad for the good of his country'. Sir Henry has been described as 'an amiable dilettante or literary amateur, with a growing inclination to idleness in his later years'. He became provost of Eton but despite his interest in education (or, as he termed it, 'moral architecture'), 'he found the boys more interesting than their work'. See Izaak Walton's 'Life of Sir Henry Wotton', *Dictionary of National Biography*, and Keith Thomas, *Man and the Natural World* (Harmondsworth: Penguin Books, 1984).
34. Smith and Helfand (eds), *Oscar Wilde's Oxford Notebooks*, pp.135, 162, 234. In his Commonplace Book, Wilde wrote: 'In the modern attempt to rest morals on a scientific basis ... A return to the old Hellenic ideal [to live by nature] can be seen', *Oscar Wilde's Oxford Notebooks*, pp.135, 191.
35. Ibid., p.135.
36. Murray (ed.), *The Writings of Oscar Wilde*, p.78. It is ironic, therefore, that Wilde spent his last years in eloquent beggary, and in Reading Gaol requested the works of Dickens.
37. Ibid., pp.106, 152.
38. Ibid., p.254. Wilde might implicitly be taking issue with Arnold's influential and more ponderous view that 'for the creation of a master-work of literature two powers must concur, the power of the man and the power of the moment': 'The Function of Criticism at the Present Time', *Essays in Criticism* (London: Macmillan, 1898), p.5.
39. Quoted by Ellmann, *Eminent Domain*, p.16.
40. Murray (ed.), *The Writings of Oscar Wilde*, p.296.
41. Smith and Helfand (eds), *Oscar Wilde's Oxford Notebooks*, p.121.
42. Ibid., p.110.
43. Murray (ed.), *The Writings of Oscar Wilde*, pp.61, 210.
44. I discuss the idea of self-realization in Moore, Joyce and other Irish writers in *Fictions of the Irish Literary Revival.*
45. Hart-Davis (ed.), *Letters*, p.448.
46. Ibid., p.467. Later in *De Profundis*, however, Wilde calls self-realization inadequate, with the wise acceptance of the enigma of man's soul being the ultimate virtue (ibid., p.488).
47. Hart-Davis (ed.), *Letters*, pp.479, 491.

48. Smith and Helfand (eds), *Oscar Wilde's Oxford Notebooks*, p.121. A second analogy which derived from Spencer but attributed by Wilde to Plato, was that between the individual and the social organism (ibid., p.109).
49. Clifford, *Lectures and Essays*, Vol.I, p.87. Smith and Helfand seem to have overlooked this lecture as a source for the ideas on p.121 of their edition of the Oxford Notebooks.
50. Smith and Helfand (eds), *Oscar Wilde's Oxford Notebooks*, p.121. Smith and Helfand do not supply a source for this remark; if there is one, it is probably Clifford, who wrote on both uniformity and the cognitive-organic analogy.
51. It is therefore ironic (despite its brevity of tenure) that among Dorian's later enthusiasms is evolutionary theory: 'for a season he inclined to the materialistic doctrines of the *Darwinismus* movement in Germany', *The Writings of Oscar Wilde*, p.146.
52. Murray (ed.), *The Writings of Oscar Wilde*, pp.74, 75, 103, 73.
53. Ibid., p.182. Arnold connected English Philistinism to the strain of vulgarity and insensitivity in the Anglo-Saxon breed signified by 'such hideous names' as Higginbottom, Stiggins, Bugg and Wragg: 'The Function of Criticism at the Present Time', *Essays in Criticism*, pp.20–5.
54. Murray (ed.), *The Writings of Oscar Wilde*, p.155.
55. Clifford develops the analogies between disease and wrongdoing, and health and moral sense (both in the individual and in society), in 'On the Scientific Basis of Morals', *Lectures and Essays*, Vol.II, pp.74–95. For a discussion of Huysmans and sickness, see Lloyd, *J.-K. Huysmans and the Fin de Siecle Novel*, pp.83–96.
56. Smith and Helfand (eds), *Oscar Wilde's Oxford Notebooks*, pp.125, 159, 159, 155. William Hunter was also an anatomist, who embalmed Martin Van Butchell's wife, and her husband kept her in a glass case in his drawing-room: see Samuel Foare Simmons and John Hunter, *William Hunter 1718–1783*, ed. C.H. Brock (Glasgow: University of Glasgow Press, 1983), p.32. In a figurative sense, Dorian Gray is embalmed, and only at the end of the novel resumes his natural *moral* age. In the light of Lord Henry's musings on self-experimentation, and Wilde's interest in William Hunter, the career of John, William's younger brother, is not without interest. It was said by several memoirists and biographers that John (pioneer of scientific surgery, anatomist, botanist, zoologist) had inoculated himself with syphilis in order to study the disease and that his death had syphilitic origins. In his biography, George Qvist is at pains to challenge the claim: *John Hunter 1728–1793* (London: Heinemann, 1981), pp.42–53. That Ellmann and others have claimed that Wilde's death had the same origin adds to the oddity of the Hunterian connection.
57. Hart-Davis (ed.), *Letters*, pp.448, 433, 440, 451.
58. The career of this concept in the nineteenth and early twentieth centuries is traced in a collection of essays, J. Edward Chamberlin and Sander L. Gilman (eds), *Degeneration: The Dark Side of Progress* (New York: Columbia University Press, 1985). The essay by Chamberlin, 'Images of Degeneration', is particularly relevant to my essay.
59. Hart-Davis (ed.), *Letters*, pp.401–2; Max Nordau, *Degeneration* (London: Heinemann, 1913), pp.318–19.
60. Murray (ed.), *The Writings of Oscar Wilde*, pp.276, 277, 276, 277.
61. Unlike Yeats, Wilde was receptive to the idea that imagination is part of the method of successful science, something that Tyndall was fond of arguing: see, for example, 'Scientific Use of the Imagination', in John Tyndall, *Fragments of Science* (London: Longmans, Green, 1907), Vol.II, pp.101–34.
62. Smith and Helfand (eds), *Oscar Wilde's Oxford Notebooks*, pp.120, 133–4. Clifford summarizes Spencer during his lecture, 'The Philosophy of the Pure Sciences', *Lectures and Essays*, Vol.I, pp.301–409.
63. Scientists like Clifford could not, however, encourage belief to go beyond inherited experience: see, for example, Clifford's review of a book bearing the Yeatsian title, *The Unseen Universe*, in *Lectures and Essays*, Vol.I, pp.268–300.
64. See, for example, Declan Kiberd's introduction to his selection of Wilde for Seamus Deane (ed.), *The Field Day Anthology of Irish Writing* (Derry: Field Day Publications, 1991), Vol.II, pp.372–6.
65. Hart-Davis (ed.), *Letters*, p.47.

4

THE WEIR: INHERITING THE WIND

The most widely and justifiably famous name in contemporary Irish literature is that of a poet, Seamus Heaney. Informed general readers outside the island could probably name, after Heaney, the fiction writers William Trevor (though they might not know he is Irish and assume he is English), John Banville (his nationality too might not be obvious) and, perhaps, the dramatist Brian Friel. Uninformed general readers would almost certainly name Roddy Doyle and Frank McCourt in place of Trevor and Banville. The weight of professional critical opinion, certainly in Ireland, supports the implied hierarchy of genre, for it is the poets, Heaney and his cohorts (Paul Muldoon, Derek Mahon, Michael Longley, Medbh McGuckian, Ciaran Carson) who attract the greatest attention, at least in Ireland, followed by the short story writers and novelists.

But whereas the best-known, and best, living poets of Ireland are those born between 1939 and 1951 (the birth dates of Heaney and Muldoon respectively), the best, and best-known, playwrights are either in their 30s or, if older, have recent reputations. If we except Friel and Frank McGuinness, then the playwrights people are talking about in Ireland are Marina Carr, Martin McDonagh, Sebastian Barry, Conor McPherson and Marie Jones. Jones is in her 50s, but came late to playwriting and has only recently achieved an international reputation, by dint of *Stones in his Pockets* (1996). McDonagh, Barry, Jones and McPherson have taken the London West End under something approaching storm conditions. Vancouver has recently had the pleasure of seeing *Stones in his Pockets* and McDonagh's *The Beauty Queen of Leenane* (1996) and *The Cripple of Inishmaan* (1997) performed and tonight will see McPherson performed.[1] It is the playwrights who appear to be reinventing Ireland and whose youthful vigour seems to reflect the vigour of all those 29-year-old Dubliners with cell phones in hand and money in their pockets: bigger, nimbler, smarter and richer than their parents. And Conor McPherson is among the best of these young playwrights. Despite having had seven plays performed, and a screenplay filmed, all between 1992 and 2001 and all to acclaim and with a mantelpiece of awards, Conor McPherson is all of 31 years of age.

I said just now 'reinventing Ireland' but at first blush this doesn't appear to be what's happening at all. Something is oddly shared by Heaney and Friel *and* these young playwrights: they are still setting much of their work in the impoverished and emigrant Irish countryside. This is the case, even though most Irish people now live in towns (the majority of people in the South of Ireland live in or around Dublin) and the Republic of Ireland is, per capita, richer than almost every other fellow-member country of the European Union – richer than Canada. Any day now I am expecting a food parcel from Ireland despatched to the relatively impoverished area of deprivation known as North Vancouver![2]

Ireland is now for the first time an *im*migrant society. Indeed, soon Ireland will have to import priests from Africa, since young men are too affluent and worldly now to wish to take orders.[3]

At first I thought that the mildly disrespectful references to the priests in *The Weir* (1997) were a reflection of the new cynical attitude to the Catholic Church in Ireland. The disrespect shown by Martin McDonagh's characters (shocking to even this Protestant) certainly *is* part of that new cynicism (even when McDonagh purports to be depicting the Ireland of 1934). But in *The Weir* what seems like disrespect is really an allusion to the age-old clash between the church and what were once called 'the elder faiths' of Ireland and to the weakness of clerical power when up against the power of the pagan Otherworld and the forces of darkness that predate Christianity. McPherson doesn't make heavy weather of this, but it is a dramatic idea as old as two famous Irish plays of the early twentieth century: *The Playboy of the Western World* (1907) and *Riders to the Sea* (1904), both by John Millington Synge. It is as if for these writers literary history carries as much weight as contemporary reality; they are revising and updating literature as much as reflecting the changes and innovations in the society around them.

So here amply in *The Weir* are what we associate with Ireland through her literature – Catholicism and Celticism, poverty and a countryside green in daylight, dark and foreboding at night. But you will hear *about* a new and recent Ireland on the stage this evening as well – of German tourists and higher education (the DCU where the character Valerie has been educated is Dublin City University, an institution more attuned to scientific and industrial Ireland than the famous Trinity College Dublin and University College Dublin). The characters who stayed put in their Sligo or north-west Leitrim obscurity are from an older but still modern Ireland, the Ireland that began in 1951 when the weir provided electricity to the countryside. They carry within themselves the conflict between that modernizing Ireland

and the Ireland of flights of fancy and belief in fairies. In one story that we are told in the play, the fairies are heard – or imagined – creating a commotion of resistance to the building of the weir. The white-wine-drinking Valerie is apparently at home in this new Ireland, and the modern city of Dublin, but ironically it is she who gives a disturbing credence to the ghost stories that she hears and that we hear, which is McPherson's clever yet serious post-modern joke. It is she who dissolves the old contest between city and country and embodies the alarmingly human and universal beneath the categories.

And you will *hear* in the play a new Ireland, an often inarticulate Ireland (however wordy), for *The Weir* is full of unfinished sentences, pauses, euphemisms and repressed thoughts. The Irish are garrulous in direct proportion to the distance between the topic and the heart. You will hear an Ireland routinely foul-mouthed instead of the customarily poetic. In 1907 Synge got into hot water for using in *The Playboy* the word 'shift' (i.e. a woman's slip under a skirt); very hot water indeed: enraged educated nationalists attempted to rearrange the architecture of the Abbey theatre at the utterance of this word (practical criticism indeed). They must be writhing in their graves when McPherson and McDonagh are performed. Yet 'shite' (an Irish adjective) and 'fucking' perform rhythmic work in *The Weir*. And the foul mouth can utter its own found poetry, the rough poetry of, say, 'a crowd of fucking headbangers'. Brendan's terminal 'fuck' has been replaced in tonight's performance by 'feck', a Dublin word that's in the play elsewhere all right, but 'fuck' has been deliberately chosen to operate as a closure and an epitaph, a nail hammered into the door that the characters close on the spooky world we've heard about in the play as we return to daylight normality and the lights go up in the auditorium.

What is interesting to me is how McPherson's pub denizens speak in a mixture of older Irish-English and new American-Irish. 'They do be around anyway', says Brendan of the German tourists; 'They do be around right enough', agrees Jim. Here and elsewhere McPherson uses Hiberno-English that derives from Gaelic grammar. The text calls for Jim to unselfconsciously use the Gaelic word 'leaba' for bed, which the director has wisely omitted for a North American audience. At the same time, McPherson's characters use constructions you will recognize from Canadian youngsters – 'And he goes ...'; 'And I'm like ...'; 'And I go ...'; 'And I was all like ...' when reporting direct speech; this is 40-something Jim telling his unsavoury ghost story. To be honest, I'm not sure a 40-year-old Irish countryman would be using this lingo. But McPherson does not want to create characters completely out of touch with the world they see on television (and the stage directions call for an old television and a radio to be above the bar).

There is of course traditional extended Irish eloquence in *The Weir*, but it is not part of the play's theme as it is in Synge, where poetry is seductive and dangerous and, ultimately, a worldview. Still, Irish talk is Irish talk, and it serves in the play – as in real Ireland – to create and then to stave off the fears, even terrors, that beset us.

With Ireland, of course, we also associate pubs and drink. Like *The Playboy of the Western World* (and many another Irish play), *The Weir* is set in a country pub. The fact that the bottles of liquor are not mounted upside down with optics in their necks but simply set upright on the shelves suggests an older-style establishment. In any case, there is a constant pouring of distilled liquid down the insides of necks during the play. Jack has eight drinks, Brendan four, Valerie three, Jim eight and Finbar five. I counted them. There is in Ireland today a growing revulsion against excessive drinking as there is against smoking in Canada. 'Let's face it', an Irish journalist wrote this summer, almost shockingly, 'we are a nation of drunkards'. Probably true, and one wonders how many atrocities of the recent past were facilitated by drink, not to speak of sightings of little people and quare happenings; but the drink is entertaining, as is the talk it sponsors, and what is said and told in *The Weir* (good and bad, wise and unwise) is inspired by ... well, to explain it all at the end of the night, Jack gestures to his glass as well as to the presence of Valerie, the attractive Dublin stranger.

I was encouraged to count the drinks because the drinking is meticulously observed. (McPherson might have learned the dramatic potential of this from such an Irish play as Tom Murphy's 1985 work, *Conversations on a Homecoming*.) Of course, it lubricates the dialogue and engenders conviviality: very Irish. As the evening proceeds, however, drinking is a signifier of mood: one offers to buy a round out of fellowship, but occasionally out of embarrassment or even loneliness (to cover the silence we Irish fear). Comically, Jack even buys a round out of one-up-man-ship, its own kind of aggression. This too is very Irish. But in the end the drink encourages characters to unbosom themselves of disturbing episodes in their lives and reveal fears and feelings normally hidden or repressed; this is not so Irish and is what helps to make *The Weir* an Irish play of unusual psychological depth.

But just as important, the drinking is elaborate stage business, by which McPherson opens the play and then punctuates the more substantial text. Dialogue – drinking – dialogue – drinking – dialogue: this is the rhythm of the play until Finbar and Valerie enter and the play changes key; but the rhythm remains – drinking – story – drinking – story – drinking. The formal value of drinking in the play is high. But by drinking I also mean the elaborate Irish mini-drama by which drinks are ordered, paid for and ceremonially acknowledged before vanishing down the hatch and signalling the start of ritual banter. McPherson is masterly at capturing a ritual that strangers can so easily misinterpret. Irish communal life is heavy with what drama critics call 'subtext': what is said is not necessarily the real subject of an exchange; gestures and expressions are not always to be taken at face value. The Irish can be a cunning and angular people; the Irish novelist James Joyce has his hero Stephen Dedalus take 'cunning' as one of his watchwords, but the Irish survived in part through cunning; so to think of the Irish, or to stage them, as merely fools or jesters, is as wrong as one can be about them. Jack may seem at times to *be* merely a fool or jester but the text creates him as a competitive, angry, sarcastic and, in the end, self-hating man. The Irish are witty and energetic but they are not all, by virtue of that, *nice* people. To depict this subtly is McPherson's success in *The Weir*.

Small talk is a ritual component of the pub experience, before it rises, as it does in the play, to good 'crack' as the Scots-Irish say: entertainingly strenuous repartee and lively anecdote, and then story and (though not in this play) song. But we know from Samuel Beckett, Harold Pinter and *Rosencrantz and Guildenstern* by Tom Stoppard the paradoxical dramatic power of the inconsequential. In drama it now induces an increasing but still half-conscious anxiety of *waiting*; and from Beckett and Stoppard we know the dramatic and even existential value of 'waiting' in the modern consciousness. During the first third of *The Weir* we are, I think, waiting for something unsuspected to happen. Small talk is also realistic: most of our talk *is* inconsequential. And so before the play seems really to get going with the entrance of Finbar and Valerie, the drinkers discuss the keg of Guinness, the high wind, Brendan's sisters, Jim's winning tip to Jack at the horses, Finbar and the new tenant of Maura Nealon's house, the likelihood of Brendan's ever getting married, and more. All seemingly trivial. But there's subtext at work, *and* cultural shorthand (only available to directors and audiences who know their Irish culture), *and* a pattern of return in these topics.

Take Brendan's singleness. Neither Jack nor Brendan can bring himself actually to use the words 'marriage' or 'children', but these are on each mind; it takes Valerie, the new woman in both senses, to take those bulls by the horns towards the end of the play. The fact is that the topic is too painful for Jack and Brendan, and pain will emerge before the play is done: that's the subtext beneath the edgy text. It is more than the Irish countryman's traditional shyness in matters of sex and marriage, but that's important too. *The Weir* exploits what Synge in *The Playboy* exploits – the way all but the most vigorous Irish countrymen and countrywomen are trapped in their isolation and by a social system in which there are too few women to go around (the young women with more initiative leave to go into service in town), parents living too long and commandeering the energies of their children, keeping a firm grip on the land and farms thereby preventing inheritance, succession, independence and real adulthood. Social anthropologists call the system – mercifully dying out – 'familism'.

Jim's 'mammy' who has been 'fading fast, like, for years' is a familiar figure of oppression in Irish country literature – a dominatrix helping to keep her 40-year-old son a boy. 'She still spoils that boy rotten', Brendan tells Valerie but he means quite the opposite. McDonagh has great gas with the grim figure of The Mammy in *The Cripple of Inishmaan* but Patrick Kavanagh had already written a savage portrait of her in his epic poem of the 1930s, *The Great Hunger*. McPherson's men are still oppressed by the society they live in and of course by themselves; they suffer a great hunger which drink and talk and story can assuage but only for a time. But at least they have a sense of humour about their wretched state of singleness; Finbar draws a hilarious portrait of country Irish bachelors which Jack plays along with; but by the end we know it is no laughing matter and that fear and loneliness are the portion of those hapless figures Synge likened to lonely jack (or male) asses. At the very least, the demographics encourage competition among the unwedded men though to reveal it is to show weakness; these men are in unadmitted competition for the attention of the sole, attractive woman. The single men are annoyed to be competing with a married man; but the men are covertly hostile to Finbar anyway because he inherited money, moved away, became successful enough to buy up half the vicinity. (There is a lot of envy, self-castigation, self-unfulfilment in this play.) But Finbar, like Valerie, will in the end dwell in the democracy of vulnerability and fear which is McPherson's real theme.

The topics of the chit-chat come round again which suggests that the small talk is bigger than that. Women, marriage, singleness, loneliness. And the wind outside – a recurring subject. It helps to know that the Gaelic word for *wind* and for *fairy* is one and the same: *sidhe*. And that the north wind is in tradition a sign of the supernatural. The wind howling past you is the passage of the trooping fairies (as distinct from the solitary fairies) – who mean you no good if you impede them. If Synge in *Riders to the Sea* took all this seriously, and William Butler Yeats too, who actually classified Irish fairies as one would species of animals, it is not because they were credulous but because they appreciated the richness of the metaphor for (or personification of) fear and misfortune into which they could turn the old literal Irish belief.

To this extent, it is fitting that we are watching *The Weir* near Hallowe'en, since Hallowe'en – or *Samhain* – is one of the nights in the Celtic calendar when the gates of the underworld open and the hosts of fairies come forth, or if you like, the hosts of our fears and regrets and self-recriminations, and half-buried incidents and episodes from one's past: it is a psychological haunting. The most frightening passage in *The Weir* should perhaps be the one in which Jack sets the scene for his story of Maura Nealon – 'And there's no dark like a winter night in the country'. Even the highly educated James Joyce admitted to a morbid fear of the Irish countryside at night. We must remember, as Jack tells us, that in the recent past that countryside was unilluminated by electricity – as high and obscure ground still is – and it was all morbidly dark indeed. Jack continues: 'And there was a wind like this one tonight, howling and whistling in off the sea. You hear it under the door and it's like someone singing. Singing in under the door at you.' Though Jack, modern (if not contemporary) man as he is, then breaks role to ask if he is setting the scene sufficiently, in a way the storyteller of old would never have done.

There is elaborate stage business concerning drinks, cigarettes and coins just before Finbar and Valerie enter and the play alters pitch. But the first three stories Jack, Finbar and Jim tell in turn might seem merely chit-chat cranked up a notch to take in 'ghosts and angels and all this', but if they are not meant to be scary they are meant I think to be disturbing. Each gets closer to the knuckle. They are like folk legends though the third is more like an urban legend with its contemporary theme of paedophilia; so too is the fourth and the most personal of all: it turns storytelling into confessionalism, which traditional storytelling never was. And it induces the last story, the most nakedly personal of all, pure self-revelation. At least it isn't a ghost story, Jack says. But I remember hearing Gwyn Thomas, the Welsh writer, on BBC television forty years ago telling how he'd met a Welsh countryman and asked him if he believed in ghosts. 'Not at all', the man replied, 'the only ghost that haunts me is myself'. It stuck with me and came back to me when I saw McPherson's play in the West End in London two years ago.

The point at which you hear the last story is the point at which you might ask yourself why McPherson entitled his play *The Weir*. We don't use this word often in Canada, if at all: we say 'dam' instead; something has been undammed in the play, as on nights of high Irish winds the gates of the underworld are thrown open and the troops of the hitherto confined and concealed issue forth. (More trivially, it might be hard for Canadians to suppress the word 'weird' in their consciousness when they hear this strange word.)

The social themes I've suggested lie above the psychological themes of guilt and remorse; and they themselves lie above loneliness. The dominant adjective in Synge's *Playboy* is 'lonesome', a poetic and presumably dialectal way of saying 'lonely'. McPherson is playing a subtle variation on an old Irish theme. The Irish are the most gregarious and the loneliest people I know; and you can spot the loneliest among them because they are the ones who are the last to suggest a nightcap or one for the road. The country Irish pub, just such a one as portrayed here tonight, is a haven, a clean, well-lighted place, a refuge from the surrounding 'nada' of living, convivial drinking a distraction and forgetfulness. McPherson's rhythm is a common one in real Irish social life: lively congregation, decline into rancour or remorse, and (not always the case) a rally for facing the stern tasks of living that lie ahead.

Loneliness is, I think, a species of fear, and fear skirts the lives of McPherson's characters. When the Irish want to bring a long evening to an end, they sometimes ask with rhetorical vigour and mock-disapproval: 'Have youse no homes to go to?' They do, but they don't want to go there. Drink, which has given them a good time to begin with, has given them the undesired insight that their real and ultimate home is the grave. Perhaps the most frightening remark in *The Weir* is, 'We'll all be ghosts soon enough'. The *Vancouver Sun* reviewer foolishly calls the play 'an insipid comedy'. But the text is neither insipid nor a comedy. It is a funny play but its humour is gallows humour; the stories told in it become whistlings past the graveyard. It is a dark play, as *The Playboy of the Western World* is despite the raucous humour, humour which can tempt actors and directors into underplaying the darkness and overplaying the humour. It is necessary to keep the caricatures and stereotypes on a tight rein in a clearly intelligent playwright like McPherson. He is exploiting them, not purveying or merchandizing them; he is skewing and even skewering them in order to depict a truer and more disturbing portrait of Ireland. 'We are a dark people', said the Irish country poet Patrick Kavanagh, 'Our eyes are ever turned inward'. *The Weir* demonstrates this again, if not with the authority of a masterpiece, then with the authority of a first-class play.

NOTES

1. This is the text of a talk, given before its staging of *The Weir*, to the Arts Club Theatre, Vancouver, 28 October 2002 in a series of pre-performance lectures. I had earlier seen a performance of the play in London's West End.
2. Nevertheless, despite these statistics, an anthropological study of small west Irish villages published in 2003 (Adrian Peace, *A World of Fine Difference*) caused a reviewer to claim on the basis of it that life has not changed much in Peace's villages since the mid-nineteenth century, that the population of the west of Ireland is declining and that there is a high rate of poverty in that part of the island. However, so fast is Ireland changing that immigration from the European Union since 2003, and technological advance since then, have already qualified such negative observations (2007).
3. Actually, priests have begun to arrive from Poland as well as Africa. 160,000 Poles have now settled in the Republic of Ireland (30,000 more have settled in Northern Ireland). As a result of immigration from the Catholic countries of Poland, Portugal, Spain and Brazil, the Irish Catholic church is undergoing a resurgence after a decade of decline and ill-repute (2007).

5

STRETCHING THE IMAGINATION: SOME TREVOR NOVELS

THE LONELY VOICE

William Trevor seems to enjoy a quietness of reputation, however firm, that befits a writer who seems to be part of no movement or clique. It would be tempting to ascribe both reputation and apartness to his prolific production of short stories and to the singular, even sequestered voice we have associated with that genre, at least since Frank O'Connor published *The Lonely Voice: A Study of the Short Story* (1963). However perfected in themselves, short stories even in cumulation can suggest that fragments and fringes of human experience are being offered, where novels attempt or achieve weight and centrality. The short storywriter can as a result be thought, almost unconsciously by us, to inhabit by virtue of a multitude of disparate viewpoints the same marginality even when there is a recurring and distinctive voice, as there is in Trevor's case. I wonder if the short story, by something analogous to the broken-wing trick of shore birds with young to protect, draws our attention away from the author back to the text. Had their author published nothing after the stories that compose *Dubliners* (1914), how inquisitive might we have been about their creator, James Joyce? But even if Trevor, unlike Joyce, has gone on to publish dozens of stories, perhaps his very dependability in prolificness, his maintenance of a superior standard of performance, has resulted in a certain self-effacement. One might read his memoir, *Excursions in the Real World* (1993) with relish, but does one do so in order to satisfy an intense curiosity about the author's life? As if in answer, the memoir resolves into a series of sketches or short stories by an author revealing little about himself but a good deal, deftly, in short compass and by virtue of something like eavesdropping, about other people, presumably real.

Yet even Trevor's novels, and particularly, perhaps, his Irish novels, could be thought of as justifying this impression of Trevor as a relatively private, even shadowy figure, a reliable producer of texts – for which 'William Trevor' is a kind of shorthand – rather than a writer imposing through force of personality his view of the world on his readers. Admittedly, when we read critics on, say, *Fools of Fortune* (1983) or *The Story of Lucy Gault* (2002), we almost invariably are offered enlightening affinities to Elizabeth Bowen's *The Last September*

(1929) and J.G. Farrell's *Troubles* (1970), but even this gesture is towards what is habitually seen as a lean tradition of Irish fiction, one which concerns itself, after all, with a minority and increasingly self-effacing population, the Anglo-Irish, fading in importance and numbers and thought to inhabit the growingly irrelevant verges of Irish history and society. Irrespective of characters' or narrators' viewpoints in these novels (and even irrespective of some dreadful events that are recounted), there is an overlying (or underlying) courteousness of narrative voice that implies a hesitancy to claim allegiance to either a tradition or a population. This may derive from the fact that the author is actually of the Irish middle class rather than gentry, with something of the discreet presence of the Irish country-town bank-manager, which is what Trevor's father was. But it may also be a kind of ventriloquism appropriate to a national minority. The loneliness of the short storywriter is duplicated by the loneliness of the Anglo-Irish.

I would like both to amend this reading of Trevor as a one-of-a-kind Irish writer and to second a reading of him as indeed a writer who has uniquely imagined his own troubled, and troubling, world. It was when I read his – to me highly disturbing – novel, *Other People's Worlds* (1980), that I realized that beneath or behind the kindly, dependable voice of 'William Trevor' I was hearing another, truly distinctive, perhaps even mercifully lonely voice that prophesies something much darker than another reliably good read.

TREVOR AND THE COUNTRY-HOUSE NOVEL

Simply by hauling the academic net, as Seamus Heaney once put it, and by selecting Trevor carefully, we can readily appreciate the extent to which Trevor has inherited the preoccupations, devices and tonalities of the Irish country-house novel, which, as I have tried to demonstrate recently, has been a populous subgenre since the Victorian period.[1] It is not simply a case of Bowen, J.G. Farrell and Somerville and Ross, but of B.M. Croker, Ella MacMahon, Katharine Tynan, Filson Young, Douglas Goldring, Dorothea Conyers and a great many others. Lahardane, Kilneagh, Carraveagh and other Trevor houses take their place amidst a host in Irish fiction. They are, as in *Fools of Fortune* and *The Story of Lucy Gault*, houses in decline, whose inhabitants embody the predicament of the Anglo-Irish, ambiguous of identity and suffering a kind of internal exile. Conveniently through what I call the Visitor to Ireland device, for example, Heloise in *Lucy Gault*, Anna Quinton, Willie's mother Evie, and Marianne in *Fools of Fortune*, the houses reflect or refract fraught England–Ireland relations. For, of course, the Anglo-Irish themselves can be regarded as Visitors to Ireland who stayed (and out-stayed their welcome, in the eyes of many native Irish). One recurring kind of Anglo-Irish relation is cousinage: we might think, for example, of Marianne and Willie.[2] The decline of the houses has been accelerated by carelessness – gambling in the case of Lahardane – or, indeed, by the very (usually female) philanthropy which traditionally radiated out from some of these houses; it is Anna Quinton's philanthropy during the Famine that becomes on her death the cause of the shrinkage of Kilneagh, her ghost appearing to her husband and instructing him to give away much of the estate. All these are the furniture and décor of the Irish country-house novel, as familiar as, say, the scarlet drawing-room that survives the fire at Kilneagh.

Trevor's country houses that are conduits for the lethal energies of the Great War, the Troubles and the Civil War cannot but remind us of those in M.J. Farrell, Edith Somerville (I'm thinking, for example, of *An Enthusiast*, 1921), and Pamela Hinkson as well as, of course, Bowen and J.G. Farrell. Philanthropic Kilneagh, set alight in *Fools of Fortune*, succeeds Bowen's Danielstown in *The Last September* (1929) that meets, indeed greets, the same fate, since its door 'stood open hospitably upon a furnace', and Hinkson's Cappagh in *The Ladies' Road* (1932) that likewise maintains its peculiar charity until the end: 'That night Cappagh lit a torch for the countryside'. The fires can seem to ignite as sunburnt grass is ignited through a lens, the country houses magnifying the malady of Ireland.

HISTORY AND TRAUMA

What, then, that is different does William Trevor bring to the Irish country-house novel? His distinctive narrative style, of course, that combination of unhurried yet relentless plot progression with its deferred increments of exposition and the carefully scheduled pay-outs of resolution (making his novels oddly seem much longer than they are); a deceptive warmth of narrative voice (whether third person or not); restrained indirect wit; and more lodgements of somehow muffled but nevertheless appalling occurrences than his predecessors – all these demanded by what reads like a paramount attention to storytelling.

But there is, I think, an unusual, perhaps unique, vision and version of history conducted by the storytelling. History may be an unseemly procession – in *Fools of Fortune*, for example, it begins in 1598 and is waymarked by 1602, the Famine, 1914–18, 1916, 1922–23, 1939, 1971 and 1983 – but it is disturbingly circular or spiral and repeats itself in odd and uncanny ways. History as Trevor's chief characters see it is chiefly deception, treachery and atrocity; the assassinated Pentecostal missionaries in *Other People's Worlds* might be let stand as one of the most graphic examples in the four novels under discussion. This view of history is not Trevor's unique perception – for Wilde history was a record of crime, for Joyce nightmare – but what *is* unique, I think, at least in its patterns of recurrence, is Trevor's demonstration of the mechanisms and agencies by which a terrible event can traumatize, transmit itself, and be inherited across generations. He demonstrates, moreover, how a collective trauma constitutes a kind of blight: it seems fitting that Anna Quinton dies of Famine fever in *Fools of Fortune*, reminding us that she is a link in the transmission of the Irish sickness. Marianne calls this blight 'the shadows of destruction'. Times change but the sickness persists (simply lying dormant at times) and an originally collective trauma, even much later, individuates itself, taking a terrible personal toll once again. In the long view, change is downward and for the bad. History in Trevor is, phylogenetically, bad news, and repeats itself ontogenetically, as it were, in the individual, in a nightmarish version of the sins of the fathers.

The initiating and later ironic English reversal of their defeat by the Irish in 1598 echoes down the centuries and construes the Irish as victims of ill-fortune, which is one meaning of the reverberating phrase that gives the novel *Fools of Fortune* its title. Yet in Trevor's world, despite the fact that history can operate *through*, rather than *on*, his characters, almost like selfish genes, personal agency is required, though the loss of true individual autonomy that this implies I find troubling. And so it is Willie's mother Evie who schools her son in the events of the sixteenth century, who later talks aloud about why Rudkin, the Black and Tan, did what he did, and later still reinstalls Rudkin in Willie's imagination after Rudkin's image had receded there, and who thereby indirectly incites Willie to commit the latest in a series of horrors: a hanging, deaths by fire, a suicide, a murder. Willie has inherited more than the family mill. Ironically, it is a different kind of possession he comes into. Just as Willie is 'possessed' by Marianne, so Marianne is 'possessed' by these terrible Irish events and transmits them to her daughter Imelda who is likewise absorbed into the helix of occurrences and who by delayed trauma is in the end indeed 'possessed', ending insane under the pressure of the past. In *Fools of Fortune* there is a curious chain of *female* transmission of history's evil that I have not noted before in Irish country-house fiction (much of it written by women) and that counters the tradition of female philanthropy we find in that genre.[3]

But the idea of fate or doom or an inherited blighted future is balanced, though conspiratorially, by the 'chance' implied in fortune. It is by her eavesdropping and chance reading of her mother's diary that Imelda catches as it were the infection that is Irish history. Trevor's narratives are filled with lost opportunities and hauntings of what might have been (such as love fulfilled instead of love starved or unreciprocated): what might have been would usually have been desirable – Daniel O'Connell's Ireland, for example, recurs in the Irish novels as a chance lost for an unviolent Ireland. What was, and is, was and is deplorable: the music of what happens in William Trevor is a harshly discordant one.

And it sounds through *The Story of Lucy Gault* likewise, even though St Cecilia, the holy patron of music, is something of a totemic figure in the novel. Despite the calm that comes after the Troubles (the novel opens in 1921), Heloise Gault assures us that the night Everard accidentally wounded an intruder won't be forgotten: Ireland's malady, revived by war, survives nominal peace. The Truce comes and nothing at root has changed. Perhaps the return of Everard Gault to a changed Ireland and a reduced Lahardane, and his befriending of the intruder Horohan, suggests something close to an ending for the enmities that have inspired Trevor. Perhaps the later peculiar friendship, if it is that, between the elderly Horohan and the elderly Lucy, and the loneliness of Lucy as she watches the fading of the day, strengthen the suggestion of final reconciliation and the imminent end of the estrangement of the Anglo-Irish. Yet the bulk of the novel is devoted to what towards the end is called the 'calamity' that 'shaped a life when, long ago, chance was cruel'; near the beginning we are told that 'Chance, not wrath, had this summer ordered the fate of the Gaults'.[4]

This is the personal and family version of a waymarked history (1921, 1922–23, 1936, 1939–45, 1949, 1955, 1972, 1990s) with which it has an inextricably symbiotic relationship. (Indeed, while in Bruges, the exiled Everard wonders if what has happened is payment exacted for the indifference of the Gaults and Lahardane while penal laws were enacted.) Reconciliation and the end of enmity, if such are presaged, have yet to receive their due and a prolonged imagining. This is true in Trevor as a whole, and the deficit, as we might construe it, has been in part justified by the extent to which the Northern Irish Troubles of the 1970s and after resumed those of the South of Ireland. In his well-known short story, 'The Distant Past', written in the early years of the renewed strife in Ulster, Trevor dashes the hopes of the shrunken Anglo-Irish family (the Middletons of Carraveagh) that they have achieved accommodation with their southern neighbours after the end of the Troubles that resulted in Irish independence, through the years of the Second World War, and through the ampler years of post-War tourism, though the decline of the Middletons continues. Even they, loyal to 'the distant past', come to believe their worship of that past is but a game – until, that is, the bombs explode in Northern Ireland in the late 1960s, the British troops arrive and tourism sags in their neighbouring town. The distant past returns and the new Troubles brew a resentment against Protestants that seeks redress this time from the elderly brother and sister, last of the Middletons, reviving the old and cruel animosity that had through the decades lain waiting and only asleep. There is, too, in this story, the violent or threatening event apparently outlived by its participants but which returns to exact its tribute of hatred, an event at once originative and serial: the night during the first Troubles when Fat Driscoll, the town butcher, invaded Carraveagh with another IRA gunman and held it as a site of ambush until the British soldiers failed to come.[5]

Any terminal gesture of reconciliation to the contrary, *Lucy Gault* is essentially a story of love starved by the indirect force of Irish history, of terrible events relived purgatorially, of a girl (an eavesdropping girl), then woman, 'possessed' by a 'terrible folly' that misshaped her life. If what happened after the wounding of Horohan seems disproportionate (and disproportionateness of event and reaction is a kind of dismaying irony common in Trevor), that is because the disproportion disappears when the event is recontextualized in the long haul of Irish history. Trevor's Irish characters live their own lives less than they do their ancestors' lives. Trauma is still the personal outcome of history. Like Imelda, Horohan is driven mad effectively by that history by which the autonomous power of forgiveness and reconciliation is removed from the individual.

TRAUMA AND IMAGINATION

Heredity and inheritance are staple notions in the Irish country-house novel, as they are in Trevor.[6] But Trevor's demonstration of his characters' relation to history is quite unusual, for in his fiction the chief mechanism of inheritance and of the transmission of history's traumatizing effects, is what might otherwise be regarded as a good but which in Trevor is often toxic – the imagination.

We see it graphically at work in young Imelda Quinton. When she is given her mother's version of Irish history, with its murders and martyrdoms, it becomes the raw material of her imaginings: she sees the lethal burning of Kilneagh and its aftermath in nightmares, which are always the same nightmare. This becomes a terrible waking vision when she closes her eyes (in Trevor there is much closing of eyes that releases or creates alternative or parallel worlds and experiences) and imagines details of the fire and its deaths she could not have been told of but which we assume to have happened in the novel's 'reality'. It is in Imelda's imagination that her English grandmother cries out, appalled by Kilneagh: 'No one could live here!' and 'This is a terrible place'. Imelda takes to reliving, by imagining, the life of her father exiled after the burning.

'As out of a fog the truth came in pieces to me' is not a statement from Imelda (her story is told in the third person) but it might have been; it is in fact the narrator of the story 'A Choice of Butchers'.[7] What Imelda does with the pieces is reconstitute them with the shaping, 'volumising' and completing power of imagination. Imelda's imaginings become increasingly atrocious: she imagines the victim's body after the gratuitously brutal murder of Rudkin, the ex-Black and Tan, by her father, urged to his violence by years of volcanic build-up of necessary reprisal. (The nearly decapitated head had already turned up in Trevor as that of the victim of the historical Constance Kent in *Other People's Worlds*, though the detail is graphically transposed to a television dramatization of the event; decapitation is referred to twice in *Felicia's Journey*, 1994.) At last ('She closed her eyes'), Imelda dwells in her imagining on the bloody murder itself, and when it combines with her waking nightmare of the burning Kilneagh, the imagined trauma pushes her over the edge of sanity.

For his part, Willie is goaded into accepting his mother's inheritance – itself imagined – of the Irish obligation to seek revenge, and surely she succeeds when she requests Willie to 'visualize' Rudkin's life in Liverpool, imagining him into the affrontery of existence for her son. Her imaginings in effect cause the murder and relive and extend history's deceptions, treacheries and atrocities by acceding to history's patterns. Trevor's biggest fools of fortune are like automatons, occupying a traumatized space into which they have imagined themselves.[8]

Throughout the Trevor I have read, characters are possessed by busy imaginings. The first story in the 1983 plump *Stories of William Trevor* ('The Table') is only several lines old when Mr Jeffs, the furniture dealer, is visualizing the woman to whom he is speaking on the telephone. Before the story is over, an entire and uncorroborated domestic drama has taken place in Mr Jeffs' imagination and it is the bulk of the story. When he meets the woman, he imagines he sees guilt in her face for mistaking him for the window-cleaner, but also imagines she is thinking he looks and sounds like a London Jew. This character's violation of the laws of point-of-view is common in Trevor and is an aspect of the blurring of fact and fiction inside Trevor's narratives. Imagination often overshoots the mark and yet supplants, and even constitutes, our only 'reality' as readers.

Trevor's characters imagine in order to supply a missing present, as Lucy Gault wishes to do since she cannot marry Ralph: she will imagine *his* wedding and married life instead; she intends to 'live a life that is all memory of our love'.[9] They imagine to improve upon the desirable or merely to conjure it into existence. In the immediate aftermath of witnessing his father kiss Bridget, the narrator of 'A Choice of Butchers' remembers how he lay in bed imagining in detail a family life other than its reality, one in which the housemaid supplants his mother (an acceptable but less preferable circumstance) and the lodger (his father's assistant) supplants his father in his mother's bed (a far preferable circumstance). In 'The Ballroom of Romance', Bridie imagines in substantial detail married life with Dano Ryan, down to such mundane details as the future repair of bedroom curtains and the whitewashing of the scullery.[10] By imagining they anticipate or foreshadow events. They imagine to console themselves in the midst of loss. In recurring dreams their imagining is out of their power. They imagine the past, the future and an alternative present. The exercise of the imagination keeps alive, and passes on, the terrible events of the Irish past; imagining them is the way Trevor's characters come into possession of history; imaginings can even seem like a contagion: they are not private but public, transmitted in a vast virtual space where nevertheless real and horrible things happen. In Trevor, history and imagination (including nightmare) are almost synonymous. Julia Ferndale in *Other People's Worlds* imagines that the story of her deception by Francis Tyte will become local legend, just as the story of Lahardane and the Gaults is coloured, enriched and re-imagined by local anecdote, in part through imported facts and motives, and memories of other country-house experiences, all to achieve, publicly, 'the tidiness of narration'.[11]

In *Felicia's Journey*, J.A. Hilditch (in the manner of Mr Jeffs) sees reflected in the facial features of the evangelizing black woman 'the thought that here is a man who is greatly changed, whose clothes are not as they have been'.[12] Set in England, this novel, like *Other People's Worlds*, suggests that final reconciliation and resolution are relevant only in the Irish context and that treachery, atrocity and trauma would in any case continue in other histories. In *Felicia's Journey*, the title character's memory of the impact on her family of the executions after Easter 1916, in which her great-grandfather was killed, retains a vestige of the lingering effects of collective trauma on her own sad and downward change. If the evangelizing woman does detect a downward change in Mr Hilditch, that change is due to the growing autonomy of his imaginings, with point of view slipping from his control.

Here again is a Trevoresque pattern. It is only slowly, and then economically (as though Hilditch is avoiding what he must not reimagine) that the traumas of past family abuse and treachery are revealed to us. Their delayed effects are more graphic than themselves. They trigger a lifetime of fantasy that grows to be as substantial as reality. Hilditch's psychopathology involves a compulsion to imagine a very different, post-traumatic, preferable life of repeatedly possible private friendships and public respect. Philanthropy privately extended might be his *modus operandi*, but to exercise it (he hopes to achieve friendship through gratitude and dependency), he himself must lie and deceive, reimagine his life for his chosen recipients. Here again is the perversion of the unambiguous philanthropy of the Irish country-house novel, and indeed, of the Irish slum-novel by W.M. Letts, May Crommelin and L.T. Meade, among others.[13]

J.A. Hilditch may require 'chance' to send him victims – it is chance, we are ghoulishly told, 'that separates the living from the dead' (p.213) – but once that happens he is an advanced technician of the imagination. 'Memory Lane is always there, always shadowy, even darkened away to nothing until something occurs to turn its lights on' (p.42). At work, he imagines Felicia installed in his house, where indeed she is, as though these images are his real reward, which indeed they are, more substantial than the self-delusion of temporary friendship. He is an inner voyeur. 'Mr Hilditch drops the lids over his eyes in the hope that the images will intensify' (p.128).

However, when Felicia remains alive, his images of her wane in strength. She has not stayed lodged in his memory bank because she is 'real' whereas his museum gallery of images requires for their maximum vividness bodily absence, death being the most graphic and definitive absence. He observes, with chillingly oblique offhandedness, that 'The Irish girl is roaming the streets, which is why he cannot see her as he sees the others, among his happy memories' (p.186).

A strange paradox occurs. Hilditch's imaginings have threatened to become public, visualizable by the evangelist to whom they might be in process of transmission. His imaginings have achieved something like autonomy. One morning, Felicia at large, his deposit of images of eternalized friendship dwindles: 'he awakes with the eccentric notion that the Irish girl has invaded him, as territory is invaded' (p.179). The image strikes back! Unsurprisingly, since it is by a radical change in point of view that imaginings turn to possess the imaginer, by which, in the Irish novels too, fresh atrocities – murder or suicide – are committed. Insanity in *Felicia's Journey* and in the other novels, awaits those possessed by their imagination.

THE TREACHERY OF IMAGINATION

But if the aftermaths of history are in Trevor constituted by imagination, which preserves their potency, so too, after all, are literary fictions. Before I opened *Other People's Worlds* (1980) – it is set in Gloucester and London – I realized that Trevor's world lies beyond Ireland. (Among other things, Trevor is a laureate of English consumer sleaze.) And that his places and pasts may be components of a parable about the stories we hear and tell and, in his case, the stories and novels he writes. (I suspect the novels are also religious parables but this idea I will put on hold.) In this perspective, eavesdroppers (we might think of Synge in the cabins of the Irish west) and adult writers of diaries both begin to suggest the activities of the fiction-writer. For Francis Tyte, the aspiring actor and apparently malevolent spirit of the novel, real people had rarely matched the shadows of his make-belief; indeed, 'Make-belief is all we have', he tells Susanna Music.[14] For months before, he imagines his imminent bigamous marriage to Julia Ferndale and talks to her of the wedding service 'as if the marriage had taken place purely for the occasion it presented' (p.141), not for any substance or implication for the future, just as Lucy Gault assured Ralph that the memory of their love would be an adequate stand in for the absence of their future love and for their impossible marriage. It is the future imagery of a past event that Tyte is after, not the event itself.

Unbeknownst to his victims, Tyte, like Mr Hilditch in *Felicia's Journey*, is indeed nothing except an agent of the imagination, of memories, fantasies and daydreams. The layering of his imaginings is quite extraordinary. Tyte entertains memories of imaginings of escape from his abuse when a boy at the hands of the lodger (the violent death of his parents is his make-believe trauma, his sexual abuse his real trauma). Then he (but it must be the impersonal narrator) summarizes the plots of recurring fantasies of escape, one an 'idyll' in an English village now replaced by one in a German city (whose plot is summarized later). Then in the narrative present (all this is during a walk in Piccadilly and Green Park) he imagines mowing down by gunfire the passers-by and visualizes their scattered bodies, which immediately remind him of the bodies (themselves an earlier imagining and the product of his fantasy) of his parents after the train crash *and* the bodies of Baader-Meinhof terrorist victims casually referred to by the director of the TV drama in which he has been acting *and* the body of the child-victim of Constance Kent, whose story the TV programme is dramatizing. When he reaches the Rembrandt Hotel we are told that Tyte had learned the prayers and responses in the Catholic prayer-book in order to make Julia believe he was a Catholic whereas he is actually an *acting* Catholic. That night, he dreams of being married and of those he has deceived or will deceive and of the long-dead murderess Constance Kent who is his closest companion. All this in the space of two pages.[15]

Tyte weaves a web of deception and treachery so skilfully that when he improvises for Susanna Music her childhood, she visualizes through his power of suggestion the fictional characters with which he populates her childhood. Later when she meets the 'real' Doris Smith, one of the victims of his fantasy life, she is 'possessed' by the notion that Doris is a figment of Tyte's imagination (p.118); not surprisingly, when she meets Doris again, Susanna remembers this possession (p.208), in a Trevoresque return. 'Real' characters will devolve, as it were, into imagined characters. Meanwhile Susanna feels herself possessed by the spirit of Constance Kent whom she is playing in the TV drama. As in the other novels, imaginings are transmittable, constituting an alternative, virtual reality. Hovering here is the true nightmare of the shared, the mutual or even communal, fantasy.

Incidentally, I had no reason to think that Constance Kent was not the product of Trevor's own imagining, until I Googled her and was introduced to a whole new sordid story: a story, moreover, of curious loose ends and doubt, a Victorian murder case that became and has remained something of a mystery, thereby putting guilt and innocence on hold, deferring blame and offering no definitive resolution.[16] Indeed, the failure of redress and resolution, the narrators' refusal or disinclination to apportion blame, or their rollback of initial blame, is a feature of the William Trevor fiction I have read. As Bernard O'Donoghue concludes of *The Story of Lucy Gault*, 'Nothing is anybody's fault ... There are no villains; all are alike victims of fate and of a series of unlikely linked misfortunes'.[17] In the context of Trevor's Irish novels this might seem like dereliction from a certain Irish perspective. But the country-house novel did not blame the gentry either (only deviant members of the caste); however, there *were* culprits of one kind or another (land-agents, for example). But Trevor's reluctance to apportion any blame at all surely distinguishes him. The autonomy of the imagination is, it can seem, the self-justifying of the imagination which implies in Trevor – worryingly when imagination impinges woundingly, even viciously, on reality – its moral neutrality.

Indeed, we find in Trevor's fiction curious inversions of moral judgement. Like Tyte, Hilditch in *Felicia's Journey* begins grotesquely to find ingratitude in the beneficiaries of his 'charitableness', as though they are not victims of his diseased imagination. Forgiveness is a large theme in the fiction but discordantly so. Francis Tyte imagines himself as a victim and by a moral logic founded on a fictional premise makes forgiveness his paramount motive and on the strength of it forgives all those whom he has victimized. Between the imagined victimization and the fantasy forgiveness he is 'careless of the consequences' (p.38). One of the consequences is the way his imaginary morality infects others. Even after his treachery towards her, Julia Ferndale 'had begun to love him for what he should have been', to love him for the food for her imagination he perversely offers. She closes her eyes and imagines their life together, her philanthropy healing him (she is a figure transposed from the Irish country-house novel): imagination in her case is also careless of the consequences (pp.195–6). Later, there is a troublingly ambiguous or foggy sentence: 'For a moment it seemed absurd that she'd ever believed in what had been a fantasy of her own: that Francis had left his vengeance behind him' (p.213), before she imagines through dream his return to her mother's Gloucestershire house.

'As out of the fog the truth came in pieces to me': the narrator of 'A Choice of Butchers' is luckier than some later Trevor characters. Julia's mother intuits Tyte's fraudulence but 'it seemed to Mrs Anstey that a fog shrouded a whole landscape. Perception couldn't cope with the mystery of that' (pp.89–90). (It is fitting that in the novel Mrs Anstey begins to read Dickens's *Bleak House*, with its memorable conjuration of fog.) After her ordeal and her awareness of the atrocities in life, Julia wonders if God is not her own illusion, 'a fog of comfort to be lost in' (p.179). Captain Gault comes to believe that his daughter Lucy has been 'possessed' by something she has broodingly imagined, 'wrapping her like fog that chilled' (p.156). It is into a fog that Felicia hurries from Number 3 Duke of Wellington Road. (This address might echo Number 12 Rillington Place, home of Christie who is mentioned at the end of the novel, as though Hilditch's life echoes that of the serial murderer.) To Julia in *Other People's Worlds*, Francis Tyte's fantasy Uncle Manchester 'belonged in the same grey limbo as the process of going through a marriage ceremony ... There were the same elaborations of pretending, with truth and lies insidiously mixed and an outcome full of other people's pain' (p.164); it is a thought transposable from this Trevor fiction to several if not many others. Fog, limbo, web: recurring images of doubt, uncertainty and entanglement in which judgement, certainty and autonomy are shrouded, consigned or ensnared.

STORIES AND DARKNESS

What *is* certain in Trevor's fiction? Stories. Yet stories, assumed to be a good and vital to our humanity, seem less obviously wonderful things in William Trevor's work. The stories inside the story or novel are usually forms of deception (and self-deception) and often dangerous beneath their plausible surface. The imaginations that spin the stories grow more obsessive as they pursue their goal of total fiction, exclusive fantasy, complete deception. They corrupt the less deceived and entangle them in their widening nets.[18] As readers we are in danger of being complicit in these stories, as, one could argue, Tyte's victims become complicit through their weird process of transmission in Tyte's fantasies. 'You write, the reader imagines: your task is to control the relationship', Trevor told Dolores MacKenna, a darker offering than would be the case were inflections of 'imagines' not sprinkled so liberally over Trevor's grimmer pages.[19] The writer controls the relationship between reader and writer; meanwhile, characters must do what they're told. Suddenly the footfalls of Tyte (though of course Julia describes him as a psychopath) and of Hilditch – another control freak – come close. One does not wish to think of the Trevor reader as a victim or to find relevance to the reader's experience of certain kinds of fiction in Julia Ferndale's observation that the murdered child in the Constance Kent case 'was the victim of other people's worlds' (p.219). Yet there are times when I'm tempted to see Trevor's fiction as a dark and conscious parable about the predatory, self-deluding and voyeuristic fictional imagination that is programmed by public history and private trauma to seek autonomy in its own satiation.[20]

Listening to Francis, it seems to Susanna Music that 'the talk could continue for hours, effortlessly inventing people and situations, changing her identity for her' (p.63). Trevor's own stories seem capable of endless invention, story after story (are there many more prolific short storywriters than Trevor?), spun webs of narration, fact and fiction that blur and blend (consider the role of Constance Kent in *Other People's Worlds* whose victim shares Tyte's first name), while our own firm sense of Irish history, of history generally, indeed of reality and truth, shivers, as the author's imaginings proliferate and draw us in. It is less that Trevor, like Tyte, is careless of the consequences of his imaginings, than that his fictive perception of the world is, beneath the amiable narration, as dark as Beckett's – darker somehow because the darkness is moral as well as existential. My recent experience of reading William Trevor has been one in which I, like Susanna Music, have sensed my own identity and my own sense of the world somehow being questioned, if not changed – and not for the better. Of Tyte's adulthood, the narrator observes: 'Even now, the stories continued'. For Tyte, amidst his 'real' and imaginary acquaintances (Uncle Manchester and the phantom best man), 'there was the usual pleasure of invention' (p.115), one he presumably shares with the fiction-writer, though Trevor bridled at Dolores MacKenna's suggestion that writing fiction is enjoyable.[21]

NOTES

1. John Wilson Foster, *Irish Novels 1890–1940: New Bearings in Culture and Fiction* (Oxford: Oxford University Press, 2008).
2. I discuss cousinage in the Irish country-house novel in ibid., pp.202–6.
3. I discuss philanthropy in the Irish country-house novel in ibid., pp.124–8 and *passim*.
4. Robert Garratt has explored the role the Irish War of Independence plays in Trevor's depiction of memory and trauma in *The Story of Lucy Gault* and two other novels: 'William Trevor and the Voices of History', a paper delivered to the Pacific Coast British Studies Conference, University of Puget Sound, 31 March 2007.
5. 'The Distant Past' was collected in *Angels at the Ritz and Other Stories* (1975) and is reprinted in *The Stories of William Trevor* (Harmondsworth: Penguin Books, 1983), pp.345–51. Perhaps in this story Trevor adds a new ingredient to the familiar recipe of Anglo-Irish 'ill-fortune' (p.345) and simmering or seething native resentment: it is the reversal of their material fortune in the South of Ireland during what came to be known as the (Sean) Lemass years that causes, as much as the Northern Troubles themselves, the Catholic neighbours of the Middletons to revisit their own anti-Protestantism and anti-Britishness.
6. In 'The Distant Past', Trevor is careful to tell us that the Middleton brother and sister 'shared a family face'. I discuss heredity in the Irish country-house novel in JohnWilson Foster, *Irish Novels 1890–1940*, pp.139–41, 317–19, 356–67.
7. 'A Choice of Butchers', from *The Ballroom of Romance and Other Stories* (1972), rpt. in *The Stories of William Trevor*, p.298.
8. 'A Choice of Butchers' offers a version of this that seems trivial because the narrator is a 7-year-old boy. He sees his father, the butcher, kissing the housemaid, the event that, one assumes, launches, in bed that night, the boy's lifelong imagination. Since the story is told by the narrator as adult, it presumably recounts a traumatizing experience. The title choice, between two ways of butchering meat – his father's crude method and the lodger's more refined method – adds an undercurrent that lends this otherwise O'Connorish story of childish misunderstanding the unpleasantness of much Trevor fiction peopled by adults.
9. William Trevor, *The Story of Lucy Gault* (New York: Viking Penguin, 2002), pp.115, 119.
10. 'The Ballroom of Romance' is a story in the volume of that title (1972) and is reprinted in

The Stories of William Trevor, pp.185–99.

11. Trevor, *The Story of Lucy Gault*, p.70.
12. William Trevor, *Felicia's Journey* (Toronto: Vintage Canada, 1995 [1994]), p.181.
13. I discuss slum-novels in John Wilson Foster, *Irish Novels 1890–1940*, pp.102–6, 179–86.
14. William Trevor, *Other People's Worlds* (Harmondsworth: Penguin Books, 1982 [1980]), p.64. For Francis Tyte, 'Real people had rarely matched the shadows of this make-belief', we are told (p.38).
15. Ibid., pp.84–6, 104–5.
16. There is a quantity of information on the murder on the internet. Since I sought such information, Kate Summerscale has published *The Suspicions of Mr Whicher: Or the Murder at Road Hill House* (2008), described as a 'dramatization' of the case.
17. Bernard O'Donoghue, 'Houses of Troubles', *Times Literary Supplement*, 30 August 2002, p.3.
18. My allusion to Philip Larkin's poem, 'The Less Deceived', is deliberate. Its chilling imagining of the 'desolate attic of fulfilment' may be just posthumous desserts for the Victorian rapist, but the deceived and deceiving rapist has committed murder in his quest for fulfilment.
19. Dolores MacKenna, *William Trevor: The Writer and his Work* (Dublin: New Island Books, 1999), p.230.
20. So liberally dropped into the narratives of Trevor novels I have read are references to other writers and literary works that I had thought of writing about Literature in the Fiction of William Trevor. Certainly the empirical data for some oblique observations on the literary imagination are there. In *Other People's Worlds* we have *Martin Chuzzlewit*, *Bleak House* and *Coral Island*. In *Fools of Fortune* we have *The Old Curiosity Shop*, George Eliot, Emily Brontë Shakespeare, Yeats, Goldsmith's 'The Deserted Village' and Tennyson's 'Vision of Sin'. In *The Story of Lucy Gault* we have Le Fanu's *Irish Life*, *Nicholas Nickleby*, Lady Morgan, *Vanity Fair*, Father Prout, Kickham, Hardy's *The Woodlanders* and *David Copperfield*. Dickens predominates, and it is a dark Dickens who does so.

21 MacKenna, *William Trevor*, p.229.

6

'ALL THE LONG TRADITIONS': LOYALTY IN BARRY AND ISHIGURO

BARRY'S OUTLANDERS

Sebastian Barry's perhaps most characteristic idiom, in novel, poem and play, is a gravid lyricism. This idiom is admirably suited to his most characteristic discourse: the monologue or soliloquy, to his most characteristic note: the elegiac, and to his most characteristic device and dimension: the flashback, recollection or vision. All are expressions of a long suspiration. There is something outmodedly unabashed in Barry's portrayals of the extended aftermath of heartbreak which is the characteristic condition of his central figures. In his play *The Steward of Christendom* (1995), surely imminent heartbreak is felt virtually, and perhaps actually, by the audience when towards the end of the play Smith reads aloud young Willie Dunne's now posthumous letter from the French front in the Great War which he did not survive and when at the play's end the long dead Willie reappears to comfort his father. Willie lies down beside him, as though after the battle, like the ghosts of enemy soldiers at the close of Wilfred Owen's powerfully affecting poem, 'Strange Meeting'.

Willie is a living ghost, but then so too is his nominally living, though demented, father. For in 1932, when the play's action takes place, both causes for which father and son fought – the British cause in Ireland and the Allied cause in Europe – were discountenanced and indeed virtually discredited among the new Irish. To an English audience for whom the Trench poets and such a play as R.C. Sherriff's *Journey's End* (1929) are cultural bite and sup, the poignancy of the figure of Willie Dunne would seem close to formulaic. But not to a Catholic Irish audience, unused even by 1995 to this kind of sympathetic figure, and whose older members would no doubt have their emotional engagement edged by a frisson of disapproval, Willie Dunne being no 1916 patriot martyr or survivor, and – worse – his father an ex-member of a police force keeping order for the British.[1]

Of course, in their fundamental situation, Willie and his father Thomas are not different from the rest of Barry's central figures outside this play, whom Fintan O'Toole has deftly summarized as 'history's leftovers, men and women defeated and discarded by their times ... misfits, anomalies, outlanders'.[2] Thomas and his daughters, who unlike Willie survive the great watersheds (however incommensurate) of the Great War and Irish independence, sustain a painful loss of status, have been marginalized and superseded in Irish society, and have felt the mortification of having their values and loyalties isolated and mocked by a new generation. Even Willie, in his letter from the front, indulges in the sad irony of thinking of Ireland as the front because of the troubles there that made some Irish soldiers feel they were already marginalized by events taking place in their absence.

O'Toole claims that Barry's casualties yet have 'an amazing grace'. This is true. But we can go farther. It is those Irish cultural watersheds that function to rescue Thomas, Willie and his sisters from an obscurity and marginality that are irredeemable from where they live and talk, but not from where certain audience members sit. These characters' unhappy condition of isolation is less existential (though it is this, and they indeed show grace in submitting to it) than cultural. They embody a whole culture driven underground into the condition of a subculture and thence the *oubliette* of Irish history.[3] They carry with them values that are yet defensible and recuperable, at least for the purposes of elegy and regret, of instruction and perhaps even of revision of our recent Irish past. These values may even prove once again viable, though the particular historical conditions have vanished forever.

Among those values is loyalty, loyalty to the past and loyalty to a soon-to-be discredited *ancien régime*. Their loyalty at first glance is foolish and justifies their apparent status as time's laughing-stocks. They are stripped of the support of history's (apparently) winning side and left exposed to failure and ridicule. But it is as if they are stripped to the bare essentials – literally in Thomas's case, as in King Lear's: clothes play a large role in the play, as O'Toole perceptively notes. But their dignity, as we (though not their fellow characters) see it, reclothes their nakedness in front of history. Instead of being foolish and reprehensible, their loyalty is revealed as core value and meaning emancipated from history and cause, from both loyal*ism* and its insurrectionary opposite. Their dignity serves not only to place loyalty centre stage as a virtue but also – and this requires some thought and empathy on the part of the audience – to cause us to re-evaluate the once deplorable loyalty to particular features of the old regime. For without distortion or prejudice, we can allow the Dunne family in their inconvenient and sometimes awkward eloquence to represent those tens of thousands of Irish who shared their values, if not always their fate, and whose voices either fell silent or fell on deaf ears when they did leave a record of how they thought and behaved during the cataclysms of world war and national convulsion. This need not blind watchers and readers of the play to the fact that Thomas Dunne, if not Willie Dunne, might have been that less than noble figure, the dupe (or someone suffering from false consciousness, as the ideologically inclined used to say), and might even have done some reprehensible things while exercising his power. Whereas we see Thomas Dunne as a figure alone on stage with his ghosts, we need to recover the culture of which he was once a part in order to measure the magnitude of his fall, his terrifying isolation. This rich sense of history, conveyed by a kind of sustained synecdoche in the economic way of drama, is what brings *The Steward of Christendom* close to greatness.

LOYALTY AND THE GREAT WAR

As late as 1916, there still were in force the opposing attractions for many Irish of loyalty to Britain and the Empire (brought to a crux by the Great War) and loyalty to Ireland (brought to a crux by the rise of Sinn Fein and the executions of the 1916 rebels). This tension we can find depicted in several neglected Irish works, including a readable novel by Mrs Victor (Jesse Louise) Rickard of Dublin, *The Fire of Green Boughs* (1918). But Rickard's is only one among several largely neglected Irish writings of the Great War, among them memoirs, novels and essays by Patrick MacGill, Lord Dunsany, St John Ervine, Robert Lynd, Katharine Tynan and Thomas Kettle. All of these writers except for MacGill represented in their work a choice between Sinn Fein physical-force activism and support for the Allies in the Great War. Sometimes it was not a clear or simple choice, as Ervine's novel *Changing Winds* (1917) shows. For one could deplore Sinn Fein militancy while remaining an Irish patriot or staunch nationalist of the constitutional or Home Rule kind. But in 1914 all of these writers, and the poet Francis Ledwidge, expressed fellowship with the Allied cause and all including Ledwidge and excepting Tynan and Lynd did so in the most eloquent way – by donning a British army uniform. Instead, Tynan sent her sons as proxies, as it were, while Lynd, Gaelic Leaguer and Sinn Fein supporter though he was, applied to join the army only to be rejected. It was possible of course to interpret one's enlistment as loyalty, not to England or the Empire, but to Europe and to Ireland, as Kettle and Lynd did. John Redmond the Nationalist leader likewise thought that Irish soldiers would be fighting for Ireland, though he also thought they would be fighting for the Empire, which he hoped (at least initially) the service of the Irish soldiers would help to alter and redirect for the moral good.

One senses in these cases an overlap or more precisely a *superimposition* of allegiances, loyalties and identities which did not demand the pain of final dissociation or peeling apart until after the war. We think of Kettle the Irish nationalist dying at the Somme as a British lieutenant, albeit a Dublin Fusilier. We think of Erskine Childers who became a British naval lieutenant *after* he ran guns for the Irish Volunteers in 1914 and before he made his unilateral declaration of Irish republicanism. And of Lynd the republican, proud of the Irish soldier's record of bravery, and proud especially of his record in the Great War. Lynd's pride was expressed in his 1919 book, *Ireland a Nation.* I would suggest that there is only the appearance but not the reality of irony here, not just because Lynd used the Irish record in the Great War as evidence of Ireland's nationality, but because the nation of Lynd's republicanism historically accommodated the virtue of fighting for the Crown and for Empire. That long tradition was not to be easily repudiated by anyone historically aware and generous in his patriotism.

The superimposition of loyalties ran down through Irish society in the early months of the Great War and was intersected by an array of positions and organizations. It is set out for us with clever hilarity at street level in a vigorous but little-known book by a little-known author, Gerald Griffin: *The Dead March Past: A Semi-Autobiographical Saga*, published in 1937 and easily bearing comparison with Oliver St John Gogarty's much more famous *As I Was Going Down Sackville Street*, published the same year and which at times it coincidentally resembles. The saga opens in the early weeks of the Great War with an enthusiastically received street oration in favour of the Allies by Reverend Dr Doherty, administrator of the Pro-Cathedral while Lord and Lady Aberdeen's vice-regal cavalcade clatters past to clamorous ovation, and the Irish Volunteers, the National Volunteers and the Citizen Army – each opposed to the others – parade about, not to speak of G-men and giant specimens of the Dublin Metropolitan Police (DMP). This ideological smorgasbord is depicted by Griffin with tempestuous humour as he remembers (or invents) pavement conversations with Augustine Birrell, Chief Secretary of Ireland, Rev. John Mahaffy, Provost of Trinity College, Tom Kettle and Francis Sheehy Skeffington. Griffin has Dr Doherty inform the crowd that the Citizen Army has threatened to prevent Prime Minister Asquith from getting to the Mansion House that night for a recruiting drive but that 'some of the good women of Dublin whose husbands and sons are fighting the Huns at this moment, have threatened to box the ears of these tin soldiers ... and to throw them into the Liffey'. 'All the Irish', Griffin recalled, 'were at present war-mad. Ninety-five per cent of them wanted to fight Germany, and five per cent wanted to fight England'.[4]

We know that for one reason or another those percentages shifted as war continued, Sinn Fein strengthened and the chief Easter rebels were executed. For a while, the sentiment of Ireland was in flux and something of a lottery, but in time the tide of opinion turned against loyalty, and Thomas Dunne and his family are amidst the debris left by the receding waters. The Troubles have begun in a realistic piece that appeared in *Blackwood's Magazine* in 1920, 'The Terror by Night', by 'An Irishwoman' (unidentified). In it a young country man who joined the British Army and fought with distinction returns to find a very different Ireland in which Sinn Fein is a power. He is subjected to a persistent and relentless persecution, boycotted and then his farm sabotaged. In his room he displays a portrait of King George V topped with a Union Jack. He is told by masked gunmen it must go; he removes it and bears his wife and child off to England in disgust. The author claims 'similar cases occur continually all over the country'.[5] And not just involving ex-British soldiers. The narrator, whose car breaks down at night, makes her way to the police barracks only to find dereliction and a message written in pebbles: 'DEATH TO THE R.I.C.' (p.29). After the setting up of the Free State, Irish soldiers of the British Army and members of the RIC and the DMP were, as sympathetic or even acceptable elements, largely written out of the story of Ireland and lodged hostilely in the popular memory.

IRELAND AND THE MONARCH

It is, in part, a vacancy in the narrative of Irish history and the popular memory that helps account for the heterodoxy and surprising success of *The Steward of Christendom*. It is the vacancy where Irishmen loyal to the Crown or loyal simply to the Army or police (and to the long traditions of service in them) ought to be. Barry rescues from near literary oblivion the loyal Irishman as hero, but in no clear-cut or agenda-driven way. The central character is Thomas Dunne, ex-chief superintendent of the DMP, in position of responsibility in Dublin Castle during the official change of regimes. 'I had risen', he recalls, 'as high as a Catholic could in the Dublin Metropolitan Police'.[6] But now, in 1932, he is lodged in a county home in Baltinglass in his 70s and prey to memories and visions. In his 'Notes on the Play', Barry acknowledges that the choice of his great-grandfather as the play's hero was 'worrying', especially since Dunne had taken part in the suppression of labour activists during the Dublin lock-out of 1913.

But this is an acutely moving play even on the page, and Dunne an acutely sympathetic figure, and the play ends with Dunne's vision of his dead son, killed in 1917 in the trenches as a soldier of the Dublin Rifles and appearing in his room to effect a posthumous exchange of love between father and son. Had he lived Willie would no doubt have suffered the minor hostilities addressed in Ireland to ex-soldiers. In a flashback, Dunne's daughter's friend is assaulted in 1922 by a woman for having seen off the Tommies as they departed Ireland for good, and the bus conductor who intervenes and tells the woman that he too had served in the War as a National Volunteer is glared at by the woman 'as if he were a viper, or a traitor' (p.29). Dunne himself recalls being spat at in the street 'by some brave boy' in 1922. The break up of the Irish units after the Treaty fills the aged Dunne with sad indignation: 'all the proud regiments gone, the Dublin Rifles and the Dublin Fusiliers. All the lovely uniforms. All the long traditions, broken up and flung out, like so many morning eggs on to the dung heap' (p.27).

An elementary point I would wish to make is that loyalty could be under the circumstances a complex fate, a difficult state of mind that was often betrayed through the cruel necessity of choice of action into the appearance of simplicity. And so in Willie's unbearably moving letter to his father from the trenches, the son reports that 'we have been told of the ruckus at home, and some of the country men are as much upset by that as they would be by their present emergency. I know you are in the front line there, Papa, so keep yourself safe for my return ... this is a strange war and a strange time, and my whole wish is to be home with you all in Dublin' (p.57). The triumph of the play is its sympathetic understanding of the complexity of loyalty which at first glance – and with the unfair and scally-eyed views of Irish posterity – can seem at worst like the mere puppetry of betrayal, at best delusion.

The terrible temptation to simplify, to turn the legitimacy of doubleness into the illicitness of duplicity, a temptation which few Irish have resisted for eighty years or more, is what Barry seemingly wishes to resist in *The Steward of Christendom*. The risk taken in front of an Irish audience lies in Dunne's easy, even natural, partnering of love of Ireland and love of the monarchy. Speaking of the unarmed DMP, Dunne recalls: 'We were mostly country men, and Catholics to boot, and we loved our King and we loved our country. They never put those Black and Tans among us, because we were a force that belonged to Dublin and her streets' (p.9). Dunne remembers King Edward praising his wife's hair when they were presented in 1903: 'All the ladies loved him. Of course, he was old in that time. But a true king' (p.25). But it was Queen Victoria whom Dunne loved most deeply, and even if Barry means the elder Dunne to be extravagant in his nostalgic half-dotage, and perhaps Barry disapproves (though I suspect he doesn't), it is still a moving testament of love.

> I loved her for as long as she lived, I loved her as much as I loved Cissy my wife, and maybe more, or differently ... The great world that she owned was shipshape as a ship. All the harbours of the earth were trim with their granite piers, the ships were shining and strong ... And men like me were there to make everything peaceable, to keep order in her kingdoms. She was our pride. Among her emblems was the gold harp, the same harp we wore on our helmets. (p.14)

Dunne's love for Victoria can seem bizarre to us but history suggests that it would have seemed less so in the early and middle portions of her reign. Assuredly we might condemn Dunne for anachronism though even that is movingly expressed in his broken soliloquies. He prays,

> Dear Lord, put the recruits back in their barracks in Fitzgibbon Street, put the stout hearts back into Christendom's Castle, and troop the colours once more for Princess and Prince, for Queen and for King, for Chief Secretary and Lord Lieutenant, for Viceroy and Commander-in-Chief. But you cannot. Put the song back in the mouth of the beggar, the tune back in the penny-whistle, the rat-tat-tat of the tattoo back in the parade ground, stirring up our hearts. But you cannot. Gone. (p.37)

But we cannot condemn Dunne for bizarrerie. Although James H. Murphy entitles his 2001 book on nationalism and monarchy in Victorian Ireland *Abject Loyalty*, his own analysis of the period is no study in abjection. 'It is presumed', he writes, 'that Irish nationalists were hostile to the British monarchy. And, indeed, by the time of Irish independence in 1922, there was an official and settled antipathy toward the monarchy both among the new governing class and among large portions of the Irish population' (the Catholic portions he must mean) but,

> The route to such antipathy, however, is long and tangled ... The perhaps startling reality is that the British monarchy, inasmuch as it was perceived as a threat by nationalists in nineteenth-century Ireland, was not a threat because it had any political power but *because it was popular in Ireland and because it was seen*

> *to symbolize a future for Ireland as a contented part of the United Kingdom that was anathema to nationalists.*[7] (My emphasis)

Even nationalists sometimes argued that Victoria was still the queen of the kingdom of Ireland. Indeed, 'Most Irish nationalists were monarchists', writes Murphy, 'of either the enthusiastic or the grudging but realistic varieties ... Monarchy seemed the natural form of government and it had the blessing of the Catholic Church ... Republicanism was the preference of only a minority in Ireland' (pp.xix, xxi).

Certainly these observations provide a context for Dunne's memories and visions that qualify their apparent dotage or falsity of consciousness. He need not even have been wrong-footed by history, which unexpressed claim is the underlying thrust of his aggrieved and unforsworn loyalty. 'The failure or rather the defeat of monarchy in nationalist Ireland', says Murphy, 'has been so great as to seem inevitable in retrospect. Yet this was not so. Monarchy might have succeeded in Ireland had circumstances been different' (p.xxxiv).

The Steward of Christendom is on one level a political tragedy, the tragedy of a man marooned in his opinions and allegiances by the changing tide of Irish history. The source of this tragedy is Dunne's resistance to the idea of changing sides, declining to accept fully the new Ireland and preferring to remain in heart with the old dispensation, that being the nobler choice. For he recalls that when Dublin Castle was signed over to Michael Collins (to whose personality he was in fact drawn), most of the men in his division of the DMP would have gladly transferred their loyalty to the Big Fella: 'And for an instant ... I felt the shadow of that loyalty pass across my heart. But I closed my heart instantly against it' (p.50). Loyalty puts honour and principle over feeling and pragmatism.[8]

On another level, *The Steward of Christendom* is a domestic tragedy – in the way *King Lear* is a domestic tragedy – about a widower with three daughters and who in the end goes mad with the weight of authority, the weight of historical change and the rewardlessness of loyalty, the weight of the years. Of these daughters it is Annie who is most incensed at how the DMP and loyalists were treated after 1922 (and to whom Barry gives a novel to herself – a sustained coherent recollection like a soliloquy – some years later).[9] Dunne himself feels aggrieved too, but not bitterly:

> We did our best and followed our orders. Go out to Mount Jerome some day, in the city of Dublin, and see the old monument to the DMP men killed in the line of duty. Just ordinary country men keen to do well. And when the new government

> came in, they treated us badly. Our pensions were in disarray. Some said we had been traitors to Ireland. (p.9)

Annie goes further, thinking her father humiliated by Collins, in her eyes the true renegade: she has become a bitter loyalist (of the kind we in Ulster know well) but Dunne on the day of transfer of power deems himself content: 'I served that King, Annie, and that will suffice me ... I don't grieve' (p.42).

SERVANT OF THE KING AND QUEEN

Above all, Barry's play is a moral tragedy about a man whose relationship with society, with the world, is undermined and transvalued by circumstances over which he has no control. At the heart of Dunne's relationship with society and the world is the notion of *service*. When Annie calls him a king, he demurs: 'That is the whole crux of the matter. I am not a king. I am the servant of a king. I am only one of the stewards of his Irish city' (p.42). This theme of Barry's play associates it in my mind with *Othello* in which the tragic hero, Shakespeare's soldier, 'invests himself in the ideology of service and obedience'.[10] Like Othello, Dunne could say, does in his own words say, 'I have done the state some service and they know't'. But in Dunne's case they do not know it and do not wish to know it because the state has undergone a sea change.

So politicized are we in Ireland that Irish readers have to work hard today to see virtue in Dunne's rambling self-justifications; he and the DMP followed orders and cleared O'Connell Street of strikers in 1913 and several men died, and we know today what we think of those who follow orders at all costs: professional duty and professional obedience can appear almost by definition nowadays as vices not virtues. But Barry puts accountings of service into Dunne's mouth and mind in sophistication far beyond these ideas, complex though these can be. It can only be adjudged by situation when a cause feeds back to de-legitimize or undermine obedience, duty, service. Moreover, I have suggested how Murphy has complicated the historical record by reminding us of the nationalist spectrum of attitude in Ireland ranging from revolutionary republicanism through to loyal – even when tactically loyal – monarchism. Republican nationalism, indeed physical-force republican nationalism, may seem to have triumphed as the purest form of nationalism in Ireland in the twentieth century – largely because we have conceded that triumph to it – but the legitimacy of other forms of nationalism

– let alone unionism – clears a space for a reconsideration of *service*. I am aware that service to revolution or subversion could appear to benefit from what I have to say, and it was with deliberate irony that Maud Gonne, the republican, entitled her memoir *A Servant of the Queen* (1938),[11] but I think there are often crucial disqualifiers at work – not the least of them on occasions, on terrible occasions, moral disqualifiers – which I will not have space to explore or even summarize.

Dunne hopes he guarded the monarchs' possessions well, for he has interpreted his service as stewardship. He was named after his great-great-grandfather who was the first steward of Humewood, a Big House and estate, a position in the family which his own father filled. Despite the solipsism of his dementia, he senses the Christian echo in stewardship: 'My father was the steward of Humewood, and I was the steward of Christendom' (p.37). He calls Victoria with the misshapenness of delirium, 'the very flower and perfecter of Christendom' (p.14). Yet there is a coherent if outdated vision of society in his broken mind: 'The world was a wedding of loyalty, of steward to Queen' (p.14). And it is a vision of family too, for just as Dunne lost his queen so he lost his wife and he tried and failed to prevent the aftermath: the 'savagery and ruin' (p.50) in Ireland that followed the Treaty and that broke his heart and the 'mire of this wasteland' (p.57) that Willie calls the front and that also breaks Dunne's heart.[12] Part of Dunne's delusion is his vague sense of responsibility as a steward who ultimately failed, and this is his tragic, Othello-like stature. But at times he realized success, in society but also at home, moments 'When you see that God himself is in your wife and in your children, and they hold in trust for you your own measure of goodness' (p.38). Stewardship is contained in loyalty, and loyalty seems like adherence to a cause or person or principle beyond the call of duty or requirement of obedience, a surplus space occupied by love and faith. Clearly loyalty can err on the side of complicity in a bad cause, person or principle, it can exhibit blindness and even abjection, but in Barry's play the loyalty in question is noble even if many readers or audience members would regard it as mistaken.

Dunne's idea of service was once no dementia, as is clear from the work of the Shakespearian scholar, Michael Neill. While discussing service in *Othello* and *King Lear*, Neill identifies its roots in sacred ritual (we speak of 'divine service') and reminds us that the early moderns saw Christ taking upon himself 'the forme of a seruaunt'. 'The faithful servant's fulfilment of his office' could be seen as 'an expression of Christian duty'. It was arguable that the Bible and Book of Common Prayer alike saw all service as belonging to God and the servant as, paradoxically, 'the Lords freeman', as St Paul insisted.[13] Neil claims Othello 'imagines his service to the state (in a secular version of the Christian paradox) as the very ground of his "free condition"' (p.22). Of course, Neil's point is that the sacralization of service was contested in the early modern period as demonstrated in these two Shakespeare plays. Anabaptists saw service as subjection and could quote St Paul's 'be ye not the servants of men' (p.14). My own point would be that we in Ireland have sacrificed so vigorously the personal and the professional, indeed even the sacred, to the political, that we have been unjust and one-eyed in the matter of service performed by Irish men and women and that Barry's play is a rare and powerful demurral. Of course, the warped nature of Ireland's political experience has skewed our perception of virtue and vice and we have settled for simplistic rather than rich stories of Ireland, simplistic stories of villains and heroes, traducers and champions in which service is servility and slavery even when freely tendered. These stories firmly exclude the notions of service explored in *The Steward of Christendom* and have encouraged their exclusion in real life sometimes at the point of a gun or the blast of a bomb.

STEVENS AND DUNNE

Service and loyalty are explored at even greater length in Kazuo Ishiguro's *The Remains of the Day*, a superlative 1989 novel that shares with Barry's play a deliberately outmoded hero and his values, and a gathering poignancy that dangerously skirts sentimentality: each is a prolonged heartbreak behind its own denial. Ishiguro's entire novel is the account by Stevens, Lord Darlington's butler, of his holiday through the west of England in 1956, an account dominated by, first, his recollections of his master's growing involvement after the Great War in friendship with, and later appeasement of, Nazi Germany, and, secondly, his developing thoughts on the perfect butler. Stevens's ponderous, if beautifully expressed, ideas skirt unintended humour, since his language, though precise, is dated, as he himself is (like the Dunne of 1932), an old-fashioned figure dressed in a 1931 suit and consulting a 1930s guidebook.

Both Stevens and Dunne are servants who reflect on the nature and virtue of ideal service. At first glance both waver for us between folly and nobility. Just as Stevens has a bizarre notion of his audience – he addresses us as though we knew and cared about the minutiae of buttling and its history – so Dunne's often elevated and poetic if confused monologues are addressed to the vulgar orderly Smith (who embodies the crass condescension of Irish posterity) and the home's sympathetic seamstress, when they are not addressed to shades and visions. This serves in both cases to render at first the respective ideas of service and loyalty anachronistic. In each case the hero is a dubious one who belongs to a previous era; moreover, both to the very end are loyal to discredited causes – in one case British administration and monarchy in Ireland, in the other the appeasement of Hitler and reluctance to confront Nazism. Stevens and Dunne could even be regarded respectively and to their chagrin as anti-English and anti-Irish.

Stevens takes his symbolic trip through the changed heart of England in the year of the Suez crisis (though it is unmentioned) that is often cited as that which signified the end of global British power. The present in Barry's play is 1932, the year Eamon de Valera came to power and the beginning of the end of those vestiges of British power in Ireland, of Thomas Dunne's Ireland, that lingered on after 1922. Stevens has been the faithful steward of Darlington Hall, guarding it through the difficult passage from Lord Darlington's ownership to a rich American's ownership (reflecting the transfer of global power from Europe to America). In his own way, though sane, rational and alert, Stevens is as mired in the past and oblivious to the present as ex-Chief Superintendent Dunne. (Dunne was in a way as oblivious to the present even when he was in active service, like Stevens.) Ishiguro's poignantly conveyed sense of an ending, the evocation of evening, the remains of Stevens's day (which gives the novel its title), has its equally poignant counterpart in the candlelight that softly illuminates Dunne's most emotional memories.

Both works reverse our expectations. A play which makes an ex-DMP member a sympathetic hero is not what we expect, while *The Remains of the Day* has downstairs in the stately home rather than upstairs as the foreground, though as the novel proceeds, what is going on upstairs, seen only through a butler's eyes, grows steadily more intrusive. In a wonderful counterpoint, Stevens's genuine concern for duty, service and loyalty is in increasing if mute contrast with Lord Darlington's apparent disloyalty to, and aristocratic disrespect for, the will of the British people and the opinions of their elected representatives. There is an evocative similarity in the way in which the deepening nobility of Dunne's loyalty must cast at least a degree of shadow over those who created the circumstances in which that loyalty was no longer a virtue; Annie calls Michael Collins and the IRA 'renegades' (p.48) and in the novel that Barry gives her in which to expand her views, she remembers Collins and De Valera as 'fierce gunmen ... savage killers'.[14]

Moreover, Stevens's almost surrealistic sense of professionalism is, we steadily come to realize, in contrast to his master's well-intentioned but – in the opinion of an American senator and Darlington's journalist godson – dangerously amateurish meddling in international politics. For *The Remains of the Day* is a secular account of loyalty, duty and service where Barry offers a sacralized account. A cardinal feature of service for Stevens is professionalism, though like Dunne his service extended into loyalty, another cardinal feature. Stevens reflects in a kind of conceptual *reductio ad absurdum* on the components of true professionalism: restraint, ability to plan, expertise, experience, insistence on high standards, and above all, dignity (a third cardinal feature), loyalty and the ability to truly inhabit the role. These, explicitly the last three, are readily applicable to Dunne of the DMP. So too is Stevens's knowledge of the tradition of his service which –whether or not Ishiguro has made it up – is fascinating and on the brink of the comic. We witness with Stevens as with Dunne a stripping away until loyalty and dignity are seen to be independent of professional livery and uniform; these are virtues humanized when man and professional role become indistinguishable.

In each work, the professional stands over against the gentleman and the amateur, yet, despite the fact that 'amateur' derives from 'lover', it is love that is hand in glove with professionalism, gainsaying our usual association. The love is repressed in Stevens's case, expressed in Dunne's. One difference between Stevens and Dunne is that the butler is utterly *compos mentis*, seemingly scrupulous in his recollections (even emending them on second thoughts), punctilious in his words and thoughts and apparently arid of heart; a far cry from Dunne's senescent confusion and unbuttoned displays of emotion. But we infer that Dunne has been undone, as it were, by the turn of historical events, that he suffers from a kind of post-traumatic stress. Stevens too has been let down by history, marooned like the Irishman in an uncongenial time and place. His obsession with professionalism and tradition – which Dunne exhibits too – may in his case be a sublimation of unfulfilled affection, love and sexuality. The vent of his feelings has been capped by these obsessions and by his Englishness, and now by his middle age and membership of a generation receding into history. In any case, his rationality is something of a carapace and underneath there is a Dunne-like disturbance he manfully keeps at bay where Dunne indulges it.

In any case, as even Dunne's life illustrates, professionalism must on occasion sacrifice the personal and familial. Dunne's domestic life has borne the brunt of his profession and his earnest, even sacralized perception of that profession. (His son and even his daughters are casualties of his career and values, and Annie the most wounded and resentful of them.) No wonder both Dunne and Stevens are tragic figures, and ones to be found in real life, though for its part Irish literature since independence has tended to be narrow in its choice of heroes and protagonists and has exhibited something of what we might now call Irish political correctness. Few businessmen, few engineers, few modern aristocrats, few Irish soldiers, few professors, few scientists, few policemen – few Thomas Dunnes – in its pages. It is as if Sean O'Faolain in his 1947 book, *The Irish*, set (or followed) the agenda and exhausted Irish society with his shrunken roster of six kinds of Irish for contemplation – priests, writers, new peasants, rebels, politicians and Anglo-Irish.

Stevens and Dunne are not without faults and it is debatable to what extent both have been unwittingly (or even wittingly) complicit in an undemocratic system. Just as it is possible that Dunne is white-washing in remembrance his role in the breaking of the strikers in 1913, so Stevens might know, and have known, more than he professes about what was going on in Darlington Hall in the run-up to the Second World War; it is unclear to what extent each is a reliable recounter of the past. But the sheer poignancy and eloquence (however different in kind) of these two characters surely endorse the nobility of their idea of service, even if the world could, and can, no longer accept it, though we, especially in Ireland, should at least acknowledge, as Barry and Ishiguro compassionately do, its previous existence.

It is the nobility that seems to count in both works. It is true that Stevens surrenders himself – like a good servant – to a perception and valuation of the world that he himself is prevented from embodying. On his travels, driving his American master's extravagant Ford, he is mistaken by villagers for a gentleman and encourages the mistake by allowing his acquaintances to believe that he had been immersed in international affairs, like the unmentioned (and apparently unmentionable) Lord Darlington. Since he has twice already denied working for Lord Darlington, one is tempted to hear the cock crow a third time. He does not come clean, thereby appearing to betray his own belief in dignity as the essence of the great butler. But he is no Judas; it is with relief he confesses his true status to the perceptive Dr Carlisle. His imposture is oblique loyalty on the part of a man who has been induced to impersonate his 'betters' (his employer insisted he take the Ford). Indeed, the dignity he has aspired to all his life requires him courteously not to disappoint the expectations of others even if that necessitates deception. When one of Lord Darlington's cronies questions Stevens about current affairs in order to show through the butler's ignorance the absurdity of universal franchise, it is uncertain Stevens is not humouring his interrogator in order to provide another instance of immaculately professional service: the servant assuming himself required to affect lack of knowledge even when he possesses it.

Yet all is not well and Stevens's trip is an attempt to redeem the past. He does this literally, by proposing to rehire a woman who had been housekeeper at Darlington Hall and his feelings for whom Stevens had, it seems, foolishly repressed out of loyalty to his profession and master. His apparently casual itinerary increasingly becomes a quest to retrieve love before it is too late, though he masks it from himself as professional necessity. He also attempts to redeem the past metaphorically by justifying Lord Darlington, and indirectly himself, in the light of posterity's condemnation. At the same time (the novel is wonderfully layered), the more prismatic Stevens's reflections become, the more we sense certainty draining from him as to the wisdom and innocence of Lord Darlington. Thomas Dunne might be regarded as engaged upon the same kind of attempted redemption of the past, even in his half-dotage, during which he too is engaging once again in the mimicry of his 'betters' yet without losing our respect.

THE LADDER AND THE WHEEL

So these are not unblemished heroes, and their visions of the world are not ours, but they surely command our respect. Dunne's vision of a world wedded by loyalties and stewardships, at the centre or top of which stood the monarch, a world now broken in Ireland (i.e. in 1932), has its more elaborate counterpart in the image to which Stevens returns again and again: the great house as a hub.

> Butlers of my father's generation, I would say [by which Stevens means before the Great War], tended to see the world in terms of a ladder – the houses of royalty, dukes and the lords from the oldest families placed at the top, those of 'new money' lower down and so on, until one reached a point below which the hierarchy was determined simply by wealth – or the lack of it. Any butler with ambition simply did his best to climb as high up this ladder as possible ... *our* generation, I believe it is accurate to say, viewed the world not as a ladder, but more as a *wheel*.[15]

Stevens clearly thinks the wheel no less undemocratic than the ladder, and he is complicit with the aristocratic disdain for democracy and Lord Darlington's preference for policy arrived at in the privacy of the great houses. There is comic and even distasteful fantasy in his image of the wheel, and yet it is Shakespearian. 'To us ... the world was a wheel, revolving with these great houses at the hub, their mighty decisions emanating out to all else, rich and poor, who revolved around them' (p.115). We might recall Rosencrantz's words in *Hamlet:*

> The cess of majesty
> Dies not alone; but, like a gulf, doth draw
> What's near in with it: it is a massy wheel,
> Fix'd on the summit of the highest mount,
> To whose huge spokes ten thousand lesser things
> Are mortis'd and adjoined; which, when it falls,
> Each small annexment, petty consequence,
> Attends the boisterous ruin. (Act III, Scene 3)

Stevens, like Dunne, is one of the doomed small annexments of the once sturdy aristocratic wheel. The wheel is an image far older than the ladder where power and status are involved, and positively Yeatsian in its neo-feudalism or neo-medievalism, though Yeats wanted the hub of the wheel to be the great houses of the 'native' Anglo-Irishry instead of the palaces of a monarch or vice-regal lodge. Dunne preferred the latter and his daughter Annie in the later novel recalls: 'My father's country had first a queen to rule it, and then a king, and then another king. It was a more scholarly, a more Shakespearean world, it was more like a story.'[16]

Stevens remains loyal to the memory of Lord Darlington and the idea of the great house, as Dunne remains loyal to the memory of Queen Victoria and imperial Ireland. If play and novel tacitly question the limits and wisdom of loyalty and service, each nevertheless seems to me to ennoble those who practised them and even those who received them. Stevens is prepared to admit that 'the passage of time has shown that Lord Darlington's efforts were misguided, even foolish' (p.201) but rejects the corollary that he should retrospectively disown his master and annul his years of loyalty. Loyalty, it seems, is in this case larger than the cause that first invited it and here includes self-esteem, even self-identity. Besides, Stevens thinks of Lord Darlington as a man of great moral stature. The young journalist, Mr Cardinal's assessment of him as an amateur bungler and gentlemanly naif is closer to the mark and Stevens may be indulging in indirect self-justification when he defends Lord Darlington; moreover, the enormity of what was at stake with the rise of Nazi Germany may be emphasized by Ishiguro's very consignment of it to 'offstage' to the novel's subplot. Nevertheless, and by the same token, Stevens's own dignity, should we grant it, acts to dignify the figure of Lord Darlington by association, the lord being served in this ironic but most loyal way by the servant. There is even a sense in which Stevens bears away from the house and on his back his master's sins, like a scapegoat.

I would be tempted to argue in similar vein that the essential nobility and dignity of Thomas Dunne in *The Steward of Christendom* – any folly and misguidedness to the contrary – retrospectively dignify appropriate cases of Irish servants of the state in pre-independent Ireland. Moreover, I would gingerly suggest that the play, apart from its intrinsic excellence and its fresh illumination of the years of the first Troubles, is a welcome contribution to the literature of our own recent and unlamented Troubles.

NOTES

1. Thanks to an Abbey Theatre rejection, Sean O'Casey's Great War play, *The Silver Tassie* (1928), was not seen in Ireland until 1935 and only fitfully thereafter. Frank McGuinness's Great War play, *Observe the Sons of Ulster Marching Towards the Somme* (1985), has tended to be discussed in the context of Northern Ireland rather than the Great War. (McGuinness's play, though, is still a double historical redress, the Great War and Ulster loyalists receiving their due.) Generally, Irish writings about the war have been sparse, though not as sparse as generally assumed, as I recently tried to demonstrate, where contemporary fiction is concerned, in *Irish Novels 1890–1940* (2008). In any case, Irish Great War writings have been fairly well neglected.
2. Fintan O'Toole, 'Introduction: A True History of Lies', in Sebastian Barry, *Plays 1* (London: Methuen, 1997), p.vii.
3. Though they are Catholic and not high class, the Dunne family share some features of fate and attitude with the descending or superannuated Anglo-Irish gentry familiarly depicted in literature. They exhibit a passivity, a gracefulness, a certain distractedness, a decline into eccentricity or even madness, an obliviousness to the modernizing world around them. (These features are continued in *Annie Dunne*, 2002: see below.) This resemblance perhaps comes in part from their emulating through proximity their 'betters': Thomas's forebears were for generations stewards of a demesne, and Thomas's tenure in Dublin Castle put him in daily sight of the rich and powerful.
4. Gerald Griffin, *The Dead March Past: A Semi-Autobiographical Saga* (London: Macmillan, 1937), p.42. Griffin was a schoolmaster, then a journalist in London and in Dublin where he worked for the *Freeman's Journal* out of the offices of which he had the distinction of being ejected, first by the Black and Tans and then by the IRA.
5. 'An Irishwoman', 'The Terror by Night', *Blackwood's Edinburgh Magazine*, 208 (1920), p.38.
6. Sebastian Barry, *The Steward of Christendom* (London: Royal Court Theatre and Methuen, 1995), p.50. All my quotations from the play are from this edition. The playwright's 'Notes on the Play' precede the text (n.p.).
7. James H. Murphy, *Abject Loyalty: Nationalism and Monarchy in Ireland* (Washington, DC: Catholic University of America Press, 2001), p.xii.
8. A brief description of the odd ceremony in Dublin Castle that Dunne recalls by which power was transferred from the British government to the new Free State government can be found in a lively memoir, 'The Last Days of Dublin Castle' by 'Periscope', *Blackwood's Magazine*, 212 (August 1922), pp.188–9. According to Michael Hopkinson, 'Periscope' was

the pseudonym of an Irishman, George Chester Duggan, a First Division Clerk in the Chief Secretary's office 1919–21: *The Last Days of Dublin Castle: The Mark Sturgis Diaries* (Dublin and Portland, OR: Irish Academic Press, 1999), pp.3, 238 n.19. Hopkinson would appear to have borrowed Duggan's title for his edition of Sturgis's diaries.

9. Annie like her father remembers with fondness the old Ireland under British rule, an Ireland that 'was another Ireland altogether' and one dominated in her memory by life in Dublin Castle when her father was stationed there: Sebastian Barry, *Annie Dunne* (London: Faber, 2002), p.95.
10. Michael Neill, '"Servile Ministers": *Othello, King Lear* and the Sacralization of Service', *The 2003 Garnett Sedgewick Memorial Lecture, University of British Columbia* (Vancouver: Ronsdale Press, 2004), p.21.
11. Gonne had a different queen in mind. She was like a mirror opposite of Annie Dunne. She was the daughter of an Irish colonel in the British Army (born in Aldershot, the army base in England) and acted as hostess for him after her mother died and when he was posted to Dublin Castle. But after his death she became an Irish republican and an Anglophobe and during the Great War campaigned against conscription in Ireland.
12. Hindsight allows Barry to assign to an unnamed character whom Thomas Dunne meets in 1922 the prediction that his grandsons 'will be feral in this garden' (p.50): an allusion perhaps to the Troubles that broke out in the 1970s and were kept alive by the activities of the republican gunmen (soon to be denominated 'terrorists') who saw themselves as heirs to Collins and De Valera.
13. Neill, '"Servile Ministers": *Othello, King Lear* and the Sacralization of Service', pp.11, 15, 14.
14. Barry, *Annie Dunne*, p.95.
15. Kazuo Ishiguro, *The Remains of the Day* (Toronto: Penguin Books, 1990 [1989]), p.115.
16. Barry, *Annie Dunne*, p.95.

7

VIRTUAL IRELANDS: MARTIN McDONAGH

ONE

The theatre programme for *The Beauty Queen of Leenane* (1996) describes its playwright, Martin McDonagh, as 'the newest "bad boy" of Irish theatre'.[1] I think this may allude to a quality of the playwright's lifestyle as well as of the plays. I'm not sure how many bad boys Irish drama has produced, but – to go back a mere hundred years – you could certainly describe Oscar Wilde as a *very* bad boy indeed, in part because he *liked* bad boys and went to gaol over the head of it. And during the lifetime of most of us, Brendan Behan was a bad boy when in the 1960s with his drunken clowning he shocked newspaper readers and television viewers but in that Irish way curiously pleasurable to the English. (I saw his notorious 1964 live interview on BBC TV with Malcolm Muggeridge – then himself an English bad boy – when he was much the worse for drink.)

In the cases of both Wilde and Behan the plays too were mildly shocking, or at least risqué. Wilde played wittily, stylishly and disrespectfully with the English class system and all its hypocrisies, and Behan likewise assaulted the class system, adding a tincture of Irish national grievance for good measure. (Behan carried out his assault from below rather than like Wilde from eye level, or even, in tone of voice, from above, like a cad or a counter-jumper with a gift for mimicry.) But finally, the lifestyle overshadowed the writing in fame, in Wilde's case until fairly recently, whilst Behan's drama has yet to be seriously revived.

McDonagh's success in England has been astounding, as the programme tells you. In 1997 he had four plays running simultaneously in London, a feat apparently unparalleled since Shakespeare's time. His success, like Wilde's and Behan's before him, is a reminder of the peculiar symbiosis between England and Ireland in the matter of literature. English (and Canadian) readers and critics like their Irish writers (indeed, their Celtic writers, if we remember another bad boy, the poet Dylan Thomas) to be confusable with the writers' own more outrageous characters and personae, to have seemingly stepped off their own pages, to act the bohemian and make rude and subversive verbal gestures at society. If not, blatant non-Englishness will serve.

Seamus Heaney, the Nobel laureate from Northern Ireland, is a good boy not a bad boy, but his poetry is all about Ireland and has an obvious 'way with the language' and the poet (with his very Irish name) has in his work rubbed shoulders with those terrible events in Ulster that because they are Irish are called euphemistically the 'Troubles'. The English critics love Heaney and write books about him, whereas a poet arguably as good, Derek Mahon, has *not* written at all about Ireland, writes a language that is not especially Irish but is wonderfully fluent, and has no books written about him and is not loved in England or present on the English school syllabus.[2]

The English grant the Irish writer a licence in language and lifestyle they do not grant their own writers; Wilde was the more readily convicted not because he was an Irishman with radical aesthetic views but because with his posh accent and public school and Oxford background he was seen as an arrogant and *Anglo*-Irish toff and thus something of a class renegade. (Although even Irishness could not have excused homosexual flaunting, or licence becoming licentiousness. If anything, that vice – as it was called then – would have been read as a denial of true Irishness.) George Bernard Shaw was another Irish bad boy of the theatre, and I wonder if friends and correspondents put up with his insufferably intelligent rudeness in life (as if traditional alcohol-induced Irish obstreperousness had been displaced into sacred cow butchery and vegetarianism) because, after all, he was *Irish* (you recall Sybil on *Faulty Towers* explaining away Manuel's charming incompetence on the ground that he was from Barcelona), even if he belonged to that line of Irish playwrights who to all intents and purposes were English – Richard Brinsley Sheridan, George Farquahar, William Congreve, Dion Boucicault – or at least Anglo-Irish, and therefore half-English. And come to think of it, James Joyce's literary reputation has been polished (or tarnished) in the marketplace by dint of his being Irish and in his own way bad, *Ulysses* (1922) being full of wordy extravagance, prosy drama and bawdy energy and Joyce in his personal life being less than pukka. Like McDonagh, both Wilde and Behan were overnight theatrical successes once they got down to writing drama, and all three stormed the London theatre scene. (Behan's success came with *The Hostage* and *The Quare Fellow*, both 1958.) Behan had the makings of a badder boy than McDonagh, since he had been a teenage member of the Irish Republican Army and had done time in borstal (reformatory) for IRA activity in England. Perhaps it could be said that literature and theatre redeemed him. McDonagh (and far more graphically, thus far, Wilde) turned 'bad' because of the writing, as part of the projected image of the subversive writer and both the theory and subject matter of the writing. Incidentally, if you want really bad Irish boys who have written literature, you will turn up Gerry Adams, Martin McGuinness and Danny Morrison, all IRA subversives who have written 'literary' memoirs (in the case of Adams) and poetry (in the cases of McGuinness and Morrison). In these instances a *real* badness preceded the writing and it is unlikely to secure redemption, though it might in the eyes of the English; the 'kidness' of the gloves with which English journalists and government officials handle Irish physical-force types never ceases to astound me. (I admit that it is touching to think that even terrorists in Ireland want *really*, if belatedly, to be W.B. Yeats or James Joyce.)

Before I leave this trifling subject of the lifestyle, we might note that the Irish – indeed, the so-called Celtic fringe people – are not so quick to grant each other such licence. It was a fellow Irishman, indeed a fellow Dubliner and fellow Trinity College man, who proved to be Wilde's Nemesis: the barrister and later politician Sir Edward Carson who broke Wilde on the witness stand. And when I was in Ireland in February, the rumour was circulating that at some banquet Sir Sean Connery – fellow Celt – took umbrage at something today's playwright said and turned into James Bond to deal with it. Whether this happened is less significant than the climate of notoriety certain Irish writers are selected to inhabit.

TWO

A more important way of being bad in theatre is to offer your audiences a disturbing evening or matinee. This Wilde did not do (his wit made his social prescriptions and proscriptions into feel-good placebos and it was his amoral aesthetic theories that disturbed readers and critics), whereas Behan did, though his depiction of prostitutes and vulgarity and the lower-class energy of his plays, which might have been menacing, were softened by Behan's love of song and his irrepressible humour into which he tended to resolve everything. (He was the funniest man in Dublin by all accounts.) McDonagh is bad in this same theatrical way, as was Shaw; and if Shaw's omnibus title *Plays Pleasant and Unpleasant* comes to mind, then we'd have to call McDonagh's works, so far, 'plays unpleasant'. But Shaw disturbed by having his characters utter serious ideas (sometimes humorously) that were unpleasant to the audience, whereas McDonagh's unpleasantness resides in what his characters do and what they say below the level of idea. His shock value belongs to the upsetting of the preconceptions we bring with us into the theatre. We are thrown off balance because we think we know the Irish, especially the Irish who live in the remote west of the island and are quaint and eloquent and bustle about cottage kitchens and country shops being entertaining (you'll recognize the set today instantly as you recognized the set of *The Cripple of Inishmaan*)[3] – Irish characters who are comic at first, romantic by turns, tragic at the last. Well, this is the trajectory you'll see this afternoon but somehow it's written in a dark minor key you may not have heard before from an Irish playwright.

When we list those characteristics of quaintness, eloquence, romance, humour, tragedy, whom should we think of but Sean O'Casey and John Millington Synge, two playwrights to whom McDonagh has been compared. Synge is the more obvious comparison because he set his plays in the west of Ireland, like McDonagh after him. McDonagh himself has claimed he is not versed in classic Irish and English drama, and this suits the image of the Marvellous Boy, the theatrical prodigy (Behan too came off deceptively like an untutored natural), but that is beside the point: cultural affinities are as interesting as confirmed influences.

In theatre history, one of Synge's plays, his most famous, was badder than any of McDonagh's could be, because it genuinely shocked a city. It is hard to know what (outside what would be considered blasphemy by certain non-Christian religions) one could depict or say on stage nowadays that would provoke a riot. (Whatever it would be would have to get beyond the reading and the dress rehearsal and the preview.) Yet *The Playboy of the Western World* did just that at the famous Abbey Theatre, Dublin in 1907. By all accounts Synge in life was a gentleman with the silent egotism of the man of genius (which William Butler Yeats said the philosopher Nietzsche likened to the egotism of a woman with child); it was behind the scenes of his play that Synge was a bad boy of Irish theatre. The first night of the play passed off without incident but enemies readied themselves for the second performance. The audience as a whole must have got restive with what they saw and heard. During those times of earnest reinforcement of Irish self-esteem we call the Irish Cultural Revival, it must have jarred to hear a father, Old Mahon, dismiss his son Christy as 'an ugly young streeler with a murderous gob on him ... the looney of Mahon's', using a word for a half-wit that McDonagh employs in *The Beauty Queen of Leenane*. Difficult, too, for a middle-class audience to accept that a son, especially an Irish son, would kill his father and be shielded by strangers, and pronounced a hero, and to have the violent crime committed just off stage, and the son tortured on stage for it, when everyone knew (even if you could swallow the crime as an anecdote) that, in the words of Pegeen Mike, 'there's a great gap between a gallous story and a dirty deed'. And then the blasphemy, with Christy foretasting love with Pegeen Mike until he'd 'feel a kind of pity for the Lord God is all ages sitting lonesome in his golden chair'.

At any rate, Lady Gregory was forced to send a telegram to W.B. Yeats (both were famous writers and effective managers of the theatre) telling him that the disorder broke out at mention of the word 'shift', the word then for a woman's slip. It can't have been the word itself, since it had been used twice in the play before Christy's marvellous haughty dismissal of the idea of other sweethearts to be had: 'It's Pegeen I'm seeking only, and what'd I care if you brought me a drift of chosen females, standing in their shifts itself, maybe, from this place to the Eastern World.' 'Shift' acted as a trigger; it was the vague notion of sexual licence, combined with the public use of a word reserved for private circumstances, and on top of that, the play's thread of pagan anti-clericalism and general defamation of Irish character that suddenly and perhaps by prearranged signal ignited the audience.

As the comedian Lenny Bruce once said, there's a difference between not liking a performance and rearranging the architecture of the theatre, but this distinction was lost on Synge's audience, who ripped up seats and caused mayhem. This forced Yeats against his artistic instinct and his own brand of Irish nationalism to call in the Dublin Metropolitan Police (the DMP, often seen then as enforcers of the Empire and alien rule in Ireland) to restore order. Synge had managed a triple whammy, to offend Irish Nationalism, Irish Catholicism and middle-class propriety.

A bra and slip will get the characters if not the dramatist into trouble in the play this afternoon and there are 'dirty deeds' I won't reveal. Actually, there's a good deal that McDonagh's dramatic world shares with Synge's despite the passage of time. From internal evidence, we know that *The Beauty Queen of Leenane* is set after 1989 (perhaps the mid-1990s when the play was composed, judging by the dominance of Australian soap-operas on Irish television that one character laments). The relative poverty of the Folans, despite the TV, radio, electric or gas stove and car, seems not that far removed from the standard of life depicted in *The Cripple of Inishmaan*, although the latter is set away back in 1934 on the Aran Islands (which like Leenane are in Connemara). It's a generalized smallness, backwardness and ingrownness of life in a remote area that strikes us. But soon it will be necessary for Irish playwrights to take cognizance of the recent and astounding Irish affluence even should they set their plays in the west. And in the play Pato, who labours in England on a building site as working-class Irishmen have done for decades, says 'It was only to see the Yanks off I was over. To say hello and say goodbye. No time back at all.' And Maureen replies: 'That's Ireland, anyways. There's always someone leaving.' McDonagh gets in by the skin of his teeth: the Republic of Ireland since around 1995 has become an immigrant society, reversing a century and a half of outward haemorrhage. (All the brickies – bricklayers – must be dot.com millionaires by now, their places on the building site taken by the immigrant Poles.) In Synge, Irish characters wander the countryside or emigrate, leaving the country and the hard life one way or another. In *Riders to the Sea*, the drownings of the young men are another form of emigration. Wakes, send-offs, desperate parties – and here they are in McDonagh as they were in Synge.

The basic dramatic setting of both *The Playboy of the Western World* and *The Beauty Queen of Leenane*, and a root cause of the trouble, is what an American anthropologist in the 1930s who studied a community in the west of Ireland termed 'familism', a system of inheritance and family relations amidst poverty, land-hunger and smallholdings that caused dissension and pitted generation against generation, son against father (as in *The Playboy*) or, as in *Beauty Queen*, daughter against mother. Christy Mahon, anthropologically speaking, has at least symbolically to kill his father before he can inherit his mantle and mature into a man. The American anthropologist, Conrad Arensberg found that in County Clare grown men were called 'boys' into their 50s or 60s, unless they had inherited land and come into their manly estate as independent farmers.[4] *The Playboy of the Western World* is a coming-of-age story that would have given Margaret Mead much to ponder.

McDonagh's characters would seem to have come adrift of their rural moorings and origins but those origins and moorings are discernible nonetheless. The poet Patrick Kavanagh in the title of his painful epic poem *The Great Hunger* (1942) translated the Irish phrase for the Famine of 1847 – the Irish like modest euphemisms: the Second World War was known to them as the Emergency – into sexual and emotional terms and depicted a farmer who grows lonely and impotent under the stern eye of a strong mother who keeps a firm grip on his life and more ... you will see something of the sort today. Mag Folan is a 40-year-old woman with the sexual and emotional life experience of a young girl. McDonagh is perversely partial to strong women ('targes' they were called in my childhood in Belfast): Mag Folan in *The Beauty Queen of Leenane* and Helen in *The Cripple of*

Inishmaan, for example. Mag Folan is the majestic Maurya from Synge's *Riders to the Sea* gone bad; Maureen is Synge's Pegeen Mike without the poetry. Helen is a less spoiled latter-day Pegeen Mike who has fashioned herself as a tomboy in reproach to the men who are too weak to romance her; both are violent by acquired default; how dearly they want to be swept off their feet and are willing to meet the men more than halfway. Today you will see something similar in another McDonagh play. I would venture to suggest that a combination of Anglo-Irish upper-class domination, the Irish priesthood and the system of kinship and inheritance called familism robbed the Irish countrymen of their manhood and drove them to drink and worse.

The sexual and emotional poverty, a kind of ethnic arrested adolescence, expressed both in Synge and in McDonagh, is accurate enough, and the land of saints and schizophrenics, as one American anthropologist called western Ireland, is a fair enough description, the wit and eloquence to the contrary.[5] A third American anthropologist, John C. Messenger, studied the Aran Islands (Inishmaan is one of the islands) in the 1950s and became *persona non grata* when he revealed the poverty of the sexual and emotional expression, its juiceless functionalism (and, as well, the aversion to nakedness that prevented the men even from learning how to swim).[6]

All of these social features we would nowadays speak of in psychological rather than anthropological terms – dysfunction, schizophrenia, paranoia, abuse – ignorantly no doubt but on the right track. It has all come home, as it were, in McDonagh in powerful and unpleasant theatrical form. The politically incorrect word 'cripple' jumps out at us, especially here in officially sensitive Canada. It's a good bet that Bord Failte, the Irish Tourist Board, is no friend of Martin McDonagh's, especially since the West is the jewel in the Irish tourist crown.

Synge was seen by some as having blasphemed against the holy Irish nation, and its ornament, the Irish peasant, but in time the *melody* of his blasphemy drowned out its dark bass chords. McDonagh has been equally iconoclastic, except that our tolerance level for cynicism and calumny and invective has risen, at least in Ireland if not in Canada where one must be far more cautious. It's harder, as the Irish poet John Montague has said, to swim against a receding tide. McDonagh's characters are disrespectful about priests (there's an allusion to the notorious Bishop Casey of Galway in *The Beauty Queen of Leenane*), about the Irish language, about America and the emigrants revisiting from there ('returned Yanks' they were called), about Irish culture (poor Delia Murphy is roughly handled), and about that intense Irish self-absorption. 'Who wants to see Ireland on telly?' asks Ray who wants to fly the country. 'All you have to do is look out your window to see Ireland. And it's soon bored you'd be' (Scene 9).[7]

Synge was iconoclastic but his language redeemed the darkness into light, negative into positive in the end of all. One critic has claimed that McDonagh's 'use of language in *Beauty Queen* and related plays is very much in the same vein as the language that Synge created', but this is hardly the case. Synge wrote that 'We should not go to the theatre as we go to a chemist's, or a dram-shop, but as we go to a dinner, where the food we need is taken with pleasure and excitement.'[8] Synge knew the diet he wished to provide audiences with: 'In a good play', he wrote, 'every speech should be as fully flavoured as a nut or apple'.[9] McDonagh writes speech like a musical score, like all good playwrights, and Pato's letter from London is a small *tour de force*. McDonagh with a good ear employs Hiberno-English, English influenced by Gaelic in syntax and rhythm. 'Me porridge , Maureen, I haven't had, will you be getting?' says Mag. That's Hiberno-English. The Irish in their native language put the verb at the end. My own mother would say something like 'Sure, he has a house in Bangor bought'. But McDonagh is too much of our own time to give us nuts and apples; he prefers lemons and sour cream that cause the mind to pucker. McDonagh avoids, perhaps wisely, the sheer poetry of Synge (which may in any case be beyond anyone not a true poet). 'Ten thousand blessings upon all that's here, for you've turned me a likely gaffer in the end of all, the way I'll go romancing through a romping lifetime from this hour to the dawning of the judgment day.' That's Christy Mahon at play's end. There's nothing like that in McDonagh, and its poetry would be beyond most dramatists, and in any case McDonagh's vision of the world wouldn't allow it except as cynical parody.

Synge also knew a good all-round medicine, despite his disavowal of the drugstore view of theatre: 'Of the things which nourish the imagination humour is one of the most needful, and it is dangerous to limit or destroy it.'[10] Luckily for him, 'In the greater part of Ireland, however, the whole people, from the tinkers to the clergy, have still a life, and view of life, that are rich and genial and humorous.' This is true in Ireland to this day, and McDonagh for his part gives us plenty of laughs, but for geniality and richness of texture he substitutes something else and you can make up your mind what it is.

THREE

Unlike Synge, McDonagh was born and raised outside Ireland, in London, and though often summering in the west of Ireland, I believe he has never lived there. His is a London-Irish voice. It is tempting to explain an odd sensation I get from watching McDonagh by that biographical fact, the sensation that the play I am watching is set in Ireland yet not set in Ireland. In *The Cripple of Inishmaan* this can be explained away, it seems, by the fact that McDonagh is playing with virtual Irelands: the Aran Islands of John Millington Synge; of Robert Flaherty, the documentary American film-maker who made *Man of Aran* (1934); of McDonagh himself; and that he is exploiting the cultural layering of the place. Add to this palimpsest of the West of Ireland the fact that McDonagh leads us astray in the plot, with twists and turns, each one a possible ending, and belonging to different modes of drama, but not an ending: he is a creatively manipulative playwright and depicts or summarizes scenes that may or may not have happened.

On top of this are all the strange anachronisms of speech in *The Cripple*. In 1934, when the play is set, the Irish referred to 'tins' not 'cans' of peas; 'miss out on' is a recent American import; I doubt if anyone outside of south Dublin had ever heard of *paella*; would anyone in the British Isles, especially in Ireland, have referred to 'the American postal system' or 'doctor–patient confidentiality' or referred to an illness as 'life-threatening'? The Irish said 'there you are now' not the American 'there you go'; they never said 'snuck' for 'sneaked'; nor have I ever heard anyone in Ireland use McDonagh's favourite word, 'anyways' for 'anyway' – it is a rural Americanism not imported even yet. One character says: 'The *Man of Aran* me arsehole. "The Lass of Aran" they could've had, and the *pretty* lass of Aran. Not some oul shite about thick fellas fishing' (Scene 6).[11] This is contemporary working-class Dublin pub talk. Understandably, the anachronisms are fewer in a play set in the 1990s, as is *The Beauty Queen of Leenane*, but yet the sense of an anachronistic Ireland (one out of time – forward or backward – as the word means) remains. It occurred to me after I read John Walsh's memoir *The Falling Angels: An Irish Romance* (1999) that there may be emerging a London-Irish voice very different from the Irish voice. (Walsh was brought up in London by his expatriate west of Ireland parents.) The London-Irish dimensions may explain in part McDonagh's unstable relationship to Hiberno-English and contemporary Irish speech.

As for the plot, I haven't quite worked out what is happening;

perhaps you can. Doubtful happenings, the hares of the plot started and coursed in different directions, the mischief (for the audience) of characters' fantasies and daydreams – they are all there too in *The Beauty Queen of Leenane.*

McDonagh's view of life is quirky and odd as he takes some measure of Irish life angle-wise, to use a phrase of Patrick Kavanagh's. My mother (who came from a long line of strong women as though out of Synge and McDonagh) when exasperated with our contrariness used to say 'you're as crooked as the arse of a willick' (willick being our dialect word for a whelk, that spiral shellfish). Well, by the time of *The Cripple of Inishmaan*, McDonagh's plots had become as crooked as the arse of a willick. One reviewer described *The Beauty Queen of Leenane* as 'a masterfully well-made play': I think the adverb is unearned, but well made it is, especially as a first play, allegedly written in eight days (reinforcing the image of the playwright as prodigy). As a dramatist McDonagh is something of a 'cute hoor', to use the Dublin expression of reluctant admiration for cleverness, cheek and streetsmarts. Which reminds me that McDonagh's favourite word is actually 'feck' and its limited inflections, which I always thought of as a harmless and exclusively Dublin-city euphemistic expletive but which McDonagh has now stamped indelibly on the west of Ireland.

Quirky and convoluted though the vision is, it is shared in some fundamentals with the American playwright McDonagh has acknowledged as a favourite, David Mamet. Indeed, I think the American drama of the Absurd, from Edward Albee to Christopher Durang, has fed McDonagh's imagination, along with specimens of what we might call the theatre – and more recently cinema – of cruelty (Quentin Tarentino and others).

Other fundamentals, of the rural Irish setting and a revisionist depiction of it, have affinities with McDonagh's contemporaries. I am thinking of equally young Irish playwrights, Conor McPherson and Sebastian Barry, who together compose a striking trio of Irish dramatists. (Marina Carr in her jarring surrealism might be an even closer affine to McDonagh.) If you get the chance to see a good production of McPherson's *The Weir* (1997), act on it; the changes these dramatists are ringing on the wild Irish west are impressive. Then there is a playwright, middle-aged in years but as young as those three in theatrical experience as a playwright, Marie Jones of Belfast, who in *Stones in his Pocket* (1996) has written one of the funniest plays I have yet seen, and like McDonagh's *The Cripple* a view of the West through the lenses of movies. In these works the West is being modernized, or if you prefer, post-modernized. Add to these playwrights the established names of Frank McGuinness, Thomas Kilroy and Brian Friel, and you realize that Irish theatre has rarely been more inspirited.

NOTES

1. This is the text of a pre-performance talk about *The Beauty Queen of Leenane* given to the Vancouver Playhouse audience in the Salon Saturday series, 5 May 2001.
2. The first critical monograph dedicated to Mahon's poetry has recently appeared (2007). I discuss the English predilection for certain Irish writers (adopting to some extent the view of A. Alvarez) in *The Achievement of Seamus Heaney* (Dublin: Lilliput Press, 1995).
3. *The Cripple of Inishmaan* (1997) was staged by the Arts Club Theatre Company of Vancouver in February–March 2001.
4. Conrad Arensberg, *The Irish Countryman: An Anthropological Study* (1937).
5. Nancy Scheper-Hughes, *Saints, Scholars, and Schizophrenics: Mental Illness in Rural Ireland* (1979).
6. John C. Messenger, *Inis Beag: Isle of Ireland* (1969).
7. *The Beauty Queen of Leenane* (London: Methuen/Royal Court Theatre, 1996), p.53.
8. Preface to *The Tinker's Wedding,* in J.M. Synge, *The Playboy of the Western World and Other Plays*, ed. Anne Saddlemyer (Oxford: Oxford World's Classics, 1995).
9. Preface to *The Playboy*, in Synge, *The Playboy of the Western World and Other Plays.* But if *every* speech, even by minor or unsympathetic characters, is flavourful, surely that narrows, as it were, the frequency across which the language of the play is transmitted and lessens the impact of those moments in the play in which richness and eloquence of speech are meant to be revelatory of character. McDonagh knows the realist value of ugly speech.
10. Preface to *The Tinker's Wedding*.
11. Martin McDonagh, *The Cripple of Inishmaan* (London: Methuen, 1997), p.31.

8

REVISITATIONS: CRITICISM AND BENEDICT KIELY

ONE

Benedict Kiely's most sustained critical achievement was his slim book, *Modern Irish Fiction – A Critique* (1950), a pioneering map of Irish novels and story collections published between roughly 1918 and 1948 (though with some backward looks). The survey has all the energetic briskness of a young critic simultaneously engaged on his own aspiring first additions to the body of Irish fiction, and the critique appears to have been written while the first novels, *Land without Stars* (1946) and *In a Harbour Green* (1949) were in the process of being written or being published. His was the earliest critical harvesting of post-independence Irish fiction and one gathered by a would-be professional writer rather than professional critic, of whom there were very few in Ireland in 1949 when the book would have gone to press.

Simply as a survey of Irish fiction by writers other (and later) than the great names of the recent Revival (Joyce, Stephens, Moore), *Modern Irish Fiction* would have been ground breaking. This must have been the first time that writers such as Brinsley MacNamara, Francis MacManus and Forrest Reid were given a hardbacked critique. Kiely was writing not only before Irish Studies was a recognizable 'field' (a word that would have been exotic in 1950, like 'Irish Studies' itself) but also before extended native criticism of Irish writing had got fairly into its independent stride. Writing between the 1890s and the 1930s, Douglas Hyde, W.B. Yeats, W.P. Ryan, John Eglinton (W.K. Magee), Stephen Gwynn, Daniel Corkery and Ernest Boyd represented the first wave of Irish critics and literary historians self-consciously devoting themselves to Irish literature. But these were primarily poets, playwrights, novelists, essayists, portraitists or literary missionaries, and only Boyd's *Ireland's Literary Renaissance*, published in 1916 before the author emigrated to the United States in 1920, kept its eye firmly on the works under scrutiny. The professional (and professionalized), dedicated and campus-based Irish criticism of Roger McHugh, Maurice Harmon and Augustine Martin was half a generation away in the future from *Modern Irish Fiction* while the American Thomas Flanagan's scholarly monograph, *The Irish Novelists* (1959) was a decade away.

As a critic, Kiely established and inhabited a kind of historical no man's land between the Revival enthusiasts and these soberer lecturers and researchers; unsurprisingly, he gave himself greater leeway than academics in the conduct of his arguments and use of 'secondary sources'. He had a Yeatsian casualness about the merely factual, especially dates: it was the spirit of the times, and the spirit of place, like the spirit of the writer in question, that gripped him. The result was that his criticism is stimulating and expeditionary rather than exhaustive or conclusive. Take away Yeats, Joyce and the Irish Revival as subjects, though, and the loneliness of book-length Irish critical surveys even in mid-century is made apparent. Certainly no one had surveyed the post-Revival fictive landscape before Kiely. He rightly called *Modern Irish Fiction* 'to a large extent a journey across uncharted country',[1] a metaphor that as we shall see has a particular pulse in Kiely's attitude to life as well as literature.

Kiely's criticism sprang from his own voracious reading and fiction-writing, and from heated and witty discussions in pubs, libraries and newspaper offices: various scenes in *Ulysses* and *At Swim-Two-Birds* might give us some sense of the critical incubation. Here, I think, are the sources of the oral and highly readable qualities of Kiely's criticism. Kiely having been a student from the country and having come up to Dublin from County Tyrone, it was perhaps inevitable that he would discover William Carleton. Yeats after all had famously awarded Carleton the Celtic palm, and Kiely would have known that, even if before he left Omagh he hadn't already heard of his legendary fellow-Clogher-Valley man by word of mouth. Inevitable, too, that he would find lively vestiges of Carleton's rough-and-tumble Dublin with its contentious journals and fierce disputes. In 1966, Kiely recalled that the writer in 1930s and 1940s Ireland 'seemed to fit in nowhere except, perhaps, in a pub, talking his guts out and doing no writing', indulging the brisk critical judgement at the expense of the creative work, though Kiely himself both got the writing done and saved enough critical breath to write an entire survey.[2] Although a history graduate from University College Dublin (and to that extent, at least, an academic), criticism for Kiely was to be an adjunct to the creative work as stimulus and expressive opportunity and, secondly, a means through journalism to help him make a living. The Dublin coterie he inhabited – which included MacManus, Brian O Nolan (alias Flann O'Brien alias Myles na gCopaleen), Patrick Kavanagh and Frank O'Connor: as near to public intellectuals as Ireland could then produce[3] – had their counterparts in New York and London where the pub and café had not yet been superseded by the academic conference auditorium and the seminar room. Later, of course, writers of distinction and some educational background and who spoke well, including W.R. Rodgers, O'Connor and Kiely (by then all veterans of Irish and British radio), were invited to American campuses as writers-in-residence and in the decades before political correctness and Perrier water, they fitted in quite well, managing to lend seminar rooms the semblance of snugs, with their Irish informality recreating as best they could their febrile native habitats.

The connection with Carleton stayed rural as well as urban. Irish writing as a 'field' was more literal than figurative. The texts in trees and sermons in running brooks that the two men from Tyrone read and heard were rather more insistent than Wordsworth's, since the congested Irish landscape was more deeply or at least more recently inscribed (one might better say incised or scarred) than the Lake District with history and bloodshed. Reading Kiely's stories, novels, memoirs and itineraries (a word to which I'll return) is to see Ireland as an immense hedge-school, a vast roofless academy and field-laboratory as busy as Joyce's streets, where one saw in the wild what one talked about in the city pubs, where one listened and learned, where life was narrated and sung (in the pub, life was more likely to be quoted), where one saw life in its ancient and protean forms. One might even detect in Kiely (as in a younger writer he early championed, Seamus Heaney) some deliberateness in hedging his feelings about academia, a conscious reversion to an elder way of connecting literature and life. In *Poor Scholar* (1947), his study of William Carleton, Kiely's recreation of his subject's education as a hedge-school pupil – an education as autodidactic as it was didactic, simultaneously half-baked and pretentious – is insightful, sympathetic and even admiring. And in his musical perambulation, *And as I Rode by Granard Moat* (1996), Kiely recalls his own Carletonesque beginnings. He opens with memories of the teachers of the Christian Brothers' school in Omagh, of country walks with Brother Walker while discussing James Joyce, of an outing with schoolfellows to the mountain-top of Mullagharn inspired by something a teacher said and a reference in a Kavanagh poem, from the top of which they looked down on Ireland (Kiely never lost his hungry bird's-eye view of the island) and sang in Irish and English. Somehow, all writing, including his own, the fiction and the criticism as well as the creative non-fiction, would be informed by place, by neighbourhood, by mountain and stream.[4]

This, however, is to distract at the outset from the serious revisionist literary history of *Modern Irish Fiction*. The book contradicts at length two post-Revival beliefs that Kiely claimed to detect.

One: that somehow peace and semi-independence by 1923 spelled the end of large-scale Irish cultural history, a belief that we can readily imagine was held by those who lived through Easter 1916, the Troubles and the Civil War. (His representative End-of-History man is Padraic Colum.[5]) His book is written by a member of the first post-independence generation who is determined to infuse Free State Ireland with significance and to demonstrate its cultural achievement and energy. *Modern Irish Fiction* is not a counter-Revival work of literary criticism (Kiely is far too respectful of literary achievements wherever or whenever they have appeared, and he never betrayed the kind of generational rivalry and *animus* Kavanagh harboured); rather it is a work that attempts to lever post-Revival fiction into the Irish tradition whatever Revival survivors might think.

Two: that the Irish society that developed after independence (and the Revival) was inimical to the kind of creativity required for the production of novels, especially novels set firmly in the 'real' world. This was famously the opinion of the dominant culture-givers of the 1930s, O'Connor and O'Faolain.[6] It has had a long shelf life, from the 1930s until the present.[7] Kiely, with some good-humoured fatigue, demurred from his late friend O'Connor's view in the pages of the *Kenyon Review* in 1968,[8] but it clearly rankled with him, as though casting doubt on the value of his own career as a novelist. He had clearly intended *Modern Irish Fiction* to be an earlier rebuttal by critical demonstration. In any event, Kiely claimed in his book that there had been proportionately more prose fiction produced by Irish writers between 1918 and 1948 than in any previous thirty-year period.

With some acidity, Kiely remembered, both in *Modern Irish Fiction* and 'The Whores on the Halfdoors' the self-justification by Professor Magennis of the Irish Censorship Board that the novels he was censoring were really short stories padded out to novel length for vulgar English readers, that Ireland had in fact few real novelists. This for Kiely ought to have been a double insult: both critical and bureaucratic denigration of Irish novels. Yet O'Faolain, for example, seems to have been incensed by the very active state censorship of the Free State government more than Kiely, who seemed, judging by his own words, to have taken censorship in his stride, or at least to have shielded any raw indignation by a sense of humour. His most sustained account of literary censorship can be found in 'The Whores on the Halfdoors' but it is an account that retroactively at least tries to laugh censorship, and the memory of censorship, into absurdity. The darkest days seem to have been the 1940s; he tells the horrifying story of *The Tailor and Anstey* yet recalled it merely as 'a gruesome interlude in the proceedings, normally ludicrous, of the Dublin censorship'. But just when things seemed to be looking up in the 1960s 'they were at their old tricks again' (a Yeatsian echo) and from the vantage-point of 1990 he recalls how John McGahern's second novel (*The Dark*, 1965) was banned and the novelist sacked as a teacher.

It is hard for me to recover what Kiely at the time felt and thought when his own early novels were banned in the 1940s. By the 1960s, he tells us, everyone knew that 'the censorship was a cod' though surely it was anything but a cod at the time, since it was not only 'steamy' scenes in novels that were being banned, but ideas and opinions (*AR*, pp.140–5). Perhaps for Kiely as an Ulsterman, and to that extent an outsider in Dublin, there was fractionally less at stake.[9] And one could always wear like a badge having one's book banned, as Kiely and some other writers seemed to have done. Perhaps, though, it was partly Kiely's temperament: he had none of Carleton's occasional spoil for a knock-down fight or O'Faolain's capacity for intellectual affront. There is a long Irish tradition of meeting oppression or suppression with scathing or oblique humour and Kiely belonged to that tradition.

Although he himself became a short storywriter of the front rank, he championed the Irish novel against the critical denigrations he recorded in his critique. What was at stake was the truth or falsity of whether post-independent Ireland was the broken, divided, barren society O'Connor and O'Faolain claimed it was, thus preventing good novels, especially good realistic novels, being written. Kiely was a life-long promoter of unity and harmony who only occasionally lost his spirit: *Proxopera* (1977) was unusual in being written in anger and despair. It was paradoxically as an Ulsterman, and a Catholic Ulster-man to boot, that he was better placed than southerners to claim through experience the essential unity of the island. Nor did he ever admit any irremediable fractures inside the Free State, be those fractures political, social or cultural. To that extent, it was necessary for Kiely to see some sort of tradition in fiction stretching unbroken across the decades of fractious politics.

The tradition Kiely sought to extend into his present and his own beginning career he outlines in his eight-and-a-half-page Foreword to *Modern Irish Fiction*, and it is one we can see expressed piecemeal in his various essays elsewhere. The first instalment of his literary tradition is now orthodoxy: Edgeworth, Lever, Lover, the Banims, Lady Morgan, Le Fanu, Griffin, Hall and Carleton were the exclusive figures of the 1800–80 period. They were followed (and Kiely's second instalment is still not orthodox in its entirety or components) by Kickham, O'Grady, Sheehan, Moore, Barlow (forgotten in 1950), Somerville and

Ross (whom he takes more seriously than did the Revivalists), Bullock (a retrieved Ulster novelist), Joyce, Corkery, Stephens and Lawless (forgotten in 1950) in the 1880–1922 period. In the first essay reprinted in *A Raid into Dark Corners* (1999), 'Ned McKeown's Two Doors: An Approach to the Novel in Ireland', Kiely adds W.H. Maxwell and Charles Maturin to the earlier period.[10] Either way, the two instalments were broadly a movement from the Anglo-Irish (Protestant) nineteenth century to the native Irish (Catholic) twentieth century.

Kiely's tradition is a procession of personalities, of individual talents, rather than a transmission and alteration of techniques or preoccupations. This concern with personality stretched to his treatment of the writing as well as the writers, with characters (and their environment) occupying the foreground of his attention. His Table of Contents in *Modern Irish Fiction* is a preponderance of human types; the chapter titles are: Rebels, Peasants, Townsmen, Heroes, History, Dreams, Exiles, Lovers and Creeds. He was aware of Liam O'Flaherty's simplified typology in *A Tourist's Guide to Ireland* (1929) – priests, peasants, publicans and politicians – for in 'The Whores on the Halfdoors' (1966) he comments on its scantiness. He is equally quizzical about Sean O'Faolain's better-known and then recent study, *The Irish* (1947), which in *Modern Irish Fiction* (p.43) Kiely thought a rather simple and personal survey of Free State Ireland. O'Faolain's typology runs: The New Peasantry, The Anglo-Irish, The Rebels, The Priests, The Writers, The Politicians. In fact, though, all three writers share a perspective on Ireland that is native and Catholic, with the peasant at its centre, the Catholic middle class off-centre, the Anglo-Irish at its historical margin and the Ulster population essentially (even in Kiely's case) off-camera. Despite its impression of diversity and democracy, it is in fact a rather partisan view that shares with the Revival's cultural nationalism the centrality of the peasantry, if not the marginality of the Anglo-Irish.

From Kiely's perspective, the most important fiction writers in the 1922–48 period are O'Faolain, MacManus, Francis Stuart and Kate O'Brien; they occupy four of Kiely's eight categories/chapters and are, as it were, his first eleven. Then come O'Connor, O'Flaherty and MacNamara. Elizabeth Bowen, Mervyn Wall, Mary Lavin, Reid and Maurice Walsh are interesting writers to whom he pays eloquent tribute but they do not alter the shape of whatever overall picture emerges. Of the important figures, O'Faolain functions like the book's tutelary genius. (Graham Greene, too, is something of an off-island touchstone, and to a lesser extent another Catholic novelist, François Mauriac.) Kiely is himself aware of what is missing from his survey but beyond his control. Having spent some lively pages on Joyce, Kiely might be right when he claims in Chapter 3, 'Townsmen', that the Irish novel has since 1922 (and by 1948) failed to keep up with the development of modern Dublin (p.47), that Dublin in contemporary novels is historical, fleeting, romantic, oblique or futuristic but almost never present and real. *At Swim-Two-Birds* (1939) by Flann O'Brien he sees as belonging to no city but rather to the 'blue parishes' of fantasy where 'wild humour can transform an undergraduate puking porter into a figure of healthy fun' (p.50). But in any case, one senses that Kiely does not deeply miss the novel of urban realism or indeed any kinds of novel he doesn't discuss.

Otherwise, he might have added to his human character-types to include (or give greater prominence to) engineers, say, or scientists, or merchants and captains of industry, travellers, policemen and detectives, or soldiers, women, residents of England and other expatriates (instead of the culturally loaded characters and authors named 'exiles'). For if it is untrue, and it *is* untrue, that there was a greater volume of Irish fiction produced between 1918 and 1948 than in any thirty-year period before the end of the Great War, the error is readily made if one has a certain, and only a certain, Ireland in mind, and an Ireland in which women were marginal *qua* women and *qua* writers.[11] For the truth is that the Ireland Kiely had in mind (and in heart) was one over which Carleton threw a shadow even larger than the one he threw over Yeats's Irish imaginary. *Poor Scholar* was heavily dependent for its biographical facts on D.J. O'Donoghue's *Life of William Carleton* (1896) but Kiely's Carleton is, pioneeringly, a figure for the Irish twentieth century, especially after the divisive events of the Rising, the Troubles, the Civil War, and partition which Carleton could be thought of as somehow presaging, he 'had in him also so much caprice, so much self-willed, unrestrained imagination', giving offence, as O'Donoghue had said, to every class of Irishman, straddling unstably all the often lethal distinctions of Irish life.[12]

Kiely made his reservations about Carleton clear: they parted ways when Carleton was judgemental and dismissive of certain kinds of fellow-Irish (though who these were varied according to Carleton's current agenda), preferring as Kiely did the huge appetite for character and incident we find in Chaucer, whose demotic embrace might come to mind as we read Kiely's own novels and itineraries.[13] Nor was Kiely impressed by, though he understood its circumstances, the fact that his subject 'never kept his two feet in the same place long enough, to find for himself a stable, logical approach to the central political problem that had so much to do with the chaos of the Irish nineteenth century' (*PS*, p.129). Kiely himself moved around Ireland a good deal (few parishes were innocent of his footprint), but Dublin was his base camp. Yet if Kiely's political position was relatively stable – on the constitutional question there was some political movement towards the centre implied in the span between *Counties of Contention* (1945) and *Proxopera* (1977) – it was not primarily logical either, being of the heart and sufficiently blurred to accommodate the political chaos of the Irish post-1969 twentieth century; Kiely too straddled deep fissures in Irish life, if not serially like Carleton, then simultaneously. The 'great heart' that he heard beating even in Carleton the propagandist (*PS*, p.146) beat in Kiely too.

And if Kiely thought he was distancing himself from what he regarded as Carleton's essential empiricism, the latter's dependence on clear memory rather than imagination which Kiely thought was never strong (here Kiely came close to contradicting himself on the matter of Carleton's inventiveness which he had already described as 'unrestrained'),[14] we are surely reminded of the elder writer when we are witness to Kiely's fictive *modus operandi* in which memory and anecdote play a huge role. For Kiely, experience is never unique or unprecedented, nor is invention the chief business of literary expression: 'every experience takes the form of a quotation', one character says in *Nothing Happens in Carmincross* (1985), but his companion amends this to 'every experience *is* a quotation [my italics] and ... every quotation is a renewed experience, a light switched on again in a darkened room to reveal familiar objects'.[15] A successful quotation requires memory while experience *is* memory. In such wise, Kiely blurs the distinction between first-hand and second-hand, between life and art, with quotation as the distillation of both and the bridge between. Fittingly, *Carmincross* opens with four quotations whose authors are not identified until the novel's last page, giving the authors the force of off-stage characters. And on the last page Kiely disclaims each of the two extremes of fictive creativity, both historical fact and pure invention: 'The earnest student of atrocities will detect anachronisms. Specimens have been moved about in time. And in place. Does it matter?' If his criticism is an elaborate form of quoting literature, so is his fiction (with its pastiche, allusion, narrative impersonations and of course quotations) while the forms of that fiction, moreover, are elaborate quotations from life.

Whatever their differences, Kiely's knowledge of Carleton's world and work is so intimate that one feels he internalized them, resulting in criticism that is steeped in fellow-feeling of an order that became out of place in later academic criticism. That sympathy suffuses the first 'establishment shot' of *Poor Scholar*, the first three paragraphs that beautifully recreate the Clogher Valley before the biographical critic zooms in to provide glimpses of this puzzling, contradictory, unsettling figure going in and coming out of cabins. It became characteristic for Kiely in his writings to begin with the evocation of place, and his sharing of geography with Carleton was a kind of brotherhood across the generations.

TWO

At the risk of writing anachronism, and for all his political tergiversations, I see Carleton as a figure theoretically at home in the Irish Free State that was dominated by the small-farmer class and the urban lower middle class. (He and O'Connell rather than Yeats, Hyde and the other Protestant Revivalists were perhaps the culture-givers of the Ireland between 1922 and, say, the 1980s. Carleton, of course, is also imaginable in the Ulster countryside after 1969, riven with sectarian animosity.) To a lesser extent than O'Faolain in terms of the general culture, but to a greater extent in terms of the novel, Kiely helped in *Modern Irish Fiction* to establish the literary curriculum of the Irish Free State. I say this despite his dissenting opinion on censorship and the impressive range of European figures he adduces in his essays and in *Modern Irish Fiction* to help place his Irish writers, including Turgenev, Flaubert, Alexander Kuprin, Gorki, Baudelaire, Voltaire, Balzac, Gide, Camus, Savonarola, Pascal and Zola. (There was a paradoxically unacademic breadth to Kiely's reading.[16]) It was partly this reading, and partly the reading of Irish authors, that led Kiely to conclude that 'the strongest force in the Irish soul is centripetal. A nation that has produced exiles and wanderers by the thousand does not seem to have produced many cosmopolitans; assuredly not one ... who has shaped his feelings into creative fiction in the last thirty years' (*MIF*, pp.129–30). This doesn't quite rise to an indignant criticism; Kiely too, his broad stretch of reading to the contrary, seems to have been quite at home in the Free State and early Republic, at home even in the partitioned island through which he freely circulated, satisfied enough with the status quo as long as it meant peace and encouraged decency.[17]

Nor, of course, need the ultimate narrowness of the curriculum, one centred on the post-independence state still in formation – and which permits Samuel Beckett, the author of *Murphy* (1938), to be omitted – obviate first-rate penetrating readings of his favourite fiction writers.[18] In *Modern Irish Fiction* there are pages on Joyce (132–6), Kate O'Brien

(139–43) and Bowen (151–8) that should be the envy of trained literary critics. These are joined by essays later collected in *A Raid into Dark Corners*, on (again) Kate O'Brien (1992), James Stephens (1946), Sean O'Faolain (1991), Thomas Flanagan (1981) and Canon Sheehan (1990s). These are essays that contemporary specialists could read with profit. He is hard on Sheehan, which is unusual for Kiely; he is normally so sympathetic that when he wishes to criticize he merely becomes condescending ('poor MacGill', he writes elsewhere, though MacGill was a writer who deserved no condescension); one wonders if Kiely in a familiarly Irish way found Sheehan's intellectuality off-putting.

But Kiely was not chiefly in the business of arranging curricula or establishing traditions, nor even of providing sustained readings of texts; his was primarily another way entirely of relating to writing: it was through writers more than texts, and writers in their native or adopted haunts. And that way of relating critically was finally indistinguishable from his other creative engines. The critic Kiely expressed himself along a continuum that involved the storyteller in him, the novelist, the short storywriter, the memoirist, the singer and reciter, the broadcaster, the *bon vivant*, the raconteur and the 'itinerant'. This horizontal chain of identity and connection was also vertical. Even more important than tradition (a rather dry category where Kiely was concerned, to be established and then left alone) was his ahistorical idea, akin to E.M. Forster's chosen way of thinking about fiction in *Aspects of the Novel* (1924). Writers form a timeless guild or company and should be read as though they all wrote at the same time, immersed in history as they wrote but read by us out of history, thereby isolating what separates them from historians or sociologists while leaving intact the place out of which they wrote.[19] He relished his own membership of this ancient guild as surely as does Seamus Heaney, whose poetry Kiely wrote appreciatively about some years before the professors.[20]

When Kiely 'placed' a writer, he did so quite literally, recreating the part of the island out of which the literature sprang. Kiely defined a realistic novelist as one 'who quietly watches his people in their environment' (*MIF*, p.35) but Kiely himself in his fiction always watched his people in their environment, quietly in the case of the short stories, noisily in the case of the novels, and to that extent he was a realistic fiction writer even when his writing could suggest a kind of magic realism: the magic lay in the reality of Ireland, not in fictional style or perception. When to 'Ned McKeown's Two Doors' he gave the subtitle 'An Approach to the Novel in Ireland', Kiely was taking the topographical metaphor fairly literally. Just as paths towards a destination can be various, so are literary judgements. In 'The Great Gazebo', he thought that the decision as to whether Somerville and Ross's novels *The Real Charlotte* and *The Big House of Inver* were greater or lesser than the Irish R.M. 'galloping reminiscences' was an arguable one 'and contingent on your mood and humour' (*AR*, p.33). This is hardly the basis for sound judgement but it was part of Kiely's sense of the contingencies of artistic appetite and not a thousand miles from the high modernist James Joyce's hospitably eclectic and unjudging penchant for parlour songs, operetta arias and pub humour.

In his musical itinerary, *And as I Rode by Granard Moat*, Kiely relished the artistic miscellany resulting from the paramount criterion of places and their associations: 'it pleases me and may have pleased them that Oscar Wilde should stand side by side with Felix Kearney, the ballad-maker from Clanabogan Planting'.[21] In the speaking of poems, he then says, 'there is a higher democracy' but for him this is clearly true for the reading of poems, and literature, and the novelist too is a kind of reader, not only of literature but of life, and Kiely like Joyce and Chaucer indulges this democracy guiltlessly. If you want your own anthology, he cautions the reader who might object to his approach and his selections (which really means his associations), make it yourself. He tells us we should never recite by category, author or theme. It is place, memory and association that are the tutelary deities of song and verse, and his criticism too aspires less to objective invidious judgement than to anthology, the very etymology of which (a flower-gathering) implies place.

Ideally for Kiely, the reading of an author whom you come to cherish and identify with inspires you to visit the author's native haunts. Criticism itself, then, is a kind of itinerary. Many of the essays collected in *A Raid into Dark Corners* involve criticism conducted *in situ*, as though Kiely were a documentary film-maker in the field; the mode of operation is most evident in his essay 'Land without Stars: Aodhagán O'Rahilly' which opens deftly: 'In autumn the reds and browns of the mountains colour the cooling air' (*AR*, p.8). (As though to fasten the connections between criticism and fiction, Kiely borrows the title for his first novel, *Land without Stars*.) Even when the writer in question is dead, the pilgrim-critic has guides, such as the tall man who had been gamekeeper to Lord Castletown and who had gone duck-hunting with Douglas Hyde around a lough commemorated by John Keegan, the Laois poet (a bonus association).[22] Often, itinerant criticism corroborates the work under consideration:

Kiely, when discussing Heaney's 'A Lough Neagh Sequence', quotes one of Heaney's sources for folklore of the eel and remembers his own successful childhood experiment by which the hair of a horse's tail turned into an elver (later discovered to be the product of a practical joke). Heaney's bull in 'The Outlaw' is corroborated by Kiely's own memory of bulls at the Mitchelstown Creamery. Kiely as critic is a kind of witness, occupying a sympathetic space halfway between detached observer and active, if belated, participant. Such a posture presupposed the stability and perseverance of the Irish countryside, a posture that must have become increasingly difficult to adopt as rural Ireland changed so much in his lifetime.

But memory has longevity.[23] The number of writers Kiely met or knew, as both stimulus to the criticism and corroboration of the writing, is impressive and violated the critical ethos that prevailed between New Criticism and post-Structuralism when authors were demoted in the critical transaction.[24] (I never asked for his reaction to the Death of the Author announced by Roland Barthes in 1967.) His first meetings with, or renewals of friendship with, Kate O'Brien, Seamus Heaney, Sean O'Faolain, John Montague, Francis MacManus, W.F. Marshall, Frank O'Connor and Thomas Flanagan enliven his criticism of their work, and in his world restore these writers to the timeless guild. If he didn't meet Yeats, he met (and chaffed) Mrs Yeats.[25] If he didn't meet Patrick MacGill, his mother did ('The Whores on the Halfdoors', *AR*, p.136). His account of meeting Alice Milligan is a memorably funny one:

> The door opened and the dear lady appeared in wreaths of smoke. There was a jackdaw in the chimney for whose invasion and occupancy she courteously apologized. We sat in the musty drawingroom and listened to her telling us how she had once spent a wonderful day with Miss Gonne and Mr Bulfin (Mr Yeats couldn't make the trip), studying druidic remains in Glencolumcille. The smoke thickened until she could be seen only fitfully, and we were set free to imagine visions of the woman Homer sung of, or of that statuesque thought from Propertius, going with the walk of a queen along that most wonderful of western glens. ('The Whores on the Halfdoors', *AR*, p.137)

Personal acquaintance has the simultaneous effect of making the writers larger than life and no larger than ourselves. On occasion the enlarging can become a dubious aggrandizing and the epithet 'great' is perhaps bandied about: if Joseph Campbell is a 'great poet' and Francis Stuart a 'great novelist', should Heaney be especially flattered to be called a 'great poet'? But these accolades are bestowed in *And as I Rode by Granard Moat* in which we can cut Kiely some critical slack, and the adjective might be used as we use it carelessly in Ireland: 'he's a great writer altogether', the verbal equivalent of a clap on the absent back.

If Kiely tracks his writers back to place, then place conjures up writers before our eyes. *And as I Rode by Granard Moat* is a circuit of Ireland, visits to places that are commemorated in song or verse, or that were the haunts of singers, composers or poets. It is an enlarged and life-affirming and secular version of the Catholic stations. Before he leaves Ulster where he begins, he has managed by association to quote and discuss W.F. Marshall, Joseph Campbell, Seamus Heaney, John Montague, M.J. MacManus, Padraic Colum, James Clarence Mangan, Thomas McGreevy, William Drennan, Patrick Kavanagh, W.R. Rodgers, Maurice Craig and Louis MacNeice. It is impossible for the reader to distinguish an itinerary in virtual time from memories of visits to places and thereby memories of writers and their work, and it would be idle for the reader to try to do so. Kiely was engaged, as novelist, short story writer, memoirist and critic, in revisiting where he had been. He calls his journeys recounted in *All the Way to Bantry Bay* 'revisits' and *Granard Moat* itself revisits, or recycles, material from the earlier itinerary as well as from essays.

By analogy, *A Raid into Dark Corners* consists of essays many of which Kiely has revisited before sending to the publisher, and these revisitations, which sometimes involve changes of opinion or heart, are occasionally difficult to keep track of. 'The Whores on the Half-doors: An Image of the Irish Writer', an entertaining and illuminating piece of literary history, is a veritable critical palimpsest. We are told in the Acknowledgements that the essay was published in *Kilkenny Magazine* in 1966, and one assumes it was written then and from the perspective of that year, yet it opens with an anecdote of an incident that took place in 1975 before in its second paragraph shifting its scene of critical action to around 1945. Only at the end of the essay do we realize that the opinions of 1945, 1966 and 1975 are framed by a critical narrative dated 1990, when presumably the book of essays, published by Cork University Press in 1999 to mark Kiely's 80th birthday, had not yet been conceived, leaving us with a bibliographical puzzle. Furthermore, Owen Dudley Edwards has stated that Kiely's essay was written at Edwards's request for inclusion in *Conor Cruise O'Brien Introduces Ireland*, edited by Edwards and published in 1969 (not, therefore, 1966). Presumably we again are in the midst of versions and revisitations.[26]

Not only did Kiely reread himself, but unlike most academic critics, he reread his authors at intervals, incited as he was by affection and a deep personal pride in authorship. He rereads Kickham for 'Charles Kickham and the Living Mountain' (*AR*, p.115), though here, as elsewhere, the essay may have been stimulated into existence by the rereading. He paused in his rereading, he tells us, to quiz his literary friends on their attitude to Kickham and by this device rehearses the case against Kickham (a propagandist, he is told) before resuming his rereading and vindicating Kickham as a novelist who brought his Ireland imperishably to life. He rereads Montague for 'John Montague: Dancer in a Rough Field' (*AR*, p.119); in 'Sean O'Faoláin: A Tiller of Ancient Soil' he confesses to a fourth reading of *Bird Alone* 'some years ago' (*AR*, p.126); a rereading of Corkery for 'Chronicle by Rushlight: Daniel Corkery's Quiet Desperation' causes him to reread Thoreau (*AR*, p.156). He believes that the best tribute one can pay to a 'great writer' on his 80th birthday is to reread him, and he does so to honour Liam O'Flaherty (*AR*, p.192), though the essay he writes as a result was first published in 1949 whilst O'Flaherty's 80th birthday fell in 1976. It is another Kiely revisitation as well as rereading.

Kiely's preoccupation is, in every genre he practised, with localities – of setting, of character, of scene of action, of dialogue, of plot – just as his patriotism is not nationalism but local pride (and affection) multiplied and extended to every shore of the island. His base unit of place that offers meaning, comfort and cause for celebration and commemoration is the country neighbourhood and unlike the more fundamentally religious Kavanagh, he does not have recourse to the parish, for that of course would be in the end sectarian. And neighbourhood is in practice inseparable from companionship: Kiely tramped and drove throughout Ireland but rarely alone (his inability to drive made companionship a practical benefit). His companions, like his writers (who were in the deepest sense also his companions), were chosen by neighbourhood. The writer came close to being the *genius loci* and critical survey was for him a kind of platonic Irish atlas. His most cherished companions when he walked abroad were the literary – scholars or creative writers who were natives or expatriates and who by courteous mutual agreement become *his* guides; he seemed to me the least rivalrous of writers.[27] In *Bantry Bay* he is accompanied on his revisits in turn by Heaney the poet, Flanagan the critic and novelist, and Kevin Sullivan the Irish-American academic. Should his writers and erstwhile companions be dead, his companions are ghosts who swell the living itinerants, as Kavanagh does in *Bantry Bay*.

His literary criticism, too, is full of companionship and place, and memories of those things. It may not satisfy the requirements of criticism today, being more essayistic and personal than scholarly and detached, for the close encounters he had with literature were not textually particular but wholesale – autobiographical and biographical, and ultimately experiential, even existential. It recalled literature to the human and humane, gave it space and body (which we gesture towards in our term 'body of work') and a personal existence, and by rendering it vulnerable to the past, like writers and readers alike, increased our obligation in both capacities to remember and celebrate and to occupy the world energetically in order to do so.

NOTES

1. Benedict Kiely, *Modern Irish Fiction – A Critique* (Dublin: Golden Eagle Books, 1950), p.160. I occasionally abbreviate this book to *MIF.*
2. Benedict Kiely, 'The Whores on the Halfdoors: An Image of the Irish Writer', *Kilkenny Magazine* (Spring/Summer 1966), reprinted with additions in *A Raid into Dark Corners and Other Essays* (Cork: Cork University Press, 1999), p.140. I occasionally abbreviate this volume to *AR*.
3. This is not quite correct. By the early 1950s Conor Cruise O'Brien had begun his long intellectual career in the public eye (though his first book was published in 1953 under a pseudonym); Hubert Butler began his early cultural interventions in the late 1940s, but out of the public eye; both of these figures later came closer to the received notion of the public intellectual.
4. The bird's-eye view, which allowed Kiely to swallow Irish geography and history whole, culminated literally in *The Aerofilms Book of Ireland from the Air* (1985) in which Kiely supplied his inimitable extended captions to the splendid aerial photographs that offer a different perspective on island time and place.
5. Colum lived on until 1972, though as Kiely reminded us in 1950, he had left for the United States in 1914. I recall a conversation (perhaps more an audience) with Liam O'Flaherty in McDaid's pub in Dublin, perhaps in the mid-1970s, when the Ulster violence was in terrible spate. When O'Flaherty proclaimed that he thought that the men of Ireland (republicans, he meant) had lost their manhood (perhaps the IRA was then in one of their temporary doldrums) and that the Orangemen were more virile, I thought I detected an End-of-History animosity towards a post-Independence generation from someone who had with perverse pride lived through the turbulent politics and literature of the 1912–22 period.
6. I discuss their ideas in John Wilson Foster, 'The Irish Renaissance, 1890–1940: Prose in English', in Margaret Kelleher and Philip O'Leary (eds), *The Cambridge History of Irish Literature* (Cambridge: Cambridge University Press, 2006), Vol.II, pp.157–9.
7. I briefly track the opinion in John Wilson Foster, *Irish Novels 1890–1940: New Bearings in Culture and Fiction* (Oxford: Oxford University Press, 2008), pp.6–7, 450–1.
8. The fine *Kenyon Review* essay, 'Frank O'Connor and the Long Road to Ummera', is reprinted in *A Raid into Dark Corners* where it is unlisted in the Acknowledgements and therefore unattributed to that journal.
9. It would be illuminating to know to what extent the proximity of a huge and, by comparison, uncensoring English-speaking country next door (of which Kiely would have been a citizen had he been born not in 1919 but 1922) took the pressure off the Irish censors. The Free State was an inward-looking society attempting to distinguish itself from godless, at best Protestant, and lately oppressing England (while England for its part withdrew its eyes as well as its troops from southern Ireland), with the result that the censorship of ideas in Ireland did not reach the ears or provoke the interest of the English. Writers, however, still had England as a market and critical hinterland so that the banning of their work in the Free State was not the kiss of death.

10. It is unfortunate that this volume did not have a professional editor so that the essays could have been fully cited. This essay was first published in 1983 in *Ireland and the Arts: A Special Issue of* Literary Review, ed. Tim Pat Coogan (London: Quartet).
11. In *Irish Novels 1890–1940*, I try to show the busyness and prolificness of Irish fiction in the 1890–1922 period, which – once we admit as evidence popular novels by Irish writers, male or female, set inside Ireland or outside – the 1922–48 period could hardly match, even if we apply the same inclusive criteria to the later years.
12. Benedict Kiely, *Poor Scholar: A Study of the Works and Days of William Carleton (1794–1869)* (London: Sheed and Ward, 1947), p.5. (I abbreviate this volume to *PS*.)
13. Kiely referred to several of O'Flaherty's books as 'itineraries' (Benedict Kiely, *A Raid into Dark Corners*, p.195) and I have adopted this useful genre coinage, from which I inflect 'itinerant', the writer of such works.
14. Kiely, *Modern Irish Fiction*, pp.91, 99. Flann O'Brien strikes me as a different kind of novelist for whom invention plays a more vital role than memory.
15. Benedict Kiely, *Nothing Happens in Carmincross* (London: Gollancz, 1985), p.39. Recognizable figures from life abound in Kiely's fiction. As it happens, a character in *Carmincross* bears a close resemblance to me: he is a red-bearded scholarly Belfastman teaching in Canada and bearing the name of Foster Wilson. The scene in which he is recalled (pp.181–3) is, as it were, an extended quotation of an afternoon Kiely and I spent in Carrickfergus, Co. Antrim while the Troubles were at their hottest. The archaeologist who accompanies 'the third man' (a major character in the novel) and Foster Wilson was in real life the late Tom Delaney, then engaged in archaeological survey work in the town. Our visit to a loyalist pub grew tense and as was usual in such sectarian circumstances, I lost confidence even in Kiely's ability to charm the bigoted and aggressive. Whether I was in fact guilty of the factual error attributed to 'me' (that someone had been abducted from the pub and murdered) I cannot now recall, though the third man later concludes: 'Not that it makes a damned bit of difference' (p.184). I think it likely that the novel is fashioned from a series of such remembered experiences (I recognize one or two set in Oregon where I first met Kiely).
16. Both near and far. I have yet to open the pages of some Irish writers Kiely mentions in *Modern Irish Fiction*: Kenneth Reddin, J.H. Pollock, Alan Downey, Dorothy M. Large and Christine Longford, for example.
17. In *All the Way to Bantry Bay – And Other Irish Journeys* (1978), however, he recalled the outrageous episode at Burntollet in 1969 when a civil rights march was ambushed by loyalists. Always for Kiely, at least after 1969, violence, by definition divisive, annulled a political opinion.
18. Timing was crucial. In 1950 it was possible for a critical surveyor to ignore the cosmopolitan author of *Murphy* (1938) and not seem hopelessly out of touch (Beckett is listed as an absentee – incongruously to us – alongside Francis Hackett, Shane Leslie, Vivian Connell and Jim Phelan), whereas eight years later to have ignored Beckett's *Molloy* (French 1950, English 1955), *Malone Dies* (1951, 1956), *Watt* (1953) and *The Unnamable* (1953, 1958) would have been fatal to the enterprise.
19. Forster asked his readers to imagine the novelists he would talk about sitting down and writing in the British Museum Reading Room at the same time.
20. Kiely, 'A Raid into Dark Corners: The Poems of Seamus Heaney', reprinted in *AR*. (In the Acknowledgements to *AR*, this essay is misdated as 1978. It actually appeared in *The Hollins Critic* in October 1970; my offprint is signed by the author who was an early admirer of the young Heaney. However, the article was absorbed into *All the Way to Bantry Bay*, an itinerary that was published in 1978 and that may be the source of the misdating.) It was no doubt the congeniality for Kiely of Heaney's native Ulster grounds that first drew Kiely to the young poet's work. Characteristically, the essay opens with Kiely's establishment of Heaney's 'native country' which is 'an old twisted land' full of thrawn men.
21. Benedict Kiely, *And as I Rode by Granard Moat* (Dublin: Lilliput Press, 1996), p.48.
22. 'The Great Gazebo', *A Raid into Dark Corners*, p.42. Benedict Kiely was my own guide around Carleton country in 1970, after I returned to Northern Ireland from Oregon with my PhD; I had written a dissertation on Kiely, Brian Moore and Michael McLaverty, having been converted by Kiely in Oregon from the study of aesthetics to the study of Irish literature. Carleton became the 'father figure' in Ulster fiction in the book I was then beginning, *Forces and Themes in Ulster Fiction* (1974), a book encouraged by my critical mentor, Kiely.

23. Kiely's legendary memory was maintained both by narrative repetition and by the tropes of oral narrative into which his experience appeared to be absorbed. It was not to be described as 'photographic' one way or the other. Certainly it was not dependent on photographs. Once when I asked him why he never sported a camera, he responded instantly (perhaps because it was an oral formula of his), 'Didn't God give me two good eyes and a retentive memory?'
24. The personal note has re-entered criticism. In 1991 I prefaced my collection of critical essays, *Colonial Consequences: Essays in Irish Literature and Culture* with what was then an unusual personal account of the originating circumstances of the essays, though I was perhaps unconsciously influenced by both Kiely and Heaney. This kind of personal intervention in Irish criticism is no longer uncommon. (My personal account included my memory of meeting Benedict Kiely in Oregon in 1965.)
25. Kiely, 'Green Island, Red South', *A Raid into Dark Corners*, p.260.
26. Owen Dudley Edwards, 'In Praise of Benedict Kiely', in *'The Waves Behind Us'*: Programme of the 6th Annual Benedict Kiely Literary Weekend (Omagh, Co. Tyrone: Strule Arts Centre, 2007), p.12. This programme includes tributes to Kiely, including my own 'Memories of Benedict Kiely'.
27. I remember when in Dublin he heard resentment expressed at the material success of the playwright Hugh Leonard (I seem to recall that an expensive car was mentioned), Kiely defended his fellow-writer and colourfully (and here unrepeatably) speculated aloud as to what *he* would do were he lucky enough to come into Leonard's money. Likewise, when Flanagan became a newly minted novelist and newly minted millionaire through the success of *The Year of the French*, Kiely delighted in the success of his old friend: a new member of the guild had prospered.

9

THE AUTOCARTOGRAPHY OF TIM ROBINSON

My Time in Space (2001) has deepened the problem of assessing Tim Robinson's likely space in time, his place in contemporary writing. This will not faze him. Classification itself is a puzzle. He has a fine disregard for prose genre, and the writing in this book, like that in its successor, *Tales and Imaginings* (2002) that has followed hard on its heels, has a conceptual, even mildly post-modernist feel to it.[1] I suspect Robinson would bristle at my second adjective, if only because his writing originates not in a fashionable penchant but in the variety of problems with which he has concerned himself so intently. And after we puzzle over which shelf to put him on, then with which department, as it were, should he be affiliated? The prodigious detail and originality of his celebrated two-part Aran Islands cartography (*Stones of Aran*, 1986, 1995) would invite his welcome as an Irish writer (and he is as conscious as Othello that he has rendered the state some service), but he reminds us in this book than on tense occasions during environmental warfare he has been dismissed as an Englishman. This while his own aggressively maverick posture seems to repudiate pre-emptively facile classifications by those he calls 'literary sceneshifters'.

And indeed, one should in the acts of reading and appreciating move out from, and through, the text rather than importing preconceptions and imposing discriminations, as Robinson works out from the essential problem or fascination (say a theorem yet to be proven) along its network of implications. But then, *My Time in Space* is a book at whose own heart is the concept of *distinction* on which the controversial and advanced calculus of George Spencer Brown (of whom more anon) is based but which really sustains these transcripts of Robinson's cognitive activities in all his chosen fields. Robinson at times suggests the predatory mental alertness of a chess master, tirelessly contemplating the possibilities of the future, in this case 'the endless interpretability of space', the 'totality of all possible forms'. Like the chess master, he chooses to put himself in the way of those problems. His obligation to solve problems is slighter than his voluntary desire to find such problems, in a kind of stern and intense play. He is, like a logician, always aware of classes and the problem arising should a class be a member of itself. His writing implicitly invites (or challenges) us to accompany him in his penetration of the thickets of experience and theory, making distinctions all along the way, though I sense that whether we do or not is of little concern to him, there being in his make-up a mildly conceited solitariness of the type I imagine chess masters to embody. His is an admirable, studied and not always congenial independence of mind. There is enough camaraderie in him to leave us the rifle and the water-canteen when we can't keep up and he must go on alone (as in the old westerns), but go on he will.

And he has chosen so widely among his fields that his peculiar versatility is also a challenge to our reception of his work. Of course, genuine essayists are by definition versatile wielders of the pen, but this historically has been, with a few exceptions, because they have thought and written below the level of professional or technical capacity: they are the writer befitting the informed general reader. Like those few exceptions he joins (Oliver Sacks and Lewis Thomas are two), Robinson has his own several expertises. He is an accomplished botanist (one might even say naturalist), cartographer and (though he might dispute this – certainly Spencer Brown did, according to the author, despite Robinson's Cambridge degree in the subject) mathematician. I have omitted *artist* simply because Robinson, while recounting in detail his early career as a conceptual artist in London, declines to illustrate his exhaustive art theories and rationales for certain of his works, leaving us sceptical in the absence of demonstration that the weightiness of the theory resulted in actual and successful artworks. But lively art theorist he certainly has been, though I myself find the theory fairly uncongenial. His topics in *My Time in Space* also include ballistics, sacredness in landscape, cathedrals, geometry, mathematical proofs and theorems, and the environment and environmentalism; these frequently invade each other's fields and all are seduced by Robinson into expanding, ever grander speculation (small solar systems of ideas swirling into galaxies); fittingly, the last word in this remarkable book is 'time'.

Yet despite his Cambridge degree, Robinson has something of the autodidact and the driven amateur in him, the faintest hint of the crank. Also despite Cambridge, I have a hunch he would steer clear of university gatherings and academic conferences, in the style of those who are not anyway party to them. Like, say, J.W. Dunne (whose name crops up in the book) he gives the impression of combining ingeniousness with the eccentricity of someone who has spent a little too much time in the loneliness of speculation. (Other more respectable affines are Bachelard, Sebald and Borges.) Occasionally his assertions have a dubious, provocative and somewhat forced certainty: 'Cities were invented to protect us from the terrors and temptations of horizons' (*MT*, p.14); 'we scan [horizons] avidly as if desperate to see as far as possible or searching for escape through the threadlike gap between the impenetrable globe and the indefinite depths of the sky' (*MT*, p.11); 'Battle is the shift and crisscross of death-lines in the hand of space' (*MT*, p.23). The vocabulary, too, has a stiff bravado to it: there are the unusual inflections and forms (*perfused*, *discarnate*, *distrait*, *resile*, *ostention*, *indue*, *madding*, *tremendum*, *extremal*), the technical terms (*plasmodium*, *loxodrome*, *chryselephantine*, *annules*, *orthogonal*, *multimen*, *aumbry*) and the neologisms (*idempose*, *echosphere*, *anthropoblemes*, *echopoetry*): a verbal and exhilarating bristle.

I was surprised to read that Robinson is 67, for his writing, despite its thoroughness, is youthful in its range and intensity of interest, but then a certain driven didacticism (or do I simply mean extraordinary versatility that can't be departmentalized in the academic or marketplace sense? 'Useful' is how he describes the bulk of his writing) is forever youthful in its passion and is outside the ripening trajectory of the fully professional career or *œuvre*. He does not quite have the professional credentials separate from the essays which Thomas and Sacks have, and there is a buttonholing, Ancient Mariner insistence with him that sometimes leaves one suspecting he is protesting too much. But one is missing nothing better by listening to him. As a thinker he moves forward with persistent close attention, slowing us as readers to his selected pace (there is an analogy to be drawn between his prose style and the detailing of his cartography) but there is room for prospecting too, and he often finds things to say memorably. Of birdsong in spring dawns, for example: 'What sounds like mere recreation is indeed recreation: the reinvention or reimposition for another day of a political geography that had lapsed overnight' (*MT*, p.6). 'The boys slid down the palmtrees like drops of rain running down a wire.' Of Spencer Brown's masterwork: 'He has been denied outlet for his papers other than as appendices to successive editions of *Laws of Form* – a shame, this, because it is a classic text, and in its current form suffers as a Palladian villa would from disproportionate extensions and ad hoc lean-to sheds' (*MT*, p.160). Of Brown's unmet brother: 'The impression I came away with of this brother was slightly mysterious; he seemed to combine an uncanny degree of intelligence with a certain mythical remoteness from the actual, like Holmes's Mycroft' (*MT*, p.148).

The wanderings (and brashnesses) of mind autodidacts and ancient mariners often display (and Robinson's is mostly an *assumption* of these roles, it seems to me, or a style that began as revolt) has its analogue in the literal space, the real places, in which Robinson has spent time, including Yorkshire, Norway, Vienna, Aran Islands, London, Cambridge, Malaya, Italy, the United States, Provence, and latterly Galway. But these are the large classes of places: wherever he is, is subjected to his minute observations, equivalent to close readings of texts, and before he mapped the Aran Islands in his imitable way he was stepping London and even before that trying to make art out of London's 'suppressed geography'. His waywardness has been barely contained by what we might call, coining a Robinsonianism, an *autocartography*. And just as maps show not the substance of things but their arbitrary if agreed signs, so his book does not permit us to grasp the author as a personality larger than the sum of his formidable parts. That too means he is elusive.

It is bold to summarize Robinson's variegated world, but it is true that he is simultaneously drawn to abstraction and form, and to their apparent opposite – experience and the incontrovertibilities of matter; to the studious asceticism of pure mathematics and the hands-on, open-air inchings forward of surveying. Basically his vision is structuralist, which the founding binary opposition I am adducing itself illustrates. He likes the theme of Spencer Brown's *Laws of Form* which he quotes: 'The theme of this book is that a universe comes into existence when a space is severed or taken apart' (*MT*, p.147). This is the theme equally of *My Time in Space*.

As for the mathematics, Robinson admits his inability to accompany mathematical geniuses (for example, Spencer Brown) all their way but is prepared to bloody his head against the bars of his limitation, as he puts it. By the same token, his own chapter, 'Constellation and Questionmark', early left me at the margin of the bog, peering fearfully ahead. (I relived the remark those of us deficient in mathematics used to make coming out of school exams; when asked how it went, we replied in mock triumph: 'I was flying up to question 1(b)'.) Pascal's Theorem, Dandelin's Proof, Spencer Brown's Laws of Form, Goldbach's Conjecture (what anchoritic beauty of contemplation these nominations distil!) – Robinson's demonstrations of these will, as the author knows rightly, lose and dismay most readers. I gave a copy of this chapter to a mathematician colleague at the University of British Columbia for his assessment; he never got back to me; perhaps he too was lost in what Robinson calls a thicket, thereby attempting to bend mathematics back upon themselves to rejoin what Francis Bacon called 'the thickets of experience'.

Robinson has crawled through actual dense thickets while surveying, as his diary entries from his first surveys of Connemara show, with the kind of detail that in his story, 'The Festival of Creation', from *Tales and Imaginings*, becomes delirious, as when the narrator, staring into the darkness of jungle, remembers that 'the silence was absolute. Then someone started to tear the jungle apart, slowly, leaf by leaf' (*T&I*, p.31). The detail of sensation, of actuality, is such for Robinson that 'every point is connected to every other point; every event is a starburst of futurity' (*MT*, p.97). In this way, the real is the site of the sacred, as much as the speculative reaches of mathematics; because God is in the details, He is everywhere and nowhere. Or one should say 'Goddess'. Perhaps his sense of a goddess in the western landscape, approached in his chapter 'Firewalking', was sharpened when he met another ex-university, eccentric treader of the west, that mobile reverist, John Moriarty (championed like Robinson by the perceptive Antony Farrell of Lilliput Press who has published them both). Robinson sees Moriarty in his early days combining shamanism with Christology where Robinson cannot quite follow; in his entertaining account of a walk in Kerry with Moriarty ('like being taken for a walk by a mountain'), he recalls Moriarty reverently unshodding himself while Robinson studiously does not, being unwilling to approve of Moriarty's 'reabsorption into the ranks of the pious'. But Moriarty strikes me as being an even intenser version of Robinson himself (where the conjunction of the finite and infinity, the conceptual and the empirical is concerned), so that there is the hint in the acquaintance of like poles if not repelling then preventing undue familiarity.

These two strange figures, Spencer Brown and Moriarty, are not Robinson's secret sharers (a theme Robinson exploits in his piece, 'Secret Meeting', which retraces in Robinsonian fashion ground covered by Joseph Conrad and Edward Thomas though not compellingly, I'd have to say) but they clearly function in part as echoes (he is much taken with echoes, as he explains in his fascinating chapter, 'The Echosphere'), as though he and these solitaries have glanced off each other in their wanderings away from the herd. After all, Spencer Brown's occupational versatility makes even Robinson seem like a sedentary: he has been a Royal Navy radio mechanic, hypnotist, racing driver, poet, soccer correspondent, psychotherapist, British Rail adviser, mathematics lecturer.

I wasn't entirely sure, in fact, that Spencer Brown wasn't a figment of Robinson's imagination and I took the precaution of using Google to inquire further. (One of the websites Robinson gives us turned up blank.) But even the facts of Spencer Brown (b. 1923) look like fiction. This 'maverick mathematician' has been called a charlatan; according to one website, the Sante Fé Institute recommends *Laws of Forms* 'just for laughs'. The 'laborious dottiness' that Robinson attributes to (his own) paintings constructed according to algorithms has been attributed also to Spencer Brown. And some of Robinson's own ratiocinations can seem like tales and imaginings while one weathers the suggestion of spoof and self-parody. Robinson descries a shamanism in Spencer Brown as well as Moriarty, and discovered something of a Spencer Brown cult and a strange 'siblinghood', to borrow from one web entry that Robinson quotes. Robinson's account of his interactions with Spencer Brown is funny and he found the mathematician 'unremittingly self-centred, so that after a few hours my own ego was struggling for oxygen'. It wouldn't be impolite to adduce the like-poles analogy again, surely. Robinson's own polite solipsism meets its match in that of the truculent calculator. *My Time in Space* (one disregards the hinted immodesty in the title beside the semantic pun) uses a great deal of self-quotation so that his prefatory observation, that the essays in the book 'hover, fascinated, about the self-mystery', is well justified. However, the solipsism is paradoxically impersonal, almost logical, a heated argumentativeness.

But if Robinson confuses deliberately the self-mystery with the universal mystery, his approaches to the latter are majestic. 'The Echosphere' is a various, uneven, brilliant piece of work. Inside it is the alarming piece he wrote as introduction to the launch of the book I edited with Helena Chesney in 1998, *Nature in Ireland*, and for which I belatedly thank him. In it the polar oppositions of form-abstraction-mathematics/sensation-detail-matter are projected in Wellsian fashion through future aeons as mind and Nature. In one scenario Nature is eventually absorbed into mind, as through the coming centuries humanity exists without Nature, without reality. 'Our consciousnesses will have been amalgamated, compressed and downloaded onto the galactic internet. Every atomic particle will ultimately be pressed into service for our data-bank, until there is nothing in the universe but information' (*MT*, p.183). He regards this prospect of the material world reduced to hallucination by technological progress as melancholy. In the opposing scenario, Nature derides mind and through some future calamity lives again without it, avenged. (This is the prospect D.H. Lawrence relished: an earth cleansed of the scourge of humanity.)

The two environmental battles Robinson took part in and recounts are contemporary small-scale episodes in these scenarios. The first was the battle to save Roundstone Bog from the ravages that an airport for Clifden and environs would have visited upon the region. This he helped Nature (as it were) win. The second was the battle to prevent the installation of three 150-foot high wind turbines on Inishmaan. This he helped Nature lose. During it, he claimed some personal responsibility (and authority) for the qualities of the islands since he had mapped them so attentively, a benign example perhaps of the author's egotism which was mocked by a local politician who sneeringly quoted Robinson's claim of responsibility. Robinson was not at home during the successful battle; he is not a natural environmentalist, disliking the bureaucracy it necessitates and resenting the notion of a vulnerable Nature environmentalism seems to require and which arouses anxiety when we are in Nature. (Hear, hear.) Characteristically, Robinson must fashion his composure in his own way. The second defeat ought to be the weightier and gloomier event but Robinson manages in a magisterial way to achieve what we might call a higher optimism.

That optimism – a kind of stoicism achieved through the long view, a kind of tragic gaiety of the sort late Yeats admired – we see early in the book when he reinterprets his 1960s attempt to retrieve London's suppressed geography as life-denying, since the city builds, tears down, rebuilds, burgeons, decays 'like the close-packed petals of a rose', a simile that will return in 'The Festival of Creation' in *Tales and Imaginings.* This becomes the visionary poetry of 'The Fineness of Things', the terminal and best essay in *My Time and Space* and which conjoins the two scenarios to essay a daring synthesis. Robinson modifies Pascal's meditation on the abysses between which human life is suspended in order to rescue the human place in the infinities of time and space. Whereas Pascal, he judges memorably, is frightening us into the arms of God by reducing us to utter negligibility, Robinson prefers to work out from 'the fineness of detail with which the world records itself' (one of the twin poles of his lifelong preoccupation). He denies that the planets pursue 'their tremendous courses indifferent to our fates', indifference being a human failing. 'Life, intelligence and love are not aliens marooned in a hostile world of iron determinism' (p.224) but participants in an existence of perpetual interaction and reconstitution. The stuff of existence creates forms endlessly through those distinctions Spencer Brown has calculated. It is as if the astrophysicists' theory of planetary creation, existence and dissolution, and Lyell's theory of the earth's changes through uniformitarian geological laws, and Darwin's organic evolution through an impersonal natural selection (competition, mutation, adaptation or maladaptation) issue nonetheless in designs, but designs that are not frontloaded like

Intelligent Design but are instead outcomes that incorporate, quite literally, ourselves. In the profusion of resulting universes, Robinson purports to discover the axiomatic truth that 'we are not desolate creatures helplessly adrift between two deathly abysses' (p.230). It is a truth with a characteristic Robinsonian chill to it, but magnificent for all that.

Tales and Imaginings is a miscellany of fictional expressions of the ideas in the earlier book, though they may pre-date the essays and be more autobiographical than they suggest. 'The Extreme Edge' in *My Time in Space* has its counterpart in 'On the Edge' in *Tales*; the 'fog of mathematics' that can enshroud the reader in *My Time* also settles in 'The Festival of Creation', and the same preoccupation with mapping and cities recurs. The latter story, which opens the volume and which like its successor, 'The River', reminds me of the druggy fantasticalities of Lord Dunsany, restates the master problem of *My Time*: 'between the indiscriminate mystic welter and the loveless systems there must be words for my awareness of the material world and my perfect continuity with it' (*T&I*, p.35). The Preface strikes a Borgesian note, with its reference to the authors as strangers whose work Robinson is publishing but who are not beyond his responsibility, a note that might have been omitted.

The tales and imaginings range from the apocalyptic nightmare of 'Visits to the Black Cliff' through the meta-travel guide of 'Approaching the Glacier' and the brief three-part suite on the Elgin marbles to the 'found' tale of 'Realism with a Human Face'. They are often dark but there is some whimsy and buoyant description, as in the cat belonging to the narrator of 'A Crystallography' that comes 'bounding across the lawn, tail superbly deployed, with a comet's indifference to all prediction or interpretation of its reappearance' (*T&I*, p.157). 'Realism with a Human Face' is one of the few pieces in which human characters convince, Robinson being far more at home amidst Nature and in the absence of people. And Mattie Laffin convinces because he is an oddity with a plastic bucket Robinson met during his travel back from a celebration of a distinguished writer whom I take to have been Hubert Butler. Laffin suffers from Tourette's Syndrome, which seems to have promoted in him a promiscuity of remark and idea. Robinson has him write his itinerary up to now and the semi-literate list might be seen mischievously as a version (minus the creature comforts, that Moriarty for his part seems to eschew) of Spencer Brown's itinerary, and Moriarty's and even Robinson's. Laffin convinces by the sum of his parts of which he is not greater. He is the oddity, the maverick wandered from the herd with whom Robinson feels at home and whom he is himself to some degree. In this Laffin resembles the bagman whom the narrator of 'The Objective Reality of Purgatory' rescues, dresses down and sends packing on his continued way through the purgatory of ordinary life.

'A Crystallography' hazards an explanation of writing, which the alert reader will realize is the verbal version of the cosmology of *My Time in Space*, with its reference to 'the spontaneous crystallization of meaning out of the limitless interplay of words themselves' and the 'tremendous datum of language' (*T&I*, p.159), but these convince more as formulae than as inescapable expressions of literary sensibility. There are good things in *Tales and Imaginings* but the volume reads like a spin-off (earlier or later as the case might be) from the more important and microcosmic profusion of ideas in *My Time in Space*, the title of which, I now realize, contains a melancholy (or more likely, stoic) acknowledgement of the author's mortality as well as an allusion to a lifelong interest and even vocation in cartography, geophysics and natural history and, of course, that signal that everything he writes is an 'I-piece', as he terms the pieces of the second volume. In any event, Robinson has now accumulated an *œuvre* of real weight and distinction and is a compelling and somewhat unsettling presence whom it seems mainstream critics have tried to ignore or underestimate out of discomfort but to their, and our, great detriment and loss.

NOTE

1. *My Time in Space* (Dublin: Lilliput Press, 2001), referenced here as *MT*; *Tales and Imaginings* (Dublin: Lilliput Press, 2002), referenced here as *T&I*.

II

WRITING AND CULTURE

10

STRANGFORD LOUGH AND ITS WRITERS

WATERS

I write this where the Ards peninsula and the mainland from which it has been prised apart begin their south-easterly turn to form the narrow channel that ends when the peninsula concedes to the Irish Sea at Ballyquinton and the County Down coastline strays south-eastwardly towards St John's Point.

Here, between Portaferry and the mainland village of Strangford half a mile away, the incoming tide is finishing with quiet determination its passage through the Narrows and has sidelined the waters loitering uncertainly near the shore. The woods wrapping Strangford are in their late spring fullness and take only mild offence at the breeze, though the trees recoil permanently from the sea so that their green tilted convexities, reflected today in the slower waters that escort the main current, are a constant invitation to the eye. Dapper in their summer wear, three black guillemots are skirmishing – or courting – on these waters and occasionally alighting on the sills or lintels of the ready-made *faux* cliff of the townhouse complex where I am. Mid-channel, arctic and common terns with chicks to feed are hunting with that peremptory, change-of-mind flight they have on these occasions, reversing on a sixpence and diving to secure an almost overlooked smelt. Swallows and house martins are swooping low above the nearby bladderwrack for insects, and a grey heron is at his sentry post. The sun is shining in a nearly cloudless sky. Right now, earth must have very little to show more fair.

However, what you see on Strangford Lough changes constantly – the water, weather and wildlife. Through autumn and winter the Strangford woods are alive at dusk with thousands of mustering rooks and jackdaws, a twilight shindig before they call it a day. Often they are silhouetted eerily against a lurid sunset; at dawn they are on this side of the Narrows and sitting side by side like omens on the townhouse roofs in a scene from *The Birds*. The terns, martins and swallows are gone. The wind might be raging and the Lough at high tide tossing seaweed angrily on to the strands and even into front gardens, a gale blowing auks into town for the disbelieving cats. In the course of a single day one might have sun, cloud, wind, rain, squall, sun again and evening calm. Things change most restlessly along the Narrows where the open sea shrinks into sea lough by virtue of 350 million cubic feet of water (by one reckoning) or 400 million tons of water (by another reckoning) that squeezes in and out each tide at a speed of up to 11 mph and in doing so causing the water in consternation to create eddies, cross-currents and whirlpools, the most notorious of the pools being the Routen Wheel. The Vikings called this dangerous passage 'strang fjord' ('violent inlet' is one translation) and with good reason: it is a formidable gateway and the water that passes through it has such force that at long last someone has decided to try harnessing it by means of underwater turbines that will produce enough electricity (they say) for the peninsula.

Yet the Lough itself seems enduring enough, lying on or shouldering Silurian rocks (slates, shale, greywacke with all their cold greys and bluish greys) and in the north Triassic sandstone, warmly red. The erodable sandstone is defiant at the promontory of Scrabo hill at the northern end of the Lough. The hill and the tower on top of it are from many places on the Lough an orientation for the sailor or fisherman and a focus for the eye. It has been suggested by archaeologists that Scrabo could have been a focal point for human activity as early as the Neolithic period yet we can forgive the tower for being only 150 years old (built in 1857 as a memorial to the third Marquess of Londonderry, son of the famous Castlereagh), so sturdy and reassuring is it. Scrabo tower oversees – sternly, one imagines – what happens on the Lough.

And often enough the Lough behaves itself, a virtue honoured in its original Irish name, Loch Cuan (anglicized as Lough Coyne) – the lough of the harbours – a name with the implication of quiet haven. Up and down the Lough can be seen those glacially formed curved hillocks called 'drumlins' and which when partly submerged form some of the Lough's many islands, islets and 'pladdies' or low banks generally covered at high water. In their famous 'basket-of-eggs' effect these drumlins are curiously restful to the eye whether they are intact and hemispherical or eroded by wave and wind to form blank foreheads or headlands, often farmed to their brink.

The geologist is of the opinion that the Lough was formed as a depression in the bedrocks (and calls it the Strangford Valley), and that the Narrows was formed by faults, perhaps helped by later erosion. The old Irish accounted for the Lough's origin differently. In one account it was the consequence of the murder of Manannán Mac Lir's son; the Irish sea-god in his rage released a burst of water that became Strangford Lough, Waterford harbour and Dundrum bay.

The ancient annalists believed instead it was an inundation of the lands of Brena in 1654 BC, one of seven lake creations in the time of Parthalon. In any event, the result overall is impressive, the Lough being 30 kilometres in length and 150 square kilometres in area: one of the largest saltwater inlets in the British Isles.

The result is also gratifying, for Strangford Lough and its shores are lessons in the picturesque, a pleasant combination of the swelling curvatures of fertility, the reactive angular shapes of inclemency, and a generous sprinkling of medieval and early modern ruins: all too pretty to be sublime but because of upstart winds and waves, not to be condescended to either. The Lough is a gift to the water-colourist interested in changeable and often remarkable skies, shapely shore-lines and lakeshore vegetation, and the visual effects of water. Yet along the 240 kilometres of shoreline (a third of Northern Ireland's entire coastline) there are a myriad colours and degrees of lightness and weight, and oil-painters have been drawn to the occasional salt-marshy inlets, small, brackish landscapes, boglike and with odd, succulent-like plants.

The biologist has already established the extraordinary diversity of the Lough. Two thousand marine species inhabit or depend upon the lough. The biodiversity on and under the water, on the shore, in the air, has been recognized by several national and international bodies. Species and subspecies unusual in numbers or unique in occurrence (whether in Northern Ireland or in Ireland as a whole) testify to the huge variety of its habitats in such modest compass and the intricacies of the interrelationships among the plants and animals. Stay for a year and you appreciate the cycles of departure and arrival among the birds, and of decay and growth among the plants, though only the biologist can fully explain the Lough-wide web that runs between wind and tide, phytoplankton and zooplankton, and the distribution, population, feeding habitats, movement and behaviour of the larger life that depends upon the Lough.

Some of that larger life is striking: seals, porpoises, occasional whales, and otters in the Lough itself, Irish hares loping down to the water across rocky beaches (even swimming), badgers, rabbits and foxes seeking their livelihood within sound of its waves. The Lough and its immediate hinterland boast three-quarters of the birds on the Northern Ireland list. Ten thousand golden plover and 10,000 knot winter here, courtesy of the 14 square kilometres of mudflats exposed at the northern end of the Lough at lowest tide. Castle Espie on the north-west corner of the Lough and the neighbourhood of the flood-gates on the outskirts of Newtownards are locally renowned expanses of bird-crowded mud. These sociable species mount spectacular displays of flight, catching the light with their plumage and improvising shapes with a wondrous aerial geometry. Nearly a third of the terns breeding in Ireland do so on Strangford Lough. Common, arctic and sandwich terns are to the eye like fairy presences, but they utter hysterical cries as if at the end of their tether. They are also tough and I have recorded sandwich terns throughout September and October and in November, December, January, February and March when they should be in Africa and when there can be rough weather indeed and they spend much of the day hunkering on the shore, beaks pointing into the wind.

But the iconic bird of the Lough is the brent goose. Strangford hosts two-thirds of the wintering population of these geese in western Europe, something like 12,000 of which start arriving from afar in September. On arrival they feed voraciously on the eel-grass at the head of the Lough, then as autumn progresses they graze their way south in dispersing groups, feeding on alternative fare and many of them peeling off and heading south to Dublin bay to see out the balance of the winter. Most of the pale-bellied brent geese that winter on Strangford Lough breed on Bathurst Island in arctic Canada, dividing their year between two continents and countries. Since I divide my own year between Canada and Ireland, I feel a fond affinity with these voyageurs of the north.

Strangford's biological diversity in a given year is nearly matched by the human diversity through history. In earlier years the chief interest of the Ards peninsula to the tourist was archaeological; later, antiquarian interest was rivalled by the attractions that awaited the amateur bird-watcher and botanist. There was also legendary shooting for the wildfowler (ducks, geese, curlew, snipe and wild pigeon galore – a flock of 10,000 wood pigeon was once witnessed) and only recently has this become a shrunken, if still active, sport. Certainly the archaeology is rich, as a major survey in the 1990s reaffirmed. The web of history woven around and on the Lough is almost as intricate as that of the natural world. The loughsiders have been figures in the familiar human pattern of settlement, invasion, confiscation, dynastic conflict, resurgence and supersession.

But Strang fjord has also been Loch Cuan. St Patrick arrived in the vicinity in the fifth century and made his first convert who built a church on Nendrum Island, changing his name from Caolan to Mahee so that in time the island became Mahee Island. One imagines that the repose the Lough often enjoys attracted the Christians who established holy sites whose ruins lie mutely around today. One of the three Cistercian abbeys built in the twelfth and thirteenth centuries, Grey Abbey's remains are substantial today at the village of that name. The monks operated a lively foreshore fishery, using rings of boulders as fishtraps, their vestiges still visible today.

In the tenth century, before the abbeys were built, there was a vigorous Viking presence, but the modern world began for the Lough in 1177 when John de Courcy led the Anglo-Norman invasion of the lands around Cuan and inaugurated the centuries of domination by great baronial families, especially the Savage family whose castle appears on a map of *c.*1568 as 'Savage castel' (now Portaferry castle) and which tower house stands as a significant ruin today. The map also shows Audley's castle, a fifteenth-century tower house across the Narrows built by the Audley family, and even in its present ruinous state, like Portaferry castle, it bristles with vigilance, its posture both defensive and assertive. Nearby are the sturdy remains of Strangford castle, a late sixteenth-century erection.

The views from these towers were, and were meant to be, commanding in the most literal sense. Kilclief castle, the earliest dateable tower house, guarded the entrance of the Narrows on the mainland side, and farther up the Lough there were Ringhaddy castle and Sketrick castle, a sixteenth-century construction. There are also the remains of Walshestown and Quoile tower houses. Killyleagh castle dates from the twelfth century. Originally a Norman defence against the Vikings, it was rebuilt in the seventeenth century. In the 1850s it was turreted, provoking Harold Nicolson to describe it as 'pricking castellated ears above the smoke of its own village and towering like some chateau of the Loire above the tides of Strangford Lough'.[1] The great scientist Sir Hans Sloane was born in a neighbouring house in 1660 and received his early education in the castle; after his death in London his collections became the nucleus of the British Museum. The castle is still inhabited, the oldest continuously inhabited castle in Ireland.

For centuries, these towers attempted to fasten Strangford in clasps of power, but in time they were abandoned (becoming instead reassuring navigation aids to mariners) and gave way to Big Houses. These houses and their demesnes girdle the Lough, and their builders appear to have been torn between the memory of highly visible tactical placement and the retreat into cultivated reclusion (with occasional charitable sorties), their power no longer military but social and on the whole secure. They are mostly Georgian or later and include Greyabbey, Mount Stewart (seat of the Londonderrys), Portaferry House, Castle Ward (whimsically half Palladian, half Gothic due to a marital dispute during its building) and numerous lesser country houses. The cultivations of the Big Houses can stretch to the shore, and over time – most notably at Mount Stewart – their exotic or unusual plants have taken advantage of, and even helped create, a micro-climate which both augments the wildlife and enhances the local picturesque effects.

Rarely challenged was the local or even national power that issued from the Big Houses. Even in the short-lived but brutal Irish rebellion of 1798, it was a combination of the waters and the Big House that put paid to insurrection around the Lough. An instigator of the rebellion in Ulster was Rev. William Steel Dickson of Portaferry, a radical thinker who ran an academy in the town. He incurred the wrath of the incumbents of Portaferry House and Mount Stewart who closely watched his movements in the months leading up to the rebellion and who inspired his arrest. When the rebellion broke out, the insurgents were to muster on Scrabo hill but they failed to materialize, though the vicinity of Strangford Lough provided most of the County Down rebels when fighting did begin.

At Portaferry, an armed revenue cutter anchored at the quay quashed the rebels' chances of success and they retreated with casualties away from the waters that had thwarted them. The unlucky (or fortuitous) presence of the cutter is minor evidence of the trade importance of the Lough because of access both to the sea and the wide world beyond and the handful of towns that grew up around its shores: Newtownards, Comber, Killyleagh, Kircubbin, Greyabbey, Portaferry, Strangford. The revenue men had much to occupy them due to the busyness and ingenuity of smugglers, an energetic and nefarious activity depicted in a local and lively best-seller by W.G. Lyttle: *Daft Eddie, or The Smugglers of Strangford Lough* (*c.*1890).

The inland town of Downpatrick exercised its trading energy through the Quoile River which runs into the Lough. Fishing was brisk and in the 1770s there was a large herring fishery that lasted from mid-July until September with 110 fishing boats sailing out of Portaferry alone. An early nineteenth-century gazetteer recorded a distillery in the town and the export of grain, potatoes and kelp to Belfast, Dublin, Glasgow and Liverpool, receiving in return timber, coal and general merchandise. This kind of trade was duplicated in ports throughout the Lough and flax-spinning mills and corn mills there were aplenty, to which the sail-less and topless windmills on its surrounding elevations bear silent witness. By the end of the eighteenth century Strangford village was one of the most important ports in Ireland.

Shipbuilding was serious enough in Portaferry in the early nineteenth century to provide vessels to bring timber from Quebec. Whether the ships were built in Strangford Lough or not, the busy maritime traffic faced a common threat and danger: the uncertain winds and waves. The opposite end of shipbuilding was ship-salvaging, which became a competitive business. The stories of the shipwrecks inside the Lough and at its violent entrance are a veritable branch of local history and include the stories of the various beacons, lighthouses and lightships to protect the shipping. Given the occasional violence of the Narrows, as the current encounters the bar off Rock Angus, it is little wonder that a successful salvage firm was started in the later nineteenth century at Portaferry, using the quieter anchorage of Ballyhenry bay just north of the town in which to scrap or repair the broken vessels. Second World War ships were broken up there, and a US liberty ship that was being towed for dismantling but sank before reaching the bay, is still visible at any tide, providing a playground for scuba divers, homes for conger eels, sea urchins, anemones and innumerable fish, and platforms for otters and seabirds.

Of course, the waters of the Lough can be treacherous anywhere and tragedies involving sailing boats and motor boats still occasionally occur. The Stewarts (later Londonderrys) of Mount Stewart were keen sailors. Edith Helen Vane Tempest Stewart, Marchioness of Londonderry, wife of the seventh marquess (a member of Churchill's wartime cabinet), was among other things a biographer, memoirist and writer of children's books. *The Magic Ink-Pot* (1928) is a delightful fairy-story she composed for her children, set on and beneath the waves of Strangford Lough. The marchioness was also a competitive yachtswoman, while the son of the Robert Stewart (first marquess) who built the neoclassical Temple of the Winds near the house (to the design of Athenian Stuart) was narrowly saved from drowning because the boy's tutor happened to be gazing out at the Lough from that remarkable building.

WRITERS

It all comes down to the tide and to the wind if it is contrary. I am not surprised, then, that the Narrows and bar mouth have been inspiring metaphors for Strangford Lough novelists. There is a fine account of a shipwreck at Rock Angus in the 1920s or 1930s in *Red is the Port Light* (1948), a realistic novel by Joseph Tomelty, novelist, playwright and actor. He is only one of three twentieth-century fiction writers of serious fiction – two of them quite forgotten, one remembered only for his plays – who were inspired by the sea, and especially by the waters of Strangford Lough. One was a son of Portaferry, one spent boyhood summers there, and one was born and raised in Kilclief.

It is Tomelty whose memory is greenest. He was born in Portaferry in 1911. He was a house-painter, playwright and actor, and scriptwriter of the beloved and legendary Ulster radio series, *The McCooeys* (1948–54). Because he is chiefly known as a dramatist, few are aware that Tomelty wrote two novels, *Red is the Port Light* and *The Apprentice* (1953), despite the fact that both have been reprinted.[2] The first is Tomelty's Strangford area novel. The action, which takes place in the 1920s or 1930s, is an episode in the life of Stephen Durnan, who is an outsider by virtue not only of being a 'by-blow' (i.e. he is illegitimate) with an unknown father and an uncommunicative mother whom he has just buried when the novel opens, but also of being a whistle-blower whose testimony as a deckhand at a shipwreck inquiry reduced the career of a Captain Norton to the humble drudgery of coasting. Durnan signs on as a deckhand on the barely seaworthy SS *Glendry* (registered in Portaferry) captained by the man he nearly ruined, and again there is a shipwreck. Norton is drowned (and buried in Ballyphilip graveyard where Tomelty himself was to be laid to rest in 1995) but Durnan survives. He falls for Norton's widow whom he marries in haste and repents in equal haste. The second half of the novel, which depicts this short, ill-fated marriage as taut melodrama, does not deliver on the promise of the impressive tense realism of the first half, but the book is nevertheless the impressive début of a novelist.

In *Red is the Port Light*, Portaferry is readily recognizable and Durnan lives a mile beyond the last house in the direction of Barr Hall. However, Tomelty also constructs a fictional geography, for 'Portaferry' is 40 miles 'up the coast' from 'Barholm' though when the *Glendry* approaches Barholm – 'a small place, inside Strangford Lough' – it passes St John's point, suggesting that 'Portaferry' is south of Barholm. The descriptions of Barholm, Captain Norton's home port, include references to Portavogie, Gun's Island (Gunn's Island on our maps), Jackdaw Island, Ballyphilip and the Gowlings. Within this partly fictional landscape and seascape, Tomelty has written some fine passages of narrative and portrayal. The *Glendry* sails from Barholm to 'Portaferry' with a cargo of potatoes, and heads towards the bar mouth *en route* to Cardiff and Bordeaux. The description of Rock Angus and the bar mouth is excellently and tightly done. Against the turbulence of this dangerous passage of water, the port light is a frail symbol of home and safety that flickers throughout this, at times, disturbing novel.

More time has passed since the death of Arthur Mason in 1955 to allow this lively writer to fall into neglect. Born in 1876, he was immensely popular in his time, especially in the United States where he seems to have lived much of his life, and I have tracked down thirteen books by him. He became a US citizen at the age of 23 but this ought not by itself to explain our neglect of him since he was published in Britain by distinguished publishing houses.

His most popular books were episodic, picaresque tales of adventure. Mason was a sailor and his stories border on being tall tales of the kind we associate with seafarers. He funnelled his taste for whimsy and hyperbole into children's writing, including the 1931 brace of stories, *The Wee Men of Ballywooden* (inspired by a Strangford area townland whose Otherworld he recreated), which with its delightful fairy characters and lively idiom and dialogue, bears comparison with the famous tales of the Dublin genius, James Stephens, author of *The Crock of Gold* (1912).[3]

Mason's popular autobiography, *Wide Seas and Many Lands* (1924), sports characters such as Liverpool Jack, Smith the Carpenter and the Old Man of Violet Rock. Mason was a romantic realist and can be classed with his equally popular contemporaries, Jack London, W.H. Davies and Patrick MacGill from Donegal. From this autobiography we learn that Mason was born and reared in Kilclief, near Strangford, went to sea at the age of 17, in 1893, and visited Scotland, the United States, Canada, Alaska, the Andes and Australia. As well as a sailor, he was a fisherman in British Columbia, a hobo in California and a prospector in Nevada.

One idea recurs in the autobiography, namely that we are all equipped with a 'clutch', a mechanism that allows us in tight spots to access our unconscious mind and thereby achieve safety and wholeness untrammelled by fear and anxiety. Interestingly, just as the shipwreck in Tomelty occurs at the bar mouth, the narrows between lough and sea, so Mason likens the connection between conscious and unconscious minds as a narrow channel. Mason grew up as a boy beside the Narrows and may have been encouraged to adopt the notion of the clutch by his memories of that crucial body of moving water connecting, we might say, the 'conscious' of the familiar lough and the 'unconscious' of the distant and mysterious sea beyond. After his wanderings 'over wide seas and many lands', Mason returns to Kilclief in 1925 and, in defiance of his disapproving conscious mind, seeks the fairies, banshees and ghosts he once saw there. (The ghosts are understandable, but the fairies are an unfortunate expatriate touch.) Here, in sight of the Narrows, he tries to get his soundings between two realities, otherworldly imagination and worldly experience, but stands forever between them, as in their own way Kilclief and Strangford do.

As forgotten a writer as Mason is Filson Young, also born in 1876 and who died in 1938. Young was a prolific and once well-known author of books on music, cars, flying, sensational trials and the sea. Sensation and the sea combined in his prompt and excellent *Titanic* (it was in the bookshops three weeks after the disaster), which is reportage with the rhythm of a novel. His two novels, the once scandalous *Sands of Pleasure* (1905) and *When the Tide Turns* (1908), also employ the sea as setting and symbol.[4]

A recurring image and idea in Young's work, fiction and non-fiction alike, is that of the tidal flow and cross-currents in human affairs. In *When the Tide Turns*, the literal version of this idea is the unnamed but clearly recognizable Narrows of Strangford Lough. (One character is called Lady Killard, a name taken from Killard Point.) The notion of cross-currents takes a figurative turn in Filson Young's eloquent and thoughtful 1903 book about Irish society and politics, *Ireland at the Cross Roads: An Essay in Explanation* (1903), the results of a two-month tour through the island in 1901.[5]

That Young's central metaphor derived from the Narrows of Strangford Lough is hardly surprising. He was born in Ballyeaston, County Antrim, son of Rev. William Young, but his connection with the Lough is revealed in P.J. McHenry's article in the inaugural issue of the *Journal* of the Upper Ards Historical Society: 'No. 8 Ferry Street, Portaferry – the History of a House' (1977). There we learn of a fee farm grant from Andrew Nugent to Dr Alexander Bell Filston (*sic*) in 1810 for No.8, which in 1866 passed to the Filston Youngs (clearly an interrelated family) who held the property until 1923 when it was bought by Dr McDonald. (P.J. McHenry bought the house in 1948.) McHenry recalled an essay he had to read at college by one Filtson Young. By then he was Filson Young, so that either he changed his name or McHenry misread the name on the house deeds and misremembered the name of the essayist.

The essay McHenry had to read as a schoolboy, 'Going Away and Arriving', recounts the long journey from Belfast to Portaferry in an Irish long car (presumably in the middle and late 1880s) and McHenry quotes a passage (no doubt from his copy of his old school reader). I traced this essay to Filson Young's *Letters from Solitude and Other Essays* (1912) from which it is clear that when the writer was a boy the

Filson Youngs made the journey every summer from their London townhouse to their large home in Ferry Street, Portaferry, with its sprawling garden and orchard, now as I write under development. The essay celebrates the glory of going away for the holidays and the joy of arriving at where the holiday would be spent. And arrival was consummated when alongside the walls of Portaferry Castle the family glimpsed the lough and the 'swift sliding tide'.

Leaving and arriving, going and coming: here again is the tidal movement that dominates Young's writings. He writes the essay, he tells us, 'in the mid-sea of life' and anticipates his 'arrival' in later years, an allegory of life inspired by those boyhood summers in Portaferry. One can only surmise that like Tomelty and Mason, Filson Young would have written, and thought, differently had he not, as we have, enjoyed the privilege of familiarity with Strangford Lough, its Narrows and bar mouth, in the ceaseless wax and wane, both in our days and our lives.

WATERS AGAIN

Young and Mason were once quite famous writers outside Ireland but are now little known abroad, rather like the Lough itself which is still a well-kept secret beyond the shores of Northern Ireland. Things are changing but at a polite rate. The same winds and waves that threaten also challenge positively the sailor, and so the Lough is ringed with sailing clubs that take advantage of the wind and exploit the Lough's waters without disturbing or overcrowding them. The previous commerce of the Lough that used the waves and winds has given way to leisure, especially yachting and wind-surfing. There is little doubt that these pastimes and others (kayaking and canoeing, perhaps) will in the future become more organized and popular, a new form of commerce, though at present visitors have the best of all worlds.

Organized leisure is, like well-organized conservation and management, a kind of domestication, though with so much of today's natural world under threat from overpopulation, development and depletion of resources this is inevitable and a price we must pay. The scenery of Strangford Lough can itself appear at times a trifle domestic, though a sudden squall, a fearsome wind, or a torrential downpour can give lie to the appearance. In any case, the landscapes and waterscapes of the Lough are subtle and immensely variegated to the keen eye. Strangford is full of nooks and creeks, bywaters and corners, overgrown ruins and wrecks, neglected beaches, sudden unexpected vistas that only the photographer or painter can rescue or commemorate. It is good to celebrate these desuetudes and oversights. Besides, the transient may be the Lough's chief currency, from the intertidal revelations to the shifting strandline of seaweed and flotsam.

Sometimes I think the allure of the Lough lies in its edges, fringes, transition zones, its meandering shorelines few can hope to trace exhaustively. These are forms of exchange: between land and water, between high tide and low tide and, supremely, between sea and lough. The seabirds testify to the variable nature of the exchanges. The manx shearwaters and stormy petrels that breed on the Copeland islands to the north of the peninsula on the Irish Sea mostly patrol just beyond the bar mouth. The gannets that breed on farther Ailsa Craig penetrate the Lough in ones or twos and seem to bring us messages from the open sea beyond. Assorted buccaneers reconnoitre the Lough, plunder and leave, arctic and pomarine skuas among them. The traffic of Strangford is ceaseless and sometimes as unexpected as shipwrecks and killer whales. But often, as they do today, the Lough and its wildlife seem composed, painterly and photographic, a scene as fair as any I can recall.

NOTES

1. Quoted in an account of Killyleagh Castle: http://www.disoverireland.com.
2. *Red is the Port Light*, published by Jonathan Cape in London in 1948, was republished by Lagan Press in Belfast in 1997. *The Apprentice*, published by Cape in 1953, was republished by Blackstaff Press in Belfast in 1983.
3. Heinemann published this volume of stories in the United States in 1930 and in the United Kingdom in 1931. *Wide Seas and Many Lands* appeared first in 1924 and in a revised version by Jonathan Cape in London in 1926.
4. These three books were published by Grant Richards in London. (*The Sands of Pleasure* was reprinted in 1912.) Grant Richards also published *Ireland at the Cross Roads*.
5. *Ireland at the Cross Roads* was published by Grant Richards in 1903 and a second edition appeared the following year.

11
BLACKBIRD

THE POETIC BLACKBIRD

The choice of the blackbird as the emblem of the new Seamus Heaney Centre for Poetry in Queen's University, Belfast is an inspired one. Anyone who knows Belfast and poetry knows 'Blackbird at Belfast Lough' ('An Lon Dubh'), the anonymous haiku-like verse in Irish from the eighth or ninth century.[1]

> The little bird
> that whistled shrill
> from the nib of
> Its yellow bill:
>
> A note let go
> o'er Belfast Lough –
> A yellow whin

It is to be found translated by the Director of the Centre, Ciaran Carson, and offered on the Centre's website in both Irish and English as lyrical marginalia in the manner of antique manuscripts. It is familiar, too, in the translations of Frank O'Connor, John Montague and Seamus Heaney, among many others'. Hurlstone Jackson in *A Celtic Miscellany* (1951) calls it an epigram, not in the Wildean sense but in the sense of a brief poem on a single subject that achieves maximum compression and force.[2]

The diversity of the translations and the formal nature of the verse, competing (it seems to me) with the mundane, if lyrical, subject of a common bird warbling from a bush, is the very emblem of the rich ambiguity of poetry to which Ciaran Carson refers in his introduction to the Centre's website. The poem has had an alluring quality for Irish poets. Translating it seems almost to be a kind of obligatory exercise of the kind aspiring musicians engage in or, one imagines, apprentice bards in the century in which it was composed. But it is easy to fancy the tantalisingly short poem mischievously welcoming translations of itself, while actually daring Irish poets to achieve the definitive version; its brevity is the enticement and the deception. And this too seems emblematic of the welcome the Seamus Heaney Centre for

Poetry will extend to poets far and wide, a welcome not untinged with challenge. Yes, indeed, an inspired logo and epigraph for the Centre.

Like Ezra Pound's famously sudden petals on a wet black bough, the poem's blackbird has the immediacy of apparition. This Patrick Kavanagh-like conjuring of small miracle out of an everyday of nature requires an incongruity, like the Monaghan poet's bluebells in a throughother landscape. The blackbird (*Turdus merula merula*) is an everyday of nature, resident with us all year round, though large numbers come in and out of Britain and Ireland in spring and autumn, and the fourth most common bird among us, up to ten million pairs strong. It is also an everywhere of nature, observable throughout our mainlands and islands, and facing the stern task of living in woodlands, gardens, town parks, uplands, thickets, rocky coasts and virtually treeless islands. William Thompson in *The Natural History of Ireland* (1849) described blackbirds as common and resident throughout Ireland: 'they likewise resort to the islands off the coasts'.[3] Thompson is never bare of anecdotes about the species he describes, and he notes that when the severe Ulster winter of 1813–14 began to relent, over a hundred blackbirds and thrushes were found floating dead on the stream flowing from a spring at Ballynafeigh, near Belfast, a stream presumably long since buried by bricks and stones.

Yet the familiarity of this abundant bird has never bred our contempt, unlike the house sparrow, a contempt we might now regret as the sparrow dwindles in numbers and deserts our eaves while its chirrupings fall silent (you don't know what you've got till it's gone, as the singer says). For the blackbird has combined abundance with caution, even hauteur. William Yarrell in *A History of British Birds* (1843) saw the blackbird as 'shy, restless, and vigilant' while W.H. Hudson in *British Birds* (1895) saw it as a skulker, ready to take alarm and flight in a trice, uttering its irritated chatter.[4] I think of the hedge-sparrow and the wren as skulkers but not the blackbird; nor is he shy, merely cautious, and bold enough on occasion. Habits change, of course: in my boyhood I had to reach the countryside beyond Belfast before I saw the wary hooded crow; now it is brazen and has penetrated the city. And there were magpies in suburban Dublin gardens but not in Belfast gardens; now they too are everywhere and may have helped drive the sparrow into decline. But the blackbird has not changed his ways much; he is still the neighbourhood watch and still utters his exasperating tic-tic from the bushes at twilight (as does the American robin), as if bedding the other species down like some scolding night nurse, then up at dawn or before and rousing his fellows awake. He will not ingratiate himself with us like the European robin and maintains his distance and dignity, and this makes him a fitter subject for the detachment of 'Blackbird at Belfast Lough'. I say 'he' and in doing so, I note Frank Finn's comment in *Birds of Our Country* (*c.*1900) that for some reason or other hens are seen far less often than cocks.[5] This is fortuitous (the hen being merely the twitcher's medium-sized brown job), but odd. Is it that the cock is simply that, seen more often because of his contrast with his backdrop? Back in British Columbia, I see seven or eight female northern harriers (what are known in Europe as hen harriers) to one male – which is not fortuitous since the male is a more splendid creature than his mate – and have no idea why.

It is the cock blackbird whose darkness sets off the almost startling brightness of his bill. Easy to see how he surprised the medieval poet with beauty. Tennyson in his poem, 'The Blackbird' imagined the 'gold dagger' of the bird's bill. In the Belfast poem, the yellow bill echoes the yellow of the gorse. The poet Montague called the Belfast blackbird 'yoke-billed'. Yet Witherby *et al.* in the once biblical *Handbook of British Birds* (1938) describe the bill as orange and so too does Ludwig Koch in his *Encyclopedia of British Birds* (1955). Yarrell chooses gamboge, the yellow pigment derived from the gum resin, and other writers too opt for yellow. But then Witherby *et al.* describe the cock's plumage as glossy and so too do T.A. Coward (*The Birds of the British Isles*, 1950) and Koch, but surely they are wrong though they are experts.[6] The starling is glossy but not the blackbird. Finn rightly notes the lack of metallic reflections in the feathers and I would describe the feathering as more matt than glossy. In any case, the colour lies in the bird's name, which the poet economically uses to achieve the black–yellow contrast in his vision of the bird. By the way, Carson's description of the bill as a nib is not just an agreeable piece of licence that neatly appropriates the bird and the poem for the institutional task he has set them. 'Nib' originally meant beak or nose and is related etymologically to 'neb': neb is the word Heaney uses in his translation ('yellow neb') and neb meant not just the nose, as I thought ('Don't stick your neb in!'), but a bird's beak. So the bird's whistle is a poet's song, neb is nib and poets are now encouraged to sing in the vicinity of Belfast Lough as of old.

Carson sees the Belfast blackbird's song as a note let go, Heaney as a 'note-spurt', Frank O'Connor as a cry tossed over Belfast Lough.[7] It is as though the original poet has frozen the song in one frame, for the joy of the blackbird's song is its continuity, which it shares with the more plangent song of the robin. (I haven't been fortunate enough to hear the nightingale.) The song thrush starts and stops, repeats once, twice or even three times (Robert Browning in his much-anthologized 'Home Thoughts from Abroad' famously settled for one repetition), but the blackbird launches into lovely arias in a voice fuller-bodied than any other songbird I've heard. The song has been described as both melancholy and exhilarating.[8] 'Flute-like' or 'fluty' is the recurring epithet in the ornithological literature. (That the Director of the Seamus Heaney Centre for Poetry is himself a flute-player is an agreeable coincidence.) In his poem, 'The Blackbird', W.E. Henley tells us that 'the blackbird plays but a boxwood flute'.[9] Everyone agrees on the disappointing falling off at song's end, but the ease of delivery that the *Handbook of British Birds* refers to is at one with this and in contrast to the beautiful but (as it were) self-conscious effort of the song thrush, as though he were trying again to get it right this time. Richard Jefferies (quoted by Hudson) thought the blackbird sings 'in a quiet, leisurely way, as a great master should?' So cool is the blackbird that he has been known to sing on the wing and recently in Derry I heard him carry on his song as he floated and looped from one rooftop to another a hundred yards off, not bothering to interrupt his aria. His is the finest song I know and the one I'd take to the proverbial desert island, though the song I'd most want to hear at journey's end would be the brief and soulful spiralling crescendo of Swainson's thrush that truly echoes like day's epitaph in the forests of British Columbia.

But we are no longer connoisseurs of birdsong because we are no longer bird fanciers. Rev. C.A. Johns in *British Birds in their Haunts* (1861) quotes Johann Bechstein (1757–1822) on the noisy nature of the blackbird's song and its unsuitability for the cage.[10] Yarrell also remarked without irony that the blackbird's song is much too loud 'except for the open air'! Ours until the mid-twentieth century was a culture of cage-birds in which linnets, mules (canary-linnet crosses), song thrushes, blackbirds and robins were prized for their song. Johns quotes from entries in Samuel Pepys's diary for May 1663 about a blackbird a house carpenter had sent him and for which the carpenter had been offered 20 shillings, 'he do so whistle', and which indeed warbled well except Pepys complained it started 'many tunes' and then left them and went no further. I like to think the blackbird was too wayward a fellow to be well caged.

THE POLITICAL BLACKBIRD

Surely the yellow bill and sweet song prevented the blackbird from the malign associations of blackness we find in the pre-Christian

Irish sagas and surviving folklore and which invest the hapless cormorants and crows. In his entry for the blackbird, John J. Watters in his *Natural History of the Birds of Ireland* (1853) quotes the Sonnah (the body of traditional sayings supplementing the Koran) but perhaps what he quotes need not blacken the name of our familiar bird: 'the souls of those in Purgatory were in the crops of blackbirds, exposed to hell fire morning and evening, until the Judgement Day'.[11] It is true that in the Early Christian voyage tales in Ireland, tortured souls in the shapes of birds are encountered frequently. By contrast, in the medieval Irish stories and poems there are expressed what the Belfast scholar Helen Waddell called in *Beasts and Saints* (1934) 'the mutual charities between saints and beasts'. Birdsong, because it is intelligible to us (though we don't hear the challenge and threat that song is often meant to mount), surely encourages mutual charity. One of the most delightful stories Waddell reproduces concerns St Kevin (d. Glendalough, AD 618) whose hand, outstretched to heaven during a Lenten contemplation, was chosen by a blackbird for her nest. The bird laid eggs and hatched her nestlings before the saint would bring himself to move. St Kevin has stretched his arm through the window of his hut for the bird's truest habitat is the outdoors where his is the indoors.[12] Heaney himself retells his story in 'St Kevin and the Blackbird' (*The Spirit Level*, 1996), but subjects the truth of it to some ambiguous interrogation. Jackson in his *Celtic Miscellany* (p.135) reproduces an epigram from the eleventh or twelfth century, 'The Hermit Blackbird', which seems to voice the holy man's envy of the bird's life without obligation, even though he sees both of them as hermits:

> Ah, blackbird, it is well for you where your nest is in the bushes;
> a hermit that clangs no bell, sweet, soft, and peaceful is your call.

The relative solitariness of the blackbird allowed the poetic monk to see the bird as an anchorite like himself. He presumably did not see parties of blackbirds on migration or in roosts; Witherby tells us of large seasonal immigrations into Ireland from Europe. In the 1950s I saw dozens of blackbirds each evening cross the old Hillfoot Road (the future A55 ring road) on the south side of Belfast, flying from the hilly hedgerows to a communal roost somewhere in the city that I was never able to locate.

In Austin Clarke's version of an eighteenth-century lay, 'The Blackbird of Derrycairn' ('Lon Doire an Chairn'), it is the blackbird rather than the holy man who is speaking. The bird recalls Fionn's discovery of the blackbird in Norway and his return to Ireland with it

to gild the branch and tell, there,
Why men must welcome in the daylight.[13]

Above all the sounds of the country, Fionn prized 'My throat rejoicing from the hawthorn'. The bird is speaking to a monk (perhaps a novice) and reminds him that 'no handbell gives a glad sound' while knowledge is found not in the monastery but 'among the branches', an idea of the roofless school later adopted by Wordsworth. 'Listen! That song that shakes my feathers/Will thong the leather of your satchels.' The blackbird seems to have played its pagan role in the contest between the elder faiths of Ireland and imported medieval Christianity.

Clarke's translation is said to have been an oblique criticism of the theocracy of Free State Ireland and the original to have been a Jacobite lay, and if the latter is the case then the bird played a rebel part. In an anonymous broadside, 'The Royal Blackbird', the bird is the Old Pretender, the son of James II. The speaker fears a fowler has taken his blackbird, which once flourished in England and is a stranger there now, though respected in Scotland as well as in France and Spain. The broadside exploits a kind of eco-politics: dealing in rarity and extinction, over-zealous hunting and adaptation – names of appropriate countries are inserted according to where the ballad was recited or printed. It first appeared around 1715 but was still popular in the nineteenth century, according to Georges-Denis Zimmermann in *Songs of Irish Rebellion* (1967), who reminds us that Patrick Dineen in his famous Irish-English dictionary translated *londubh* as 'a blackbird; a Jacobite, a rapparee, a hero'.[14] As I have pointed out elsewhere, a curious feature of Irish nationalist culture in the eighteenth and nineteenth centuries is the way natural elements or species were invested with political symbolism.[15] Irish nature was recruited in order to advance the cause: in the famous song of the 1798 rebellion, 'The Croppy Boy', the sweetly singing birds change their notes from tree to tree, 'and the song they sang was "Old Ireland free"'. Birds and animals could help disguise political protest and conspiracy. The blackbird, dark-robed, singular, whistling with deceptive innocence, often skulking and fleeing, was a natural for the part.

The title of one broadside from the Year of Revolutions, 1848, 'Granua's Lament for the Loss of her Blackbird Mitchel, the Irish Patriot', identifies the latest role assigned to the bird. The ballad is full of the circumstances of the Fenian John Mitchel's arrest for sedition and deportation and there is little extension to the metaphor of the bird itself.[16] The Irish republican and dynamiter Jeremiah

O'Donovan Rossa in his *Recollections 1838–1898* (1898) performed an interesting volte-face with the blackbird. He remembered that a blackbird once tried to lure him away from its nest by feigning injury, something known to ornithologists as the 'broken-wing trick' and practised by certain shore-birds, though I have never seen it practised by a blackbird. Later, he says, the blackbird uttering its false wounded cry, 'chuc-chuc-chuc-chuc-chuc' (in reality, I think, a response to danger and sounding like disapproval), came to remind him of Gladstone whose 'chuc-chuc-chuc-chuc-chuc' is the seductive promise of Home Rule luring the Irish away from their plight and their freedom. In fact, writes Rossa, the 'Gladstone blackbird' as he named it (and it names his chapter also) maintains the destruction of the Irish whereas the real blackbird was trying to *save* her young from destruction.[17] In 1881 new words were set to the air of 'The Royal Blackbird' and turned Charles Stewart Parnell into 'The Blackbird of Avondale'.[18] It is a female Ireland who laments Parnell's imprisonment as she lamented Mitchell's banishment, and as in the Jacobite ballad, it is a base fowler who captures and carries off the bird. Besides the obvious political circumstances there is also an implied story and cultural context involving a beautiful woman who has a pet blackbird that sweetly sings but that is snared by a trapper presumably netting or 'liming' songsters for the cage, a common professional and amateur occupation until the early twentieth century. In the blackbird's absence, it is the linnet and thrush who must warble, but with their sadder notes.

Since the speaker of 'The Blackbird of Avondale' is expressly unconsoled by the song of the nightingale (which is absent from Ireland on natural grounds), either the broadside was distributed in England as well as Ireland, or the birds are simply generic presences. Certainly the blackbird became an adaptable figure detached from real nature. The traditional Irish song, 'If I was a Blackbird', reduces the bird to a mere figure of flight; in this secular rather than political love song, the lovelorn speaker simply wishes for the power of flight that she might follow the ship in which her sweetheart sails in search of fortune; under the circumstances she would have been better off wishing to be, say, a blackheaded gull. But in the song the landlocked lover would, were she a blackbird, build her nest in the ship's rigging, and one can almost imagine a real blackbird doing the same, fond as she is of odd choices of location for her nest, whilst migrating perching birds do sometimes make landfall on a moving ship and stay for a while. Older readers may remember the hit that whistling Ronnie Ronalde made of this song in the 1950s, its title subjunctivized.[19] And no more real, ornithologically, is the bird in the even more famous and curiously moving 'Bye Bye Blackbird', composed in 1926 by Henderson and Dixon. This is an American Tin Pan Alley song and since none of the various American blackbirds are songsters, the composers have a bird in mind as fictional as Vera Lynn's bluebirds that were to fly over Dover's white cliffs. That is, unless Henderson and Dixon when they write of the blackbird singing the blues all day outside the speaker's door are thinking of the curious bluesy warble of the redwinged blackbird.[20] (And we could argue that Lynn's bluebirds are familiar legendary embodiments of happiness that will appear when the tide of war turns against Hitler and in favour of Britain.)

The base fowler makes a comeback in one of the few poems by Francis Ledwidge to gain fame: 'The Blackbirds', which Padraic Colum entitled for an anthology 'Lament for the Poets: 1916'.[21] In a natural progression, the mourning young maiden of 'The Blackbird of Avondale' has become the keening old woman of Irish sorrows, the Shan Van Vocht (or Poor Old Woman) who mourns the capture of her blackbird by the fowler at dawn and who grieves 'the silent bills', in this case the singing of Pearse, MacDonagh and Plunkett, executed for their part in the Easter Rising. When this tragic week happened, Ledwidge was otherwise engaged in service for the Crown in the Great War, though Ledwidge like many of the Irish volunteers saw himself as fighting for Ireland as much as for Britain. When the Old Woman predicts that the skylarks will dip their wings when they fly over the graves of the martyrs, we have an image that suggests the gesture of respect made by airplanes which Ledwidge would have seen in action in the skies above Europe. And in future dawns, blackbirds will appear, singing with love of the executed. That a patriotic Irish soldier in British uniform laments the dead republicans in Dublin casts Ledwidge's lines in a secondary and poignant light.

Ledwidge wrote several poems about the blackbird, one entitled 'To an Irish Blackbird at Dawn' in which 'yella bill' sings in gladness to mark the refusal of grief by the speaker, either an Irish small farmer mourning a lost child, or a woman of the countryside mourning a sweetheart who died young.[22] In 'Lonesome Song' (p.45), a lyric in the manner of the early Yeats, a blackbird says '"Amen!"/To the vesper hymn of the forest's choir' and announces thereby the night and its release of the poet's memories that 'pitch their camp' on the fields of his dreams. 'To a Blackbird On a Sign-post' (p.202) is a richer, denser performance with the bird again a gatekeeper of memory. The apostrophized singing bird allows the poet briefly but intensely and movingly to escape a weary landscape of 'nomad winds' likened to old men or 'comrade hinds' (labouring farm-workers): 'for in your eye/I see the twilight of some woodland pool' in which light he is transported to the busy pastoral world that started up the figures and similes in which his poetry began. The structure and movement of the poem resembles that of Keats's 'Ode to a Nightingale'.

Patrick MacGill, the poet and novelist who was also an Irish volunteer in British uniform, recalled in his memoir, *The Red Horizon* (1916), one dawn in the trenches when 'a blackbird hopped on to the parapet, looked inquiringly in, his yellow bill moving from side to side, and fluttered away' and a skylark rising and falling, nature's life mocking mankind's death, but also offering the consoling and encouraging idea that life goes on despite the trenches and will go on after them.[23] Clearly, the blackbird is a bird for all seasons and the Seamus Heaney Centre has done well to recruit its potent reality and equally potent symbolism.

NOTES

1. This is a lightly revised version of 'Blackbird', written for the inaugural issue of *The Yellow Nib* (2005), the journal of the Seamus Heaney Centre for Poetry.
2. Hurlstone Jackson includes the poem in a section called 'Epigrams', *A Celtic Miscellany* (Cambridge, MA: Harvard University Press, 1951), p.135.
3. William Thompson, *The Natural History of Ireland*, Vol. I, *Birds* (London: Reeve *et al.*, 1849), p.142.
4. William Yarrell, *A History of British Birds* (London: John Van Voorst, 1843), Vol. I, p.203; W.H. Hudson, *British Birds* (London: The Library Press, 1923 [1895]), p.49.
5. Frank Finn and E. Kay Robinson, *Birds of Our Country* (London: Hutchinson, n.d. [1900?]), Vol. I, p.18.
6. H.F. Witherby *et al.*, *The Handbook of British Birds* (London: H.F. and G. Witherby, 1943 [1938]), p.136; Ludwig Koch, *The Encyclopedia of British Birds* (London: Waverley Book Co., n.d. [1955]), p.72; T.A. Coward, *The Birds of the British Isles and Their Eggs* (London: Frederick Warne, 1950 [1920]), First Series, p.229.
7. Frank O'Connor (ed.), *Kings, Lords, & Commons: An Anthology from the Irish* (London: Macmillan, 1962), p.27.
8. W. Percival Westell is particularly enamoured of the bird's rich song and reminds us that in those pre-RSPB days the blackbird flourished 'in spite of the persecution meted out to him by the fruit grower and gardener' – a melancholy fact that oddly chimes with the political meanings of the blackbird I discuss below: *British Bird Life* (London: Unwin, 1905), p.1.
9. In Louis Untermeyer, *Modern British Poetry* (New York: Harcourt, Brace and Howe, 1920).
10. Rev. C.A. Johns, *British Birds in Their Haunts* (London: Routledge, 1909 [1861]), p.9.
11. John J. Watters, *The Natural History of the Birds of Ireland* (Dublin: James McGlashan, 1853), p.36. Watters also quotes *Cormac's Glossary* (*Sanas Chormaic*), the encyclopedia of Irish oral tradition by the tenth-century priest-king Cormac mac Cuilennan: 'Sweet the warbling of the blackbird/About the lonely Rath of Fiach'.
12. Helen Waddell (trans.), *Beasts and Saints* (London: Constable, 1934), p.137.
13. Austin Clarke, *Collected Poems*, ed. Liam Miller (Dublin and London: Dolmen Press and Oxford University Press, 1974), pp.203–4.
14. See Georges-Denis Zimmermann, *Songs of Irish Rebellion* (Hatboro, PA: Folklore Associates, 1967), pp.119–21. The outlaw (or rapparee) and the royal personage combine in the exiled

pretender to the throne; Westell, *British Bird Life*, p.1, calls the blackbird 'one of the kings of song'.

15. John Wilson Foster, 'Nature and Nation in the Nineteenth Century', in John Wilson Foster and Helen G. Chesney (eds), *Nature in Ireland: A Scientific and Cultural History* (Dublin: Lilliput Press, 1997; Montreal-Toronto: McGill-Queen's University Press, 1998), p.414.
16. Zimmermann, *Songs of Irish Rebellion*, pp.240–2.
17. Jeremiah O'Donovan Rossa, *Rossa's Recollections 1838–1898* (facs. ed. Shannon: Irish University Press, 1972 [1898]), pp.61–3.
18. Zimmermann, *Songs of Irish Rebellion*, pp.277–8.
19. In another version of the song, the blackbird is the speaker and is already on the wing in the wake of the ship; this version is entitled 'A Blackbird's Lament'.
20. Nor is the bird in the American poet Wallace Stevens's famous poem, 'Thirteen Ways of Looking at a Blackbird' our *Turdus merula*, if we wish to seek Stevens's original bird and take our bearings from the line 'He rode over Connecticut'. Stevens's bird would be either the rusty blackbird or the redwinged blackbird.
21. 'The Blackbirds', in Francis Ledwidge, *The Complete Poems*, ed. Liam O'Meara (Newbridge: Goldsmith Press, 1997), p.192; 'Lament for the Poets: 1916', in Padraic Colum, *Anthology of Irish Verse* (New York: Boni and Liveright, 1922).
22. Ledwidge, *The Complete Poems*, p.42.
23. Patrick MacGill, *The Red Horizon* (London: Caliban Books, 1984 [1916]), pp.96–7.

12

GUESTS OF THE NATION

CULTURE AND CATEGORIES

Categories – religious, political, ethnic – have been an important engine of the Irish Problem.[1] Like Philip Larkin's 'days', in the poem of that name, categories it seems are where we live, and there are times when we wish to be in them and times when we wish not to be, times when we categorize others; and times when we are troubled by the category we customarily place *ourselves* in. I think a lot of pro-Union people in Northern Ireland were troubled in this fashion by the recent unrest at Drumcree church near Portadown which has seen a stand-off between Orangemen and the Royal Ulster Constabulary. Even from the distance of Vancouver, 6,000 miles away, I was troubled in a new way by what I saw on television or read in the newspapers.

As no doubt was the case everywhere, Canadian newspapers had a field day with the stand-off. The articles, editorials and cartoons (often depicting sashed dinosaurs) beamed Canadian superiority to such Jurassic Park goings on. It would have been idle to point out the problematic innocence of residents' groups, the remote descendancy of the IRA from the eighteenth-century Defenders, and the origins of the Orange Order in 1795, not, as Madelaine Drohan of the Toronto *Globe and Mail*'s European Bureau thought, in 1690 immediately after the Battle of the Boyne. (One recent windfall: we all know a little more about the Orange Order, this important, secretive and controversial organization.) 'The long-standing local feuds between Protestants and Catholics in the Ulster counties', Edmund Curtis tells us, 'came to a head on September 21st 1795 in an affair called "the Battle of the Diamond" in Armagh, when in an armed encounter between the two sides some twenty or thirty Defenders were left dead. The day closed with the institution of the Orange order "to maintain the laws and peace of the country and the Protestant Constitution, and to defend the King and his heirs as long as they shall maintain the Protestant ascendancy".'[2] All of this was shrunken at Drumcree to freedom to walk the 'Queen's highway'.

In a curiously depressing way, it has been *déjà vu* all over again. On 10 July 1796, Lord Gosford, Governor of County Armagh, wrote to Edward Cooke, Under-Secretary to the Lord-Lieutenant, Dublin

Castle (after visiting Portadown) on the occasion of the Orangemen's plan to parade (for the first time) on the Twelfth of July:

> I wish your letter had come some time sooner. At present I know not what measures can be taken with propriety and prudence to put a stop to their assembling on Tuesday. They have gone to considerable expense in banners, orange ribbons, *etc*. By every enquiry I can make, they profess loyalty to the King, and their determination is not to disturb or offend anybody, but after walking through different parts of the country to return peaceably to their homes.

He adds: 'What is most to be dreaded is the power of whiskey.'[3] (I wonder what has been the role of alcohol in vicious acts of the last thirty years; William Carleton remarked on how Orange yeomanry primed themselves with whiskey when setting out on nocturnal devilment.[4]) Gosford also adds: 'I fear they [by which he means either the Orangemen or the people generally: it isn't clear] only wait a favourable opportunity and very little encouragement to revive the spirit of religious quarrel, and to renew the animosity which for a time so unhappily subsisted between the Presbyterians and Catholics'.

In any case, watching the television, this Protestant (of sorts) felt, like the French-Algerian schoolmaster Daru in Albert Camus' story 'The Guest', 'a sudden wrath against ... all men with their rotten spite, their tireless hates, their blood lust'.[5] (Televised events in the Balkans have induced the same reaction in many of us, I'm sure.) I found myself in a position resembling Daru's (without of course his very real and immediate dilemma of what to do with the Arab prisoner foisted upon him): 'he cursed at one and the same time his own people who had sent him this Arab and the Arab too who had dared to kill and not managed to get away'. It is involvement Daru resents, entanglement in something he wishes to escape. And since we feel and see and think across oceans and continents now – through newspapers, satellite television, facsimile, telephone, the internet and electronic mail – this undeclared war (as the Algerian war was undeclared in Camus' story), comes to those of us from Northern Ireland as the two men, gendarme and Arab prisoner, come to Daru ineluctably in the story's opening sentence.

It would have been equally idle perhaps to have reminded Canadians that the Quebec Question and the Ulster Question are of identical vintage (early seventeenth century), that there was the matter of 1763, that Quebeçois car licence plates carry as motto, not 'Beautiful Quebec' (as in 'Beautiful British Columbia') but 'Je Me Souviens', and that while there has been no Drumcree-type stand-off between Quebec and the Rest of Canada, this may be because the conciliation of Quebec (some call it appeasement) has been extraordinarily tireless, and that there was a deadly First Nations–Quebec stand-off, at Oka several years ago. This was all conveniently forgotten by Canadian editorial writers covering Drumcree. A.T.Q. Stewart reminds us in *The Narrow Ground*, that 'whereas the English believe that compromise is the answer to all disputes, Ulstermen believe the opposite is the case'.[6] Well, the first proposition is debatable, but the second is largely true. Hence the recurring symbolism of the stand-off and siege, the prolonged protest, the hunger strike, in Ulster history. I do think this is changing, but we must expect terrible reversions to the old solution.

I confess to having felt during Drumcree a very real estrangement from the events. I felt for the first time that here is something archaic and rural that may indeed have to do with civil liberties of assembly and movement but is really an ancient feud between two sides to which I do not belong, that I am a mere spectator. I remember the moment: when an Orangeman answered the question put to him by a television reporter: 'What will happen if you aren't allowed through?' 'The country will burn', he declared. 'We'll burn it. It's ours and we can do what we want with it.' Perhaps later he regretted the remark (especially after the lethal arson attack that took the lives of children), perhaps the heat of the moment fired him; perhaps he was in a tiny minority. But it was 1796 and like Daru I was disgusted by both parties to the quarrel.

But what if my reaction is a reprehensible luxury, rather like E.M. Forster's narrator's confession (or declaration) in *Howards End* (1910), a novel that places an otherwise immense range of English society under scrutiny: 'We are not concerned with the very poor. They are unthinkable, and only to be approached by the statistician or the poet'.[7] The narrator (or Forster) gives himself licence to avoid the duty of extending his first-hand knowledge of a large – the impoverished – portion of England, while appearing to register its importance, if only by the distancing effect of irony. But surely it was in 'darkest England' – as General Booth ironically called the part of the imperial mother country afflicted by poverty, unemployment, drugs and prostitution – that the etiology of England's late Victorian and Edwardian problem could best be found? Maybe so, but not everyone (and rarely the liberal) has the stomach to investigate the heart of darkness, 'darkest Ireland'. Drumcree and Garvaghey – anglicized in John Montague's 'rough field' – need to be diagnosed but I have found myself turning away.

Forster's distance from the core of the problem – what economic and political system can be devised to eradicate poverty and maximize happiness? – is achieved by his courteous liberalism: the equal distribution of viewpoints and the chronic sense of irony. It is not an existential problem, as is Camus', but a strategic problem that omits vital and accessible data. To Camus it seems as a universal truth that one cannot be just *and* partisan. He is aware in his story 'The Guest' (but not, according to Conor Cruise O'Brien, in his novel *The Outsider*) that the category one inhabits – or is *perceived* to inhabit – endangers one's freedom of neutrality, one's benign *self*-involvement. (To O'Brien, *The Outsider*'s Meursault is in fact a liar and indifferent to truth, while Camus' implication that the court is impartial between Arab and Frenchman sustains the unjust colonial fiction.[8])

There is copious published research by social anthropologists and psychologists on the structure and structural dynamics of categorization and grouping in Ulster, especially the categories of 'Catholic', 'Protestant', 'unionist', 'nationalist'. I read recently that only 15 per cent of marriages in Northern Ireland are 'mixed': this struck me as extraordinary, an indictment of the society and sad evidence of the diminution of the possibilities of emotional life and development in that small place. Think of by how much *love* has been diminished, and sexual fulfilment. I have yet to read an exploration of the individual and collective effect on each of us from Ulster of having against our will to occupy and represent these categories, of having imposed on us a hierarchy of identity (for example, in a hypothetical case, Catholic first, Irish second, nationalist third, woman fourth, professional consultant fifth – or some such). It is the permanent awareness of the categories, 'Protestant', 'Catholic', 'nationalist', 'unionist' that works its psychological damage.

The extent to which we assume the roles required by the categories is illustrated by Carleton in his account of the invasion of his home by a group of Orange yeomanry one night some years after 1798. The yeomen, ostensibly in search of weapons held by rebel Catholics and knowing full well that the Carletons secreted no such arms, insulted his father and slightly wounded his sister with a bayonet. But although the yeomen spoke to the Carletons as though to enemy strangers, 'My readers', remarks Carleton, 'may form an opinion of the state of society, when they hear that there was not an individual present that night in this gross and lawless outrage with whom we were not acquainted, nor a man among them who did not know every one of us intimately' (p.39). The social (and sociable) self was doffed and the sectarian and hostile self donned.

'Protestant' and 'Catholic' – those are the most damaging roles, categories and selves, *even if one is a Catholic or Protestant!* At times a comic existentialism suggests itself – as though one were permanently aware that one was a Big-Endian and not a Small-Endian, or a

Tramecksan and not a Slamecksan. (Not that Swift wished to eradicate categories – he knew the hierarchy of religious and party political categories he wanted to maintain in Ireland and England.) And they are present even in denial; they are paradoxically highlighted in government affirmative action-type programmes aimed at their dissolution, in a manner that suggests Orwell rather than Swift.

In his celebrated book, *The Colonizer and the Colonized*, the Tunisian writer Albert Memmi speaks of 'the colonizer who refuses' (that is, refuses to inhabit and practise the category of colonizer).[9] It is an ironic category: by his refusal, the colonizer who refuses identifies himself as a colonizer! Just so in Northern Ireland. Shouldn't the enlightened Ulster woman and man refuse the roles to which history has consigned him and her? Were she or he to do so, identity politics, ethnic politics, inherited party politics, the politics of heredity, would be impoverished. By the irony of quotas in furtherance of equity, such refusal is itself refused by the government. Anyone working for the government in Northern Ireland who declines to identify herself as a Catholic or Protestant must suggest which category she would be 'perceived' by others as inhabiting. Is this not Camusian irony? In 'The Guest', Daru at the end is perceived not just as French but as anti-Algerian, ironically so since he demonstrated his neutrality by offering the Arab prisoner the choice of walking to freedom or walking to prison. For his part, the Arab, by choosing the road to prison is choosing, unconsciously or no, the category which imprisons him.

Today, what a colleague calls 'categorism' has entirely colonized the academy as it has the wider society (government, the justice system), certainly in Canada.[10] Individualism is mocked (save as competitive individualism in professional sports and possessive individualism in economic life), likewise liberal humanism: it is probable that Forster's quirky and once celebrated liberalism has been partially sheltered from mockery by his recent status as a gay writer. Orwell the dissenting independent seems to have lost ground in the academy. Camus' species of existentialism now reads oddly, too, as though he were trying to escape the self-condemning categories of whiteness, Europeanness, colonial Frenchness, maleness all of which – it is fairly easy to see – informs much of what he says, certainly about Algeria. I fully realize that he is a vulnerable harbour I am trying to sail into.

THE PULL OF THE TRIBE

One does not always wish, or find oneself able to escape the taxonomies. O'Brien has shown how Camus in the late 1950s reverted, if that is the word, to a pro-French position on Algeria. Camus proposed, for example, that the French government announce a disposition to grant full justice to the Arab Algerians but make no concessions on the question of the rights of the French of Algeria. He wrote: 'I believe in justice, but I will defend my mother before justice'. His 'long hesitation' in choosing between justice and his mother seemed to many like neutrality, writes O'Brien: 'now Camus is beginning to take the side of his own tribe against the abstract entities' (pp.92, 102).

Surely this is a measure of how difficult it is to abandon the tribe, at least later if not sooner, and when it seems to be in peril. It is that gravitational pull we recognize in Seamus Heaney despite his description of himself in *North* (1975) as an 'inner emigré'. I recognized it in myself when I read, for example, the apparently and abstractly exemplary *Agreement Reached in the Multi-Party Negotiations* (1998), otherwise known as the 'Belfast or Good Friday Agreement'. I would have voted for the *Agreement* had I had, as every good American has, an absentee vote; I wished like many to 'give peace a chance'. But I have short reservations about parts of this hard-headed constitutional document that offers no cherry-picking or notwithstanding clauses (to borrow a constitutional Canadianism), and a 'long hesitation' about all of it. I am being candid. But I think if the spirit in which the *Agreement* is implemented is generous, then it will prove to be lasting and beneficial.[11] Let me list a couple of my hesitations.

The proposed Article 3 of the Republic's Constitution envisages an island united 'in harmony and friendship', but ... it is the 'firm will of the Irish nation' that this take place. The 'Irish nation': surely at the moment that is the problem and not the remedy. Since the Irish nation presumably does not exist until the harmonious and friendly unity takes place, there is no nation – only Dublin – to express such a will. Does the proposed amendment not then subvert itself? Am I wrong to find the firm will of the Irish nation still threatening, even in amendment?

Under the section entitled Economic, Social and Cultural Issues, there is a presumably tongue-in-cheek reference in the *Agreement* to the 'Ulster-Scots' language which, having been duly noted, can be quietly shown the door.[12] Not so the Irish language, to promote which in Northern Ireland no fewer than eight major steps are to be taken. Is there evidence that the Irish language in Northern Ireland has not – regrettably, and despite the efforts of the Ultach Trust and other bodies – been used primarily as a vehicle for a sectional nationalism? Since I suspect that loyalist culture is more visual than verbal and nationalist culture more verbal than visual, I think that the *Agreement* is seriously imbalanced culturally. Actually there is no evidence of cultural analysis in the *Agreement*, certainly of or from the unionist side, which has always been backward in cultural awareness and promotion.[13] Anyone who believes that the literature, visual aids and infrastructure of tourism, for example, is an exclusively economic matter and not a cultural matter of great importance – telling and depicting as it does the *story* of the visited place – knows little about culture. Already the Northern Ireland Tourist Board is engaged in joint advertising with Bord Failte, and in Great Britain – but not in Northern Ireland – promotes 'Ireland's North Country' ('twelve neighbourly counties') with the friendly slogan (with huge political implications) 'Is there a difference?' across a borderless north. Tellingly, this advertising feature is unclaimed in the advertisement by either tourist board, knowing as both boards do that they are literally and surreptitiously redrawing the map of the island. If Sinn Fein were ever in joint government, they would be smart to seek the Ministries of Art and Tourism.[14]

But surely there is little cause for unionist alarm. Surely the 'cherishing' of the Irish language underlines its minority status, suggesting it *needs* to be cherished, whereas – which might be the implication – the British culture of Northern Ireland is as pervasive as it is in the Republic of Ireland (where it isn't acknowledged either), and needs no more mention than camels in the Koran (to borrow Jorge Luis Borges, who thought that the absence of camels proved the authenticity of the Koran, since a forged Koran would have had caravans of camels winding through its pages). Perhaps, but I think the pro-Union negotiators should have held out for at least a brisk statement of this truism with the solemn promise that this British culture would be encouraged, however apparently pervasive.

I trust I'm not being 'intransigent' here (to use the standard anti-unionist epithet, the pro-unionist epithet being 'staunch'). Camus feared the eviction of the French from Algeria, retraction of the rights of the French there, the threat of erasure to his mother. Frankly, and without being alarmist, I feel uneasy about the future of the Ulster-Scots culture, and the British cultural identity in Northern Ireland. I fear that what has been called the 'long retreat' of the Protestants in Ireland is being hastened in Ulster by uncaring British administrators.[15] If I am right in claiming (as Kennedy would) that it is an error to think of Ulster Protestants as colonialists in the way the French were in Algeria (republican cries of 'Brits Out!' to the contrary), then my fear has more justification than Camus'. Anyone who thinks Northern Ireland is essentially a colonial situation and supports the Belfast

Agreement is using the *Agreement* as a trick and a trap.[16] But the ambivalence about the *Agreement* from the republican side must be as deep, perhaps deeper: one has only to think of the negative resonance of Stormont as a site of government (even a watered-down Assembly with input from the Republic of Ireland), guarded as it is by the aggressive posture of Edward Carson's statue with his 'raised claw', to borrow John Montague. Perhaps opposing ambivalences make a right.

It may be that Protestant tribal fears have less ground under them because of the unforeseen changes that have taken place in the Republic, changes that ought to worry traditional republicans from Ulster. If Ulster-Scots culture is at risk it may be chiefly from globalization from which no culture is safe except as a saleable travesty of itself. Globalism, it might appear, is dissolving the old categories and the pull of the tribe is superannuated. The threatening nationalism of the South may by now be merely what we could call 'Riverdance nationalism' or 'Temple Bar republicanism' – theme culture and theme politics that both disguise and facilitate the real global consumerism now motivating the South, it seems. An American sociologist recently described our global choice as that between 'Jihad' (religious and political fundamentalism) and 'McWorld' (global consumer capitalism).[17] The challenge posed for the free-standing self as a citizen of McWorld, exchanging the problem of imprisonment for the dreadful and illusory freedom of consumer choice, is best left for another day. Meanwhile, McIreland, as we might call it, has already made an appearance on the island and cannot be a welcome sight to the tribal elders. A reconstructed Stormont, a democratic Northern Ireland inside the United Kingdom, may be far less of a threat to genuine Irish nationalism.

Yet post-nationalist Ireland, if not McIreland, may not be exactly as it seems, and the old tribal wind-sniffing may not be an outmoded and unnecessary reflex. Several Irish historians and critics have rewritten the old nationalist 'Story of Ireland'.[18] In this rewrite, the Republic is European; we are all European; we are all modern, indeed post-modern; the old ways, the old divisions are dead, the old discourse silenced; it is the end of Irish history. In a recent lecture in Paris, Declan Kiberd offered an interesting boosterizing twist on the rags-to-riches, vassal state-to-buoyant nation story of Ireland.[19] It is hardly more reassuring to me, despite its colourful elasticism and the characteristic humour and verve of its author. After each modernist article of the argument there is a nationalist codicil.

Article. The surrender of the Irish language in the nineteenth century had the effect of deracinating and reorientating the Irish, of landing them as global pioneers in 'a modernizing predicament'. *Codicil*: the English language became the language of separatism, while nostalgia for a Gaelic past was a result of Irish modernization.

Article. In the nineteenth century, the Irish participated in several social and educational reforms and experiments that had the effect of modernizing them ahead of the British. *Codicil*: the British for colonial purposes sponsored these reforms and conducted these experiments, but are debited, not credited, for doing so.

Article. Easter 1916 was an event of social modernity, lamentably ahead of its time; it was also a feminist event. *Codicil*: Connolly's homology between the socialist landholding future and the Gaelic landholding past was a 'representational tactic', an example of the 'archaic avant-garde'.

Article. Ireland is post-Catholic. (Omitted *Codicil*): only since the 1990s can this be claimed.

Article. De Valera was a prophet of 'community values' from whom Tony Blair has borrowed; he was a prophet of the Green Party, who echo his 'eco'. (Omitted *Codicil*): De Valera's arch-nationalism must be okay since he was these other post-modern things.

Some of this is provocative, some preposterous, some undoubtedly true. But Northern Ireland, Protestant Ulster, figures nowhere, though the Belfast *Agreement* is seen in one sentence as offering 'a postcolonialist version of overlapping identities'. The total absence of the industrial North in Kiberd's story of modernizing Ireland suggests to me that it is very difficult, if not impossible, even for sophisticated 'nationalist' commentators and critics to play host to my experience (as I – to be fair to myself – have played host to theirs). What is in operation is what we might call selective or exclusive pluralism. If McIreland does indeed come about, as a branch plant of McWorld, it is probable that there will be McNationalism too, of which Riverdance might be a precursor.

THE POETICS OF DESTINY

One of the ways in which one's identity can seem to be decisively out of one's hands is to feel that the direction of the times one lives in is already perceived to be concluded, foregone. One is required to inhabit the categories that support this perception because it needs as butts and culprits those who have provoked it. And so to the foregone conclusion story of Irish history one can feel as a unionist at best simply an observer, at worst a villain inside it. A guest, if you like, either tolerated or discouraged.

And so one could see a constitutional trajectory in the *Anglo-Irish Agreement* (1985), the *Downing Street Declaration* (1993), the *Framework Document* (1995) and the Good Friday (or Belfast) *Agreement* (1998). It is a trajectory arching away from London towards Dublin. Plotting this trajectory is something that united both fearful unionists and confident nationalists. The counter-coordinates, the concessions from the Republic contained in these documents, are real but objectively less worrisome to most Southern Irish people. The narrative silently contained in the trajectory is the familiar one: the firm will of the Irish nation to be itself once again, via the annual stepping-stones of 1798, 1803, 1848, 1916, 1922, 1972, 1985, 1993, 1995 and 1998. (One could insert in this list other stepping-stones, only the last one of which did not sink when stepped on: 1886, 1893, 1912 and 1920, i.e., the years of the Home Rule bills.) It is a teleological narrative of commemoration, reparation and consummation, the kind ordinarily frowned upon in the academy but permitted to the Irish even in the academy. Of the early 1920s, the historian J.C. Beckett wrote: 'To begin with, at least, it was on the conduct of affairs in the Irish Free State that future developments most obviously depended; for the government in Dublin was confident that the Six-County area would shortly be brought under its control; and even after these hopes had been disappointed, it continued to regard the extension of its own authority over the whole country as no more than a matter of time.'[20] Surely that is the position of successive Irish governments in our own time, though expressed with increasing guardedness. It is certainly the position of the formulators of the *Anglo-Irish Agreement*.

I came to consciousness in Northern Ireland in the appallingly stultifying atmosphere of Unionist Ulster; later, that was replaced by the remorselessness of Irish republicanism; two kinds of unhappiness, one shrunken and fast going, the other ever-present. To have one's identity under permanent sentence is a curious form of unhappiness I have yet to see explored. I have envied the Americans and the English for having escaped this peculiar chronic anxiety, a milder form of which afflicts Canadians too. (And though I am a Canadian also, I have not suffered the effects of the 'two solitudes' as deeply as a native-born Canadian.)

Unionist fears have to be put in the historical context of the widespread Irish belief in Irish exceptionalism, of Irish irredentism since the 1920s, and of the predestinarian element in Irish republicanism. Someone as political (i.e. interested in the art of possibility) as Charles Stewart Parnell spoke of wishing to come in sight of 'the Promised Land' when he addressed his party in Committee Room

No.15 and when he addressed an audience of supporters at the Rotunda in Dublin on 10 December 1890.[21] Patrick Pearse, of course, wrote in the *Proclamation of the Irish Republic* of the 'august destiny' to which Ireland was called in 1916, and even allowing for the understandable Henry V rhetoric of summons to arms, it is clear that Pearse believed that an Irish Republic was God's wish. Irish republican rhetoric – in song, verse and speech – has as common trope the idea of an Irish nation that once existed and that it is imperative to re-achieve. In this way the future *ideal* of a republic is justified by the past *reality* of, if not a Republic, then a nation unnaturally prevented from *being* a Republic. The future Republic will both *repeat* ('a nation once again') and *complete* history. The dream or reverie in Irish republican discourse can dissolve into the waking reality of political and military effort to live the resumed dream or reverie in the coming days.

Michael Collins knew, as he said, that 'No freedom when realised has quite the glory dreamed of by the captive',[22] but he acknowledged the legitimacy of the 'full republican ideal' and was hypocritically prepared to subvert the new *agreed* statelet of Northern Ireland to bring the ideal closer. And if he acknowledged the limited availability of Platonic Ireland, he justified the Anglo-Irish Treaty (and surely to himself and not merely to the anti-Treatyites) on Aristotelian grounds of almost certain development of the 26- county 'pupa' Free State into the 'imago' 32-county Republic.

It may be that the contemporary Sinn Fein/IRA has reluctantly followed constitutional nationalism by substituting an Aristotelian for a Platonic conception of a united Ireland. It is hard to tell, for the major manifestoes of Irish republicanism seem to have long since dried up.[23] This may be partly because of internal ideological divisions, chiefly between republican socialism and Catholic nationalism. Perhaps Sinn Fein/IRA is now post-ideological, leaving only momentum: power of some sort going on (to adapt Philip Larkin), 'if only that so many dead lie round'. But this may be a naïve inference. In any case, even if Platonic Ireland has been abandoned, an Aristotelian concept of the island maturing into a united Republic would allow contemporary Sinn Fein/IRA to add the dates of the recent documents I've mentioned to the stepping-stone dates I also mentioned, to continue the teleological narrative.

I have never heard unionists use the word 'ideal'; theirs instead is the rhetoric of resistance and reaction: stand-off or siege their necessary posture, their site of refusal the 'narrow ground'. They have been plagued by what we might call the 'Canute Complex'. Or, if you like, the 'Cuchulain Complex', which would be doubly, if ironically, apt: Cuchulain's Men of Ulster fight the Men of Ireland (and depicted doing so in an east Belfast loyalist mural) and Yeats's Cuchulain fights the ungovernable tide of history, fancifully here of Irish republicanism.

Bad as those Complexes are, unionists have also suffered what we might call chronic British appendicitis: the grumbling sense of endlessly being but an appendage of the British body politic, an irksome role and thankless condition but preferable, it seems, to the perceived alternative: finding themselves in the belly of the Irish whale. Nationalists, who have suffered from British appendicitis also, mostly in the past, recommended surgical removal. Of course, the behaviour of unionists over fifty years (like the behaviour of the British and Anglo-Irish in the South over centuries) has caused deformations and malformations in the Catholic and nationalist body politic as well, as though the Daru-like imprecation, 'a pox on both their houses' became a detectable pathology.

I have coined the phrase 'the poetics of destiny' as complement to Michael André Bernstein's fine phrase 'the prosaics of the quotidian', which he coins in opposition to what he calls apocalyptic history. Bernstein's formulations are courageous because he is writing about narrations of a past supreme in its painful challenge, the Holocaust.[24] Bernstein rejects historical inevitability as a theoretical model: he substitutes for apocalyptic history what he calls 'sideshadowing', which means 'learning to value the contingencies and multiple paths leading from each concrete moment of lived experience, and recognizing the importance of those moments not for their place in an already determined larger pattern but as significant in their own right' (pp.70–1). To do so is to avoid, among other errors, what the English historian E.P. Thompson famously called 'the enormous condescension of posterity'. It also enables us to escape what Conor Cruise O'Brien has called the 'ancestral voices' that in Ireland prophesy war self-fulfillingly.[25]

Among those to whom Irish exponents of apocalyptic history have condescended enormously (as though the culprits ought to have known how Irish twentieth-century history was going to turn out) are members of the Royal Irish Constabulary, Dublin Metropolitan Police, Irish volunteers in the British armed forces in two world wars (this is changing now, I'm glad to say), Redmondites and supporters of the Anglo-Irish Treaty, Irish scientists and engineers – and, of course, Irish (especially Ulster) Protestants. As Bernstein reminds us: 'a prosaics of the quotidian requires a willingness to remain receptive to the voices from the shadows in order to safeguard itself from becoming either a new kind of reductionism or a blind affirmationof whatever has triumphed sufficiently to flourish in the glare of actuality' (pp.7–8).

Bernstein points out the irony attendant on any Jewish attempt invidiously to grade pre-Nazi Jewishness and establish an ideal: 'It was Nazism that denied Jews any right to choose their identity or degree of communal affiliation, reducing all Jews to a single, undifferentiated category with one common destiny' (p.37). Has not an ideal of Irishness, and an ideal of Irish polity, fuelled Irish republicanism, South and North, and been used too often as a weapon of judgement? The other side has its fundamentalism too, of course, its allegations of betrayal, its normative idea of loyalism; but unionism by definition is other-directed as well as self-directed (it wishes to stay united with a larger entity), just as Sinn Fein by definition prides itself on its autonomy ('Ourselves!') and ideological endogamy. Sinn Fein/IRA embodies the notion of exceptionalism: it regards itself as above and beyond ordinary political discourse; any debate it enters into is purely for tactical purposes; there is really nothing to debate, after all, except the schedule and details of its inevitable victory.

The prosaics of the quotidian – how that phrase evokes James Joyce! – do not refer only to our 'daily pleasures and troubles' (as Bernstein puts it) for it is clear that, as he goes on to say, 'concern with one's ethnic identity, with the welfare of others in one's community, and with the nature of the political dispensation under which one lives, are themselves also local and personal matters' (p.71). But a genuine community of desire can arise only out of the shared aim and hopes of individuals; he decries the proposition of one novelist: 'Personal experience was simply not worthy of recall ... Suffering by itself did not merit attention – unless it served a collective purpose' (p.71). The mere rhetoric of victimization, which can become the pragmatic welcoming of victimhood, is to be avoided. It was Liam Kennedy who tongue-in-cheek identified the MOPE syndrome among the Irish – their belief that they are the Most Oppressed People Ever. He did so in order to satirize reflex rhetoric and implicitly to challenge the apocalyptic theory of history he sees espoused by Irish republicans. It is otherwise with real suffering: he himself has taken up the cause of those who have suffered as individuals and often been ignored or treated as embarrassments or inconveniences – those who have received so-called punishment beatings administered by the paramilitary groups.

'Sideshadowing' – a reading of history but also a reading of our experience, of our community – is alive to the contradictions, unusual mutualities and privacies of the past and, I would add, alive to emerging realignments, phenomena, eventualities – what were hitherto unforeseen and unforeseeable. Who in the first twenty years of the Troubles could have foreseen the vigour with which the South of Ireland has plunged into the European mainstream? Who could have foreseen the rise of popular western culture in Ireland to which traditional culture has had to respond by repackaging , reinventing and popularizing itself in like manner? Who could have predicted the growth of 'theme-Irishness' and its worldwide commodification? Who could have daydreamed such affluence, and foreseen Ireland's economic transformation and enthusiastic embrace of the electronic world? Who could have foreseen the loosening joints of the United Kingdom, to the point where a distinguished historian can write a history of 'the Isles' and omit the adjective 'British' not only because long history does not warrant it but also because he believes the imminent future does not warrant it either?[26] All's changing, but not changing 'utterly', i.e. apocalyptically. The old moulds are being broken (to borrow John Montague), but they still have power, and will have lingering effects.

HOSTS AND GUESTS

'Unforeseen' – 'the very word is like a bell to toll me back ... to my sole self'. I'm being factitious, but the sole self is where Frank O'Connor's great story, 'Guests of the Nation' comes to rest and it is a story in which this word 'unforeseen' plays a pivotal role. It is worth setting this story beside Camus', since in each the host becomes, ironically, the guest, a guest in his own house or nation. His identity is defined by a nationalist cause which apparently triumphs. The irony is even greater in O'Connor's story because the host-turned-guest is himself the nationalist, but in Camus the tribe is itself a guest (more like that of the Ulster Protestants) and therefore Daru's pain is the more complex.

The original title of the Camus story is 'L'Hôte'. This could be translated as 'The Host', which is how it is translated by Germaine Brée,[27] and Daru plays unwilling host to Balducci the gendarme and his captive, the unnamed Arab. In doing so, Daru is entertaining against his will the undeclared war between the French and their colonized subjects, the Algerians. The inhospitable and remote terrain in which Daru has chosen to live has been the landscape of a man's retreat and removal from his inherited past. As the story opens, it becomes for readers the allegorical simplicity of the colonial situation from which Daru cannot, ironically, distance or remove himself. It is also the stark landscape of dilemma: what should Daru do when Balducci delivers the Arab and tells Daru he in turn must deliver him to prison? Daru refuses but cannot refuse consignment of the dilemma, since he signs a receipt for his 'guest'.

Left in temporary custody of the Arab (that is, forced to take responsibility for his own identity and position as a French Algerian), Daru offers simple hospitality and extends the hand of fellowship but it is not taken. Daru is unvigilant and wishes for the prisoner to escape, but he doesn't; Daru's dilemma (to deliver the Arab to prison or not) remains his alone. He is joined to Balducci by citizenship, by race, by law. Yet he is joined to the Arab by joint habitation of this aboriginal landscape. He tries again to offload involvement and dilemma by delivering the Arab to a crossroads and granting him the liberty of choosing between prison and freedom. The Arab chooses prison presumably because to choose justice or conscience is somehow to lessen the dreadful freedom of choice and in turn makes prison perhaps preferable to the trackless free path towards friendly nomads. But the dilemma returns again to Daru, and this time resolved: on the blackboard is a chalked indictment and threat from the Arab's 'brothers' (ambiguously relatives or comrades). They must have thought Daru was taking their brother to prison, but anyway, even the Arab's *choice* of prison would be enough to condemn Daru. Irrespective of his intentions, his thoughts and actions, Daru is categorized as the enemy, a colonialist (a kind of hostage to the past); is it by mistake or misunderstanding, or by racial identity, ethnic politics?

But in truth, only in an abstract sense is Daru non-aligned. He tells Balducci that he is willing to fight the Arab Algerians should he have to, but he will not hand them over. His rejection of the moral authority of the French colonial authorities does not mean complicity with Algerians or even neutrality or pacifism. His abstract desire for freedom and justice is subverted by reality; *he cannot escape the categories*. Presumably Camus' depiction of this paralleled his real-life reversion to the tribe. Of the Algerian region, Camus writes: 'Daru had been born here. Everywhere else, he felt exiled.' It echoes what the Ulster poet John Hewitt wrote at the end of his poem 'The Colony', a poem apparently about the Roman Empire but surely about Ulster and Ulster Protestants:

> ... this is our country also, no-where else;
> and we shall not be outcast on the world.[28]

But Daru *is* outcast on the world. 'Daru looked at the sky, the plateau, and, beyond, the invisible lands stretching all the way to the sea. In this vast landscape he had loved so much, he was alone.' He achieves at the end, with some irony, non-alignment, but it is the non-alignment of loneliness. This is the loneliness of the individual but also the loneliness of his tribe, the French Algerians. 'L'Hôte' is usually translated as 'The Guest', and in a reversal of roles, Daru turns out to be the guest, the Arab the host: an unwanted guest, l'étranger who wishes estrangement upon himself, loses it, and ends with a greater, more dreadful estrangement than he wished for. He is both identified and categorized – as an enemy and a colonizer by the Arabs, as an unpatriotic citizen by the gendarme. He is consequently nullified, rejected by the landscape he thought was his but is really the natives'. Daru declares unilaterally a kind of independence, loses it, and ends up with a greater, more dreadful, independence than he wished for. The tribe has never been a comfort and became a prison, and now it is loneliness itself. In this way personal and political, individual and communal traffic. I do not believe Ulster Protestants ever found tribal comfort in themselves as the Irish did and that Protestant Ulsterness is a necessary butinsufficient and comfortless affiliation.

Daru's terminal sense of loneliness succeeds and subtends the 'daylight' brotherhood with Balducci (and France) and the 'night-time' brotherhood with the Arabs. The second is an imposed fraternity, a 'strange alliance ... in the ancient community of dream and fatigue', a kind of sleepwalking. It is such an alliance, I would venture, that Protestants and Catholics share in the countryside and in the working-class streets of Belfast. The Carletons and the Orange yeomen shared it that brutal evening, though the yeomen implicitly denied it. When we educated or urban revert to the tribe we share it too, though we feel lonely because we cannot successfully revert *or* escape.

One would like to think that the placards held up recently in the Catholic areas of Belfast for the parading Orangemen to see, reading 'Our Future, Not Your Past', referred to the future of multiparty agreement and cooperation. But one wonders if it wasn't a message from the Arabs' brothers. It wouldn't be surprising if it were: Catholics, like Algerian Arabs, were for half a century guests unwanted by many in Northern Ireland and it is proving hard to avoid payback time. In being so, they continued the status that William Wolfe Tone, Theobald Wolfe's son, referring to the 1790s, identified in 1828 in his edition of his father's autobiography: 'This wakening of the spirit of liberty, roused ... the oppressed and degraded Catholics; who, by a strange anomaly, forming the original population of the country and the mass of the people, were, at that period, and are still in some respects, aliens in their native land'.[29]

WRESTLING WOLFE TONE

Theobald Wolfe Tone is the host of the pilgrims of Irish republicanism. Like Daru he is the colonizer who refuses, but unlike Daru he does so actively by making common cause with the oppressed and breaking with his birth religion, the Established Church, and race, the Anglo-Irish.[30] More than common cause: he wished to lead them, enjoying, like later Anglo-Irish nationalists, the exotic thrill of spearheading *les autres.* For good or ill, Tone's greatest achievement, I assume, was his origination and prophecy, as Marianne Elliott puts it, of 'an ideology which continues to dictate the shape of Irish politics'.[31]

I have been grateful for the chance during this bicentenary of the 1798 rebellion to come to grips, if gingerly, with Tone, a figure who up to now has sat in my blind spot, who has not been visible in my rear-view mirror. Having read his *Life*, I see him as that recurring (usually Anglo-Irish, Anglican) figure who identifies with the 'Irish' but for mixed or obscure motives – the guest of the nation who decides to assume the role of host. But if the odious categories I have mentioned need to be transgressed, why does a transgressor like Tone still worry one?

Well, there are his famously strange proposals in the late 1780s and again in 1790 for a British military colony in the South Seas to thwart Spain. When the first was turned down, Tone, he tells us in 1796 from France, 'made something like a vow, that, if ever I had an opportunity, I would make Mr. Pitt sorry, *and perhaps fortune may yet enable me to fulfil that resolution*'.[32] He guilelessly recalls himself in 'a transport of rage'. Although it was turned down a second time, Tone as late as 1796 describes it as 'a measure which I still think might be attended with the most beneficial consequences to England' (p.44). Yet six months before, he purports to 'abhor and detest the very name of England'. It occurred to me, while reading the *Life*, that this might be the sort of man who would conjure a rebellion and invent an ideology in order to secure private revenge. Might that explain why he is long on plans for separatism and short on plans for post-separatist peace and administration?

I am reminded that Swift too suffered a deep disappointment (that of preferment in England) and became an Irish patriot in a way that can be called a result. Presumably revenge patriotism is an understandable condition of thought.

In his two celebrated separatist passages in the *Life*, the eloquence of vision and nobility of intention seem to be empowered by the demonization of England – 'the radical vice of our government', 'the never-failing source of our political evils' (pp.39, 62). Transport and hyperbole are a feature of many of Tone's pronouncements and this indicates to me an unstable relationship between political plan and personal determination. I wondered if the intensity and hyperbole derive from Swift, verging on unintended satire and therefore without the purpose of satire. In his *Argument on Behalf of the Catholics of Ireland* (1791), Tone writes: 'Religious intolerance and political bigotry, like the tyrant Mezentius, bind the living Protestant to the dead and half corrupted Catholic, and beneath the putrid mass, even the embryo of effort is stifled'.[33] Even allowing for the fever of pamphletese, this seems to me a kind of delirium.

Tone's misunderstanding of the Dissenter mind similarly suggests to me that he was on the outside looking in, and looking in with a hint of ideological prurience. He might have been right to think that the differences between Catholic and Dissenter flourished in times of adversity, but was surely in error to think that bad times therefore *caused* the differences. He was also wrong, surely, in believing that the Dissenter is exclusively patriotic and anti-English rather than (now as then) inclusively Irish and British. Probably wrong, too, to think that denomination was paramount among the differences and that racial or ethnic self-perceptions were of no account.

Was there not an element of reversion in his compromise with the Irish government over the Jackson affair[34] and his disclaimer at his trial that he wasn't in Ireland when atrocities occurred and therefore couldn't be held responsible? Beside his disclaimer and his weak expression of 'regret' we might set down what *did* happen: according to Roy Foster, 'The 1798 rising was probably the most concentrated episode of violence in Irish history. Mass atrocities were perpetrated in circumstances of chaos and confusion ... By the end of the summer, the death-roll on both sides, from various causes, has been estimated at 30,000.'[35]

The Tone of the *Life* is a likeable fellow – daring, cavalier, clever. I like to think I would have been a United Irishman too, at least before the oathbound departure from reform. Tone's vanity is entertaining but in the end worrying. In his journal entry for 24 February 1796 he writes in lightly mocking self-congratulation: 'I am a pretty fellow to negotiate with the directory of France, pull down a monarchy and establish a republic; to break a connexion of 600 years standing, and contract a fresh alliance with another country' (p.147). I wondered if he felt more keenly the blow to his vanity than the threat to his life when he was not treated as a prisoner of war, an Adjutant-General in the French military, though he tried to make amends by appearing at his trial in full ceremonial French uniform: cocked hat, cockade, pantaloons, laced garters. He seems lonely to me at the end – he wouldn't see his family, insulated in his own dream of rank, gallantry and sacrifice.

The dream of 1798 has been recorded by modern historians as a series of errors, disappointments and follies. I will not tally them but they can be found listed and discussed in the pages of Roy Foster, A.T.Q. Stewart and Conor Cruise O'Brien. This does not in any way compromise the original intention to right wrongs and relieve the bulk of the Irish of impositions and injustices. But the unrealities that inspired the rising were matched by Tone's own increasing loss of realism. Elliott writes:

> In France he had become increasingly detached, a pure, uncompromising conscience rising above the unpleasant realities of republicanism in operation. The same notions of honour and dignity he brought to his role as French officer, and he could compartmentalize his life sufficiently to see that role as separate (and increasingly so) from that of a United Irishman. When confronted with the word 'traitorously' at his trial some weeks later, he was taken aback.[36]

This makes him sound like Camus' just and unconnected man. Or perhaps he was starring in his own melodrama that he had written, but with a quite different ending. I think that at his trial he sat as a guest of the nation, knew it, and took his leave.

It was the private melodrama that was adopted and made public, in the process becoming the romantic legend that Elliott refers to. He represented that 'delirium of the brave' Yeats ambivalently honoured in 'September 1913', and it is a sad irony that during his last hours (Elliott believes) he was literally delirious and most certainly in his own fashion brave.

GUESTS AND THE NATION

The French connection reappears in Frank O'Connor's masterly 1931 story, 'Guests of the Nation', a short story set during the guerrilla war against the British 1919–20; one wonders if Camus read it before writing 'The Guest'. (Neil Jordan certainly did before making *The Crying Game* as he did Brendan Behan's play *The Hostage*.[37]) The narrator, one of the Irish captors of the two English soldiers, bears the name Bonaparte, though he is no ideological or sartorial dandy, but a simple man with a loose grip on English grammar, yet observant, good-hearted, a foot-soldier in this war and this life.

The story is the more chilling for recreating the domestic circumstances in which the soldiers are held – the hearth, games of cards, banter and fellowship, all presided over by the aged woman of the house, 'a queer old girl, all right', remarks Bonaparte, and so she proves.[38] It is wilfully 'unforeseen' of the author (to use a key word in the story, and meaning in one sense 'inconsiderate') not to warn the reader that a lethal brutality lies behind the camaraderie, that these household gods are sponsors of death. For at first the reader enjoys the ways in which the deadly wartime distinction between *English* and *Irish* is undermined and transgressed by 'unforeseen' permutations of lifestyle (rural and urban), temperament and manner, political persuasion, religious belief.

Treated like guests, the soldiers, it transpires, are hostages; Bonaparte's early description of them as 'our guests, as I may call them' is in retrospect a grim ironic euphemism. Fellowship and wartime duty cannot coexist, it turns out; the hard man Jeremiah Donovan (echoes of the Irish-American republican Jeremiah O'Donovan Rossa) has been 'unforeseen' (in both senses) in allowing friendship to develop among the group, but unlike the narrator he has been inured against fellowship by his hatred of the English (which Bonaparte sees naïvely as mere dislike). For Donovan, the English clearly are unwanted guests in Ireland: as the story progresses the allegory and history assert themselves against the domestic minutiae and affective experience (the prosaics of the quotidian).

Irony is the signal that the openness of event and experience is foreclosed by a history waiting to happen, and therefore allegorical. On a second reading of the story, when we know that the soldiers will be shot and buried hugger-mugger, the early warmth is chilled by double intention. At the start of the story, Bonaparte remembers:

> I couldn't at the time see the point of me and Noble guarding Belcher and Hawkins at all, for it was my belief that you could have planted that pair down anywhere from this to Claregalway and they'd have taken root there like a native weed. I never in my short experience seen two men take to the country as they did.

Take to the country they will – at the edge of a bog after being shot in reprisal. In the early domestic scenes, Belcher walks in and out 'like a ghost'. The old woman is confusable with the Shan Van Vocht or Cathleen ni Houlihan, and her prayers at the end seem in part like national contrition (that such deaths are necessary), in part like religion's prurient complicity in the whole masquerade of death. She may be an even queerer figure, a representative of the hidden and unforeseen powers that mysteriously govern our lives, but if so that is O'Connor's return of the unforeseen to the realm of the metaphysical. Incidentally, if as Ulsterman I find myself identifying with the English soldiers, with the dubious guests of the nation, and not at all with the IRA men (save for, perhaps, Bonaparte), I don't know if O'Connor would have been bothered.

But the story is not just Irish history and allegory; it gestures towards the universally human. Bonaparte is the agent of the story's universality. Like Daru, he has been given prisoners to guard; and like Daru this is, when it becomes clear they are to be punished, against his will. Like Daru, he wishes the prisoners would escape and let him off the hook. But unlike Daru he follows orders; it is only the glimmer of a moral dilemma that confronts Bonaparte, fitting perhaps the case of a simple man.

Yet the end of the story anticipates the end of Camus' 'The Guest': Bonaparte has an indescribable feeling after the executions and burials,

> as if the patch of bog where the Englishmen were was a million miles away, and even Noble and the old woman, mumbling behind me, and the birds and the bloody stars were also far away, and I was somehow very small and very lost and lonely like a child astray in the snow. And anything that happened me afterwards, I never felt the same about again.[39]

Life has proven 'unforeseen'; Bonaparte is a guest in his own nation, detached surely from the cause. It would be too clever to say that the story's final irony is that the soldiers have gone native and changed places with their captors. But the narrator's name lends a 'Tonal' unreality to the story; it is an unreality – that strange and estranging combination of deadly earnestness and surreal game – that I have always thought the Irish 'struggle' to be.[40] The real final irony, since irony is dislocation, is the turning of us all into guests – at our own lives, at our country's most intimate, conspiring and lethal fellowship, at our own deaths and burials.

Bonaparte's loneliness and desolation must have been duplicated hundreds of time in the last thirty years, but it is rarely if ever recorded: the real Bonapartes of Ireland rarely write their own stories to warn us, while the Donovans are praised and commemorated, reprehensibly guests in our own degraded imaginations.

There is nothing we can do about the existential loneliness, about being and nothingness. But there is something we can do about the historical and political causes of that loneliness. The recurring venue for these guests I have discussed is 'the nation'. All I can suggest is that we cast a cold eye on it and try instead to make a house of this island in which we can all feel welcome and at home.

NOTES

1. Under a different title, this essay began as a plenary lecture to the International Association for the Study of Irish Literatures, University of Limerick, July 1998. Its perspective is that of 1998 although I revised the essay in 2003.
2. Edmund Curtis, *A History of Ireland* (London: Methuen, 1950), pp.336–7.
3. Public Record Office of Northern Ireland, Education Facsimile 66 ('United Irishmen').
4. William Carleton, *The Autobiography* (Belfast: White Row Press, 1996), p.37. This volume is a version of the 1896 two-volume *Life of William Carleton*, ed. D.J. O'Donoghue.
5. This and other quotations from Camus' story (originally published in volume form in 1957) are from *Exile and the Kingdom*, trans. Justin O'Brien (London: Penguin, 1962).
6. A.T.Q. Stewart, *The Narrow Ground: Patterns of Ulster History* (Belfast: Pretani Press, 1986; facsimile ed. of 1977 Faber edn), p.101.
7. E.M. Forster, *Howards End* (Harmondsworth: Penguin, 1941), p.44.
8. Conor Cruise O'Brien, *Camus* (London: Fontana), 1970), pp.21, 23.
9. Albert Memmi, *The Colonizer and the Colonized*, trans. Howard Greenfield (London: Earthscan, 1990), pp.85ff.
10. See Graham Good, *Humanism Betrayed: Theory, Ideology, and Culture in the Contemporary University* (Montreal-Kingston: McGill-Queen's University Press, 2001).
11. Ten years on, the Agreement has not been wholly or satisfactorily implemented, and deep ideological differences lie underfoot beneath the procedural wrangling (2008).
12. This reference turned out not to be tongue-in-cheek at all, though it might have been included with rolled eyes. Northern Ireland Assembly documents are translated into Ulster-Scots as well as Gaelic, but there is a good deal of amused scepticism about this 'language', even on the part of unionists; the amusement it causes may be a kind of petard on which earnest unionists are hoist (2008).
13. Máiréad Nic Craith, a lecturer at the Academy of Irish Cultural Heritages (University of Ulster) has made an interesting distinction: unionists, she says, are more interested in citizenship, nationalists in culture (research project proposal: see www.arts.ulst.ac.uk/academy/) (2003).
14. As it turned out, the Unionist party surprisingly chose the Culture portfolio in the first Northern Ireland Assembly (2003).
15. Liam Kennedy and Kerby A. Miller, '"The Long Retreat": Protestants, Economy and Society 1660–1926', in R. Gillespie and G. Moran (eds), *Longford: Essays in County History* (Dublin: Lilliput Press, 1991), pp.31–61.
16. Actually, the cry of 'Brits Out!' is heard more rarely in the land than it was even in 1998. This I take as a sign of progress. It was as retrogressive and stupid an exclamatory imperative as 'Taigs Out!' The difference between Algeria and Northern Ireland would not be in the length of time Protestants have been in Ulster or the changing nature of the political structures there between the early seventeenth century and the present – or rather it would not reside in these exclusively – but in the cultural resemblances between Catholic and Protestant Ulster people which undermine a colonialist–native binary division, official preoccupation with sectarian affiliation to the contrary. Both communities share a British-Irish culture. See Hugh Roberts, *Northern Ireland and the Algerian Analogy: Suitable Case for Gaullism?* (Belfast: Athol Books, 2003 [1986]).
17. Benjamin R. Barber, 'Jihad vs McWorld', *Atlantic Monthly* (March 1992), revised as *Jihad vs McWorld* (New York: Times Books, 1995).
18. Roy Foster is one of these. He has written a book about this story, trying by doing so to unravel it: *The Irish Story: Telling Tales and Making It Up in Ireland* (London: Allen Lane, 2001). But unlike other sophisticated revisionists, including Richard Kearney and Declan Kiberd, Foster does not revert at important junctures to an old nationalism in new bottles.
19. Declan Kiberd, 'Romantic Ireland's Dead and Gone', *Times Literary Supplement*, 12 June 1998, pp.12–14.

20. J.C. Beckett, *The Anglo-Irish Tradition* (Belfast: Blackstaff Press, 1983), pp.150–1.
21. *The New York Times*, 10 December 1890.
22. Collins, 'Arguments for the Treaty' (1922), Searc's Web Guide to 20th Century Ireland: http://www.searcs-web.com/collins.html. Collins spoke of the 'full republican ideal' in 'Clearing the Road' (1922): see Historical Publications & Reports in http://www.generalmichaelcollins.com.
23. The last one appeared in 1973.
24. Michael André Bernstein, *Foregone Conclusions: Against Apocalyptic History* (Berkeley, CA: University of California Press, 1994).
25. Conor Cruise O'Brien, *Ancestral Voices: Religion and Nationalism in Ireland* (Dublin: Poolbeg, 1994).
26. Norman Davies, *The Isles: A History* (Oxford: Oxford University Press, 1999).
27. Germaine Brée, *Albert Camus* (New York: Columbia University Press, 1964).
28. 'The Colony' appears in John Hewitt's *Collected Poems 1932–1967* (London: MacGibbon and Kee, 1968).
29. Theobald Wolfe Tone, *The Life of Theobald Wolfe Tone*, ed. William Theobald Wolfe Tone (London: Hunt and Clarke, 1828), p.7.
30. Curtis tells us that the Trinity College-educated Tone was 'born in the Established Church' but like many of the advanced of the time adopted Deism (Curtis, *A History of Ireland*, p.330). Owen Dudley Edwards tells me (pers. comm.) Tone's mother was Roman Catholic, which the handful of historians I consulted does not mention. In Ireland of course one deals often with cultural upbringing rather than heredity; and in any case professed religion and apparent ethnicity are frequently out of alignment.
31. Marianne Elliott, *Wolfe Tone: Prophet of Irish Independence* (New Haven, CT and London: Yale University Press, 1989), p.419.
32. Tone, *The Life*, pp.32–3 (my emphasis).
33. In John Killen (ed.), *The Decade of the United Irishmen: Contemporary Accounts 1791–1801* (Belfast: Blackstaff Press, 1997), p.19.
34. Tone, *The Life*, pp.101–16.
35. Roy Foster, *Modern Ireland 1600–1972* (London: Penguin, 1989), p.280.
36. Elliott, *Wolfe Tone*, p.392.
37. Neil Jordan in his Introduction to *The Crying Game* cites both *The Hostage* and 'Guests of the Nation' (which he mistakenly calls 'Guest of the Nation'): *The Crying Game* (London: Vintage Books, 1993), p.viii.
38. I am using the version of the story in Frank O'Connor (ed.), *Classic Irish Short Stories* (Oxford: Oxford University Press, 1985), pp.172–87.
39. If he didn't feel the same about anything in the future 'again' this must mean that it was familiar experiences that were never the same again; the prosaics of the quotidian were subsumed in the poetics of destiny, something Bonaparte could hardly begin to understand, but which – one hopes – O'Connor believes is at best tragic, at worst tyrannical.
40. Although it is of course an allusion (and as the credits roll, a reference) to a pop song, the title of Jordan's film, *The Crying Game*, shares this sense of a lethal duality; it is signalled too in Dominic Behan's ambiguous song, *The Patriot Game*.

13

GETTING THE NORTH: YEATS AND NORTHERN NATIONALISM

YEATS AND ORANGE ULSTER

Strands in Yeats's background might lead a beginner student to suppose his broad sympathy with the people and culture of the North of Ireland. After all, until two generations before the poet's birth, his English forebears had included merchants, and the North had always been busily mercantile. After 1800 those forebears had also been demonstratively Protestant, with several ancestors Church of Ireland ministers, one a rector in County Down, where his father, John Butler Yeats, was born. (The poet himself was born into the Church of Ireland.) The North had always been predominantly Protestant in numbers and ruling ethos. The poet's mother was a Pollexfen, a member of a mercantile family in the north-west county of Sligo who were loyal Protestants, active Freemasons, suspicious of Roman Catholics and Irish nationalists. In short, here is a family history that in its cultural components many Irish unionists shared and many Northern unionists still share.[1]

In his boyhood and early youth, Yeats was faithful to the blueprint. He later remembered wanting as a boy to die fighting for the Orangemen against the Fenians. Yeats's later recurrent imagining of Cuchulain's death while fighting for the Men of Ulster against the Men of Ireland was an odd transposition of the boyhood fantasy, both a version of it and an inversion of it. (Cuchulain as an Ulster champion has recently appealed to hardline loyalists in Northern Ireland, to which a gable mural in east Belfast testifies; but of course Yeats was to identify the mythic figure with Patrick Pearse and Irish republicanism.) And as a youth, the poet displayed a passion in Sligo for the collection and study of Lepidoptera (*WBY*, pp.28, 32–3, 35). He might, it would have seemed, have gone on to emulate one of those nineteenth-century Protestant clergyman-naturalists, or even become a Robert Lloyd Praeger, that younger contemporary who became the island's leading naturalist though only one among a veritable swarm of Northern scientific students of Nature.

However, not only did the maturing Yeats discard the blueprint (though not as decisively as is sometimes thought, a point upon which contemporary Northern nationalists and I agree), but the blueprint was in fact partitionist in its tendency. The latter is a claim that Northern nationalists have not as far as I know advanced, since for them unionism is unionism and can be partitionist only from the direction of the North, not from the direction of the South, from which direction Yeats felt and spoke. Nor are they likely to admit that Yeats's nationalism grew out of his Southern unionist background, like Standish James O'Grady's, Lady Gregory's and Douglas Hyde's; normally it would have been against the grain of that background, but under the conditions of the time cultural nationalism was the natural, indeed illegitimate progeny of unionism. Nor are they likely to agree that his was an identifiable species of Irish nationalism – of an articulate, forceful, executive kind – one that Pearse at first repudiated and then shrewdly made common cause with. Nor that there is a partitionist strain in the Southern Irish nationalism that triumphed against Britain in 1920, be it Yeats's or Eamon De Valera's, Pearse's or Hyde's.

Yeats's grandfather William Butler Yeats, the rector in County Down, disliked Presbyterians, Hone tells us, 'and could never come to an understanding with the aggressive North, because his Evangelicalism belonged to the cultivated classes' (*WBY*, pp.5–6). Social class and religious denomination would have early instilled in Yeats a distaste for the bulk of his co-religionists in what in his lifetime became Northern Ireland. When young George Russell (Æ) visited the Yeats household in Dublin, John Butler 'was a little critical of this friendship, for he detected in Russell, already spoken of as the religious leader of the future, the ethical complacency of the Ulster Protestant. "A saint but raised in Portadown", he would say' (*WBY*, p.46).

So Yeats inherited his distaste for religious Dissent (especially Presbyterianism), and would have likewise inherited a distaste for industry, the factory city, the labouring class and the clerical workforce, all of which contributed to the regional distinctiveness of the North of Ireland. To explain Yeats's finding of Northern Protestants 'alien' in terms of a 'mutual incomprehensibility between northern and southern Protestants' – as Edna Longley has recently done – is perhaps to posit an equality of respect between these two Protestantisms which Southern Protestants would have rejected, and still do reject.[2] Quite early, of course, Yeats's inherited prejudices and inclinations played their parts in the poet's developing and ever more complex philosophy and poetic. Some of them were overturned; thus science, especially the scientific study of Nature, was banished, and Protestantism disavowed. However, if the repudiated science found its counterpart in the mystical pseudo-science of *A Vision*, Hone (and

Maud Gonne) were surely right in seeing Yeats's enthusiasm for secret societies – from hermetic orders to republican brotherhoods – as a transposition of the Pollexfenian Freemasonry (*WBY*, pp.29, 47, 85–6). In like manner, Ulster for Yeats was chiefly the embodied opportunity for both rebellion against the ancestors and a disguised expression of ancestral attitude.

Before the Yeatsian system generated its own momentum, there would have been an element of pleasurable shock value in the youthful inversions. An even more graphic example than Yeats's is the career of Charlie Johnston who was the son of the 'staunch' (as they say) Unionist Westminster MP for South Belfast – celebrated throughout the pro-Union North as 'Johnston of Ballykilbeg' (his memory was green for my grandmother and her true-blue Unionist cohorts in Belfast even as late as the 1950s). Johnston *fils* was a fellow pupil with Yeats at the High School (Dublin), who was converted to Buddhism, interested Yeats in the subject and started with the poet a hermetic society. He travelled to London to interview Madame Blavatsky in 1886. (This was the year of the first Home Rule Bill and of the potent symbolic expression of future Ulster resistance, when Lord Randolph Churchill rhymed, 'Ulster will fight, and Ulster will be right' – which political situation young Johnston was clearly fleeing.) He married the great woman's niece (Yeats remarked with amusement: 'If you only heard madame Blavatsky trying to pronounce Ballykilbeg', *CL*, Vol.1, p.101), later gave Yeats introductions to the London theosophists, and later still wrote tirelessly for American magazines in the furtherance of mystical Irish nationalism (*WBY*, pp.47, 49, 69; *LTWBY*, p.26). Here was Orange Ulster (as Yeats called it) upended indeed, and by a son of one of its most illustrious embodiments. Whether this was, as I suspect, a case of a son's rebellion against a respected father might only be determined by a biography of this remarkable but little-known figure, a biography that would necessarily engage with many of the chief components of the Irish scene at a crucial time in the island's history.

Yeats spent a week in July 1891 at Ballykilbeg, County Down, visiting the Johnstons. He relished the notion of being in alien country, not just because it was Orange Order territory but also because it was Ulster-Scots territory. He recalled later: 'I left Dublin next day to stay somewhere in Orange Ulster with the brilliant student of my old Dublin school, Charles Johnston.' ('Somewhere' is characteristically Yeats: the grand general threat of the place occluding its particular location.) After the visit, he reported: 'I have been away in County Down, looking almost in vain among its half-Scotch people for the legends I find so plentiful in the West'. He was to recall another visit to the North as 'an expedition into Ulster', as though Ulster were like the wilds of Connemara or Kerry (*Mem*, p.45; *LNI*, p.53).

At this time Yeats clearly thought that through Ulster – the birthplace not just of Cuchulain in antiquity but of Sir Samuel Ferguson and William Carleton in modern times – coursed 'that wild Celtic blood' the poet claimed in 1892 (in a letter to *United Ireland*) coursed through his own veins (*UP*, Vol.1, p.256). Ferguson's work was praised by Yeats in 1886 for its 'barbarous truth' and the poet described as 'the greatest poet Ireland has produced, because the most central and most Celtic', Ferguson's Protestantism and unionism swept aside as irrelevant (*UP*, Vol.1, pp.87, 103). Yeats wished Ulster to mean an inspired peasant Carleton and an aristocratic Ferguson in the real world, and Cuchulain in the unreal world, a place that had produced the figures that mattered most to Yeats: peasant, artist, aristocrat and hero.

But such a view of modern Ulster could not be sustained in the real world and Yeats gave up on the North as a bad job. Scots Ulster, Presbyterian Ulster, became indeed a kind of antithetical cultural self. In 1895 he thanked Sarah Purser for an embroidered 'book cover [which] is at this moment helping to civilize a novel all about North of Ireland presbeterians [*sic*] & succeeding as well as could be expected under the circumstances' (*CL*, Vol.1, p.474). Yeats did not invent his abstract portrait of Protestant Ulster: Daniel O'Connell before him, and many a celebrated Southerner after him, found the place galling, refractory. Those beliefs, values, modes of thought, bodies of expression to which Yeats became converted – Irish nationalism, Celticism, mysticism, folklore, nationality of literature – largely and perforce excluded Ulster. Of course, even for Yeats these were beset (Yeats might have said enriched) by ambiguities and contradictions, but in the midst of all 'the North' remained a simple and uncongenial place. There were attempts to make contact, going there to help start a branch of the Irish Literary Society, or joining Maud Gonne on one of her errands of political mischief (*Mem*, pp.58, 59, 131), but they were half-hearted or inappropriate: lecturing to the Belfast Naturalists' Field Club in 1892 on fairies, for example.[3] (It's an entertaining talk, almost a parody of biological systematics, but what must the amateur scientists have thought?) It became clear that as far as Yeats was concerned, any involvement of the Northern Irish in his Revival meant their self-transformation in order to satisfy the requirements of the Revival, and it is a measure of the magnetism of Yeats and the Revival that certain Ulster writers changed their names and went, figuratively but usually literally too, to Dublin: Samuel

Waddell remade himself as Rutherford Mayne, Alice Milligan (on occasion) as Iris Olkryn, Anna Johnston as Ethna Carbery, George Russell as Æ, Harry Morrow as Gerald MacNamara, Joseph Campbell as Seosamh Mac Cathmhaoil.

There was in Belfast a radical tradition that might have been congenial to Yeats. Charles Gavan Duffy had edited the *Belfast Vindicator*, an O'Connellite organ, and he had also founded with John Dillon and Thomas Davis the *Nation*, an anti-Union paper, the management of which he handed over to John Mitchel, an Ulster Presbyterian nationalist (*CL*, Vol.1, p.483). But this tradition did not much engage Yeats. Nor was he much exercised by the partition of Ireland as far as I can tell, having been engrossed by the War of Independence (as it came to be called) and about to be engrossed by the imminent Irish Civil War. On 17 October 1924, after the dust settled on the island, he did speak wisely in the Irish Senate on the subject of Northern Ireland when he said, 'I have no hope of seeing Ireland united in my time, or of seeing Ulster won in my time; but I believe it will be won in the end, and not because we fight it, but because we govern this country well. We can do that, if I may be permitted as an artist and writer to say so, by creating a system of culture which will represent the whole of this country' (*SS*, p.87). This was perhaps too much to expect from an overwhelmingly Catholic country celebrating its cultural as well as political independence by enshrining in law its differences from Britain (and therefore Northern Ireland), but Yeats knew that if it was too much, then the claim to Ulster should be dropped.

However, I cannot think Yeats was entirely ingenuous in the matter of Northern Ireland, which I believe was a pretext by which he could doubly defend Protestants in the new Free State. In 1925 he made his celebrated Senate speech accusing the new state of infringing upon Protestant freedoms in preparing to pass anti-divorce legislation. But his noble and often quoted defence of Irish Protestants as a racial stock with a great cultural tradition was not intended to include Ulster's Protestants, who in his eyes were decidedly *not* the people of Burke, Grattan, Swift and Parnell. In fact, they were beneath his notice. His warning that by passing Catholic legislation the Free State would never 'get the North' (a phrase he repeats) seems not to challenge, rather to express, an irredentism that culminated in the territorial claim in the 1937 Constitution of the Irish Republic (*SS*, p.92). It may be that Yeats was tactically affecting the language of irredentism, hoping to appeal to that sentiment in order to sabotage legislation bearing directly upon Southern Protestants.

Either way, the North in Yeats never materializes. In his brief retrospective, 'Ireland, 1921–1931', published in the *Spectator* of 30 January 1932, Northern Ireland is never mentioned. The article contains some expression of regret that he had once seen nothing in Protestant Ireland but its faults, but the Protestant Ireland that he rehabilitates is strictly Ascendancy Ireland, and he declines to turn his gaze north (*UP*, Vol.2, pp.486–90). In the late 1930s, when the IRA staged an anti-partition campaign, Maud Gonne sought his support for it. Yeats told her that, in the words of Hone, 'he found the inhabitants of the lost province of Ulster so disagreeable that he hoped they would never reunite with the rest of Ireland' (*WBY*, p.469). After all, he felt (as Hyde did) that the Protestant north-east ruptured the continuity of Irishism and made impossible that 'unity of culture' he hopefully refers to in his *Vision* papers: 'When people have unity of culture the transference of thought & image goes through the whole people. In the past pure races have been made by blood, but bloods are now so mixed that in the future they will have to be made by culture' (*YVP*, Vol.3, p.63). The political unity of an Ireland sundered from Britain would have been an ideal expression of that unity of culture and might have permitted or facilitated that 'unity of self' and 'Unity of Being' he also extolled during his preparation for *A Vision* (*YVP*, Vol.3, p.27). The disobliging reality of Ulster has pained and irritated more Irish figures than Hyde and Yeats who persist to this day in seeing reality as a despotism to be overthrown; or if they concede that the despotism is not removable, they simply eclipse it from their minds.

THE YEATS QUESTION

Until recently, there were no identifiable Northern attitudes to Yeats, his life, art and thought, with the exception of Patrick Kavanagh's. Æ, Forrest Reid and St John Ervine were all Ulstermen, but because Yeats's national politics were not admitted as an issue, they wrote about him from no regional or sectional point of view. Like Louis MacNeice in the following generation, they assumed an all-Ireland perspective which freed them to respond in appreciative or explicatory modes, the poetry and plays in the forefront of their attention.

What added a new note to the critical reception of Yeats in Ireland was the coming to maturity of the first generation of Roman Catholics in Northern Ireland to receive higher education courtesy of the Butler Education Act (GB, 1944, extended to Northern Ireland in 1947). It may have been their distrust of Protestants, because of their early experience in Ulster and their later experience of the Troubles from 1969 onwards, which caused them to look askance at the nationalist credentials of a Protestant from the South. Whereas those who see in Northern unionists the chief obstacle to a desired island unity ought to be gratified by Yeats's disregard for Northern unionists, I do not recall ever hearing such gratification expressed. Rather, the chief issue has been how far Yeats was a real nationalist and how far he truly escaped his Protestant, unionist background. Given Yeats's received stature as a culture-giver to the new, mostly Catholic Ireland, this is ironic. There is also irony in the fact that whereas Yeats rather ignored the North because of his dislike of Protestant unionists, a cold (that is, scrutinizing) eye has been cast on him by the other Northerners whom he abandoned as readily as did the new Free State – those from the community of what we might loosely call Catholic nationalists. Now he is 'getting the North' in a way that must astonish his shade.

The local pressures operating on readers in Northern Ireland in the past quarter-century have been augmented by the pressures operating on literary critics generally, especially those in British and American universities. Such pressures, issuing from fashionable feminist and post-colonialist readings, have resulted in the 'interrogation' of major figures, especially from ideological perspectives unlikely to be congenial to a male writer who wrote what can be construed as Romantic work while being prominently and in the end notoriously involved politically and whose nationality was not of an unalloyed minority kind. Only Yeats's claim to Irishness and a presumed continuity of sorts between his Irish nationalism and contemporary Sinn Fein/IRA have, I suspect, prevented him in the current chilly Anglo-American critical climate from being ideologically arraigned more than he has been. (Anglo-American humanities students have a sentimental attraction to the glamour of Irish 'revolutionaries'.)

An Irish university teacher such as Seamus Deane inhabits that climate, though he knows when it is not applicable to Ireland: knows the difference, for example, between Yeats and the IRA. Given the chance by Northern nationalism (in the guise of the Field Day Theatre Company, of which Deane is the guiding light) to gauge the political direction of Yeats's work, Edward Said (whose knowledge of Ireland is admittedly modest) must have surprised the editors by analyzing Yeats as 'a poet of decolonization' (i.e., a poet who furthered the cause of decolonization), when he might have been expected to follow its own lead and seen through the poet's nationalism; the consolation must have been that Said trounced imperialism and colonialism and therefore by indirection (it could be imagined) British policy in Northern Ireland.[4] More congenial to Field Day would have been recent remarks on Yeats by Terry Eagleton, another Field Day guest pamphleteer: 'In seeking to replace the detestable abstractions of politics ... with the connections of myth and image, he seems unaware that this is just another form of politics – that a conservative politics is usually one which denies the very category of the political itself'.[5]

There has been fallout from Northern Ireland in the rest of the island too. Perhaps a truer sense of where the Irish think Yeats stands on the 'National Question' can be achieved through a kind of critical 'triangulation', to borrow a concept from surveying. I am aware that the three perspectives I am about to list might remind Irish readers of the three Irelands that F.S.L. Lyons identifies in his controversial book, *Culture and Anarchy in Ireland* (1979), but it is no surprise either that Lyons's three Irelands should have generated their own critical perspectives or that those perspectives should be apparent in Yeats Studies in Ireland. Yeats's career coincided with great and terrible events in the life of Ireland – rebellion, secession, division of the island in two, civil war, enduring suspicion between the two reconstituted Irelands – and his voice sent its echoes into the future to trouble the ears of those struggling to understand and help solve the problem of Northern Ireland. More than any other Irish writer in history, Yeats, his art and thought, has become a *locus* as well as a focus, an *arena* as well as a field of study.

From our first of three 'stations', one might see in the responses to Yeats of Edna Longley, Roy Foster and Terence Brown a family resemblance, though these three critics are individualistic, subtle and of mixed background. In their reading, Yeats is unambiguously Irish and benignly nationalist, and their painstaking historical revisionism would defend him against a sectarian and excluding nationalism. From our second 'station', one might see a second perspective and it would be my own; in this perspective Yeats is both a cultural nationalist and a literary unionist, at first promoting extra-constitutional nationalism in the mistaken belief that it could be contained by the literati, then retreating from hard nationalism when it proved its sectarian and recalcitrant insularity and philistinism; all the while he partitioned off Ulster yet helped to create the climate of attitudes and feelings in which hard nationalists have waged unrelenting war against it. Conor Cruise O'Brien represents a less exonerative anti-nationalism (without becoming explicit unionism, leaving breathing-space for moderate nationalism), whereby Yeats's mystical nationalism led him into a deplorable fascist enthusiasm.[6] The third perspective is that of a more importunate but often disguised nationalism and it is this perspective to which I devote the rest of this chapter. We find it graphically but not exclusively articulated by literary critics of Northern Catholic background. In this perspective Yeats (the merit of his poetry bracketed off) is a literary unionist but not an authentic cultural nationalist, nor even a literary unionist who unwittingly promoted the cause of authentic nationalism.

Patrick Kavanagh (1906–67), the poet from Monaghan, held such a view, though he might have derived it in part from Daniel Corkery (1878–1964), the influential Cork critic. There have been extenuating historical and biographical circumstances for this view, and it must be clear by now that recent Irish criticism of Yeats has a demonstrable autobiographical dimension. Kavanagh's smacks at Yeats were uncoordinated, personal and eccentric. Kavanagh brought a sense of grievance and envy from his backwater North and resented Dublin and metropolitan reputations such as Yeats's (which is perhaps in part why he famously extolled the virtue of parochialism); it was as if his northernness – he came from an obscure border county – was too remote from Dublin for him to accept the narrative of Irish nationalism that had installed Yeats as hero. Kavanagh's views of Yeats and the Irish Literary Revival were bound up in complicated ways with his own poetry, a poetry at once forceful and lyrical that had a liberating effect on the youthful Seamus Heaney.[7] And they do represent a critical point of view that can be, and has been, expressed in a sophisticated manner by Seamus Deane, who was also keenly aware of Kavanagh.

It may be, then, that Deane and Heaney inhabit a similar problematic northernness as did Kavanagh, even though all three moved to Dublin as to their natural capital. Deane and Heaney, after all, grew up in Northern Ireland, which had been separated from the rest of Ireland for forty years by the time they entered university; Belfast, not Dublin, was their administrative capital, and the Northern city of Derry in some ways their cultural headquarters (the founding of Field Day in Derry rather than Dublin being recognition of that fact). In the case of Kavanagh, it may be less that Yeats seemed not quite Irish enough than that he was too centrally Irish, a Protestant who had usurped (ahead of time) Kavanagh's place in the story of Ireland.

The career since 1920 of Catholic-Gaelic Ireland (one of Lyons's three Irelands alongside Anglo-Ireland and Protestant Ulster) explains the quandary of Northernness, and it created the circumstances out of which the sophisticated elaboration of Kavanagh's attitude emerged. A major fault line in this Ireland was created by partition in 1920, after which Northern and Southern Ireland grew apart, the North becoming more officially Protestant (and marooning Northern Catholics, many of whom more or less abstained from participation), the South more officially Catholic (against Yeats's initially loud protests and the diminishing protests of the Anglo-Irish, themselves diminishing in power and population).[8] Sadly, the cut-off Catholic population of the North came culturally and in other ways to resemble an ox-bow lake, history like new water failing to course through it.

Ironically, it was the British education system that stirred and ertilized the waters. But when the grievances, talents and ambitions of the Northern Catholics were given voice in the 1960s (when the first beneficiaries of higher education reached their 20s), the emerging voices were out of harmony with Catholic voices elsewhere in Ireland. They sounded in the beginning fresh, indeed alarmingly fresh to Ulster unionists, but as time went on they began to sound on certain issues curiously old-fashioned, baying after quarry everyone assumed had been long since captured, despatched or liberated. When the Field Day Theatre Company began its pamphlet series, there must have been many who were surprised to find William Butler Yeats (reborn as gentleman, unionist, Protestant, enemy of Catholic Ireland and, even if nationalist in some peculiar way, nevertheless at heart West Briton) listed among the legitimate targets.

Yet these were not simply unkennelled hounds from the past, outmoded nationalists giving tongue after half a century of enforced silence in an Orange state. They were sophisticated readers and gifted writers, indeed poets themselves some of them, and they helped to create a literary scene in Ulster that was sometimes referred to as the Northern Renaissance. And the Field Day pamphlets, as well as the critical books of those I have in mind, were welcome stimulants to thought in Ireland. But on the 'National Question', the effect of these new figures in the landscape nonetheless was to suggest, almost subliminally (they made no explicit constitutional claims or demands), the illegitimacy of Northern Ireland and the legitimacy of the reunification of Ireland. The Irish Republic, having apparently moved on from partition, satisfied with its twenty-six counties (more than enough of a handful), was suddenly brought with a shock back to 1920 or something passingly like it.

Never mind the Irish body politic, it was all an injection of adrenalin in the Irish body poetic, and Seamus Heaney's achievement, for example, has been acknowledged far beyond the borders of Ulster, far beyond Ireland. But the authentic tension of Ulster, an intense localism of engagement, has remained nevertheless in the work of Heaney and Seamus Deane. (Even Heaney's poetry achieved a paradoxical newness in the beginning by 'resuming the dark' like Kelly's unlicensed bull in Heaney's poem 'The Outlaw', setting in verse notions of Ireland – female, mythic, undefeatable, boggy, resurgent – that the Republic of Ireland had all but abandoned, and that more resembled those of early Yeats than, say, of MacNeice, Kavanagh, Austin Clarke or Thomas Kinsella, and that might be partly explained by the time-warp of Catholic Northern Ireland and the way in which Northern Catholics had become 'unlicensed' nationalists, as far as many Southerners were concerned.) To demonstrate this it is only necessary to compare the criticism of Heaney and Deane (and of Longley) on the subject of Yeats with the criticism of Declan Kiberd, a Field Day pamphleteer and an athletic intelligence. Because there is less politically and personally at stake (and because, I am compelled to say, he lacks the others' knowledge of Northern Ireland), Kiberd's criticism can afford more *jouissance*, and it is not surprising that he is more creatively exercised by Oscar Wilde than by Yeats. His criticism has a spring in its step that the criticism of Deane, Heaney and Longley does not, freighted as theirs is with the problems of articulating North.[9]

The tensions and intensities of engagement were buried in the work of another critic and were exhumed less by the urgencies of the Troubles than by the challenge posed by the Northern Catholic writers and readers of Yeats. Denis Donoghue, born in the South of Ireland and eventually a Professor of American Literature in New York, might have been content to ply his reputable international wares, had not the Field Day pamphleteers reminded him by example that he too had been reared a Northern Catholic (in Warrenpoint, Co. Down) and had suffered disabilities now to be freshly voiced if not freshly remembered. However, he had been a sympathetic critic and admirer of Yeats, and so his aroused fellow feeling for other Northern Catholics was complicated by the matter of where he stood on Yeats. To take issue with Field Day, as he did, was to take issue with them on the subject of Yeats. For at times in Ireland, the 'Yeats Question' can seem very like the 'National Question', a measure of the crucial importance of that poet in Irish cultural and even political dispute.

SEAMUS DEANE

Seamus Deane's unruffled account of Yeats's art in *A Short History of*

Irish Literature (1986), with its nimble transitions and summary eloquence, can only appear approving. Having quoted the famous last stanza of 'The Statues', with its fellowship of Pearse and Cuchulain, the critic is content to explain:

> Momentarily the hero and the race are in accord with one another. In the poems on his own life and his great friends, Yeats had rewritten his account of modern Ireland as a place haunted by heroes. At the end of his life, he called for that heroism again, both from Irish writers and from the Irish people at large. Although he also saw that heroism was at a discount, that was merely in the oppositional nature of things. The murderers of Cuchulain, the convicted cowards, the representatives of the common mob, find their opposites too: 'They had changed their throats and had the throats of birds'.[10]

This evenness of tone is a far cry from the heated scrutiny to which Deane had subjected Yeats's idea of heroism in his celebrated Field Day pamphlet, *Heroic Styles: the Tradition of an Idea* (1984).[11] The difference may not be just one of occasion and genre (a short history versus a polemical pamphlet, professional explication versus engaged critical reading) but of deep-seated ambivalence about Yeats at the heart of Deane's ongoing response to the writer.

Yeats's 'heroism' in *A Short History* was in *Heroic Styles* 'spiritual heroics' and Deane's neutral explication was then harsh judgement. Deane claims in *Heroic Styles* there are two dominant ways of reading Irish literature and history: the Romantic way and the Pluralistic way; these are also two modes of Irish writing, the first represented by Yeats, the second by Joyce.

The romantic mode when it is engaged in 'restoring dignity and power to what had been humiliated and suppressed', can work in the service of nationalism. One imagines one hears in the phrase 'humiliated and suppressed' an autobiographical note sounding from Derry City (where Deane was born and reared), but Yeats is not the figure who can redress the wrongs. For in the Ascendancy Revival, 'the restoration of native energy to the English language is seen as a specifically Irish contribution to a shared heritage'. 'Cultural nationalism', writes Deane, 'is thus transformed into a species of literary unionism'. In this regard, Deane allows no difference between Yeats and Ferguson, since both beat the strategic retreat of the Ascendancy from political to cultural supremacy. Whereas Catholic Ireland could provide Yeats with a language of renovation ('regeneration', Deane calls it in *Celtic Revivals*[12]), the art and civilization of

Yeats's new Ireland came from the political connection between England and Ireland. Whatever its connection with Irish nationalism, Yeats's programme 'was not, finally, a programme of separation from the English tradition'. Deane then quotes from Yeats's 'A General Introduction for My Work' (1937) – the passage that includes the claim that 'I owe my soul to Shakespeare', etc. – to exemplify 'the pathology of literary unionism'.

The inference is clear: unionism is a disease. Also: nationalism is the cure, but only a nationalism that is literary as well as political, that is full-blooded and liberationist and admits of no reservations or complications. Aside from the milkier satisfaction of pointing out certain incongruities in Yeats's philosophy (and for what ideological gain?), why else would Deane assail Yeats on the grounds that he was not a real nationalist unless he, Deane, felt *himself* to be a real nationalist?

Clearly some of Deane's premises are unexceptionable. I have seconded Deane's proposition (first advanced by Conor Cruise O'Brien in 1966) that the Anglo-Irish nationalism of the Cultural Revival was the attempted transformation of Anglo-Irish power, not its surrender. (It failed, and became a surrender.) Moreover, Yeats's nationalism was indeed in many ways problematic. He 'became definitely a nationalist' in the 1880s (Hone), but claimed in 1937 (when the mischief had been done and nationalism was a nasty notion; 1937, moreover, was the year De Valera's anti-Protestant Constitution for the Republic of Ireland was adopted) that, 'I am no Nationalist, except in Ireland for passing reasons' – an astounding retreat from responsibility (*WBY*, p.54; *E&I*, p.526). He promoted Gaelic but said English was his mother tongue (*E&I*, p.520). One moment he would speak for 'we Irish', the next claim merely that he was '*joined* to the "Irishry"' (my italics, his inverted commas), a rather different notion of alliance instead of self-identification (*E&I*, p.526). He thought (or affected to think) of the English as foreigners but was much among them and claimed that 'everything I love has come to me through English' (and he meant the literature written by the English, not literature in the English language) (*E&I*, p.519). He sought to encourage the formation of a national literature in Ireland yet complained to Lady Gregory that the Easter rebellion overturned 'the freeing of Irish literature and criticism from politics' (*L*, p.613) – he who was even then contemplating the poem that became 'Easter 1916', though it is arguable that the impulse of that poem is precisely the transformation of political action into myth, courtesy of the dynamic removals of the poetic imagination.

These cross-currents are evidence of Yeats's fierce energy and involvement in Ireland, though some of them are psychologically and socially explicable in ways that may not always endear the poet to an Irish reader, especially perhaps a Northern Irish reader. No one was more aware of the anomalies than Yeats himself who attempted to absorb them into a system that rested on the very notion of contradiction, opposition, antithesis. The poet often wrote in the rag-and-bone shop of the system, where mere doubts had not become things as grand as antitheses: 'we sing', Yeats wrote of poets, 'amid our uncertainty' (*Myth*, p.331). Yet Deane is correct in seeing a fundamental unsatisfactoriness in Yeats's understanding of, and role in, the 'Irish Question'. The condition of the Anglo-Irish after Catholic nationalism got into full swing from the 1880s onwards *was* a kind of pathology. My own view is that Romantic nationalism, as much as unionism, was the source of the disease and that the incoherence Deane attributes to Yeats in 'Yeats and the Idea of Revolution' would have been lessened had Yeats been more unionist and less nationalist, been truer to a cultural reality that Romantic and mystical nationalism helped to disguise.

The blank that the North constitutes on Yeats's inner and outer map of Ireland guarantees the unsatisfactoriness. Deane is right when he complains, as he did recently, that 'the island Yeats knew excluded the Northern Ireland I knew. I had to find out how he managed to invent the place so that I might possess it for myself in terms that seemed to me more responsive to its realities.'[13] His conclusion ought to have been that the map of Southern nationalism, not just of Yeatsian nationalism, is blank where Northern Ireland is. Despite the reference to reality, I detect in Deane the chronic and romantic disappointment of Northern nationalism in Southern nationalism, a disappointment which possibly underpins Deane's rejection of Yeats's 'hot rhetoric' of Irish nationalism. It may also underpin his rejection in *Heroic Styles* of what he calls Joyce's alternative 'cold rhetoric', which he finds to be a 'harmony of indifference'. Underneath the dissatisfaction with pluralism, does one detect here the note of abandonment sounding from Derry City or (an allusion that will become clear later) from Warrenpoint revisited (and, by extension, from Catholic Northern Ireland)?

If Yeatsian nationalism is really unionism and a pathology, might it not explain the 'disease' of Ulster unionism? Yes, says Deane, and proceeds to claim that 'the cultural machinery of Romantic Ireland has ... wholly taken over in the North', that unionism is Paisleyism and that Paisleyism is romanticism and therefore comparable to

Yeatsianism, indeed somehow the spawn of Yeatsianism, but a Yeatsianism partitioned off and grown stagnant. Elsewhere I have set out the trouble with these equations.[14] But I would draw attention here to a certain inequality of example. Deane calls in salutary fashion for the rejection of the romantic mystique of Ireland; to accept this mystique 'is to be involved in the spiritual heroics of a Yeats or a Pearse'. But whereas Deane is detailed in his assault on Ulster unionism as romantic mystique (a largely unsustainable thesis), he is next to silent on the obviously more applicable case-study, that of Sinn Fein/IRA, a movement that produced the cult of Bobby Sands. Instead, the counterweight to Paisley is held to be John Hume, 'the minority's agent of rational demystification'. The IRA is explained away by one terse phrase: the IRA as the minority's 'agency of millenial revenge', a phrase that manages to excuse while apparently indicting. Deane claims that Pearse was 'our [*sic*] last romantic' in politics as Yeats was our last romantic in poetry, which makes odd his subsequent claim that Ulster politics is rife with romanticism, unless 'our' means 'Catholic Ireland's' and the implication is that Catholic nationalism is now rational, leaving only the unionists as romantic anachronisms. Indeed, one suspects that Deane's real target is unionism, whether Yeatsian unionism (as Deane sees it) or Ulster unionism, and *not* romanticism or nationalism.[15]

To put it another way, it is Yeats's particular *kind* of nationalism to which Deane takes great exception. He calls Yeats 'dangerous' because 'his work had found an originating impulse in a theory of racial essences and identity' and promoted '*a brand of nationalism* which was the product of a colonialism of which it thought itself the opposite' [my emphasis].[16] This interpretation is given an extended outing in 'Yeats and the Idea of Revolution', during which the adjectives 'hysterical', 'effete', 'authoritarian', 'strident' and 'incoherent' are attached to Yeats's project and later poetry. Yeats's spiritual heroics are explained as deriving from his colonialist mentality. Deane would agree with O'Brien on Yeats's 'savage politics', but whereas O'Brien traced them to Yeats's fascism, Deane traces them to his colonialism (i.e., his unionism) which his fascism was in reality. But on the issue of whether Yeats's colonialist nationalism actually furthered the cause of Irish liberationist nationalism (helping to bring into existence the Irish Free State), as Said believes it did, Deane is peculiar. 'To describe Yeats's politics, and to a large extent his achievement, as colonial is not at all to diminish it.' (How does Deane expect his Yeats to survive the barrage of those epithets?) He seems to approve when he writes:

> [H]is demand was always that Ireland should retain its culture by keeping awake its consciousness of metaphysical questions. By doing so it kept its own identity and its link with ancient European culture alive. As always with Yeats, to be traditionalist in the modern world was to be revolutionary ... It is a conviction which has a true revolutionary impact when we look at the history of the disappearance from the Western mind of the sense of eternity and of the consciousness of death ... In its consciousness of death, the culture would become truly alive ... [Yeats] was a revolutionary whose wars took place primarily within himself.[17]

It is bewildering to find Deane re-admitting the very metaphysics and solipsism he elsewhere labours to repudiate. And I'm unsure quite what the revolutionary nature of death-consciousness is.

Because Yeats's nationalism was colonialist, not native or Catholic, it was not the genuine article: that is Deane's implication; it was forged from above, not from below through humiliation or suppression. Deane is opposed to nationalism *only when it is Yeatsian*: that is the conclusion I have come to after reading his work over the years. Deane's reading of Yeats seems to me a case not of Marxist anti-colonialism colliding with romantic colonialist nationalism but of one nationalism colliding with another, one being Anglo-Irish (colonialist, in Deane's phrase), the other being Northern Catholic. Given Deane's acute intelligence, we can explain his inconsistency on the subject of Yeats only by reference to – dare I say it? – the pathology of Northern nationalism. It is an ideology which feels itself pre-empted by Southern, indeed Anglo-Irish, nationalism, but which nevertheless must be advanced, though (in the light of nationalist excesses by Sinn Fein/IRA) by oblique means that will not offend the liberal humanist academic establishment.

The troubling irony of Deane's response to Yeats is that when he leaves Yeats in order to contemplate other Irish writers (including Joyce) or other aspects of Irish culture, he sounds to this ear like a nationalist, and a nationalist moreover who mystifies by omission – as he has accused Yeats of being and doing, particularly in the matter of the North. Deane closed *Heroic Styles* by calling for an anthology of Irish literature from the beginning that would in total effect demystify Yeatsian Irishness (deriving in part from Ferguson and Arnold), revealing a literature 'unblemished by Irishness', but nevertheless also secure a sense of Irishness so as to avoid Joycean pluralism and disinterestedness. The anthology would supersede Yeats's 'literary unionism' and install a literary nationalism. The distinction between a blemished and a secure Irishness is perhaps too nice. In any case, in its conception and execution, the project actually bore much resemblance to Yeats's own early attempt to rescue from the past (and from the West British professors), and to encourage in the future, an Irish national literature whose writers would 'include only those who have written under Irish influence and of Irish subjects', but, of necessity, in the English language (*UP*, Vol.1, p.360). Yeats's project, though fitful compared to Field Day's, was so successful that in planning his anthology, Deane used the same criterion, merely extending it in order to reread as Irish, writers whose work Yeats initially ignored as failing the nationality test (Swift, Berkeley, Sterne), writers normally subsumed under English literature (Wilde, for example), even British writers who merely wrote about Ireland (Giraldus Cambrensis, for example, and Spenser) and whose claim to Irishness, made on their behalf, resembles that of certain Republic of Ireland soccer players.

The anthology came to pass as the huge, three-volume *Field Day Anthology of Irish Writing* (1991), with Seamus Deane as General Editor.[18] But there was a limit to the extensions Deane was prepared to entertain. Most of the omissions are traceable, I suspect, to the Northern nationalism that pervades the anthology.[19] It is an immensely useful assemblage and Deane laboured on it with great fortitude of love and duty. Among its many omissions, though, one must register in the present discussion an 'unblemished' Ulsterness. Ulster and unionism are offered to the reader only as a pathology. (In Ireland we seemed to have developed germ warfare as a supplement to guerrilla and electoral warfare.) Deane does to unionist Ulster (i.e., the bulk of the North) what he accused Yeats of doing to Northern Ireland. Like Yeats, Deane inscribes on the thither (north-east) edge of his known Ireland, 'Here be strange beasts'. Whereas Deane's repudiation of essentialism in *Heroic Styles* was a potentially liberating and reconciliatory intervention in the Irish cultural debate, he chose in that pamphlet and in the organization of his anthology to invest the Northern unionists and Protestants with a negative mystique and to erase them categorically. Unfortunately neither the Southern Protestant nationalist nor the Northern Catholic nationalist can bear very much reality where the Ulster Protestant is concerned, an ironically convergent antipathy for Yeats and his critic Deane to meet in.

DENIS DONOGHUE

The internal difficulties of Northern nationalism have lately been revealed in another and surprising location: the Irish criticism of the worldly Denis Donoghue. In that criticism, no less than in Deane's criticism, those difficulties find their curious counterpart in the internal difficulties and contradictions of Yeats's attitude to Ireland and Irishness. Donoghue's long-standing loyalty to the poet has been challenged by affairs in Northern Ireland, including the advent of Field Day, and caused him both to revise earlier readings of Yeats and to resist having to make such revisions.

To give title to his 1986 collection of Irish criticism, Donoghue wrote an essay called 'We Irish'.[20] The phrase is from the last stanza of 'The Statues' ('We Irish, born into that ancient sect'), inspired by Berkeley's repudiation in his journal of English abstractionism *and* English materialism ('We Irishmen cannot attain to these truths'). Donoghue appropriates the phrase, too, in order to reclaim his own Irishness, prompted in part, surely, by the long years in semi-exile. But in the reclamation is preserved an expatriate ironic distance: Donoghue, unlike Deane, does not wish to get mauled by the Irish situation, an experience Cruise O'Brien offered as a virtual definition of Irishness.

Yeats, Donoghue tells us, believed there is a special Irish mentality, deriving the idea partly from Berkeley, for whom 'the Irish', Donoghue concludes, meant powerless but prestigious upper-class Protestants. Donoghue calls the notion 'bizarre' and reduces it to Berkeley's wish to counter English philosophy. Yet Donoghue defends Yeats's preoccupation with a distinctive Irishness against Deane's attack in his Field Day pamphlets on the romantic mystique of nationhood, defending even the essentialism from which it issued. Indeed, Seamus Heaney, also a Field Day man, is shown to have the same preoccupation as recently as *Station Island* (1984). In 'We Irish', Donoghue is reluctant to concede the incoherence of Yeatsian Irishness to Deane, whom he stops at seeing as an anti-nationalist revisionist instead of a different kind of nationalist, which further inquiry would have revealed.

Like Deane, Donoghue regards Joyce's view of Irishness as an alternative to Yeats's. He takes issue with Joyce's ghost in *Station Island* (i.e., with Heaney) for telling Heaney that the issue of Irishness doesn't matter, yet praises Stephen Dedalus in *A Portrait* (i.e., Joyce) for riskily attempting to escape his Irishness. Donoghue concludes that there *is* a distinctive Irish experience but that it is an experience of proliferating 'division'.

'We Irish' ends with a reminder that Berkeley lost interest in defining an Irish mentality and increasingly regarded himself as English.

Donoghue quotes the philosopher wondering aloud if it isn't the duty of the Irish after all to cultivate their love for England, and the critic adds: 'The only way he had in view was that of being unfailingly biddable'. The reader might wonder aloud if this is meant to be a nationalist sneer at a West Briton. In any case, in this one essay as elsewhere, nationalism and romanticism in one corner, and pluralism and revisionism (a reactive, more culturally versatile liberal humanism) in the other, can be seen contesting the field of Donoghue's Irish criticism and in a way that might baffle the reader.

Yeats's ambiguities (as Donoghue sees them) are analogues, as it were, of Donoghue's own ambivalences on the matter of Yeats and Ireland. In 'Romantic Ireland' (1980), Donoghue sets Yeats's career-long Romanticism against the poet's recognition that Romantic values had failed. In 'Yeats: the Question of Symbolism' (1977), Yeats's symbolism, with its attraction to essence and vision, is countered by 'the scruple which prevented him from making his entire art with Symons and the Symbolists', that scruple arising from 'the roughage of daily experience, chance, choice, and history' (*WI*, pp.39, 44). In 'On *The Winding Stair*' (1965), Yeats is seen as running his course between extremities, of which his dialogue between self and soul, and all they imply, is the case in point.

Donoghue attempts on Yeats's behalf to resolve these ambiguities. He sees Yeats as a legendizer, legend being a middle term between symbolism and history, and between essence and existence: Yeats absorbs history into his *own* history, situating himself between contraries. Deane had said something similar in 'The Literary Myths of the Revival' in *Celtic Revivals*, but went farther when he identified one of Yeats's appropriations of history as his 'seductive historical fiction' of the dignity and coherence of the Ascendancy, which amounted to a myth *of* history and which distorted history in the service of continued Ascendancy power. (Unlike Donoghue, product of a more dominantly liberal humanist era in criticism, Deane does not concede the sovereignty of the subject.) More problematic is Donoghue's defence gambit in 'Romantic Ireland' that the idea in the essay's title is one that has been endlessly celebrated or satirized in Irish literature, and has now (1980) been temporarily 'sequestered', removed from dispute until a calmer, more hospitable future arrives. Four years later, Deane's *Heroic Styles* and the Field Day project showed him in error, for Deane assailed Romantic Ireland in his pamphlet, though in no unproblematic fashion, as I have tried to demonstrate.

Having loyally defended Yeats, Donoghue proceeds a few years later in 'Yeats, Ancestral Houses, and Anglo-Ireland' (first seeing print in *We Irish*) to undermine the poet's romantic concept of the Big House with a few well-chosen observations on the ground from Arthur Young, Carlyle and Froude. Perhaps sensing some contradiction, Donoghue attaches a personal postscript. We are told that Yeats's politics and occultism caused the critic difficulty from the start, though he was reading the poet under the aegis of New Criticism, an American methodology that required the reader to extend latitude to the work of art as artefact. It seems that young Donoghue accepted R.P. Blackmur's notion of doctrine-as-emotion. Nowadays, Donoghue admits uneasily, latitude is denied by Marxist and Irish anti-colonialist critics alike. 'My own stance is that of a latitudinarian, and I would hold to its concessiveness until a particularly extreme outrage makes me ashamed of it' (*WI*, p.66).

Yeats is a test case for latitudinarianism. At the outset of both 'We Irish' and 'Yeats, Ancestral Houses, and Anglo-Ireland', the most outrageous, violence-mongering, anti-democratic Yeats Donoghue can recruit (the Yeats arraigned on these nominal charges by Deane) establishes the threshold of Donoghue's tolerance for Yeats. He manages to find Yeats's occasional late hysteria 'touching in its appalling way'; Yeats was at the end of his tether, allows Donoghue, and therefore exonerable; it was society's fault for provoking Yeats's violent anti-democracy; it was not the subject's vice.

Latitudinarianism and sequestration are defensive concepts Donoghue has been forced to deploy to defend Yeats against his hostile readers, among whom he has counted the Field Day writers (wrongly) as pluralists and revisionists, left-leaning anti-authoritarianists. More than Yeats is at stake, as he knows, for the poet is simply one example of 'the subject' which is under a barrage of attack by ideologues in the American university literature classroom under the banners of Women's Studies, Feminism, Gender Studies, Gay and Lesbian Studies, African-American Studies, Marxist Criticism, Psychoanalytic Criticism, Deconstruction, New Historicism, Cultural Studies, Post-Colonial Studies. All of these he has recently taken on gamely if briefly in 'Doing Things with Words: Criticism and the Attack on the Subject', in which the countering concepts of latitudinarianism and sequestration become an object of study for literary critics: i.e., Bakhtinian dialogism (something he had tested out in an essay written especially for *We Irish*, 'Bakhtin and *Finnegans Wake*').[21]

Under pressure of contemporary criticism, Donoghue's response to Yeats has become marked by increasing ambivalence. On the one hand, he has become a revisionist in an Irish sense; that is, he is now inclined to a pluralist notion of Irish culture and chary of Yeats's mystical nationalism. He is, after all, a man of international perspective, living and teaching in a cosmopolis. This has caused him to rethink his attitude to Deane and Field Day, whom he had at first repudiated *because* he thought they were pluralists and revisionists. (And yet in any case, Yeats for Donoghue is a privileged, different-order figure who escapes the strictures of revisionism.) On the other hand, his original review of Field Day (which he was honest enough to reprint above his second thoughts, in Hutchinson's hardback version of the pamphlets) shows him to be a nationalist, yet not ready to leave the field to 'revisionist pedagogy' (as he calls it in 'At Swim', a 1983 essay in *We Irish*) or loosen his grip on Romantic Ireland and the 'sorrowful legend of Ireland', as Stephen Dedalus cynically called it.

His quarrel with Field Day is more of an illusion than Donoghue believes. He fails to see that these Marxist and anti-colonialist critics are in Ireland neo-nationalists and so believes he is defending Yeats from attacks from the fashionable left rather than from new Irish nationalism that assails Yeats nominally for being ultra-conservative but really for being a Protestant and Anglo-Irishman (a colonialist) and an *inauthentic* nationalist. Latitude and sequestration would normally be evidence of a liberal humanism in its New Criticism (serious) or quasi-Bahktinian (playful) guises and closer kin to pluralism and revisionism than the nominal pluralism and revisionism of Field Day. But instead, I believe Donoghue's loyalty to Yeats is a loyalty to Irish cutural nationalism of the Anglo-Irish kind that before academic new Marxism, post-colonialism and Field Day came into existence, used to be the only respectable variety for a critic or professor.

In other words, it is not simply loyalty to that notion of the aesthetic which underpinned Anglo-American critical practice when Donoghue came to maturity, and which then was the alternative to the pluralism and revisionism of today. Under protection of the notions of the aesthetic and of the inspired individual, Yeats was then a great and complex world writer to be explicated and appreciated and, when necessary, excused. (Actually, at that time the aesthetic response, which ought to have stood over against it, cohabited with a polite routine Irish nationalism, for appreciators and explicators of Yeats simply accepted the poet's versions of Ireland.) Whereas Donoghue wishes to extend latitude to Yeats the mystical, romantic nationalist, he disapproves of latitude when he spots it in Irish revisionist historians such as T.W. Moody, F.S.L. Lyons and Roy Foster who have wrongly 'played down the story of revolution and drawn more attention to the latitude of personal, social and political experience which the history of Ireland entails'.[22]

What we overhear in the quarrel of Donoghue and Field Day over Yeats is an unadmitted quarrel between two kinds (and two generations) of Irish nationalism, both forged in Northern Ireland, but Field Day's forged under pressure of the Troubles, Donoghue's forged in quieter days. There is, then, a generational difference and perhaps a rivalry. 'I left Northern Ireland before it became necessary for me to deal with its wretched system', Donoghue tells us in 'Castle Catholic', a revealing book review in *We Irish*, and so he is forced to watch from the sidelines while the younger generation tries to see something through. It is an irony that it was an enterprise Donoghue mistook for an anti-nationalist enterprise, Field Day (as he thought, cleverness at the expense of the suffering forebears), that stung Donoghue into re-examining sympathetically his Irishness, at first primarily through the medium of Yeats and most recently through the medium of autobiography, in which Yeats nevertheless looms large.

When I reviewed his collected Irish criticism in 1988, I wrote:

> *We Irish* has a psychological subtext: a belated and faltering redress. Quite what is being redressed is never spelled out. The subtext's provenance, however, is probably autobiographical and it breaks the surface of the text at those points where politics and ideology, even the critic's own life, demand expression, a thrashing-out.[23]

Two years later, the autobiography of his childhood and young manhood appeared.

Whereas *Warrenpoint* (1990) exploits 'the latitude of personal, social, and political experience', it does so in order to set straight from an autobiographical point of view the record that the revisionists (among whom he still numbers Deane) have distorted. And part of the record distorted is the work of Yeats. He allows that 'it is a difficult issue', but believes that Yeats, even though 'poetic images harbour a corresponding disposition to carry their energy into action', was not responsible for violence in Northern Ireland, that poetic language 'holds the reader's mind for as long as possible in a fictive or otherwise gratuitous space' (sequesters the political issues, one might say; *W*, pp.167–8). Here we see adherence to the aesthetic (he recruits Susanne Langer's concept of 'virtuality') consorting with unreconstructed nationalism, as of old; for 'what the revisionist spirit in the reading of Yeats mainly shows [especially in Deane] is the reader's resentment' (*W*, p.168).

This is odd, for *Warrenpoint* is full of barely repressed resentment. Not only does Donoghue defend the Catholic ethos instilled in him by the Christian Brothers, with its anglophobic nationalism and disloyalty to Northern Ireland ('the sorrowful legend of Ireland' with its unquenchable 'flame of freedom' and 'heroic men') – this ethos that is derided in the fashionable quarters that Donoghue resentfully derides in turn – but he relives and promenades anti-Protestant sectarianism which the intervening years have not softened through examination or reservation. (Donoghue cares to know as little about Ulster unionists as Deane – or Yeats.) A childhood once fled has now been re-accepted in its entirety, along with the story of his country told to him in childhood. It is a story of the indomitable Irishry acted out grimly by Bobby Sands and imaginatively propelled by Yeats. Indeed, Donoghue believes the entire country (i.e., the Republic of Ireland) needs the story: without it, he says with a Yeatsian flourish, Ireland 'is merely a member of the EC, the begging bowl our symbol' (*W*, p.172).

This childhood is re-anchored in the father, and the book's central act is homage to him. And the father, we are told, embodied 'purpose' and 'truth' and, it transpires, political conservatism. Although at times similarly moving, *Warrenpoint* is the mirror image of Gosse's *Father and Son* (1907) in which the son wins liberation from the father: here, Donoghue surrenders his freedom to the father. There is, though, a resemblance: against the odds, the father is in the end immensely sympathetic, as was Philip Henry Gosse. Because the father, a Catholic, born in Kerry, member of the disbanded Royal Irish Constabulary, went north after partition and joined the Royal Ulster Constabulary, Donoghue cannot find it in himself to denounce the RUC in which his father served, which his neo-nationalism requires, though he allows himself the opinion that his father's religion prevented his promotion. (I'd prefer to think he is wrong but have to accept that he could be right.) The father's situation necessarily modifies the son's from what it might have been, an unlicensed republicanism, into a constitutional, quietist nationalism, which inside the text seems to sublimate its frustration through the virtual revolutionism of Yeats's poetry and plays.

What also complicates Donoghue's nationalism is his resentment at the Irish Free State and Irish Republic for abandoning Northern nationalists: 'the rhetoric of Irish politics since 1932 has been a cynical exercise in bad faith. It is dishonourable for Irish governments to persist in a claim upon the unity of Ireland and to make that claim ... with studied silence' (*W*, pp.161–2). His resentment is so great he finds himself defending Yeats's *Cathleen Ni Houlihan* against Cruise O'Brien and comes close to defending the IRA.

Somehow Yeats, the nationalist Southern Irishman, is the depository of the deep ambivalence felt, or suffered, by the Northern nationalist who refuses the invitation of the physical-force tradition. Even in *Warrenpoint*, a remarkable document of reversion and reaction, there are hesitations about Yeats beyond the ones I've mentioned. Donoghue was born, he tells us, in a small Southern town, and adds, seemingly gratuitously on the first page of his story: 'it is the kind of town that Yeats hated'. Why drag in Yeats? Well, Yeats would have hated it, we are told, as he passed through it with distaste 'on his way to Coole Park, Lady Gregory's estate in Gort, County Galway'. In his quarrel with Deane, Donoghue tells us that Yeats was not interested in understanding Irish history in terms of class or social formations, and we are meant to assume that Donoghue believes Yeats to have been right: Yeats's is the world of transcending mythology, of intensified narrative, the anti-bourgeois story of Ireland that allies virtual peasant with virtual nobleman. Yet earlier in *Warrenpoint*, Donoghue remembers with resentment the subtle way in which the Yeats scholar T.R. Henn slighted him and did so from the vantage point of Protestant cultural superiority, the vantage point, in fact, of Yeats's adopted Anglo-Irish Big House culture (*W*, pp.49–50). We suspect that Yeats would have slighted him in a similar manner had the occasion arisen; Donoghue's resentment at (Yeatsian) Protestant superiority smoulders throughout *Warrenpoint*.

SEAMUS HEANEY

When I reviewed *We Irish*, I somewhat whimsically likened the Yeats of the Northern Catholics to Freud's primal father, a figure invested with an undesirable but irresistible authority. Their battle with him is beginning to resemble that Irish tale type, The Everlasting Fight. He is the nationalist they want and the higher-class Protestant nationalist they don't want, the pre-eminent purveyor of a myth of Irishness that they know has enthralled them and that has nevertheless insulated them in their Northern Ireland existence and given their life there (since they refused participation in the society of the province) meaning. He is the Ireland they have 'betrayed', either by leaving – like Donoghue – or by staying and outgrowing the old simple nationalism – like Deane, but the Ireland they still wish to propitiate; but he is also an impostor, being a Protestant.

Donoghue has, after some anguish, explicitly accepted Yeats's authority as he has accepted the authority of Irish nationalism and of his own reimagined father. At the end of his memoir, he admits that his father's characterization is not well rounded but reduced (in my opinion, by the diet of his son's reactivated nationalism – though he is still a moving figure) to the dimensions of authority, purpose, conservatism, single-mindedness, duty, 'truth'. In my review I said that, like Jacob, these critics are grappling with Yeats the father to discover their real names (the name of their country). But in *Warrenpoint*, Donoghue expressly rejects the Freudian theory that the son's struggle with the father is necessary to avoid neurosis. And so Donoghue writes his book in order to affirm the father without struggle. And for 'father' read also Yeats and Ireland, 'a nation once again'.

I suggested in my review that there are three ways in which Irish critics can come to grips with Yeats and solve the 'Yeats Question'. They can 'kill' him symbolically after an authentic struggle and walk away into freedom and maturity. O'Brien has tried this and succeeded; Deane has tried it and failed. Or they can engage him in the deferential, essentially exegetical way North American academics used to engage him. Or they can go on grappling painfully and inconclusively with him (which Deane is doing), which is brave and honest as long as it is clear that there is not some other struggle going on, which in the case of Deane I believe there is, and it has to do with Northern Ireland. Donoghue would seem to offer a fourth course: acceptance of Yeats after self-interrogation; but I believe that the painful, inconclusive struggle is yet going on with him and it has to do likewise with Northern Ireland. I see no end in sight.

Which is what makes the prospect of Seamus Heaney's intervention in Irish Yeats Studies so appealing. Heaney as a poet will surely recuperate the aesthetic response (the poem as artefact; poetry as a sovereign space and discourse) and reconfirm the necessity of the realized self, detaching both from ideology, be it the old ideologies of romanticism (the transcending self) and nationalism or the new ideologies of pluralism and revisionism. His, one expects, will be the successful fourth way of engaging with Yeats that Donoghue was not able to achieve and that Heaney can because he is a poet. Heaney's interest, like Donoghue's and Deane's, is of course that of a reader, of a professional teacher and critic, and of an Irishman. But it is also that of a fellow-poet, teaching himself all that can be learned from a master; he has, as he remarks of his interest in Hopkins, 'the slightly predatory curiosity of a poet interested in the creative processes of another poet'.[24] This being the case, and Yeats's poetry being self-evidently exemplary as creative achievement, Heaney will have no truck with any ideological or political belittlement of Yeats. 'Fifty years after the death of Yeats ... it would be both stupid and insensitive to think of him or his art or the figure he cuts as being anything less than dignified, heroic and epoch-making'.[25]

Above all, Yeats was a poet and his interests and his statements – many of them troubling in their propaganda quotient – 'refer to the ambitions of a poet, not to the operations of a promoter' (*FD*, Vol.2, p.785). The latitude Heaney extends to Yeats here is in the first instance an unfashionable sequestering of the poetry, not just by a reader like Donoghue (*Warrenpoint* has some poignant and honest pages on Donoghue's lack of creativity), but also by a fellow-poet. Heaney's exemplar was no ideologue, nor did his imagination 'function like an obedient seismograph', even if 'the historical shocks that ran through the world did affect Yeats' (*FD*, Vol.2, p.787). Apart from anything else, Yeats 'possessed a robust, sceptical intelligence and his grasp of what was happening in his own times was at least equal to that of the most secular and topically focussed minds of his generation' (*FD*, Vol.2, p.787). Yeats as a masterful voice is in active, even aggressive, transaction with society and history; he is no mere amanuensis through which society and history dictate themselves. Therefore we can't simply read back from the poetry to history and society without distorting the uniqueness of the poetry, i.e., both of the poem (poem as artefact, as embodiment of the aesthetic) and of the poet and the ultimate privacy of his agenda (poet as autonomous self). One senses here Heaney's memory of critics who in the 1970s wished Heaney to write directly and reactively about the Troubles in Northern Ireland and how he sought to deflect their desire.

This is an essential but insufficient part of the story for Heaney, however. In fact, Yeats was in search of a third space, which both denied and utilized the importunities of the self and of society (which through time is history). And 'space' implies both breathing-space and clearance for action and flight, at once empowerment and closure. Yeats 'merged history and his biographical self into the representative figure of the poet/seer, and he spoke as one both empowered and responsible beyond the limits of a private self' (*FD*, Vol.2, p.788). This too sets up echoes for readers of Heaney's poetry, with its claim to the vatic in the poetic speech and act, and with its declaration of poetic independence from the taxations and unwanted citizenships of society and nation. Poetry is poetry, a country unto itself.

Heaney's latitude would seem to resemble Donoghue's and to be opposed to the interrogationist, demystifying approach to Yeats practised by Deane. Besides, Heaney is a poet whose own effects have been often those of a powerful mystique, and whose poems reconstituted an

Ireland mythic in its power and in some ways a Northern Catholic updating of Yeats's poetic mythology of Ireland. Not just as a poet, but as a poet of a certain tendency and temperament, Heaney has a vested interest in defending the accomplishment of his great predecessor. Whatever Yeats's social standing or pretensions might be, whatever his politics might be and whatever his religious background might be, Yeats was first and foremost a poet, membership in which masonry or guild must command Heaney's first loyalty. There is something noble about a Northern Irish poet's conviction that poetry transcends the otherwise fierce and deep differences of sect, politics, class.

Yet very early into his Introduction to Yeats for his selection of the poet in the *Field Day Anthology*, Heaney shows eagerness to bring Deane on-side. 'Quite recently', Heaney writes, 'Seamus Deane (in his *Celtic Revivals*, 1985) has insisted that there is a disparity between the social, political and intellectual realities of the eighteenth-century Anglo-Irish world and the mythic version of them that Yeats's poems both derive from and project'. And yet, he asserts, 'Deane would be the first to acknowledge the unique necessity of Yeats's work in the evolution of the consciousness that would criticize it' (*FD*, Vol.2, p.784). But if this is true, it is a claim that imputes no real attraction by Deane to Yeats: it is akin to saying that the bourgeoisie were necessary to the triumph of the proletariat or that the vole is necessary to the marsh-harrier. And Heaney continues in this vein: Deane, he allows, does indeed expose 'the recalcitrance of Yeats's mind. Yet, equally, he displays a relish and a gratitude for the integrity of the recalcitrance itself'. I have ransacked Deane's perceptive criticism in vain for evidence of that relish and gratitude.

Is this a contributing editor's loyalty to the General Editor? A wish to present an unbroken anthological front? The informal obligations of an old camaraderie? A well-learned reluctance to show division to the enemy (whoever they might be)? A gentle desire to influence an old friend? Or is it a wish to put in words what he believes Deane really feels about Yeats but cannot for ideological reasons state? For it may be that Deane and Heaney converge more than is apparent in their response to Yeats. According to Heaney, national regeneration (of Ireland) was of vital and original importance to Yeats, and it survived failures to give it political form. 'Yeats's radical devotion to the potential and otherness of a specifically Irish reality should never be underestimated', Heaney tells us in his Introduction (*FD*, Vol.2, p.785). This surely echoes Deane's sentiments in 'Yeats and the Idea of Revolution' (it is also the ontological statement of the Field Day project), both critics managing to rarefy Irish nationalism beyond offence while attempting a usable metaphysics of republicanism.

I have discussed at length elsewhere the implication of Heaney's own poetry in the social and political realities of Ireland, despite his notion of the sovereignty of poetry.[26] Moreover, even though Heaney has utilized to eloquent, even visionary poetic effect the admission of such implication, and has poetically marked the progress of the implication *en route* (i.e., within the preoccupations – stylistic and thematic – of the poems) to an attempted third space, the truest poetry, even the space he has achieved is not without its political implications. Fascinatingly, the process so far has accompanied Heaney's almost continuous readings of Yeats.

Heaney has identified Yeats with the actions and ambitions of 'control', 'alerting strain', 'equestrian authority', 'urge to mastery', 'bony structure' and 'masculine elements', and elsewhere in his scheme of things has interpreted the Vikings, the Anglo-Saxon language, North, the English, the Anglo-Irish and the Ulster Protestants (in short, invasions, overmasterings, colonizations, imperialisms) as exemplifying maleness. The earth (Nature), Ireland, Irish Catholicism, poetry in its most natural expression – these are exemplars of the feminine. Heaney has identified himself with the feminine set of imbrications but has expressed admiration for the 'masculine' (including decisive political intervention, for instance in Northern Ireland) and has lamented (with paradoxical eloquence) its rarity in his work.[27] (It seems fair to assume that his directorship in Field Day must have satisfied the expressed desire in him for Yeatsian political partisanship.) His suggestion in one early essay that Yeats entertained at last 'a motherly kindness towards life' is hardly convincing.[28] Yeats remains in Heaney's criticism the proud Protestant and his work remains politically (because culturally) infused, and therefore applicable, like it or not, to Northern Ireland.

With an almost Yeatsian engagement with antithesis, Heaney has struggled against the tide of evaluation of Yeats that Heaney's own scheme of things helped to create, whereby Yeats is implicated in the Protestant *misrepresentation* of Ireland (in several meanings of that word) and in the Protestant subjugation of Catholic Ireland, as a man arrogates to himself the lawful right to subjugate a woman. He has struggled against the tide of nationalist desire (by which as an Ulster Catholic he is naturally carried), whereby Yeats misrepresented Ireland by remaining a literary, if not political, nationalist. He has shouldered, though without spelling them out, the difficulties of being a Northern Catholic. But the outcome is still in doubt.

A recent solution essayed by Heaney coincides with the express nature of his recent poetry, which aspires to a new spirituality, a 'neuter allegiance', truancy, freedom, 'ungovernment'. In his inaugural lecture as Professor of Poetry at Oxford, he identified 'transcendent equilibrium' as the preferred destination of poetry, and offered examples.[29] Lately, Heaney has begun to reread Yeats in the grip of this new light. *Through* history and *through* nationalism (and *through* maleness and femaleness, one might add), Yeats's poetry reached and created 'the place of meditation, the place of writing, the place where the second, imagined life is possible'.[30]

I have suggested in 'Heaney's Redress' that the place of transcendence unavoidably has political dimensions. The ideal republic of poetry is indistinguishable under the evolving circumstances from the ideal republic of Ireland; its political philosophical version can be found in the work of another Field Day pamphleteer, Richard Kearney, as Ireland's 'fifth province', the republic in Platonic guise. I believe my suggestion is vindicated by Heaney's own recent claim for the utility and applicability of Yeats's 'nobility' (as Heaney names the state of Yeatsian poetry):

> There is surely political meaning, *at once realistic and visionary*, in his sense of life as an abounding conflict of energies; in his recognition of the necessity as well as the impossibility of the attempt 'to hold in a single thought reality and justice'; and in his conviction – overriding his sense of hierarchy and election – that even among the Paudeens of this earth, 'There cannot be ... A single soul that lacks a sweet crystalline cry'. (*FD*, Vol.2, p.790, my emphasis)

What reality must the place of transcendence assume? Heaney offers only one political reality. He paraphrases what Yeats admitted ('I am no Nationalist, except in Ireland for passing reasons') – 'His nationalism', Heaney tells us, 'was essentially another avenue towards an ideal if unattainable "Unity of Being"' (*FD*, Vol.2, p.790).

But from the perspective of a Northern unionist (routinely erased by all of the writers and critics I have discussed), these would-be unities of being, culture and island are not quite the good they seem to Yeats and Heaney. The story I have tried to tell in this chapter has been the progress of, and reasons for, the engagement of Northern Catholic critics with the work of W.B. Yeats. It has been a dialogue of peculiar intensity, but it has also been an *intimacy* of peculiar intensity. It has been a rivalry rather than a radical opposition. The point at which Yeats's unities would converge is the point at which these Northern readers of Yeats would converge. It is also the point at which they in turn would converge with Yeats, however genuine the differences before that point is reached.

NOTES

1. I borrow the details of Yeats's ancestry from Joseph Hone, *W.B. Yeats 1865–1939* (London: Macmillan, 1965 [1943]), hereinafter abbreviated as *WBY*. In this chapter I employ the following abbreviations for cited works of Yeats. *CL*: the multivolume John Kelly and Eric Domville (ed.), *The Collected Letters of W.B. Yeats* (Oxford: Clarendon Press, 1986, 1994); *E&I*: *Essays and Introductions* (London: Macmillan, 1961); *L*: Allan Wade (ed.), *Letters of W.B. Yeats* (London: Rupert Hart-Davis, 1954); *LNI*: George Bernstein (ed.), *Letters to the New Island* (London: Macmillan, 1989); *LTWBY*: Richard J. Finneran (ed.), *Letters to W.B. Yeats* (London: Macmillan, 1977); *Mem*: Denis Donoghue (ed.), *Memoirs: Autobiography* (London: Macmillan, 1972); *Myth*: *Mythologies* (London: Macmillan, 1959); *SS*: Donald R. Pearce (ed.), *The Senate Speeches of W.B. Yeats* (Bloomington, IN: Indiana University Press, 1960); *UP*: John P. Frayne (ed.), *Uncollected Prose by W.B. Yeats* (London: Macmillan, 1970); *YVP*: George Mills Harper (ed.), *Yeats's* Vision *Papers* (London: Macmillan, 1992).
2. Edna Longley, 'W.B. and Cultural Politics Today', *Yeats: A Fortnight Anniversary Supplement (Fortnight Magazine)* (March 1989), p.4.
3. *Irish News and Belfast Morning News*, 22 November 1893, p.8.
4. Edward W. Said, *Nationalism, Colonialism and Literature: Yeats and Decolonization.* Field Day Pamphlet No.15 (Derry City: Field Day Theatre Company, 1988).
5. Terry Eagleton, *Heathcliff and the Great Hunger: Studies in Irish Culture* (London: Verso, 1995), p.308. Eagleton wrote a Field Day pamphlet in the same series as Said (*Nationalism: Irony and Commitment*, pamphlet no.13) but did not discuss Yeats.
6. The work of Longley, Brown and Roy Foster is widely available; Foster is writing the authorized biography of Yeats, and Brown an unauthorized critical biography. [Both now published: Brown's critical biography in 1999 and Foster's two-volume authorized biography in 1997 and 2003 – JWF 2008.] My own views are set out in *Fictions of the Irish Literary Revival: A Changeling Art* (Syracuse, NY: Syracuse University Press, 1987). I find a view of Yeats not dissimilar to my own in Norman Vance, *Irish Literature: A Social History* (Oxford: Basil Blackwell, 1990). For O'Brien's earlier and pioneeringly fearless critique of right-wing Yeats, see 'Passion and Cunning: An Essay on the Politics of W.B. Yeats', in A. Norman Jeffares and K.G.W. Cross (eds), *In Excited Reverie: A Centenary Tribute to William Butler Yeats* (London: Macmillan, 1965), pp.207–78.
7. John Wilson Foster, 'The Poetry of Patrick Kavanagh', in *Colonial Consequences: Essays in Irish Literature and Culture* (Dublin: Lilliput Press, 1991), pp.97–113.
8. See Clare O'Halloran, *Partition and the Limits of Irish Nationalism* (Dublin: Gill and Macmillan, 1987) and Dennis Kennedy, *The Widening Gulf: Northern Attitudes to the Independent Irish State 1919–49* (Belfast: Blackstaff Press, 1988).
9. See, for example, Kiberd's *Anglo-Irish Attitudes*. Field Day Pamphlet No. 6 (Derry City: Field Day Theatre Company, 1984).
10. Seamus Deane, *A Short History of Irish Literature* (London: Hutchinson, 1986), pp.159–60.
11. Seamus Deane, *Heroic Styles: The Tradition of an Idea*. Field Day Pamphlet No. 4 (Derry City: Field Day Theatre Company, 1984).
12. Seamus Deane, 'Yeats and the Idea of Revolution', *Celtic Revivals*: *Essays in Modern Irish Literature 1880–1980* (London: Faber, 1985), p.38.
13. *Guardian* Symposium on W.B. Yeats (27 January 1994), quoted by Longley, 'W.B. and Cultural Politics Today', p.4.
14. John Wilson Foster, 'The Critical Condition of Ulster', in *Colonial Consequences*, pp.215–33.
15. A demystified unionism is advanced throughout John Wilson Foster (ed.), *The Idea of the Union: Statements and Critiques in Support of the Union of Great Britain and Northern Ireland* (Vancouver: Belcouver Press, 1995).
16. *Guardian* Symposium on W.B. Yeats, quoted by Longley, 'W.B. and Cultural Politics Today', p.4.
17. Deane, *Celtic Revivals*, pp.49–50.

18. Seamus Deane (gen. ed.), *The Field Day Anthology of Irish Writing* (Derry City: Field Day Publications, 1991). Hereinafter abbreviated as *FD* Vols.1, 2, 3.
19. Glaring omissions or inadequacies include nature writing, women's writing, feminist writing and serious unionist apologetics.
20. In *We Irish: The Selected Essays of Denis Donoghue. Volume 1* (Brighton: Harvester, 1986). Hereafter abbreviated as *WI*.
21. 'Doing Things with Words', *Times Literary Supplement*, 15 July 1994, pp.4–6.
22. Denis Donoghue, *Warrenpoint* (New York: Knopf, 1990), p.167. Hereafter abbreviated as *W*.
23. The review, originally published in the *Irish Review*, is reprinted as 'A Complex Fate: The Irishness of Denis Donoghue', in *Colonial Consequences*, pp.206–14.
24. Seamus Heaney, 'The Makings of a Music: Reflections on Wordsworth and Yeats', in *Preoccupations: Selected Prose 1968–1978* (Oxford: Oxford University Press, 1980), p.61.
25. Seamus Heaney, 'William Butler Yeats', *Field Day Anthology of Irish Writing*, Vol.2, p.783.
26. John Wilson Foster, 'Heaney's Redress', *Colonial Consequences*, pp.168–205.
27. These equations are discussed at length in ibid.
28. Seamus Heaney, 'Yeats as an Example?', in *Preoccupations*, p.113.
29. Quoted in John Wilson Foster, 'Heaney's Redress'.
30. Seamus Heaney, 'Yeats's Nobility', *Yeats: A Fortnight Anniversary Supplement* (March 1989), p.3.

14

WAS THERE ULSTER LITERARY LIFE BEFORE HEANEY?

NO JOHN THE BAPTISTS

Many college students of Irish Literature, clamouring to write their essays on Seamus Heaney and 'the North', apparently believe that Northern Irish literature began *ab ovo* with the publication of *Death of a Naturalist* in 1966. Their belief is in part a sign of our current cult of celebrity that can stifle in all but the brighter students interest in the complexities of the past and the uncertainties of the present. But then, only recently (say in the past quarter-century) did serious criticism discover that there were Irish writers of the Revival other than Yeats, Synge, O'Casey and Joyce who merited extended discussion, so the understandable small tyranny unwittingly exerted by the Major Figure may also be in play. Heaney, particularly for North American undergraduates, has threatened to become synonymous with 'the North' as Yeats for long was synonymous with Ireland.

I say this because Sean McMahon has in his literary life-story of Sam Hanna Bell drawn attention to the generation of Ulster writers who immediately preceded Heaney.[1] It is important not to regard them – when they do come to our attention – as minor John the Baptists paving the way for the Major Figure. (Or Major Figures, if you include those excellent poets, Michael Longley and Derek Mahon, who have to date only one critical monograph apiece devoted to them, whereas I have lost precise count of the books on Heaney as they crowd the thirty mark; I have augmented that total myself.) Nor in any important way were these writers Sons of Sam. The actual writing aside, the Ulster society which Bell and his contemporaries grew up in, lived in, and enjoyed their heyday in, was divided from that of Heaney and his contemporaries by crucial first-hand experiences – the aftermath of the Great War, the partition of Ireland, the hungry and ideologically convulsed 1930s, the Second World War, and the minor post-war British cultural revival the official form of which we might see as the Festival of Britain of 1951. Heaney and Co. in turn had their own crucial experiences which helped initiate and shape their own generation: the first fruits of the Butler Education Act of 1947 (NI) which enabled Ulster children of parents of modest means to receive free grammar school and third-level education through 'merit', i.e. by examination, and the Civil Rights movement that roused Ulster Catholics from their resentful slumber.

(It is a mark of the traditionalism of what we might otherwise think of as the radical departure of Heaney and Co. that only James Simmons – a fractionally elder contemporary who could be allowed to bridge the broader political enthusiasms of Bell and Co. and the surprisingly apolitical 'literary renaissance' of the 1960s and 1970s – seems to have been influenced by that other massive post-war British and American cultural revolution: the explosion in pop music, including modern jazz, folk-music and, above all, rock 'n' roll, and with their far-flung cultural fallout. And in years to come it might seem strange that for twenty-odd years Heaney wrote extensively and intimately of his county Derry boyhood apparently unimpacted by the sensibility of post-war modernity or the Cold War.)

It is arguable that the continuities of Ulster society, with its largely dormant or camouflaged Catholic population, its stifling official Presbyterian puritanism and killjoydom, and its Unionist Party's grey hegemony, survived the experiences that shaped Bell's generation, but if they did, it was only by a few years; by the time of Heaney's third volume in 1972, all was changed, changed utterly. Bell by then was 63. McMahon's biography is more than incidentally a portrait of a previous age. Bell and his peers lived on, of course (biology being oblivious to cultural epoch-making): Bell died in 1990; Roy McFadden died in 1999; John Boyd died only this year (2002), while Robert Greacen is happily still with us.[2] Greacen, born in 1920, eleven years after Bell, published his *Collected Poems* in 1995 and a spirited autobiography in 1997, *The Sash My Father Wore*; but styles in poetry and memoirs alike had changed, and these are valuable contributions to Ulster (and slightly less valuable contributions to British and Irish) literary history. As indeed is McMahon's literary life of Sam Hanna Bell.

BELL'S DIVERSE COHORT

The social history of the literary generation in question is certainly interesting, and I will return to it. But whereas (and probably not unusually) I have in my own criticism made space for only a few Ulster names from the three decades, 1930s to 1960s – John Hewitt, W.R. Rodgers, Michael McLaverty and Bell himself – Bell's cohort as a whole (Ulster writers born between, say, 1905 and 1920) need yield little to the generation of Heaney, at least in terms of the demographics of accomplishment. Bell the novelist, short-storywriter and theatre historian, Hewitt the poet and historian of Ulster verse, Boyd the playwright and editor, McLaverty the novelist and short-storywriter, Greacen the poet and editor, McFadden the poet, Rodgers the poet, Joseph Tomelty the playwright, novelist and actor, Richard Rowley (R.V. Williams) the poet, Sam Thompson the playwright: this was only the Belfast contingent of writers of some distinction whose work is discussed in the standard and contemporary histories of the three genres in Ulster – by Terence Brown in *Northern Voices* (1975), by this writer in *Forces and Themes in Ulster Fiction* (1974), and Bell himself in *The Theatre in Ulster* (1972).[3] These books have been credited with providing a little creative stimulus for other critics, but they also wrapped up a Northern epoch and helped form the threshold of a new one.

Louis MacNeice was a fitful Ulster congregant; as a BBC man he was often in Belfast where BBC Northern Ireland was active in the arts, but not resident since after graduating from Oxford University he worked for the BBC in its London headquarters, to where he invited Rodgers. Brian Moore (who was born in 1921 and died in the same year as McFadden) was a maverick, though *An Answer from Limbo* (1962) would lead us to believe that he was in his youth part of a satellite literary scene in Belfast. In attendance on the Belfast literary scene were figures of more shadowy achievement: John D. Stewart, J.J. Campbell, Denis Ireland, Jack Loudan, James Boyce. There were painters of quality too: William Conor, John Luke, Mercy Hunter, George MacCann. And I was pleasantly surprised to learn from McMahon that Estyn Evans, the eminent geographer, consorted with Bell, Boyd and the others up in Murlough Bay (Co. Antrim) as well as in the chosen Belfast restaurants. (The most accomplished contemporary Northern writer of all, Forrest Reid, lived reclusively in Belfast and was of no use to anyone contemplating a literary movement or even public coterie; Greacen recalls sending him his writings as a schoolboy and then being summoned to visit him in his disappointingly un-Bohemian suburban house in south Belfast imposingly filled nevertheless with books.[4] Reid lived until 1948 but was of a previous generation, having been born in 1875. Another Belfast writer of the previous generation, St John Ervine, was born in 1883 but although he lived on until 1971 his career was pursued outside Northern Ireland, in England or Dublin.) All in all, whereas the South was in a healthier literary state through the 1930s, 1940s and 1950s, the residents of which included, among others, Frank O'Connor, Sean O'Faolain, Peadar O'Donnell, Flann O'Brien (Brian O'Nolan), Patrick Kavanagh and Benedict Kiely (the latter three Catholic migrants from Ulster), the Belfast scene was lively enough.

To be sure, there was a good deal of croneyism, and an almost exclusively male croneyism at that, but hardly more than what obtained in the 1960s and 1970s when there was a similar sense of literary huddle with writers (smaller in numbers, in fact) deploying themselves like musk-oxen against the besieging Unionist and low-church Protestant philistines and comforting and inspiring each other with verse letters and mutual dedications and, no doubt it will be revealed in time, posted letters. And until the advent of Medbh McGuckian, the Ulster 'Literary Renaissance' of the 1960s and 1970s was pretty well a 90-per-cent male phenomenon, with a strong component of literary 'laddism' among the youngest and most famous. An important difference between the generations, though, was the conscious, almost wilful provincialism of Bell's cohort, whereas Heaney, Mahon and Longley early had broader horizons (thanks in part to their university education) and were determined to succeed in London and Dublin, and through the best publishers.

But the word 'provincialism' needs to be qualified. Bell and company were the first generation to reach literary maturity in the devolved state of Northern Ireland and in addition were inheritors of the desire of the generation before them – the generation of Rutherford Mayne (Samuel Waddell), Bulmer Hobson, James Cousins and Gerard Macnamara (Harry Morrow) – to fashion an Ulster equivalent of the Irish Literary, especially Dramatic, Revival. This was provincialism that bethought itself something of a national movement, since Northern Ireland was constitutionally meant to approximate in weight the Free State. (This was an illusion that persevered in Ulster until Westminster unilaterally prorogued Stormont in the early 1970s; any remnant of the illusion was destroyed by the Anglo-Irish Agreement of 1985 – a pact trumpeted on both sides as one between two sovereign states, the United Kingdom and the Republic of Ireland.) Besides, Belfast was a large enough city, with more than 400,000 inhabitants, to be in theory a capital, even a cultural capital, but by the 1940s it was losing its industrial heft and its cultural pretensions were, as they are now, with Belfast vying to be European City of Culture in 2008, problematic.[5] By the 1940s, Belfast, like the down-at-heel Dublin of the turn of the twentieth century (as Joyce saw it), 'wore the mask of a capital'. Devolution may have created Northern Ireland and given it a parliament, but it was, and is, an anomalous, indeed paradoxically unique 'province' of the United Kingdom and is often referred to by the pro-Union Northern Irish and English as 'the Province'.

WAR AND AFTER

This odd provincialism was betrayed, in the contradictory senses of 'sabotaged' and 'revealed', by the quasi-bohemianism of Bell's generation. The writers frequented coffee houses, held colourful international left-wing opinions, enjoyed group weekends in country cottages, creating echoes of both Auden's open-air 1930s and London's Fitzrovia of the 1940s and 1950s. Their social heyday seems to have been the Second World War. Life in Belfast was largely protected by distance and the Irish Sea and this permitted sub-bohemian life to continue, though the Belfast 'Blitz' in April 1941 gave them an alarming taste of metropolitan danger so that they had it both ways. In 1962 Denis Ireland recalled in 'Scenes from Irish Life: 1941–46' (in *The Dubliner*) an evening of gramophone music (Mozart, Grieg, Chopin, Bach) in the Lombard café in downtown Belfast with the black-out curtains drawn down and lamps lit within and the drone of bombers overhead: European high culture and sunken European barbarism somehow cosily juxtaposed. In *The Sash My Father Wore*, Greacen recreates an 'identikit' morning in Campbell's coffee house during the war after a German air-raid. It is all rather exciting, with Yanks in Jeeps scuttling by outside, the sun shining on the imposing City Hall across Donegall Square, the witty Denis Ireland, the bow-tied William Conor, the business-suited Richard Rowley and others dropping by and engaging in crisp, humorous repartee and discussion; Joe Tomelty pops in, followed by the English novelist living in wartime Belfast, F.L. Green, author of *Odd Man Out* (1945); young painters are in a corner arguing about recent art exhibitions in Belfast; those hungry for a first-class meal make plans to travel to neutral Dublin to secure it. It would appear to be a weekday and no one seems to have a nine-to-five job to go to.[6] It is difficult to read Greacen's recreation without a little envy, world war or no, though one has to suppress the memory of Myles na gCopaleen's (Flann O'Brien's) withering reference to Dublin's own 'velveteened, work-shy Marxist toads'. But then, almost everyone I know who lived through it in Belfast seems to have had a 'good war' and remembered it with affection. In my childhood, adult relatives seemed to wear the Blitz (never the far more serious-sounding 'Blitzkrieg') as a badge of civic honour. Recalling a meeting of the Irish Branch of the literary association, International PEN, in a mansion on the shores of Belfast Lough, where drinks and live piano music soon superseded the Society's official agenda, Denis Ireland (perhaps working from a diary) wrote in his *Dubliner* contribution, 'Scenes from Irish Life', of 'the drenched green island that, if it had the worst of the nineteenth century, is now having the best of the twentieth'.

The Free State seems to have been temporarily transmogrified for Ulster Protestants and even deep-dyed unionists – with some hypocrisy – from an alien and suspect state to the warm and hospitable provider of black-market eggs and butter, restaurant meals and physical safety, and even fire-engines and firemen after the Blitz: dear dirty affable Dublin surrounded by opulent farms that yet allowed the luxurious frisson of fear at the border, the fear coming from the possibility that the customs officials might close the border for the night with you and your car on the wrong side of it (though even I recall a time when the border would be kept open for a solitary returning bonded car from the North!). There was also drama as well as good food on offer in the Free State, and Denis Ireland remembered an entertaining, but ultimately uncomfortable, mounting of Wilde's *The Importance of Being Earnest* (while bombs were flying over London) attended by 'mountainy young women from remote Georgian country houses' and 'hungry-looking authors, even respectable bookmakers and publicans'.

But from the literary historian's point of view, the biggest difference from the next generation was the fact that Bell lived, aspired and wrote outside the university. *Before* the university one could say, since only after the Butler Education Act kicked in by producing the first scholarship graduates around 1958 did it become *de rigueur* for writers to come out of, and often go back into, the university. What the university – with its creative writing courses, its seminars, its conferences at home and abroad, its readings and festivals, its cafeterias and Student Union – became for Heaney's generation, the BBC and, to a lesser extent, the Central (public) Library and Linenhall (subscription) Library and the newspaper, and the city-centre pubs and restaurants, were to Bell's generation. The Linenhall Library in central Belfast was of inestimable value to that generation, and McMahon fittingly begins his biography with a memory of his Saturday meetings with his subject in that library in the 1980s. And what the pub and later up-market restaurant were for Heaney's harder-drinking generation, the modest restaurant and coffee house were to Bell's, especially Campbell's coffee house in Donegall Square North, the Lombard café in Callender Street (that survived as a grammar school pupil afternoon hangout into my teens in the late 1950s and indeed is there to this day) and the Chalet d'Or restaurant in Fountain Street. Drinking stout would have been a way for Protestant writers to signal their small rebellion from their orthodox community (the majority of Protestants sixty years ago being teetotal) but the mores of that community would have prevented Bell's generation from engaging in the heedless indulgence of the 1960s generation of Mahon, Longley and Heaney. Without the benefit of the post-war welfare society and the cushion of subsidized education, those who were determined to be full-time writers in those days often faced the stern task of living through professional writing, through hack work glorified by the opportunity to create literature simultaneously. The BBC even more than the newspaper created this opportunity, and Bell was for most of his working life a BBC producer, script-writer and broadcaster. Greacen remembers that it was largely through the good offices of MacNeice that Bell got into the Beeb.[7] For his part, McMahon tells us that Bell, who attended a lowly National School (before post-Partition primary schools) and then went to work, dearly wished for some academic standing; the BBC (Arts, Talks or even Schools department) for him and for others was as an institution the next best thing to a university in the matter of intellectual status.

It was in the offices of Broadcasting House, Ormeau Avenue, the Belfast home of BBC Northern Ireland that I met Bell, and accidentally, for the only time. He entered the office where I was talking to the producer David Hammond and his colleague Maurice Leitch, about to publish his first novel. I had brought Hammond some folk-songs I had written – in the 1960s one could write 'folk-songs' without waiting tediously for anonymity, the passage of time and the mechanisms of transmission. Despite my youthful shy arrogance I felt the lazy creative buzz around me in that BBC office; it was a couple of years before I conceived an interest in Ulster writing that issued ten years later in *Forces and Themes in Ulster Fiction* and I am sorry to report that I had no particular wish back then to meet Bell. I was studying aesthetics and D.H. Lawrence under Philip Hobsbaum at Queen's University, don't you know, and about to leave for the rumoured state of Oregon to study for a doctorate, and ignorantly thought Bell an incorrigibly provincial figure. I was Pip among Trabb's boys. I see from McMahon's useful list of the programmes produced or written by Bell that Leitch and Bell were collaborating on several talks around that time, just before Leitch lit out for London. It shocks me now to realize that Bell would have been only 55 or 56, Hammond about 35, Leitch probably in his late 20s: oh, Lawrence's 'relentlessness of life'!

Those programmes produced or written between 1949 and 1969 during Bell's tenure at the BBC and in the early 1970s after retirement stood his stories and novels in good stead. One envies him the valuable legwork and fieldwork around Ulster that they required and which must have played the part that hours in a library play for most fiction writers, though clearly Bell researched his programmes too, no doubt at the Linenhall and Central libraries. Bell, like his slightly younger Ulster contemporary Benedict Kiely, came to know the geography, history, dialect and folklore of Ulster intimately and it shows in *Summer Loanen and Other Stories* (1943) and *Erin's Orange Lily* (1956), as well as in his novels, *December Bride* (1951), *The Hollow Ball* (1961) and *A Man Flourishing* (1973). I wonder if the technology and foresight of the time allowed any of those wireless programmes to be preserved: if they exist, they would be a valuable cultural archive.

The provincialism of lifestyle and regionalism of literary style had their virtue. Whereas MacNeice, Patrick Kavanagh and Kiely, like earlier Ulster writers such as St John Ervine, Æ and Robert Lynd, fled the North of Ireland to the capital, be it London or Dublin, Bell and Co. stayed; someone after all had to mind the store and keep the home fires burning. Throughout the 1970s, 1980s and 1990s, Michael and Edna Longley performed the same essential service, and it is good – despite the misspelling of one of the names that I have corrected below – that McMahon quotes Michael Longley's posthumous tribute to Bell in 1990: 'For me Sam Hanna Bell ranks alongside Lloyd Praeger, Estyn Evans and John Hewitt as one of our prophets'. High praise indeed, and by 'prophets' Longley means Ulster culture-givers. Evans arrived in Ulster from Britain in 1928 and stayed; Hewitt after a lengthy spell in Coventry returned to Belfast and lived during the Troubles in Stockman's Lane, one of the Belfast 'interfaces'. (I remember Hewitt using this euphemistic neologism with bemusement on one of my visits to him.) There is surely the distant implication in Longley's statement that to remain at one's post through thick and thin deserves recognition. But if we think of Praeger who left Belfast for Dublin around the turn of the twentieth century, then the virtue of deep regional study (which the naturalist Praeger conducted in Ulster) must also inform Longley's honorific. All these writers were masters of the Ulster Experience at its deepest levels, those of geography and folkways.

In his youth Bell regarded himself as a socialist and McMahon tells us that he wrote for a socialist news-sheet called *Labour Progress*, which issued from a Belfast office that was the focus of Belfast's socialist activity in the depressed 1930s and was also the Northern Ireland distribution centre for Victor Gollancz's Left Book Club. Hewitt, Greacen and many of their writer friends thought of themselves as left-wingers during Auden's dishonest decade and the succeeding war. Looking back fifty years later, Greacen in *Brief Encounters* recalls wartime Saturday nights in a Belfast flat rented by Bell and Bob Davidson when talk about Marx and socialism flowed as generously as the Guinness. Greacen remembered Bell as 'a man whose socialism was idealistic and rooted in concern for the underdog' (p.19). For his part, McFadden was drawn to pacifism, socialist realism and cultural anarchism, though how deeply or seriously would need to be discovered.[8]

This is in contrast to McMahon's memory of the 1980s when he and the elderly Bell would meet in the Chalet d'Or with other survivors among the novelist's contemporaries, including Hewitt, Tomelty and Greacen (visiting from London where he lived and where I myself visited him a couple of times around then on my way to Belfast from Canada). Politics, McMahon says, was a rare topic and we can supply the reason why: it was the tense and terrorized decade of the hunger strikes, bomb atrocities and the Anglo-Irish Agreement. One did not discuss these events in public, nor did one risk serious disagreement between friends on matters about which one privately felt deeply.

The contrast between the 1940s and 1980s in this regard is telling. Pre-war socialism was a way in which Northern Irish writers could overcome, however precariously, their prior and largely involuntary primary identities as either Protestant or Catholic, unionist or nationalist and take part, first and foremost, in an unpartitioned and recognizable intellectual and artistic community (or, at worst, coterie); as a bonus, it was a way too of defining oneself as an artist and dangerous. After the more extreme British left parties dwindled after the war (including the Communist Party), the Northern Ireland Labour Party (NILP), which harboured those sympathetic to the arts and some artists themselves, was a tremendously important asylum to the artistic or merely arty, and we know that the party foundered in the 1970s when the rupture between unionists and nationalists became so deep during the Troubles that the NILP could no longer contain Protestants and Catholics. Its adherents scattered: Catholics of nationalist persuasion who abjured physical force joined the new Social Democratic and Labour Party (SDLP); the Protestant working class came adrift and then transferred much of its allegiance to Paisley's Democratic Unionist Party (DUP). For its part, the arts crowd fell politically silent or circumspect: socialism was of no use now in the face of IRA guns and bombs, loyalist retaliation, and the need to be either for or against the Union of Great Britain and Northern Ireland. If the NILP's demise was tragic, then Paddy Devlin and

Gerry Fitt were its tragic heroes on the Catholic side (realizing in time that the SDLP was a Catholic nationalist party first and foremost, whatever its socialist allegiance), Sam Napier, Billy Blease and David Bleakley on the Protestant side (watching the rump and now largely Protestant NILP being wiped out by the DUP and Ulster Unionist Party (UUP). The British Labour Party was the NILP's nemesis, scandalously deserting it in favour of the SDLP and to this day adhering to the miserable and at base sectarian (anti-Protestant) and nationalist (anti-unionist) policy of disqualifying Northern Ireland residents from membership of the party. The same British party (in its reincarnation of New Labour) went on to become the nemesis too of the Official Unionist Party, thereby helping to destroy non-sectarian and centre-ground politics in Ulster and paving the way for triumph by the DUP and Sinn Fein/IRA.

Socialism was also a means by which such Protestant literati as Bell, Hewitt, Greacen and others could cock a snook at the prevailing atmosphere of Unionist Northern Ireland which starved artists of sufficient oxygen. They were, of course, wishing to participate in the publicly intellectual *Zeitgeist* in Britain, but left-wing opinions served the more proximate purpose of *épater le bourgeois*, the bourgeois in question being Belfast burghers, abounding clergymen and po-faced Unionist politicians. Socialist views were a purchase on art and intellect and also a way of being anti-Unionist without being nationalist and (to use an offensive phrase of the day) a 'Fenian lover'. Yet the posture actually presupposed the stability of Stormont and the sectarian state of Northern Ireland as it was then. George Moore somewhere said that he supported public and orthodox morality the better to enjoy offending against it, and one suspects an analogous attitude on the part of Protestant artists and intellectuals even today: they discountenance Trimble, Paisley and the others, but don't commit themselves to a coherent or public constitutional position. A quiet unspoken unionism underneath a noisily ambiguous anti-Unionism has been a feature of Protestant intellectual and artistic life for decades. This does not rebut what Greacen remarked of Bell: 'I know that he thought of himself as an Irishman first and an Ulsterman second'.[9]

THE ARTS IN ULSTER

I say anti-Unionist with a capital U to distinguish a ruling party and establishment from a fundamental constitutional position. Any unity of artistic community that obtained in Ireland was, after Partition, incapable of entirely superseding the constitutional divide. Going to Dublin and drinking in public houses with fellow writers, sitting in Belfast lounges and trashing the more innocuous Stormont idiocies – these were one thing; but working for the very British BBC and knowing London to be your capital and wanting, really, to stay British – these were something else again and the more powerful thing by far. To say this is, I know, to engage in a kind of 'outing'. So Bell and his friends were at most what I would call soft nationalists, and even this is to overstate their take on constitutional politics. Denis Ireland recalled in 1962 that at the wartime PEN meeting in someone's Big House on the upscale shores of Belfast Lough, the whiskey and music seduced the artists and critics away from official business until at the end politics crept in, and of course it was sentimental nationalism, though most of the members would have been, I surmise, Protestants. The singing of 'My Lagan Love' gave way to the singing of 'The Three Flowers' ('For Emmet, Tone, and Dwyer I'll keep,/As I do love them all') and eventually – with grey warships outside riding at anchor – 'The Bold Fenian Men'. Then the members would have tipsily returned to their small *u* unionist lives by car or taxi.

McMahon has interesting pages on the making of the critical anthology, *The Arts in Ulster* (1951) which Bell was commissioned to edit, with John Hewitt, George Buchanan (an interestingly experimental novelist from Co. Antrim) and Nesca Robb (apparently a wealthy scholar) as associate editors.[10] The book was part of Northern Ireland's participation in the Festival of Britain of 1951. It is a good and useful book but there is a committee whiff of fustian about it; not surprisingly, since the committee of editors often disagreed before compromising and was in turn overseen by the Council for the Encouragement of Music and the Arts (CEMA), a forerunner of the Arts Council of Northern Ireland and presided over by the Stormont Minister of Health, it being a NI government body. McMahon quotes an editorial letter by Bell desiring less fustian in contributors' comments, but of course it probably came with the territory of government work, since what artists were to be included and which omitted and which political and historical observers were acceptable and which unacceptable were only in part a matter of art history; they were also a matter of contemporary political sensibilities and positions. McMahon remarks that Patrick Kavanagh was omitted from the account of Ulster poets, an omission impossible today. But it wasn't impossible even in 1974 when I omitted Kavanagh from *Forces and Themes in Ulster Fiction*. Were I to rewrite this book, I would include *Tarry Flynn* and *The Green Fool*. But it was less a critical oversight on my part than an almost unconscious cultural-political attitude. What has changed since 1974 is the cultural-political landscape, which has made the boundaries of purview more elastic. Protestant writers and critics are all now more soft-nationalist if in a different way from Bell and Co., a difference I will not go into here; but many of us are still small *u* unionists.[11]

My point would be that Bell, Boyd, Hewitt and others willingly took part in the government project of *The Arts in Ulster*. Why? Because in the end, Bell, Boyd, Hewitt and the other Protestant writers of their generation were Ulstermen, i.e., writers whose natural hinterland was the six counties, i.e. Northern Ireland, with a more distant but still natural hinterland in Britain and, pretty much an exceptional case, certain pubs in Dublin. They were lower-case unionists, the only kind of unionism that at the end of the day counts and to which trendy socialism and soft-cultural nationalism subordinate themselves in a crunch.

I wouldn't wish to suggest that these writers were cowardly, confused or hypocritical. I would rather imply the difficulty of their position caused by the way in which their preferred political position lay athwart their literary allegiances and affinities which when those allegiances and affinities originated in Ireland inclined the writers towards a cultural nationalism. The position of the Northern Irish Catholic is almost as difficult, witness the tangled issues provoked by Heaney's inclusion in Blake Morrison and Andrew Motion's *Penguin Book of Contemporary British Poetry* (1982). McMahon quotes from a letter that Heaney's mentor, Michael McLaverty, wrote to Bell, requesting that a photograph of himself not appear in *The Arts in Ulster*: 'Surely you don't expect an Irish nationalist like myself to subscribe, implicitly or explicitly, to Festival activities.' But McMahon does not quote him as writing firmly: 'Please excise all references to me from your book', presumably because McLaverty wrote no such thing. His Irish nationalism seems, on the evidence of McMahon's anecdote, no more whole-hearted than Heaney's during the Penguin affair. Greacen in remembering his friendship with McLaverty in wartime Belfast remarks: 'I was always amused by his suspicious attitude towards Dublin which, in some ways, differed little from that of a typical Orangeman ... He tended to think that the city was a trap for the writer who would squander his energies and ideas in tavern talk'.[12] Behind McLaverty's possibly temperamental puritanism lay perhaps a deeper, 'Northern' ambivalence. I suspect that in the cases of Heaney and McLaverty the Northern Irish Catholic had to make certain anti-unionist gestures while either keeping a low profile and wearing camouflage (McLaverty's tactic) or changing suits and conveying the gestures to one's more strident anti-unionist colleagues (Heaney's apparent tactic).

From the evidence of this very useful biography, Bell can do sterling duty as a case-study of what I have been talking about. The background and early life are exemplary. He was born in Glasgow in 1909 of a County Down mother and a Scots journalist father of County Antrim extraction. He was baptized in the United Free Church of Scotland. When his father died prematurely in 1918, young Bell and his family returned to the farm of his maternal grandfather in County Down, a stoutly Presbyterian and oppressively Sabbatarian figure. Here is the unsurprising childhood of the author of *December Bride*, one of the most characteristic Ulster Protestant novels and for which McMahon provides a useful annotated paraphrase. McMahon quotes Bell from his 1970 BBC talk, 'A Country Childhood', on his boyhood returns to Ulster from Scotland: 'We were doing no more than treading a path beaten over the sea by generations of my father's ancestors.' Bell's mother in the five years preceding her marriage lived in working-class and lower middle-class Protestant east Belfast (the very streets where my own parents had grown up) and this underlines the graphic typicality of Bell's background. After some years in his grandfather's country home, the Bell family removed to Belfast where Bell experienced adolescence, reached manhood and worked at a number of jobs before fetching up in the BBC. Belfast and the Ulster Scots countryside were his twin real-life and fictional locales.

The veteran literary commentator Sean McMahon has performed a fine service with his book. In some ways, it is a book written by a writer congenial to his subject, with whom he shares an ambivalent relation to scholarship. Unfortunately there are no full citations for primary or secondary sources and no listing of secondary sources at the back to supplement the useful checklist of Bell's books, articles and programmes. The author does not seem to have consulted many critical books and articles on Bell and Ulster literature. There is only one photograph, a frontispiece portrait of Bell. Blackstaff Press have lost an opportunity to enliven the text and provide a valuable photographic essay on a literary generation; individual and group shots of MacNeice, Rodgers, Greacen, Hewitt, Boyd and the rest, with illuminating captions, would have done wonders for the book's archival value. The author and publisher could have searched the photographic and illustrated book archives of the BBC Hulton Library, the Ulster Museum, the Ulster Folk and Transport Museum, the Linenhall Library among others.

Nevertheless, I hope Blackstaff thinks about commissioning other life stories of the chief Belfast literary and cultural figures of the last century, the better to fill out our knowledge and sense of Northern Irish writing before Heaney and Co. and to complicate profitably our typically simple picture of life and letters in Ulster. I'm sure the Arts Council of Northern Ireland would support the venture as it has supported this worthy addition to Irish biography.

NOTES

1. Sean McMahon, *Sam Hanna Bell: A Biography* (Belfast: Blackstaff Press, 1999). My review article on his book appeared in 2003.
2. Robert Greacen alas died in 2008 (2009).
3. The appearance of these three critical surveys within three years suggests that the creative ferment in Northern Ireland we associate with Heaney, Longley, Mahon, Simmons and others was accompanied by a new critical awareness of the distinctiveness of Northern Irish writing and culture. Both accompanied, of course, the new awareness of the distinctive and unhappy politics of Northern Ireland. The three surveys were preceded by Michael Longley's pioneering critical anthology, *Causeway: The Arts in Ulster* (1971), a sequel to *The Arts in Ulster* (1951), which I discuss later. The Arts Council of Northern Ireland where Longley worked (and which published *Causeway*) contributed considerably to the renaissance of creative sensibility and critical perceptiveness in the province. It is the case, however, that the fresh awareness of the literary distinctiveness of Northern Ireland (or, in various definitions, Ulster) was exactly contemporary with the emergence of Ulster critics and writers of a robust nationalist (or at least, anti-partitionist) hue and persuasion. The latter writers and critics, who were graduates of the new meritocratic education system, joined or initiated movements and magazines for which *Crane Bag* and Field Day can function as shorthand, while their Northern-orientated counterparts became identified with what became known as revisionism.
4. Robert Greacen, *The Sash My Father Wore: An Autobiography* (Edinburgh and London: Mainstream Publishing, 1997), pp.111–18; *Brief Encounters: Literary Dublin and Belfast in the 1940s* (Dublin: Cathair Books, 1991), pp.7–14.
5. It has been announced (2007) that this bid has been unsuccessful. There was some debate in Northern Irish circles about the extent to which Belfast could lay claim to culture in the past, but as it turned out the bid relied upon the perceived need for Belfast to *have* culture *in the future*, and thus an opportunity was lost to define culture in such a way as to include applied science (especially engineering) and commerce in the achievements of which Belfast once shone.
6. This portrait, and much else from *The Sash My Father Wore*, first appeared in Greacen's *Even Without Irene: An Autobiography* (Belfast: Lagan Press, 1995).
7. Robert Greacen, 'Sam Hanna Bell: An Appreciation', in *Brief Encounters*, p.18.
8. Sarah Ferris of the Institute of Irish Studies (Queen's University, Belfast) has written a useful summary of McFadden's poetic career and belief system: see http://researchservices1.qub.ac.uk/Sarahferis/rpy.htm.
9. Greacen, *Brief Encounters*, p.19.
10. *The Arts in Ulster: A Symposium* (London: Harrap, 1951).
11. But perhaps in this matter of Kavanagh I am unfair to myself; thirteen years later, in *Fictions of the Irish Literary Revival* (1987), I discussed the kinds of works that in 1974 I would have deemed inadmissible to any discussion of fiction. Genres too have become more elastic since 1974 and perhaps I thought Kavanagh's two works both too poetic and too autobiographical.
12. Greacen, *Even Without Irene: An Autobiography*, p.143.

15

BLOOMSDAY'S JOYCE

CULTURE ON THE MAKE

I confess I am not a fan of Bloomsday as a date on the cultural almanac. All of a sudden it has become a fixture on the Irish tourist calendar. As such, it is a kind of mock-festival, like Frank Costanza's entirely made-up Festivus holiday in the *Seinfeld* sitcom (a sitcom, incidentally, that goes in for some Joycean, if vastly simpler, arrangements of theme, motifs and plot line), his tongue-in-cheek alternative to Christmas. Bloomsday also puts me in mind of those recent attempts in some Canadian cities to supplant Christmas with a Multiculturalism holiday, with a Holiday Tree or even Multiculturalism Tree in the city square, instead of a Christmas Tree. Bloomsday indeed is part of the widespread *festivalization* of culture, of which the very use nowadays of the word 'culture' is itself a symptom. And, of course, Bloomsday comes close to being a form of Kitsch or camp. Just this week, John Banville in *The Irish Times* called the Dublin Bloomsday celebrations 'a more than usually depressing extravaganza of kitsch'.[1]

Now Joyce himself, as Banville reminds us, relished Kitsch: we know he liked operettas, sentimental songs and things campy; he couldn't have written *Ulysses* (1922) as we know it had he not at least skim-read rubbishy dailies and weeklies, penny romances and novelettes, and listened to parlour recitations and Victorian tear-jerking songs around the piano. I seem to remember that in his house abroad he had a picture of Cork and when Frank O'Connor looked closely and asked what it was, Joyce said it was a view of Cork; I know that, said O'Connor, but what's the frame? Cork, replied Joyce. I think that whatever the people liked (what we would call popular culture, especially the culture of street and pub), *he* liked, or at least commended to memory, sought out, even researched while composing *Ulysses*. Joyce's real take on popular culture is as ambiguous as his real attitude to his chiefly lower-class Dubliners. Joyce's own attitude is overwhelmed by so many points of view and judgements in *Ulysses* that it is impossible to identify *from the texts* the real Joyce as a man of known opinions. For all his formal experimentation, was he a sentimentalist or a mocker of sentimentality? Will the real Joyce please stand up? No, he won't. Still, the popular culture is there, laid on with a trowel. It is a culture that W.B. Yeats hated, preferring as he did an eloquently rewritten and aristocratized, and anti-sentimental, popular *country* culture. Yet to take popular culture away from Joyce's work would perilously leave little more than the pedantry of Stephen Dedalus and the curiously effete drawing-room poems of *Chamber Music* (1907).

It's not Dublin working-class culture, by the way, nor is it middle class. Rather it is lower middle-class culture, the lower middle class having no coherence or class solidarity and making do (however energetically and pleasurably) with scraps of culture from above and below. Many of Joyce's characters are on the fringes of respectability; the cleverer are like Lenehan in 'Two Gallants', a story in *Dubliners* (1914), who holds 'himself nimbly at the borders of the company until he was included in a round. He was a sporting vagrant armed with a vast stock of stories, limericks and riddles.' Joyce and his family seem to have declined from the middle class to the lower middle class and so he was at home – at least artistically – with the incredibly piecemeal culture of his Dubliners that let him plunder their sayings, jokes, mottoes, half-baked knowledge (a parody of the wisdom Yeats sought among the peasant Irish); no wonder *Ulysses* is packed with lists, inventories, catechisms – cultural flotsam and jetsam.

Moreover, Joyce has an impeccable ear for the language of the Dublin lower middle class that is at its most vigorous in banter, behind which lie envy, greed, one-upmanship and a ruthless rush to judgement: an attitude to others that always assumes the worst and for which we in Belfast had the term 'pass-remarkable'. Such language reads comically, even hilariously on Joyce's pages (as on Flann O'Brien's pages) but in real life, in my youth, I disliked and rather feared the banter that passed for conversation in lower middle-class Belfast, though I later commended to memory and notebooks as many of the withering sayings and ironies as I could remember. Some of my mother's sayings I later found to my delight in *Ulysses*: 'she's not as green as she's cabbage-looking'; 'he has a belly on him like a poisoned pup'; someone is 'a mean scut'; someone Bloom sees is 'foostering' over change (which is misprinted in my Penguin *Ulysses* as 'fostering'); some drouth 'would suck whisky off a sore leg', and from the pub, those smart-alec ripostes: 'I beg your parsnips' and 'could a swim duck?'

My mother was teetotal and had a large range of sayings as colourful as any of Joyce's Dubliners, but there is no doubt that drink fuelled many of the sayings in Ireland. We relish Irish pub talk, yet Bloom –

who gives his name to this Joycean holiday – is right when he refers to 'drink, the curse of Ireland'. So strictly speaking, Bloomsday ought to be a public celebration of moderation, tolerance and prudence. (Bloom is referred to by one character in *Ulysses*, with typically hurtful understatement, as 'the prudent member' – a demeaning sexual *double entendre.*) Fat chance of such a celebration in our current culture of excess. *Ulysses* is set at a time of ferocious drinking because of promiscuous licensing by corrupt magistrates and a time of energetic temperance campaigns by Catholic and Protestant societies – 'Ireland sober is Ireland free' was one nationalist catch-cry – and I believe that that time has come again, though the coming temperance campaign in Ireland will have to be waged by government rather than religious organizations. Ireland will be far less funny than it was in the time of *Ulysses*, but healthier and wealthier. Not good news for the realist novelist, however.

So: given the role of popular culture in *Ulysses*, why *shouldn't* Dublin City Council, Failte Ireland and the Department of Arts, Sport and Tourism try to popularize Joyce by taking him at his word (his spendthrift thousands of words)? Moreover, if Banville is talking about Kitsch put to commercial ends, then we can remind ourselves that Joyce made the hero of his most famous novel a commercial gent, canvasser of newspaper ads. Yet there remains a pretty large gap between the serious, astoundingly uncommercial quality of Joyce's fiction, a fiction wrought with monk-like tenacity to the point of the author's near blindness and various personal and family deprivations, and the Tourist Board's transparently commercial machinations to get people to visit Dublin (or get out to various events if they live there) and spend money. Admittedly, I can think of no author more preoccupied with money than Joyce. Each and every story in *Dubliners* turns one way or another on money, and every other page of *Ulysses* mentions money – as coin, base or otherwise, as debt, as payment, as Judas silver. And we know that Joyce was in pursuit of the legal tender much of his life and was open to borrowing money freely even if he wasn't quite in Dylan Thomas's league as a cadger. But there's all the difference in the world between the money of reality and the money of fiction which in Joyce's case is part of a currency of metaphor and meaning and takes its place in their extraordinarily complex network and circuitry. One might feel better if Joyce's shade benefited from the serious money that will be made in Dublin this summer and every summer, but then Joyce's shade of opinion is hardly less mysterious than the living Joyce's.

Well then: why not praise the secular, come-all-ye nature of

Dublin's Bloomsday celebrations? We aren't, after all – and just as well, given Joyce's fiction on the subjects – talking about celebrations motivated by old-style Irish Catholic nationalism. I say this, even though, courtesy of some Irish 'chit from matron', somehow Joyce's deep reservations about Catholicism and nationalism were regarded as no obstacle whatsoever on the path of progress of these two forces or movements after 1916 and 1922 when *A Portrait of the Artist as a Young Man* and *Ulysses* were respectively published. His novels were largely unread in the South (there was no need to ban *Ulysses* in the Free State – it was simply unavailable) and when they were, they were regarded as merely academic. This proves, I think, that Joyce's use of popular culture was actually as abstruse as the arts to which the fictional and scholarly Stephen Dedalus resolves to devote himself.

Indeed, somehow Joyce managed to remain in everyone's eyes a Catholic writer (the way Yeats remained a Protestant writer even when an avowed paganist and an Irish nationalist) and a writer who enlarged Ireland's nationalist sense of itself every bit as much as Yeats did. Yet this was a writer whose French passport, as late as 1940, identified his nationality as 'Britannique'. He chose not to proclaim like a later Irish writer, 'my passport's green', though this was perhaps because British nationality might have provided more protection in a dangerous wartime Europe than an Irish Free State one. One suspects Joyce was essentially pragmatic in the matter of passports, but this in itself is telling.

But if Joyce wasn't in the strictest sense an Irish Catholic or Irish nationalist writer, he didn't become what you might expect if you didn't know better. That is to say, he did not become British or Protestant. Unlike many Irish writers seeking fortune and fame, he didn't hasten to England but instead vaulted over England to Europe. We recall Stephen's famous and, let's face it, sectarian remark to Cranly in *A Portrait* that although he has lost his Catholic faith he hasn't turned Protestant: 'I said that I had lost the faith ... but not that I had lost selfrespect'. This is a well-remembered passage from the novel; would its counterpart by a Protestant novelist be as fondly recalled? The phrase '*the* faith' is telling, there clearly being only one faith. This remark is often quoted, and with evident relish, by critics, Irish and otherwise, though it is just possible that Joyce meant Dedalus's reply to reflect his pretentious hyperbole.

Joyce was not quite as secular and come-all-ye as we might think. For example, Ulster and Ulster people fare as badly in Joyce as they do in Yeats. The student MacAlister in *A Portrait of the Artist* has an accent that offends Stephen Dedalus, an offence anticipated in Mr

Alleyne's 'piercing North of Ireland accent' in *Dubliners*. The schoolmaster Garrett Deasy in *Ulysses*, Stephen's paymaster, and whose ancestors came from the 'Ards of Down', adopts his motto in good received/perceived Protestant fashion from the English (as he believes): *I paid my way*. Stephen immediately does a list in his mind of all *his* outstanding debts. Deasy believes that 'money is power' and is seen by Stephen as an Ulster Orangeman identifiable with those who put the croppies down. And Belfast, capital of 'The black north and true blue bible', is where Blazes Boylan will have Molly to himself over 25 June (when she will sing in the Ulster Hall), though Bloom seems more concerned that the smallpox 'up there' doesn't get worse. (I assume the newspapers of the time and the archives of the Royal Victoria would corroborate the factuality of this epidemic.)

So Bloomsday celebrations can hardly be recruited in the post-dated service of the Belfast Agreement of 1998 and its cultural subclauses. But everyone is welcome and Bloomsday is clearly now a post-Tiger Ireland festival, not the obscure pre-Tiger festival it used to be.[2] American hash browns have suddenly become naturalized Edwardian-Irish nosh in the O'Connell Street (Joyce's Sackville Street) 'fry-up' that is happening as I speak. (My guess is that Poldy's beloved calf's kidneys and chicken livers and nutty gizzards will not be on offer – it will be chiefly, I suspect, American hotdog-stand food, times being what they are.) Culture and capital now inextricably couple, it seems, and their progeny we call *Heritage*, and Heritage, paradoxically, must be available to everyone. Heritage is the opposite of what we used to regard Culture as being; it is comprehensive and unifying, not divisive or distinctive. Culture and Heritage are now reasonably priced commodities. We no longer aspire to Culture; it is freely available to all and sundry if they put money in their purse. So James Joyce is now himself Heritage, which means you don't have to read him. Heritage is culture in capsule form; it is, as it were, the book review, not the book. To foreigners and young contemporary Irish, cubs of the Celtic tiger and emancipants from bad old Catholic Ireland, Joyce on the page must be an opaque writer, but there is no need to grapple with him in order to celebrate him, it seems. True, Joyce proved in fiction what his astute contemporary, Thomas Kettle, claimed in an essay in 1910: 'Ireland, a small nation, is, none the less, large enough to contain all the complexities of the twentieth century.'[3] But if Joyce is not read, then Bloomsday's Joyce is not the Irish novelist James Joyce but some commercialized impostor: 'The Cultural Icon James Joyce Formerly Known as The Novelist James Joyce'.

But if we shrink from this year's Bloomsday celebrations, no whole-hearted reader of Joyce can be squeamish or scrupulous any more than a whole-hearted reader of Geoffrey Chaucer. However, if we do shrink from them, what can we offer to celebrate in their stead? Why should Bloomsday *be* celebrated? And what in Joyce's life and his great novel *Ulysses* is worthy of celebration on a grand if not vulgar and commercial scale? If I try to answer these questions, I have to confess that I'm not a Joyce specialist and you will probably know already much of what I have to say. For these remarks, I simply reread *Ulysses*. Some of it once again (for example, the notorious Nighttown episodes) gave me the head staggers, and much of it left intact many of its difficulties and riddles. Yet once more I was stirred into deep admiration and given pleasure after pleasure.

THE WHOLE GHESABO

What you will certainly know is that Bloomsday, 16 June 1904, is the date of the events of *Ulysses*, chosen by Joyce in commemoration of the day on which he first walked out with Nora Barnacle. They strolled at Ringsend and Richard Ellmann rather grandly interprets the significance of the evening out: 'On June 16 he entered into relation with the world around him and left behind him the loneliness he had felt since his mother's death.'[4] But since this first date with Nora is not itself in the novel (and might even be seen as being mocked in Bloom's lascivious thoughts throughout the day, in the visit to the brothel, and in Boylan's and Molly's indoor date), this can be seen as one of Joyce's private commemorations that ought not to detain us.

It makes sense to celebrate the day (the only day, uncommonly enough) on which a great novel is set, though frankly it would make even more sense to me to celebrate the day the novel was published. Indeed, 2 February is the date both of Joyce's birth and the day in 1922 when the first two copies of *Ulysses*, complimentary copies for the author, rolled off the press. That way, Bloomsday would mean the anniversary of the novel *Ulysses* itself. But then in the uncertain greyness and touristlessness of an Irish February, the attractions of summer in the city would be lost to the Tourist Board and to holiday-makers themselves. I see that the Rejoyce Dublin 2004 Bloomsday Centenary Festival is running from 1 April (April Fools' Day) until 31 August: in other words, the entire summer tourist season for 2004. Presumably Bloomsday will resume centrality in 2005, but not exclusivity, given the annual Joycean summer schools and seminars. It is right and proper for Dublin to take advantage of its having been the setting for a very great novel, though Joyce's Dublin of 1904 has four-fifths of it (if we are talking about the housing) gone. I take my statistics from a fine article by Frank McDonald in *The Irish Times* Bloomsday Supplement of 12 June. McDonald notes sadly that Joyce's assertion that in the event of catastrophe Dublin could be rebuilt using *Ulysses* as a blueprint is now unsustainable, since so much of Joyce's Dublin has had an appointment with the wrecker's ball. Moreover, McDonald reminds us it never was rebuildable in the manner of Joyce's boast, since the writer was visually undetailed when it comes to the architecture of the city that Stephen Dedalus and Leopold Bloom wander through. Still, if only Belfast had some comparably focussed and spacious work of art by which to be commemorated. Indeed, we in Belfast suffered the indignity of having the setting of Brian Moore's fine novel, *The Lonely Passion of Judith Hearne* (1955), moved from Belfast to Dublin when it was filmed, an indignity that I am still amazed was not protested by critics and filmgoers, since *Judith Hearne* is a Belfast novel through and through. Imagine the outcry had John Huston shifted the setting of Joyce's 'The Dead' to Belfast!

So to celebrate Bloomsday is to celebrate Dublin, but this requires no *Ulysses*, no Joyce, no 1904. The odd thing is that Bloomsday on the face of it is Bloom's Day, the Day of Leopold Bloom, the Ulysses of *Ulysses*. It is a fictional Day that borrows the illusion of a real day and is composed largely by the thoughts, actions and feelings of a fictional hero. Real events are registered in the novel – the winning of the Ascot Gold Cup, report of a catastrophe in New York harbour, a fireworks display as part of the Mirus Bazaar in aid of Mercer's Hospital, a Vice-regal parade to the inauguration of the bazaar, arrival in Dublin of the three-masted schooner *Rosevean*, and so on. But they are all contorted by, and absorbed into, the inner consciousness of Bloom and Stephen and several other characters (for example, the unnamed swaggering 'I' – the seeing 'eye' – of the Barney Kiernan's pub/Cyclops episode, with his monocular view of Ireland and Irish history) and the governing but fitful consciousness of the overall narrator, unnamed, unbodied, a voice merely.

There are so many voices, angles of vision, prose styles, characters and scene settings in *Ulysses* that there is no single 'take' on the world that we can fasten on, the way we can fasten on a D.H. Lawrence take on the world. Joyce was an extraordinary pedant so there are some very big Greek words he uses in the novel to explain indirectly in scientific terms what he is endeavouring to do. One is *parallax*: differences in an object's position or direction, and appearance, relative to the observer's own position and direction. Joyce has fun with this in nineteen short scenes that make up the Wandering Rocks episode and in which characters criss-cross and we see or glimpse characters from different angles. Another is *metempsychosis*, a word Molly Bloom has stumbled on (and stumbles in pronouncing) in the novel she's reading, *Ruby: The Pride of the Ring* and that she asks her husband Poldy to define. He knows its meaning, being a bit of a cultured man: it is the transmigration of souls or reincarnation, and Joyce offers us all kinds of transmigrations of identities in *Ulysses:* mothers, fathers, sons, daughters, brothers, for example, are inhabited by various substitutable individuals; Hamlet becomes a whole series of Hamlets, some of them fictionally alive in 1904. The very word *metempsychosis* migrates or mutates into *met him pike hoses* (Molly's faltering attempt to pronounce it) with its appropriate sexual double entendre. But Joyce was also a mock-pedant. According to Richard Ellmann, Joyce claimed there wasn't a serious line in *Ulysses.*[5] Perhaps Joyce subscribed to Bloom's own deflationary idea about the big words: 'Only big words for ordinary things on account of the sound'. This is Joyce having it both, or many, ways.

This idea of recurrence and shape-changing (advanced by the repetition of words and bits of words, of sayings, phrases, ideas – in one episode the telling phrase 'as said before' recurs) suggests to me that Joyce was demonstrating in his novel the idea of the Eternal Return. Consider the multiple meanings of the title *Finnegans Wake*; declaratively, 'the awakening of the clans or families Finnegan', but since the natural form of the title is the possessive *Finnegan's Wake*, which is how it is frequently and wrongly printed by printers and even editors, to the infuriation of critics and scholars, the title means too 'the wake for Finnegan' (as in the traditional song from which Joyce borrowed his title). And of course there is more inside this portmanteau phrase: 'Fin(n)' = end, '-egan' = -again, thus End and Again, Finish and Begin again: verse into chorus into verse into ... 'Wake' is a mourning after death but also a reawakening into life, a new morning, both composing an eternal rhythm: Finneganbeginagain, both a description of nature and a cosmic command. Bloom remembers he wooed Molly in June and thinks: 'The year returns. History repeats itself.' There is nothing new under the sun, Bloom concludes.

But Joyce isn't consistent, which must be his point. Bloom also thinks of life as 'flowing in a stream, never the same ... Because life is a stream'. And he thinks of his eye contact with Gerty McDowell on the strand as 'Chance. We'll never meet again.' I remember the late Anthony Burgess in a lecture at Queen's University in the early 1960s describe *Ulysses* as a *roman fleuve*, a river-novel. The 'stream of life' required in a story a 'stream of consciousness': a narrative method Joyce perfected. So Joyce has it all ways, always. *Finnegans Wake* is a river novel with a vengeance. Another big word in *Ulysses* is *omphalos*. Yet another is *entelechy*. We could be clever about those too, simply by imitating in our own humble way Joyce's own supreme, occasionally fatiguing, cleverness.

Rereading *Ulysses* for this occasion, I have been stunned by the brilliance of it all and I was wondering as I read if being stunned is the proper condition of a reader. Joyce seems to me about as different from D.H. Lawrence as one novelist could get from another. Suitably, they hated each other's work. Lawrence thought that a novel was the nearest thing we could get to a quick, direct, unmediated representation of the our most natural and elemental human reality, our bedrock emotions, instincts, bodies, sexuality. So he avoided as many formal contrivances and structural arrangements as was compatible with achieving this goal. Joyce is the opposite, because he thought that life as he knew it had, if sometimes only beneath the surface, its own formal contrivances and arrangements: life *was* a contrivance and arrangement. He both promoted and reflected its patterns by superstitiously commemorating, indeed almost fetishizing, recurring numbers and dates, including birthdays and anniversaries. Surely it is relevant that Lawrence was brought up a Nonconformist Protestant whose religion valued spareness, directness and unmediated communication with the divine, Joyce an Irish Catholic whose religion was replete with ritual and terminology, and had a full calendar of observances, and a very long history. *Ulysses* is a very Catholic, even medieval Catholic, work. Would it be impertinent to detect in Joyce an almost adolescent conspiratorial mind produced by a surfeit of youthful learning and the various suppressions of an Irish Catholic boyhood that produced more than the usual boyish indulgence of the hidden and forbidden, while craving freedom and individuality?

Ulysses is Catholic and medieval only on one level, of course. For it is a novel beloved of the literary Modernists who praise *Ulysses* for its architectural wonders, its stylistic pluralities, its making good on Joyce's claim that it would keep the professors busy for fifty years ... plus thirty, by now, as it turns out. Such a happy hunting ground for Modernists is *Ulysses* that it seems to prove their theory that, really, language itself is writing the book. Joyce himself is absent like the artist Stephen Dedalus imagines in *A Portrait*, off-stage, paring his nails. (Perhaps, however, the novelist is the mysterious man in the brown macintosh who fleetingly appears now and again in the story – until indeed he becomes the fictional-fictional Mackintosh – the way Alfred Hitchcock would appear fleetingly in his own films as creator and character.) It is the novel *as novel* the Modernist critics are interested in, not the events or characters of the novel as moral entities or empirical representations. I know this may be foolish waywardness on my part, and it is certainly against the critical odds, but I can't help thinking that despite the stupendous mature accomplishment of *Ulysses*, the humbler *Dubliners* (itself no slouch in the formal department) is Joyce's perfect work that achieves life amidst paralysis but without the sledgehammer blows of relentless multiple demonstration.

Bloomsday means nothing to lovers of Modernism except as a clever coinage that rhymes with Doomsday yet affirms life amidst death, as Leopold does in Glasnevin cemetery, thinking living thoughts amidst corpses. Well, we all know the cryptic crossword pleasure of decoding and unravelling the pages of *Ulysses*, its patterns and puzzles. I hadn't realized before this current reading, for example, the importance of the word and concept of *key* in the novel (and its inflections; for example *Keyes* the potential ad-placing firm) or indeed the abundance of money references. I will offer one episode-sized example that I've tried to work out for myself in the last few days.

In the Nausicaa episode, Gerty McDowell with two girlfriends Cissy and Edy and three children sit on the rocks at Sandymount shore. Leopold Bloom is there too, a figure apart as usual and quite soon playing pocket billiards. The episode follows after the rough male banter of the Cyclops episode set in Barney Kiernan's pub and the first half of the episode (from Gerty's point of view) is written in a 'female' style that suggests the stories in the *Lady's Pictorial*, Princess series of novelettes, and the novels of Miss Cummins, author of *The Lamplighter* and *Mabel Vaughan*, all of which Gerty has read. Needless to say, Maria Susanna Cummins was a real author (1827–66) and the two novels, real novels; *The Lamplighter* was reprinted many times between 1854 and 1906. I'm surprised Joyce doesn't mention another of her novels, *Haunted Hearts*, for it could subtitle both Bloom's and Gerty's day (Bloom haunted by the early death of his son Rudy and the awareness of Molly's adultery, for Gerty a 'gnawing sorrow is there all the time'). But maybe he does and I've missed it. And perhaps he left it to the professors to discover that Maria Cummins also wrote a novel called *Little Gerty, or The First Prayer*, which I found out for myself only a couple of days ago.

In any case, Gerty's thoughts are couched in soft sentimental-romantic feminine literary language which allows Joyce to confuse imagination and narrative reality. Gerty is attracted to the foreign-looking figure in mourning black and she daydreams a romantic fantasy about him that is chastely sexual but which she acts out seductively. Cissy asks Bloom, who is nearby, what time it is, but he discovers when he takes out his watch that it has stopped. At this point one might realize that *Time* dominates the episode. The episode is famous, of course, for the description of the rockets and Roman candles that seem verbally to enact Gerty's orgasm. It was the periodical publication of this episode that got Joyce into hot water with the American authorities. 'Periodical' is, however, ironically apt. Earlier, Gerty feels a 'warm flush, a danger signal always'; soon after she 'felt a kind of a sensation rushing all over her' and realizes that 'that thing must be coming on because the last time too was when she clipped her hair on account of the moon'. Some minutes later she excuses her own sexual thoughts because they were 'on account of that other thing coming on the way it did'. The ecstatic rush of language as the Roman candle bursts and gushes *suggests* – in the Joycean imagination that transcends the limits of gynaecology – both orgasm and menstruation. Bloom detects pre-menstrual edginess in Edy but Joyce has planted this.

In any case, the breathy gush of language does double duty in also representing Bloom's ejaculation. The narration shifts post-climactically from Gerty's to Bloom's point of view and the prose style from that of what we might call 'expectant female Harlequin Romance' to Bloom's customary commonplace, realistic yet suppressively sexual mode of thinking. The style changes when Gerty gets up and Bloom sees the reality: her lameness. (Though he does imagine writing a story for *Titbits* about himself, 'The Mystery Man on the Beach' but typically, on coining the title, thinks immediately of remuneration: 'Payment at the rate of one guinea per column'.) Bloom is as much the creature of time as a menstruating woman. Even ecstasy in Joyce is time-bound as it never is in Lawrence. Bloom wonders if his watch, which stopped at half past four, did so at the moment when 'he' and 'she', i.e. Blazes Boylan and Molly, completed the act. And even *because* they did the act. For he now wonders if there is some magnetic attraction 'between the person because that was about the time he...', a typically uncompleted Bloom thought. Magnetism is behind it all, he thinks. It causes movement. 'And time?' he asks himself. 'Well that's the time the movement takes.' (We love Bloom for his curiosity.) 'Because it's all? arranged', he says of 'the whole ghesabo'. (This might be Bloom's misunderstanding of the word 'gazebo' but since there appears to be no such word as 'ghesabo', this is possibly his affectionate use of one of Molly's malapropisms.) He remembers that Molly met Boylan at a dance where she wore black: 'Good conductor, is it? Or bad?' Anyway, Joyce is the conductor in the orchestral sense as he deploys his characters in the act of conduction or attraction, and repulsion, in the physicists' senses of those words.

By the way, the dreamy action at Sandymount has as accompaniment a men's temperance retreat in a nearby Catholic church with the conducting of the mass as background to Bloom's arousal and Gerty's girlish daydreams. She recalls her father's drunkenness and how 'that vile concoction which has ruined so many hearths and homes had cast its shadow over her childhood days'. I suppose it's fitting that the hope of Ireland's being sober should be expressed in an episode written in the romantic language of daydream and wish-fulfilment.

Bloom muses on Molly's malapropism – Ben Dollard's having a 'base barreltone' instead of bass baritone voice. (But how would Bloom know Molly was saying 'base' rather than 'bass'? Isn't this Joyce's pun, not Molly's? Besides, since Molly is an accomplished singer, she would know the word 'baritone' so that her malapropism must be deliberate, a stroke of Joycean wordplay and hence not strictly a malapropism.) He thinks: Big Ben has legs like barrels and you'd think he was singing into a barrel. Plus, Dollard was a powerful man at storing away Number One Bass. Barrel of Bass. 'See?' Bloom says pleasurably to himself. 'it all works out'. (But unlike 'base' and 'bass' in music, 'base' and 'Bass' as in beer are not homophones.) After another mildly convoluted exercise in association, this time social association rather than word association, he comments to himself: 'Wheels within wheels'. The cliché does not invalidate its structural truth for *Ulysses*. For so the novel is: wheels within wheels and it all – with the exception of riddles at present apparently not decisively solved by the critics (what is the 'U.P.:up' on the postcard business? Who is Martha Clifford? Who is the man in the macintosh?) – works out.

FUNFERALL

However, it is not the Modernists but the liberal humanists who could make a case for a real Bloomsday celebration. For Leopold Bloom has been seen by liberal humanist critics as representing Tolerant Man, Loving Man, Cultured Man, Flowerchild Man, and Victimized Man. He is the Jew who is also a genuine Christian, unlike the nominal Christians of the novel, and whose name is contained in the phrase on the throwaway flyer thrust into his hand: *Bloo*d of the La*m*b

(Joyce having it all ways again). He is Euro-Man (Irish, Jewish, Hungarian), even Everyman (no narrow, intolerant religious or nationalist bigot) who is yet Irish Man in its potentially best sense, neither Catholic Irish Man nor Protestant Irish Man (who each causes all the bother). 'What is your nation if I may ask', challenges the figuratively one-eyed super-patriotic Citizen. 'Ireland, says Bloom. I was born here. Ireland.' Also Solitary Man, Exiled Man. Simply, Man (or Humanity as we would nowadays say). Bloomsday conceived along these lines would certainly seem to be worth celebrating and commemorating, though it probably hasn't motivated organizers of the Bloomsday carnival.

Yet on rereading the novel I became conscious of two flies in the ointment. The nature of Bloom and the liveliness and livingness of his enemies. I suppose we are meant to dismiss the venom directed at Bloom by the unnamed narrator of the Cyclops/Barney Kiernan's episode as typical Dublin witty contempt. Bloom is referred to as 'lardyface' and the episode enacts in micro-version the expulsion of the Jews from Egypt, or in this case the desired-for expulsion of the Jews from nationalist Ireland, Catholic Ireland as we know being rather anti-Semitic in the time of *Ulysses*. So the characters' attitude to Bloom in the novel is a deep prejudice. The problem is that the bigotry and sectarianism in the novel are so comically expressed for the most part and the expulsion so comically depicted that it's hard to feel hostile to these fierce Irish nationalists. With extravagant inadvertent ironies, the citizen shouts: 'By Jesus ... I'll brain that bloody jewman for using the holy name. By Jesus, I'll crucify him so I will. Give us that biscuitbox here.' It's a Jacob's biscuitbox, of course, and therefore made by a Quaker firm, an irony in the light of the Citizen's violence. Meanwhile a street slut shouts after Bloom who is on a jaunting car with Martin Cunningham: 'Eh, mister! Your fly is open, mister!' Flann O'Brien thought the second 'mister' proves the accuracy of Joyce's ear for Dublin street speech. Bloom's expulsion exceeds even Exodus and becomes his ironic Assumption into Heaven on a chariot as the prophet Elijah, amid clouds of angels ascending 'to the glory of the brightness at an angle of forty-five degrees over Donohoe's in Little Green Street like a shot off a shovel'. This is Joyce's surplus of irrepressible narrative energy: he didn't always know when to stop and everything between here and eternity was fair game.

But anti-Bloomitism is also based on the assumption (remember, always believe the worst) that he has won on the Ascot Gold Cup and is keeping mum. The narrator thinks Bloom is stingy (as a Jew he would be, of course): 'Gob, he'd let you pour all manner of drink down his throat till the Lord would call him before you'd ever see the froth of his pint.' But we know Bloom is a temperate man where drink is concerned. We also know that Bloom lent Joe Hynes three bob three weeks before. True, Bloom hasn't forgotten it and is virtually obsessed with money. (Of course, money may be in part Joyce's metaphor for reality.) Only one character, the leech Lenehan, defends Bloom and I assume we're meant to see the justice of his remark: 'He's a cultured allroundman, Bloom is ... He's not one of your common or garden ... you know ... There's a touch of the artist about old Bloom.' (Which in part explains the might-have-been artist's later communion with the would-be artist, Stephen Dedalus.)

But Bloom might not, if we think about it, get off so lightly nowadays as he used to. He's offered to us as a masturbating voyeur. He thinks a lot about his daughter Milly's emerging sexuality and when Gerty McDowell has departed, Bloom would like to be the rock she sat on. Gerty is 21 and is afraid of being left on the shelf, but she is an arrested adolescent who looks young (she is still 'sweet seventeen' in the episode's fantasy) and who blushes easily and Bloom thinks: 'I begin to like them at that age. Green apples. Grab at all that offer ... Also the library today: those girl graduates.' Today these would be seen as the thoughts of a stalker and groomer. In the Oxen of the Sun episode, Joyce in the person of an anonymous orator even makes the case against Bloom as a hypocrite, prudish and salacious by turns, a masturbator, a man who sexually neglects his wife and whose 'marital breast is the repository of secrets which decorum is reluctant to adduce'. (The amazing and sometimes dispiriting thing is that anything you want to say about Joyce's characters in *Ulysses* Joyce has already said!)

Then there's Bloom's complaisance as a cuckold. He even thinks he *might* be a bit of a chump for aiding and abetting Molly and Boylan: 'I am a fool perhaps. He gets the plums and I the plumstones.' Before wondering if his watch stopped in commemoration of his wife's infidelity, he thinks – combining money with complaisance – 'Suppose he gave her money. Why not? All a prejudice. She's worth ten, fifteen, more a pound. What? I think so. All that for nothing'. And then there is his clandestine sexual correspondence with 'Martha Clifford', a form of adultery by letter while he passively encourages his wife's adultery in letter (if not in spirit). We know that Joyce himself engaged in a clandestine sexual correspondence with a Marthe Fleischmann in Zurich in 1918, which became Bloom's correspondence with Martha Clifford, just as the girl Stephen sees by the shore in *A*

Portrait was based on the girl Joyce saw in 1898, as was Gerty McDowell, a version de-idealized for Bloom through a debased romanticism. We also know that Joyce flirted with the arousing idea of his wife Nora's infidelity.

So if we want to celebrate Bloom we have to take him warts and all. Either we emulate Joyce's hugely encyclopaedic view of humanity, and take the long and the panoramic view (and could a Bloomsday celebration do or promote such a thing?), or let Bloom remain a vague symbol of the little man's passive and conscientious triumph against the big forces and the big words, an almost Charlie Chaplin-like figure with his moustache and black mourning garb. But that seems an unlikely figure for present-day go-getting, mobile-phone brandishing, tigerish Dublin to celebrate. (I rather think that Bloomsday is vaguely regarded instead as sanctioning enthusiastic eating and drinking as though commemorating the gargantuan appetite of the novel itself rather than Bloom's prudence and peccadilloes.) Speaking of Bloom, warts and all, he himself hides his profile from Gerty, knowing he is not handsome but perhaps because he has an aquiline nose, which Gerty wonders if he has. Still, he thinks he can't be too bad if Marion Tweedy – Molly – married him.

Ah, Molly. Somehow, Bloomsday incorporates Molly Bloom too and adds generosity, femininity, affirmativeness to the qualities we attach to her husband. The eating and drinking I mentioned could be regarded, almost subconsciously, as honouring, by implication, Molly's alleged sexual appetite and appetite for life. She is of course an adulteress; whether once or several times over we don't know, but surely the text suggests the latter: Bloom *assumes* that Boylan's bringing the programme for the Belfast concert to Molly is actually a tryst, implying it has happened before – unless it is a wish-fulfilling daydream like Gerty McDowell's but which comes true – while the unnamed narrator of Cyclops assumes Boylan's contribution to the concert will be 'Blazes doing the tootle on the flute', though the narrator always thinks the worst anyway and is an unreliable witness. Bloom's so-called friends seem to assume an affair between Molly and Boylan, or Molly and *someone* (Bloom being only a 'half and half' in their bloodshot eyes) but this could be Dublin cynicism.

In any event, even in these Politically Correct times, any errancy of Molly's is absorbed into her quasi-feminist status as an allround-woman (to borrow from Lenehan). The way we perceive her may be as vague, as devoid of outline, as her character itself. We base that on her mighty and mollycoddling soliloquy which is self-justifying and therefore Molly-justifying. For we hardly see her from the outside, as it were, only from the inside. And when we *do* see her from the outside, it is through others' eyes. One character remembered dancing with her and finding her 'an armful'. Lenehan remembers coming home from an annual dinner at Glencree reformatory and sitting beside Molly on an outside car with Bloom and his own wife and getting aroused by Molly's 'fine pair': 'His hands moulded ample curves of air'. An allround-woman, indeed. The unnamed narrator of Cyclops sees her avoirdupois rather differently: 'The fat heap he married is a nice old phenomenon with a back on her like a ballalley'. So to celebrate Molly, we have to take her part and parcel, bit and bundle, as we have to Leopold. I see no way into *Ulysses* for moral discriminations.

So maybe, after all, the fun-for-all the Centenary celebrations promise is the way to go. And after all, *funferall* is a portmanteau word Joyce coined, combining as it does *fun for all* with *funeral.* Anything goes with Joyce, and everything goes. So if I'm contradicting myself, perhaps I'm only honouring the spirit of his extraordinary novel, *Ulysses.*

NOTES

1. This is the text of a public Centenary Bloomsday talk delivered in the Linenhall Library, Belfast, 16 June 2004.
2. Ironically, my use of the phrase 'post-Tiger' suggests the Ireland in current recession, whereas in 2004 I meant Ireland in triumphant Tiger mode (2009).
3. Thomas Kettle, *The Day's Burden: Studies, Literary & Political and Miscellaneous Essays* (Dublin: Browne and Nolan, 1937 [1910 without the miscellaneous essays]), p.xi.
4. Richard Ellmann, *James Joyce* (New York: Oxford University Press, 1959), p.163.
5. Ibid., p.538.

16

BETWEEN TWO SHADOWS: KETTLE, LYND AND THE GREAT WAR

CHANGING WINDS

During the Great War Lord Dunsany joined the Royal Inniskilling Fusiliers. He was wounded but not while serving at the front; rather he was wounded in Dublin during the Easter Rising while helping to crush the rebellion. He was far from being the only Irish writer who was caught in the fierce cross-winds created by the War and the Rising, but Dunsany's *Tales of War* (1918), thirty-two short narratives, are generated exclusively from his Great War experience.[1] One feels it would have been impossible for him to have transferred his allegiance from the British Army to Sinn Fein, but that is what Harold Firbank, the hero of Douglas Goldring's novel *The Fortune* (1917), does.

Firbank is an Englishman who enlists in the army, becomes a captain, sees combat and is invalided home after being wounded by a sniper. Recovered, he arrives in Ireland to visit a friend and take up a War Office posting in the Curragh; his heart is not in the suppression of the Easter Rising; the 'crack-brained' rebellion could be quelled by English magnanimity but stupidity loses the day. In what is not entirely a tragic irony, since he has effectively changed sides, Firbank is shot dead by one of his own men as a rebel spy. Firbank's Irish widow rediscovers the depth of her Irishness and the last chapter speaks of 'the saintly Pearse, poor Joseph Plunkett', Firbank's posthumous conversion complete. Aldous Huxley, who supplied a Preface to the 1931 edition, called *The Fortune* 'the earliest, indeed the only contemporary, fictional account of War-time pacifism',[2] but in an Irish context, the novel comes to rest with sympathy for the physical-force republican martyrs. Although Goldring's adopted pro-Irishness seems firm, he is not otherwise easy to pin down, despite George Orwell's later outing of him as a crypto-Communist; he described himself variously as 'a libertarian, Little Englander, pacifist and someone with leftwing views'.[3] In *The Fortune* he writes as an Irish rcpublican.

A novel that crosses some of the same turbulent terrain as *The Fortune* is *Changing Winds* (1917) by St John Ervine from Ballymacarrett, near Belfast. It is a baggy work like Goldring's and similarly involves a group of young talented friends who are buffeted by the cross-winds of public events, ideas and movements, climaxing in the violent double-headed apotheosis of the Great War and the Easter Rising. If Goldring's unique contribution to the theme is Conscientious Objection, Ervine's is a portrait of an Ulster Protestant, Henry Quinn, behind whose fear of being a coward lies the built-in ambivalence of his 'thrawn' Protestant Ulsterness. Quinn is a man who loves England and Ireland but doesn't always love England and doesn't always love Ireland and who is a unionist whose love of Ireland can nevertheless become support for Home Rule: in short, the familiar cross-winds that blow across the Protestant Ulster Irish. But Quinn's Home Rule is very different from the republic that is envisaged by John Marsh, his tutor, a Gaelic Revivalist and Sinn Fein republican. Quinn's admiration for Tom Arthurs of Harland & Wolff's suggests a different kind of Irish Revival: industrial expansion, educational reform, broadening of community service, reorganization of what we would call infrastructure, and seeing off the premises the priests, publicans, politicians and poets: freedom from the bondage of religion, drink, sectionalism and romance. His is the Revival that Didn't Happen though wished for by many. Such a Revival is pre-empted in the novel by the Easter Rising which Quinn witnesses in Dublin, where he has gone to get papers for his marriage to an Englishwoman. Marsh is killed as a leader of the rebellion, deluded but brave, whereas Quinn is dogged by his cowardice. Quinn's youthful English friends have already enlisted and been killed in France. The War is the Shadow that hangs over Quinn as he hangs back from participation. In the end, returning from Dublin to England, he resolves to marry and enlist and is sure he will be killed. But the uncertainty of his fate mirrors the uncertainty of Ulster and Ireland themselves after the War; since the novel appeared in 1917, Ervine himself could not know their post-War political outcomes.

The physical scale of the Easter rebellion and the Great War was of course incommensurable. Robert Lynd pointed out that 'there were not enough Irishmen in the Dublin insurrection of 1916 to make up even one battalion of the Irish Guards ... For every Irishman who shouldered a rifle on the insurgent side, nearly a thousand Irishmen bore weapons on the side of the Allies'.[4] Yet through the power of symbolism and changing political winds, the Rising took its place alongside the War to complete a potent emblem of duality, one that inspired and troubled writers of the time but lost its potency after the War when the Rising occluded the War in the popular and even literary imagination. Katharine Tynan was aware of the duality, and in *The Years of the Shadow* (1919), her reminiscence of the war years, she recalls a sunny day in April 1915. In the morning she encountered in St Stephen's Green a group of casualties, and her military companion spoke to two soldiers who had been wounded at Ypres. In the afternoon she watched 500 Irish Volunteers embarking on a route march in the Dublin mountains 'where they acquired their deadly skill at marksmanship. Easter Week, 1916, was yet more than a year away'.[5] Tynan had been a Parnellite and briefly alienated from the priests, then a Redmondite and Revivalist writer; but when the War broke out she became a kind of confessor and consoler by correspondence, receiving and answering a hundred letters a week – often from the bereaved – after her poem, 'Flower of Youth', appeared. Her elder son fought in Palestine and her younger in France and she was deeply engaged emotionally throughout the War. Hers is the perspective of a mother: 'Things we shall never have to suffer happened to these children of ours.'[6] But the Irish mother whose sons were away fighting in the War to end all Wars became a forgotten figure beside the Shan Van Vocht and Yeats's Kathleen Ni Houlihan.

Yet for a few years the struggle between Irish commitment to participation in the Great War and Irish commitment to independence seemed roughly equal and no stark crossroads had been reached.[7] But an Ireland torn between loyalty and rebellion was unstable and it is caught without fanfare by Ella MacMahon in nineteen pieces, humorous and poignant by turn, that were first published in serial form under the title 'Vignettes' (the earliest between 1920 and 1921) and then in book form as *Irish Vignettes* in 1928. They exist appropriately somewhere between short stories and essays. There are references to both the Zeppelin air raids on London and Easter 1916. One character with marvellous duplicity (or is it merely doubleness?) shouts 'Up the Irish Fusiliers! Up the Rebels!' The characters are suspended between 'a bygone day' and a 'new Ireland' of the period 1914 to 1918; Sinn Fein is on the rise but the Troubles have not begun. Among the 'peasants' (her word) whom MacMahon writes of in the guise of a travelled and cultivated Irishwoman there is a new 'impidence' (as one of the country cast calls it); there is an increasing dislike of England and a discernible pro-Germanism.[8] The rural Irish are caught between 'purely feudal predilections' and 'modern democratic opinions' but the latter could themselves – though this is only implied – favour either Sinn Fein populism or continued unionism. The author herself seems similarly suspended in sympathy and opinion between two Irelands but retains an alert ironic detachment. But the Great War–Easter 1916 duality lost its potency quite soon after the War which, astonishingly (the magnitude of the Great War considered), the

Rising all but erased in the Southern Irish popular and even literary imagination.

In Tynan's novel, *The Golden Rose* (1924), that potency is lost before the Great War is half over and her novel takes as one of its themes the supersession of the War by the Rising in the hearts and minds of Tynan's farmers and peasants in Connaught, even while Irishmen were fighting and dying in France and Belgium. *The Golden Rose* registers early signs of the massing of the Irish in hostility against England and those Irish who were fighting for her in Europe and does so from a preponderantly female perspective.[9] Whatever its modest literary merits, it is a brave and illuminating novel that is honest in its implied narrator's confusion when caught between, on the one hand, the imperatives of instinctual love of son and brother and traditional loyalty to the Irish soldier fighting for the British cause, and, on the other hand, the imperatives of Irish patriotism and social need of neighbour. At first no choice is necessary, when the War effort, and the Irish boys who helped make it, are supported by all but die-hard Sinn Feiners, but even before the Easter Rising in 1916 the waters are muddier than they were at first. But the waxing tide of popular sentiment is clear and, of course, writing her novel from the perspective of 1923 or 1924, Tynan knew that the Irish heroes-in-making of the Great War had been prematurely expelled from the nationalist pantheon.

More than the novel's rural romance, the course of the War as it is received in the west of Ireland lends *The Golden Rose* its interest for us. The novel's heroine, Carmel O'Reilly, is the reader's custodian of the companionable and talkative Ireland before the War, which she keeps alive in her memory, though recalling how soon after the War's outbreak Ireland grew darker and tenser. At first the exploits of her father and her brothers at the front thrill his patients and neighbours and the tidings of his son's death fill them with apparent sorrow. Carmel remembers the days 'when, before a soldier, the heart melted, the hands went out'.[10] But, in fact, ever since the War began 'there had been a steadily growing distaste and dislike of it among the people. It was too early yet to call it hostility. That was to come: but a good many things had happened in Ireland since civil war threatened in 1914 to break up the peace, which some people thought sluggish, of the years before the war.' Tynan alludes here to Ulster's resistance to Home Rule. By early 1916 the people, very few of whom had been touched by the War, are 'oddly indifferent, almost hostile' to the O'Reillys, the War, and the Irish soldiers fighting it. Ireland's temper is obscure, uncertain. The change in the people is 'subtle ... they were less friendly, less respectful.' The unfriendliness is 'strange', the hostility is 'mysterious'.[11]

In Dublin, however, even as late as March 1916, 'there was everywhere the friendliness of the war' (p.146). Then happened the definitive watershed of the Easter Rising, from the other side of which Carmel in early 1917 is recalling events. She and her mother are in France visiting the dangerously ill doctor, and into this strangely beautiful weather and spring flowers 'there came something violent and terrible hurtling into the peace as though a shell had dropped upon them. It was the news of the Dublin Rebellion' (p.169). The latest crossroads has been reached. Carmel takes it hard; she breaks down and weeps 'for Ireland, for the Irish soldiers in the war, betrayed and deserted as they would see it, for the madness of it all and for what was going to happen' (p.170). Her father too thinks the rebellion a wicked betrayal. Back home he claims that the rebellion had corrupted the kindly people, and this is remembered against him. Even before the rising, his neighbours had decided that he had been wrong, not heroic, in abandoning his patients to a *locum tenens* in order to join the War. Now in the wake of the Rising, the Royal Irish Constabulary (RIC) become the enemy and some families are split in their loyalty, one brother in the War, one in the rebellion ('the same spirit in both of them', p.188), a kind of Irish civil war of the affections. The Irish soldiers are no longer heroes, or even victims, but misguided fools, even traitors: 'There was no heroism now but that of 1916', Carmel realizes in early 1917.

THE WAR AND THOMAS KETTLE

A transitional Ireland pivoting on Easter 1916 and concurrent episodes of the Great War is amply pictured, then, in contemporary Irish fiction.[12] The novels, of course, merely reflected the tensions in many Irish hearts and minds, including some of the biggest hearts and strongest minds in Ireland. The rebellion in 1916 was sudden, graphic and short-lived and its immediate aftermath of executions and bitterness changed the attitude of many Irish to the Great War, which was by contrast an anticipated, arduous and drawn-out affair. Yet the rebellion was an outcome of Sinn Fein politics unforeseen only in its timing; the tension had been rising for some years. What we might call the political culture of Sinn Fein was inimical not only to Irish participation in the Allied resistance to Germany but to the political and social values and prescriptions that made that participation necessary in the eyes of many Irish who simultaneously considered themselves unequivocal nationalists. The opposing attractions that created a dilemma for many thinking Irish were not those of the Great War and Irish nationalism, but the Great War and Sinn Fein republicanism. We see the dilemma at its most eloquent and painful in the life and writings of Thomas Kettle. This accomplished and tragic figure shrank in post-Rising, post-Treaty and post-Civil War Irish memory in tune with the shrinkage both of what we might call the Irish Great War and of the constitutional Home Rule nationalism that helped wage the War.

Kettle resolved his dilemma through brave and ethically motivated action on one side of the equation. In the summer of 1914 Kettle had crossed to Belgium to buy guns for the Irish Volunteers; Erskine Childers's yacht *Asgard*, engaged in the same mission, was on the seas. However, while Kettle was abroad war was declared. The parallel with Childers (a political activist also of literary bent) appears the closer because the desire to make an impact proved, after the search for guns, fatal. But unlike Kettle, Childers seems to have been less torn in his loyalties than equipped with a renegade capacity to superimpose them. He began as a patriotic, even imperialist Briton, but turned Irish nationalist and ran German guns for the Volunteers in 1913. Then when the Great War broke out, he turned patriot again and fought for Britain against Germany, before returning to Ireland to become an Irish republican rejectionist in which current phase of disloyalty he was executed.[13] And whereas historical chronology allowed Childers to attach greater ultimate importance to Irish independence than to the War (which ended with the Irish Question still unanswered), Kettle stayed on in Belgium as a war correspondent, realizing that Prussian aggression in Europe far outweighed English sins in Ireland. In his despatch, 'Under the Heel of the Hun', he sized the situation up: 'It is as simple as it is colossal. It is Europe against the barbarians.'[14]

Kettle's despatches, reprinted in *The Ways of War* (1917), were heated, purplish and memorable; they were by turns descriptive and denunciatory, ranging from the angry fable of the Rat-Kaiser to quiet, superb eye-witness account. He visits the town of Termonde torched by the Germans and walks every destroyed street. At such times he strikes the modern note of a George Orwell in Spain. Amidst the indignation there can be an un-Orwellian softer feeling.

> On the other side of the town, a battery of artillery, magnificently horsed, was waiting under the trees for any alarm. Most of the horses were Irish. I felt a little *nostalgia* as I rubbed the

> sensitive nose of a roan mare. I wished that I had with me a poet or two of the Celtic renaissance to make a poem telling her how she had begun at the fair of Ballina, or Moy, or perhaps Ballsbridge itself, and how she would wander the white roads of Europe – not white now, but red – and die at last over there on the banks of the Rhine near pleasant Coblenz, or many-pinnacled Cologne. There being no poet about, I could but scratch the butt of her ears and give her some chocolate.[15]

Kettle's credentials as an Irish nationalist were impressive and his nationalism was more than nostalgia and hardly in doubt. He had been Nationalist MP for East Tyrone, had co-founded the Volunteers and was prepared to translate his desire for Irish freedom into action. He had defended the economics of nationalism and could even echo uncomfortably Pearse's mystic Catholic politics: 'Destroy nationalism, and you extinguish the sacrificial flames about which the greatest nobleness of the world has gathered in abnegation. You shatter the altar vessel in which the precious wine of freedom has been passed from lip to lip.'[16] In 'The Philosophy of Politics', transcript of a 1905 Presidential Address to the Young Ireland branch of the United Irish League, Kettle summarized the importance of nationality to the nineteenth century and checklisted the criteria of nationhood which he believed Ireland met.[17] Like an organism, a nation strove to realize itself and he saw economic nationalism as essential to this 'self-realization' or 'national self-direction'.[18]

But Kettle associated nationalism with the other crucial nineteenth-century movement, democracy, and he had little truck with the Big House neo-feudalist nationalism of Yeats. His nationalism was democratic and outward-looking, and fully engaged in reform, improvement and steady gain, in that 'continuous adjustment of internal and external relations' that he said characterize adaptation, development and evolution in organic life.[19] Moreover, Kettle's instinct for democracy trumped his instinct for nationalism. J.B. Lyons quotes him: 'It is a confession to make, and I make it. I care for liberty more than I care for Ireland.'[20] His thought was unconfined by any hint of 'Sinn Fein' (Ourselves). In 1910 he agreed that his generation had for its first task 'the recovery of old Ireland' (the business that the Irish Revival was about) but thought that its second task was 'the discovery of the new Europe'.[21] The second task, which did the work of democracy and freedom, was compulsory: he ended his 'Apology' for his essays in *The Day's Burden* (1910) by insisting that to become deeply Irish, Ireland had to become European. His paper of 1912, 'The Economics of Nationalism' closes: 'If it helps you to join up the dreams – as yet unformulated – of the Irish nation with the intellectual tradition of Europe, then I shall not have wasted either your evening or my own.'[22] In his 'Apology' he anticipated a nationalist sniff at the essays' un-Irish content and replied that 'Ireland, a small nation, is, none the less, large enough to contain all the complexities of the twentieth century'.[23] His old school-pal, James Joyce, was to demonstrate the same proposition in *Ulysses* (1922) over hundreds of pages. Even after Kettle's death, Lynd called him one of the voices of the 'New Ireland', and today, in European Ireland, he ought to be hailed as a forebear. And this is not in spite of, but because of, Kettle's advocacy of Irish involvement in the Great War, which he saw as the corollary of Ireland's embracement of Europe.

What was true for space was, for Kettle, true for time. Unlike Pearse, Kettle reposed no hopes in a catastrophically or apocalyptically achieved (we might say, Pearsian) republic. In 'The Philosophy of Politics' he identified the nineteenth-century 'thought-climate' called evolution as defining the new age: ethical principles develop, 'as we hope, towards a fuller realization'.[24] This was the philosophic basis of Kettle's democratic nationalism. (Yeats's nationalism for its part was undemocratic, anti-Darwinian and apocalyptic.) A theme in *The Day's Burden* is that life is 'incomparably vaster, more various, and more complex than any theory of it' and that we mustn't believe in the 'expectation' of finality which is an 'illusion'.[25] Again, it was Joyce who demonstrated that theme at vast and complex length. Only in death, thought Kettle, could we escape the temporal and spatial circumstances of our daily existence. In his essay, 'On Saying Goodbye', he suggested that in death ('normally encountered', he added in order to exclude suicide) 'We shall bid our first real adieu to those brother-gaolers of ours, Time and Space'.[26] (What he wanted were good lines and a timely exit in the fifth act, Lynd reminds us, and Lynd believed that he got both.) Kettle was consistent and remained loyal to his own philosophy. We can see in his attack on Sinn Fein in 1908 an expression of views that later were the basis of his decision to join up and denounce the Easter Rising. In the pages of the *North American Review* he published 'A Note on Sinn Fein in Ireland', a riposte to Seumas MacManus's 1907 article in the *Review*, 'Sinn Fein: Its Genesis and Purpose'. Kettle, writing as a nationalist MP of the Irish Parliamentary Party, intended to scatter MacManus's claims that Sinn Fein had been the only begetter of the Irish language revival, Fenianism, the temperance movement, the cooperative movement, Catholic Emancipation, land reforms and other nationalist achievements among its 'Whitmanesque catalogue'.[27] On the contrary, Sinn Fein, Kettle insisted, sprang from the head of one man, Arthur Griffith, and far from being the indigenous movement it claimed, and wished, to be, borrowed its ideas from Hungary. National advances, according to Kettle, had been achieved through realistic political understanding and activity and not through visionary intervention. He thought the Irish Parliamentary Party stood for 'realism' whilst Sinn Fein stood for 'ideologism'.

Kettle's politics were at base naturalistic and it is clear that it had absorbed, and perhaps been informed by, the theory of organic evolution from which he borrowed his narratives and metaphors. Whereas Sinn Fein is static, parliamentary nationalism is explicable through evolution: 'It has gone forward in a minute obedience to Herbert Spencer's formula; it has been a movement from "an indefinite, incoherent homogeneity to a definite, coherent heterogeneity" ... The development of Ireland has been like to growth of a great oak' (pp.56–7). Sinn Fein, by contrast, is too fond of the 'catastrophic and sensational type of change' (p.57). He reminds Sinn Fein, anticipating a major theme in *The Day's Burden*, that 'Life is more complex than we once thought it' (p.57), 'once' meaning before Darwin and Spencer. The Darwinian notions of complexity, adjustment and adaptation, growth and development, and evolution itself all underpinned the politics of parliamentary and consensual reform and national self-realization.

To nationalism and democracy, then, we can add realism and evolution as crucial components of the nineteenth-century *mentalité* that formed Kettle's politics and consequently his attitude to the Great War, which embroiled Europe and thus Ireland, and to Easter 1916, which was the brainchild of the catastrophists and apocalyptics. 'There is no such thing as finality of achievement' (pp.57–8), Kettle was sure. Ireland suddenly free, prosperous and beautiful was a Platonic vision, a mirage. If Kettle was an Aristotelian beside the Sinn Fein Platonists, his view at least allowed for the teleology embodied in the organism's (or nation's) growth into its own realization, though even self-realization was an unending process. Of course, the Great War was a calamity, a catastrophe, but it gave Ireland the opportunity through participation to enter a Europe in which its own self-realization could be steadily advanced in a properly enlarged theatre of culture. Kettle's awareness of the interconnectedness of events and impacts, of nations and continents, necessitated in his mind Ireland's involvement in the War and was surely sharpened by his knowledge of the role of interconnectedness in Darwinian evolution. And the significance of Europe was why the War changed everything: Germany threatened the very Europe he saw as essential to Ireland's self-realization. Home Rule agitation (never mind armed republicanism) was to be suspended in the face of the greater crisis – and for perfectly self-serving national reasons, if such were demanded. German conduct in Belgium instantly justified suspension of the belief that Ireland's nationality required her to stand aloof from England in the latter's resistance. Moreover, in Germany's invasion of Belgium Kettle saw the anti-Christian philosophy of Nietzsche made flesh even if, as Lyons points out, he could still appreciate the style of that philosopher's 'lucid brutality'.[28]

Returning to Ireland from Belgium, Kettle became a recruiting campaigner (making some 200 speeches) and was regarded in some quarters as a renegade from Irish nationalism and a lackey of imperialism. But he made it clear that he cared for liberty more than for Ireland; a free Ireland, yes, but first a free Europe; Home Rule, yes, but German defeat first. According to Lynd, Kettle regarded Pearse and Connolly as having at Easter 1916 'all but destroyed his dream of an Ireland enjoying the freedom of Europe'.[29] He surely saw the Rising as a needless rupture, an unnecessary catastrophe. Lynd described Kettle as fighting in the streets of Dublin to suppress the insurrection (like Lord Dunsany, though for opposite reasons).[30] According to Lyons, Kettle later referred to 'the Sinn Féin nightmare'.[31] Yet Kettle at the same time raged against the manner of British suppression of the Rising.[32]

Kettle's take on the European crisis permitted him to see Irish soldiers as constituting the first Home Rule Army; he insisted that when he enlisted he would be fighting for Ireland and Europe not for England and her colonies. He hoped that joint experience of the War could reconcile Ulster and Ireland, Ireland and England in a post-War world.[33] When he debated the anti-recruiting figures of Patrick Pearse and W.B. Yeats, he turned up (a little drunk) in the uniform of a British soldier, Lieutenant, 9th Royal Dublin Fusiliers.[34] While wearing that uniform he was killed at Ginchy, at the Somme, in September 1916. He would not have allowed that *his* self-sacrifice was any less for Ireland than Pearse's at Easter in the same year.

I have recruited Thomas Kettle as a figure who contemplated and rejected a catastrophist view of the Irish past and Irish experience, in favour of a gradualist or evolutionist interpretation and prescription. We could recruit Pearse or Yeats as representative of those who see Irish history as essentially catastrophic and in which shock-waves never entirely receded but merely presaged the next catastrophe. If

Kettle's politics were in part influenced by Darwinian evolution (in its guise not of lethal competition among organisms but of adaptation and progressive evolution over time), Pearse's were surely influenced by the kind of eschatology and Judaeo-Christian explanatory narrative (involving apocalypse and salvation through miraculous intervention) that Darwin was forced to turn away from when faced with the data of the natural world.[35]

DR JEYKLL AND MR LYND

Kettle has been called an enigma. But was he an enigma? Many Irish, including Yeats (at least at first) thought the rebellion at Easter a gross error, even if the aftermath horrified them more than the rising itself. Many Irish, though not Yeats, supported Irish involvement in the Great War. True, the vicissitudes of Goldring (judging by *The Fortune*) and Childers came to rest on republicanism, but it is perhaps noteworthy that both were Englishmen and that Childers tried for years to straddle both sides of the epoch-making divide. For their part, Dunsany, Ervine, MacMahon and Tynan, though torn in their allegiances and instincts, could not in the end turn their backs on the War or on Europe – the larger theatre of action, thought and culture.

Moreover, that the Irish regiments composed the first national army was John Redmond's idea as well as Kettle's. 'Irish blood has reddened the earth of every continent', Redmond wrote in February 1916, but 'never until now have we as a people set a national army in the field'. (Redmond's imagery is less an inadvertent echo of Pearse than a commonplace of the day.) Redmond even thought that the Cause of Ireland had passed into the safekeeping of the soldiers; their service was down-payment on post-War independence but was in no wise mercenary or mindless. In fighting alongside 'sister democracies', Ireland would 'help to bend the British Empire to a mission of new significance for humanity'.[36] Redmond clearly seized the opportunity of the War to try to elevate Ireland from subaltern to first lieutenant status, as it were; to substitute voluntary collaboration from the whole island (behaving thereby like a nation pondering its policy) for the reflex obedience expected of a colony by the colonizer and the colonized alike. This was a subtle construction of the idea of loyalty, turning it from something taken and assumed to something given on reflection. As for the island as a whole: Kettle believed that an incidental good that would flow from Irish participation in the armed conflict would be the achievement of 'the two reconciliations of which all statesmen have dreamed, the reconciliation of Protestant Ulster with Ireland, and the reconciliation of Ireland with Great Britain'.[37] In his last political testimony, written from the front and published after his death, Kettle wrote that he had consorted much with Protestant Ulstermen and knew they would agree with him that 'Colonial Home Rule for Ireland' was 'essential as a prologue to the reconstruction of the Empire'.[38] Even if 'reconstruction of' was not code for 'emancipation from', this notion he shared with Redmond that by fighting in the Great War Ireland would radically change the British Empire was a startling one. Kettle's anthology, *Irish Orators and Oratory* (1916) concludes with Redmond's intervention in the House of Commons debate on the declaration of war, 3 August 1914, offering Britain the opportunity to withdraw troops from Ireland, leaving the safekeeping of the island from invasion to the two bodies of Volunteers, Irish and Ulster. Given his argument, it was fitting for Redmond to refer to the 36th *Irish* Division, not Ulster Division, before this Division's heroism at the Somme. The argument that the Irish fighting men were to be the first Irish national army was also Robert Lynd's. Lynd, as I shall suggest in a moment, is a far more enigmatic figure than Kettle on the issue of the polar attractions of the Great War and republican rebellion.

Events may have put Redmond and Kettle on the wrong side of history, but time may yet restore them to the right side. Robert Lynd called Kettle 'a soldier in the lost cause of the intellect in national and international affairs'.[39] As for Lynd himself, we used to think of him as the greatest Irish exponent of the English essay, a genre pioneered by Addison and Steele, continued most notably by Lamb and Hazlitt, by Stevenson, by Chesterton and Belloc, by Woolf and by Orwell. It is a genre which cannot by definition accommodate the fanatic or extremist. Lynd's essays often brought up the rear of anthologies read by British and Irish schoolchildren between the 1920s and 1960s, many of the literary buds among whom began to bloom in imitation and emulation of him and other English essayists. He was born in Belfast, a son of the manse, and educated at Royal Belfast Academical Institution ('Inst'). He left for England in 1901 and stayed there, contributing weekly essays to the *New Statesman* over what became the famous initials Y.Y. These essays display the miscellany, wisdom and whimsy of the genre, behind which could lurk an affected worldliness and a mild snobbery, familiar ingredients also of the genre; his writing shows the inventive flair for character andanecdote that characterizes the work of the finest essayists. 'The Gentle Art of Idling', 'The Pleasures of Ignorance', 'In and Out of Bed', 'Why

We Hate Insects': these offer the wilfully affected dilettantism at one end of the genre's spectrum, though in fact Lynd practised each of what one literary historian has identified as the four subgenres of the essay: the moral essay, the travel essay, the critical essay and the autobiographical essay.[40]

Lynd's prolificness and multiversity were not what we associate with the single-minded political writer. The cultivated and very English Richard Church edited Lynd's essays on books and writers in 1952 and remarked that Lynd 'was universally loved both as a man and as a writer', a professional writer who never made an enemy and enjoyed a personality that exhibited 'gentleness, tolerance, humour, scepticism', whose interests were characteristically English ('town and country, village life and solitude, football crowds and Fleet Street pub'), whose philosophy represented 'the fine flower of European humanism', and who as 'a liberal humanist' always stood staunchly between extremes, and displaying the virtues of 'healthy protestantism'.[41]

But there was another and very different Lynd, and presumably not the one for which he received a Litt.D. from his Alma Mater, Queen's University, Belfast in 1947. It was not unknown for Ulster Protestants (especially Presbyterians) to become Irish republicans, as Lynd did (Sean McMahon puts Lynd in the tradition and company of such Ulster Protestant literary nationalists as Bulmer Hobson and Alice Milligan),[42] or for Irish republicans to live in England, as Lynd did. Yet there is, when we step back from his life and work, an essential tension in Lynd that ought to make him an intriguing Jekyll-and-Hyde figure rather than the neglected figure he is – and neglected under both hats: that of a tolerant, unideological, merely observing English essayist and that of a hard-nosed Irish writer and political interventionist. For as well as being a rambling and congenial (if prolific and disciplined) English essayist, Lynd was a literary propagandist for vigorous Irish nationalism (a kind of literary Childers), a topic that did not encourage the whimsy or unfocussed tolerance of the anthologized essay. He learned and taught Irish, attended the Gaelic League (where he met his future wife), as 'Riobard Ua Floinn' wrote for the nationalist magazine *Uladh*, and was to edit the works of James Connolly. Sean McMahon identifies Lynd's political mentors as Thomas Davis and Arthur Griffith.[43]

In *Home Life in Ireland* (1909) Lynd set out the wares of Sinn Fein who were striking what he called 'the New Note in Politics' in Ireland and endorsed its programme of economic self-reliance and its plan to withdraw from Westminster and set up a *de facto* Irish parliament in Dublin. McMahon describes Lynd's early approach to Irish self-regeneration as Gandhian, Lynd believing that non-violent agitation would help preserve the unity of the island.[44] In Sinn Fein's Ireland, fewer Irishmen would enter the British Army and those who did would forfeit employment in Ireland thereafter, an idea Lynd appears to endorse as a necessary or desirable corollary.[45]

Despite his English residence and the English cultural ambience he enjoyed, Lynd was still a supporter of Sinn Fein even after the bloodshed of Easter 1916. Written after the Great War, his book, *Ireland a Nation* (1919), begins with a chapter entitled 'Why It is Important to Realise that Ireland is a Nation'. He denies that Sinn Fein is a policy of armed insurrection and says Easter 1916 'was not a Sinn Fein but a Fenian insurrection'. At the same time, Sinn Fein, he says, did not claim armed rebellion was wrong, only impractical. Lynd does not know how the insurrection came about, though he is sure that the Carsonist introduction of physical force into the Home Rule equation made it inevitable. He cannot bring himself to say that the rebellion was wrong but does admit that it was not a success until fifteen men had been shot and one hanged because of it. He is clear on the way most Nationalists saw it at first as a rebellion 'not against England, but against Ireland' and on the way women of the slums, many with husbands in the War, were enraged by it. He agrees with the view that 'when the [Great] war started, the vast majority of Irishmen were in sympathy with England'. And if in 1919 much of Ireland is Sinn Fein, he attributes this less to the aftermath of Easter 1916 than to the War itself, which he thinks was waged in defence of nationality against aggressive imperialism; he saw the move from Home Rulism to separatism happening throughout Europe, sweeping Ireland along with it.[46] This was a post-hoc extension of Redmond's and Kettle's belief that Irish participation in the War would promote Irish autonomy in post-War Europe. Given the post-War choice the Irish gave themselves between support for the War and support for Sinn Fein, it is an irony that Lynd believed his defence of Irish participation in the Great War and his extolment of the Irish military tradition to be an outgrowth of his Irish nationalist pride and promotion of Irish sovereignty.

His European defence of republican separatism to the contrary, Lynd's exposition and defence of Sinn Fein and Easter 1916 seem lukewarm next to his fascination with the Great War and with Kettle, whom he called a mathematician, economist, barrister, philosopher, bohemian and scholar.[47] For Lynd, Kettle, it seems, was a one-man counterweight to the Irish insularity that (officially at any rate) won the day in the Irish Free State and that has characterized Sinn Fein from Lynd's day to the present. It was Kettle's albeit constitutional nationalism that brought what unity there was in Lynd's career. In his published writings, he kept returning to his dead friend – in 'T.M. Kettle' (1916, collected in *Essays on Life and Literature*, 1951) in which he announces the death of 'the most brilliant Irishman of his generation'; in 'The Work of T.M. Kettle' (1919, posthumously collected in *Galway of the Races*, 1990) which sees his friend as 'the Hamlet of modern Ireland'; and in 'The Soldiers' Sacrifice' and 'Voices of the New Ireland: [4] T.M. Kettle', both chapters in *Ireland a Nation* (1919).

For all his persistent republicanism, Lynd sided with Kettle's view of the Great War and with much of what that subtended. Perhaps his personal attachment to Kettle helps to explain Lynd's frankly enigmatic politics, or rather the contradiction of his political philosophy by his cultural being. There is in Lynd something approaching a fundamental contradiction; indeed, something that reads like a double life, and one sharper than, though similar to, that lived by that other Northerner, Ervine's Henry Quinn. Lynd exhibits the deep-lying ambivalence of the northern Irish protestant of nationalist or republican conviction, for which ambivalence the Easter Rising and the Great War can stand in Lynd's case as iconic embodiments.[48]

Yet I cannot help but see Lynd's attitude to the Great War and his affection for the memory of Kettle as expressions of his truer self. He named as 'patriotic faith' the cause for which Kettle and thousands of Irishmen died, and like Kettle himself tried hard to see the latter's Europeanism as a possible bridge between Sinn Fein and the Orangemen. In 'The Irish Soldier', a chapter in *Ireland a Nation*, Lynd, like Redmond and Kettle, believed that 'the war with Germany was the first war in history in which the Irish soldier fought, *qua* Irishman, on the same side as England' and that, whatever reasons motivated some (hunger, adventure, cheap emigration) 'Irish soldiers fought consciously as Irish patriots in a way in which they never fought before'.[49] Lynd asserted that 'the evidence of the national spirit of the Irish troops in crisis after crisis of the war, in addition to their gaiety, fidelity and daring, is overwhelming' (p.113). Indeed, so proud is Lynd of Irish participation in the War that in 'Ireland's Record in the War' (another chapter in *Ireland a Nation*) he called for a full list of the Irish war dead so that everyone could see the extent of Irish participation and sacrifice (p.120).[50]

If Lynd the Sinn Feiner, Redmond the Home Rule Empire-man, and Kettle the Home Rule European were right, no bad faith exercised by England after the War could make them wrong. Lynd bemoans the neglect and even belittlement of Ireland's record in the War – which he rehearses with pride – but he sees them originating outside Ireland among enemies of Irish freedom, citing the case of the Irish presence at Gallipoli, which he accuses the English as having suppressed until Redmond raised a storm (p.123). Surely Lynd must have come to see – and it must have pained him – that the neglect and belittlement had begun in Ireland too (Tynan was to chart it in *The Golden Rose*), and among those who saw themselves as promoters and guardians, no less, of Irish freedom, and that it continues today.

NOTES

1. I discuss Dunsany's *Tales of War* briefly in *Irish Novels 1890–1940: New Bearings in Culture and Fiction* (2008).
2. Aldous Huxley, 'Introduction', to Douglas Goldring, *The Fortune* (London: Desmond Harmsworth, 1931 [1917]), p.xxiv. Goldring was born in 1887 in Greenwich and educated at Oxford before going to London where he became an editor under Ford Madox Ford at the *English Review*. He enlisted in the army when the Great War broke out but was invalided out and became a Conscientious Objector and a 'propaganda novelist'. He travelled to Dublin to investigate the events of Easter Week, set out to meet the Irish, met his future wife there and wrote *The Fortune*, which was published by Maunsel. He traced his Irish connections in *Odd Man Out: The Autobiography of a 'Propaganda Novelist'* (1935).
3. The description is that of Goldring's grand-daughter, Polly Bird, reacting to a *Guardian* article on Orwell's 'crypto-outing' of Goldring and others; his son Patrick Goldring reacted similarly: 'Letters', *Guardian*, 28 June 2003.
4. Robert Lynd, *Ireland a Nation* (London: Grant Richards, 1919), p.118.
5. Katherine Tynan, *The Years of the Shadow* (London: Constable, 1919), pp.174–5.
6. Katherine Tynan, *The Wandering Years* (London: Constable, 1922), p.72.
7. We can find a vivid and satirical portrait of a confused, uncertain and multiple Ireland on the eve of the Great War in Gerald Griffin's neglected *The Dead March Past: A Semi-Autobiographical Saga* (1937).
8. Ella MacMahon, *Irish Vignettes* (London: John Lane The Bodley Head, 1928), pp.220, 75, 1–4, 74, 132.
9. There is an excellent account of the waxing and waning of Irish commitment to the War, set inside the Home Rule-independence debate, in Patrick Maume, *The Long Gestation: Irish Nationalist Life 1891–1918* (Dublin: Gill and Macmillan, 1999), pp.147–214.
10. Katharine Tynan, *The Golden Rose* (London: Eveleigh, Nash and Grayson, 1924), p.81.
11. Ibid., pp.140, 138, 141–2, 143, 138.
12. I discuss other examples, and the present ones at greater length, in *Irish Novels 1890–1940*.
13. I discuss Childers in *Irish Novels 1890–1940*. Childers's broad switch from British imperialism to Irish republicanism resembles that of Wolfe Tone and Roger Casement.
14. Professor T.M. Kettle, 'Under the Heel of the Hun', in *The Ways of War* (London: Constable, 1917), p.106. This volume is a collection of Kettle's war journalism, made by his widow Mary Sheehy Kettle.
15. Kettle, *The Ways of War*, p.119.
16. T.M. Kettle, 'The Economics of Nationalism', in *The Day's Burden: Studies, Literary & Political and Miscellaneous Essays* (Dublin: Browne and Nolan, 1937 [1910, without the miscellaneous essays]), p.133.
17. Kettle, *The Day's Burden*, pp.10–11.
18. Ibid., pp.10, 147.
19. Ibid., pp.6–7.
20. J.B. Lyons, *The Enigma of T.M. Kettle* (Dublin: Glendale Press, 1983), p.278.
21. Kettle, 'Apology', in *The Day's Burden*, p.xii.

22. Kettle, *The Day's Burden*, p.147.
23. Ibid., p.xi.
24. Ibid., p.7.
25. Ibid., pp.2, 7.
26. Ibid., p.105.
27. T.M. Kettle, MP, 'A Note on Sinn Fein in Ireland', *North American Review*, 187 (1908), pp.47–8.
28. Lyons, *The Enigma of T.M. Kettle*, pp.256, 266.
29. Robert Lynd, 'The Work of T.M. Kettle', in Sean MacMahon (ed.), *Galway of the Races: Selected Essays* (Dublin: Lilliput Press, 1990), p.105.
30. Ibid.
31. Lyons, *The Enigma of T.M. Kettle*, p.297.
32. Robert Lynd, 'T.M. Kettle', in *Essays on Life and Literature* (London: J.M. Dent, 1951), p.53. According to Patrick Maume, Kettle may have developed some late doubts about his military involvement: *The Long Gestation*, p.185.
33. He reiterated the first hope in a letter from the trenches and saw the hope justified in the splendid deeds of the Ulster Division: Lyons, *The Enigma of T.M. Kettle*, p.298.
34. Lyons, *The Enigma of T.M. Kettle*, pp.271–2. R.F. Foster tells us that Yeats at this meeting tried to dissociate himself from Pearse because he did not wish to be seen as an 'advanced nationalist' of a Pearsian stripe but that Yeats noted (presumably with some satisfaction as an anti-recruiting campaigner) that when Kettle appeared in uniform he was booed: R.F. Foster, 'Yeats and War: Poetic Strategies and Political Reconstruction from the Easter Rising to the Free State', *Transactions of the Royal Historical Society*, 6th series, vol.11 (2001), p.127.
35. We know now that the history of life on earth included mass extinctions, catastrophes, bold punctuations of evolutionary equilibrium. And there may be irony in the fact that past natural disasters in Ireland are now coming to light, at a time when the influence is at last waning of those who promote catastrophe (past and impending), apocalypse, end-game in Irish history and politics. But in this respect at least, it is important to distinguish nature from culture.
36. John Redmond, 'Introduction', to Michael MacDonagh, *The Irish at the Front* (London: Hodder and Stoughton, 1916), p.5.
37. Kettle, 'Why Ireland Fought', in *The Ways of War*, p.71.
38. Quoted by his widow in her 'memoir', *The Ways of War*, p.10.
39. Robert Lynd, 'Voices of the New Ireland: [4] T.M. Kettle', *Ireland a Nation* (London: Grant Richards, 1919), p.54.
40. Graham Good, *The Observing Self: Rediscovering the Essay* (London: Routledge, 1988).
41. Richard Church, Foreword to Robert Lynd, *Books and Writers* (London: J.M. Dent, 1952), pp.v–vi.
42. Sean McMahon, 'An Introduction', to *Galway of the Races*, p.10. McMahon's is a good survey of republican Lynd. Desmond McCarthy's Preface to Lynd's *Essays on Life and Literature* is, like Church's Foreword, a brief survey of English Lynd.
43. Sean McMahon, 'An Introduction' to *Galway of the Races*, p.21.
44. Ibid.
45. Robert Lynd, *Home Life in Ireland* (London: Mills and Boon, 1909), p.257.
46. Lynd, *Ireland a Nation*, pp.54, 64, 68, 74, 56–7.
47. Lynd, 'The Work of T.M. Kettle', in *Galway of the Races*, p.101.
48. In a brief interesting essay, G.K. Peatling sees Robert Lynd as a writer 'acting out' or 'working through', concepts derived from Dominick LaCapra who concerned himself with writing and trauma. Peatling reads Lynd as an Irish cultural revivalist and promoter of an Irish essentialism undercut by his deployment of paradox and levity and working through at some psychological level an underlying Anglophobia to achieve an express admiration of English culture. This might be true but Peatling doesn't quite come to grips with these elements in Lynd's life and work, nor does he identify a disturbance in Lynd even remotely approaching trauma. The Great War or Thomas Kettle or the Easter Rising as cruxes might have helped him to focus on the troubling cross-currents he rightly senses in Lynd. It would have been beneficial, too, to have inquired into the nature of Lynd's Ulster Protestantness and into the symbiosis of Lynd's nationalism and unionism. The 'revivalist Ulster-based periodical *Uladh*' to which, Peatling reminds us, Lynd contributed might be the unidentified link between that

unionism and nationalism. See 'Robert Lynd, Paradox and the Irish Revival: "acting out" or "working through?"', in Betsey Taylor FitzSimon and James H. Murphy (eds), *The Irish Revival Reappraised* (Dublin: Four Courts Press, 2004), pp.167–74.

49. Lynd, *Ireland a Nation*, pp.109, 112.
50. If statistically feasible, such a list would at the present time be timely and perhaps epoch-making.

INDEX